WINCHESTER CATHEDRAL

Nine Hundred Years

1093-1993

Tower and south transept from the south-west. *John Crook*

WINCHESTER CATHEDRAL

Nine Hundred Years

1093-1993

Edited by

John Crook

Phillimore

1993

Published by
the Dean and Chapter of Winchester Cathedral,
in conjunction with
PHILLIMORE & CO. LTD
Shopwyke Manor Barn, Chichester, West Sussex

ISBN 0 85033 852 2

Printed and bound in Great Britain
BIDDLES LTD
Guildford, Surrey

CONTENTS

FOREWORD BY THE DEAN OF WINCHESTER

I am deeply grateful to the scholars who have contributed to this important and fascinating volume. Those of us who are fortunate enough to play some part in the life of Winchester Cathedral today are aware that we are serving in a church whose history is as awe-inspiring as its architecture. The reading of the pages that follow can only heighten the sense of wonder and gratitude.

It is significant that over the course of the centuries the huge building has evoked not only awe but also affection. Winchester is a greatly loved cathedral and this finds expression both in the large number of people who contribute voluntary service and money, and in the warmth of atmosphere often remarked upon by its multitudes of visitors. It is undoubtedly a place where, in the words of T. S. Eliot, 'prayer has been valid', and where infinity is made visible.

Affection for the cathedral extends far beyond the ranks of the Church of England's own membership. The celebration of mass in the Lady Chapel by Roman Catholics, the holding of celebratory services in the nave by the Free Churches, and the enthusiastic involvement of all the churches in ecumenical worship is a clear sign that this House of God is 'home' to the entire Christian community of the region.When money is required for the restoration of the fabric or the development of the ministry, contributions come from many whose religious beliefs cannot easily be defined.

In an age when religious faith and acceptance of Christian values are evidently in decline the importance of cathedrals as centres of worship and mission can hardly be exaggerated. And there is ample evidence that when those responsible for these ancient shrines approach their task with vigour, imagination and sensitivity they win a ready response. Their full potential has still to be realised.

The world in which the 900th anniversary of Winchester Cathedral's consecration by Bishop Walkelin is being celebrated is vastly different from anything that could have been imagined by the monastic community that first worshipped within its walls.Yet the fundamental needs of human beings have not changed since those days—a purpose informed by hope—and it is the task of those entrusted with the stewardship of the cathedral in every age to reinterpret the vision of its founders to enable these needs to be met.

This latest contribution to the study of Winchester Cathedral's long history will be of the greatest value to all who are involved in the making of contemporary history and by their engagement in dynamic worship and mission are affirming the building's deeply spiritual character.

TREVOR BEESON

Ash Wednesday 1993

EDITOR'S PREFACE

It is unlikely that Bishop Walkelin could ever have dreamed that his cathedral would still be standing 900 years after its first consecration; its predecessor, the Anglo-Saxon Old Minster, had survived in its final form for scarcely more than a tenth of that time. Yet Walkelin's cathedral remains with us, still recognisably the church into which the monks of St Swithun's Priory first made their entry on 8 April 1093, and—just as remarkable, perhaps—still broadly fulfilling the purpose for which it was designed.

Throughout nine centuries the physical fabric of the cathedral has altered in a way which reflects evolving patterns of worship, liturgy, and artistic taste. While this volume does not pretend to be a complete history of the cathedral as a social institution, the broader history of the building is in fact mirrored in its actual fabric, a document that can be read as clearly as an historical text. It is to be hoped that the articles in this book will help a wider audience to understand the way in which the story of Winchester Cathedral is chronicled in its very stones.

All the major periods of architectural and artistic development are richly represented in the cathedral, and the diverse articles in this book underline the extent to which Winchester was at the forefront of creative endeavour: in sculpture, wall painting, wood carving, music, and many other fields. With the recent introduction of exciting new works of art, it continues to be so.

The thanks of the editor are due above all to the authors, who freely gave of their time to carry out completely new research on their various subjects; many of them undertaking to read the contributions of their fellow-authors, thereby helping to provide a more integrated text. In particular, I should like to thank the Dean and Chapter of Winchester Cathedral for their support and encouragement throughout the venture; Brenda and Tom Kipling, who carefully read the early proofs of the chapters and made many useful suggestions; John Hardacre, for proof-reading, suggesting many improvements, and answering countless queries; and Noel Osborne, Managing Director of Phillimore, and his team—especially Helen Chadwick, who ably saw the volume through the press.

JOHN CROOK

March 1993

ix

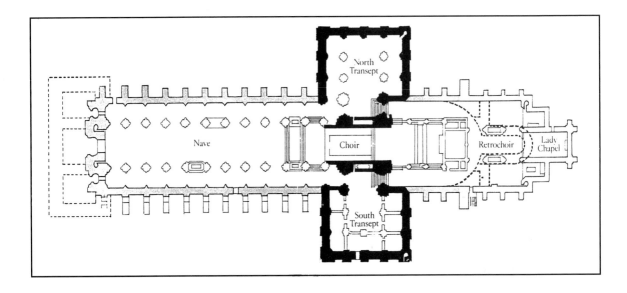

Plan of Winchester Cathedral

BISHOP WALKELIN AND HIS INHERITANCE[1]

Christopher Brooke

There have been various moments in the history of the English Church when worldliness and devotion have been most bewilderingly entangled, and the reign of Edward the Confessor was one of them. The Old English Church enjoyed an Indian summer; many monastic communities flourished; it was a golden age of English craftsmanship. Yet the Confessor lent his complaisant patronage to Archbishop Stigand, who contrived to be archbishop of Canterbury, bishop of Winchester, and master of several abbeys besides, without being a monk: a scandalous combination of offices which Thomas Wolsey himself would have envied.[2] Stigand's translation to Canterbury had been irregular, and his role was one of William the Conqueror's best excuses for interfering in the affairs of England. He was also a notorious abuse. Yet William moved cautiously; and it was not till after the rebellion of 1069, in which his family were implicated, that Stigand was formally deposed. At the Easter Council at Winchester in 1070, Stigand was removed from office along with his brother Æthelmaer of Elmham; and a cosmopolitan group of clergy already well established in the Norman church ruled in their stead.[3] Lanfranc of Pavia, abbot of the Conqueror's foundation at Saint-Etienne, Caen, became archbishop of Canterbury; Walkelin, royal chaplain and canon of Rouen, was made bishop of Winchester; Herfast the royal chancellor, bishop of Elmham.[4] It was a crucial turning-point for all three sees and for the English Church at large.

Lanfranc was an elderly man still possessed of immense energy and force of character; he was intimately acquainted with some of the leading figures in the papal curia in the heyday of the papal reform of the 11th century. He had been a central figure in the flourishing monastic world of Normandy for nearly thirty years. He brought to England a cosmopolitan experience of the Church of his day, and some powerful assumptions, which he was still not too old to modify. One of his first acts was to prepare for the destruction of the old cathedral at Canterbury and its replacement by a new Christ Church based on the best continental models. Eadmer, who was already a monk of Christ Church in Lanfranc's later years, assures us that he virtually completed the new cathedral in seven years, a statement often doubted by modern scholars; but Eadmer was describing the building which was the centre of his life.[5] Lanfranc came to accept the curious English custom (as he seems at first to have thought it) of having a monastic community as his cathedral chapter.[6] It is likely indeed that he gave firm encouragement to his colleagues to foster monastic chapters, and in his later years and soon after his death their number was increased from three to nine.[7] There are indications that Lanfranc's firm support of the movement for clerical celibacy and the spread of monastic institutions throughout the Church kept at bay the formation of secular chapters on the usual Norman pattern—comprising canons enjoying individual incomes (or prebends) and living in their own

1

houses, often with concubines and families—till after his death. There is a striking passage in Eadmer's *Historia Novorum* in which he asserts that Walkelin, the secular clerk, had collected almost forty clerks with the tonsure and in the habit of canons to oust the monks from Winchester Cathedral, and that it was only the firm opposition of Lanfranc which prevented this. He goes on to quote a letter of Alexander II describing a similar attempt on Canterbury Cathedral itself by 'certain clerks'. It may even be that Lanfranc himself had hesitations. In the event, Lanfranc became a fervent supporter of the monastic cathedral chapters, and Walkelin, in spite of his secular origin, seems to have become a faithful disciple of the archbishop, fostering the local traditions of his see by providing the monks with magnificent new buildings and St Swithun with a splendid new setting for his shrine.[8]

Walkelin's early career is quite obscure, but he seems to have won his way both in the chapter of Rouen and in the royal court.[9] He was favoured by the distinguished monk-archbishop Maurilius, and his brother Simeon was a monk of the abbey of Saint-Ouen at Rouen, prior of Winchester, later abbot of Ely.[10] His nephew Gerard, son of Osbert and Anne, was to be precentor or perhaps archdeacon of Rouen, bishop of Hereford and archbishop of York.[11] David Spear has argued with great probability that Walkelin was a canon of Rouen; he was certainly a royal clerk.[12] His connections linked him both to the secular chapter of Rouen and to the monastic order of his brother. In some respects the two orders were worlds apart; and they were often in conflict. Yet they co-existed, and there were many links between them. Perhaps the most dramatic link of the next generation comprised Abelard's concubine and wife, Heloise, who had been brought up as a child in the secular cathedral close at Paris, yet in later life was a greatly respected nun and abbess, foundress of a small religious order.[13] In a rather more conventional way Walkelin spanned the secular church and the monastic, of which as bishop he was a very notable patron.

In some respects the early Norman bishops were very much a team, in others they were intensely competitive. One striking feature of the many churches for which Lanfranc was responsible, or personally influenced, is their extreme plainness and absence of orna-ment. It is true that we know too little of the original scheme of painted decoration to be sure of their precise original appearance.[14] But the absence of sculpture is very striking.[15] The cushion capitals in the crypt of St Mary-le-Bow, apparently the London headquarters of Lanfranc, have been well preserved, and are entirely plain.[16] So are those in the crypt, transepts and nave of Winchester Cathedral, and in many other churches of the first Norman phase. In contrast, the choir pillars at Durham of the 1090s already show a marked ornament, and the Canterbury crypt built in the generation following Lanfranc's death, at the turn of the 11th and 12th centuries, has a riot of sculpture on the capitals. The plainness of early Norman Romanesque has many continental parallels, especially from the early 11th century. But it stands in striking contrast to such influential buildings as the third church at Cluny, begun in or about 1088, and the cathedral of St James at Compostela, begun in the 1070s.[17] Here we may see the tastes and fashions of Normandy mingling with the personal attitudes—dare we say puritanism?—of Lanfranc himself.

Yet the Councils of Winchester and London of 1072 and 1075 were dominated by rivalries between the bishops and the issue of primacy and precedence.[18] Lanfranc was able to assert for a time the new-found primacy of Canterbury over York; and the bishops of London and Winchester were able to win recognition of the precedence of their sees. In due course London was to be the dean of the province, Winchester the precentor; the rest had to take precedence in order of consecration. In the years which followed, one after another of the bishops—and many of the abbots too—embarked on extremely ambitious building schemes. By about 1130 every cathedral and most of the larger abbeys had complete—or nearly complete—new churches. The late 11th and early 12th centuries saw elaborate building programmes in many parts of Christendom, but none quite so far-reaching and all-embracing as the building explosion of early Norman England.

The two churches which were built by Lanfranc to be his own homes, Saint-Etienne, Caen (Fig. 1.1) and Christ Church, Canterbury, were only about 90 m. long: a little short of some of the major continental churches of the day, and only half the length of the third church at Cluny.[19] In contrast, Winchester Cathedral, when complete, was 164 m. long: by an ample margin the longest in Britain, and after Cluny the second in the Europe of its day. It was built, so far as we can tell, in two campaigns. The first began (if we may accept the dates in the late 12th-century *Winchester Annals*) in 1079 or 1080 and completed in time for a formal dedication in 1093.[20] This probably comprised the east end, choir, crossing and perhaps three or four bays of the nave.

Fig. 1.1   Caen. Saint-Etienne. The west front. *John Crook*

The nave itself, which gives the cathedral its spectacular length, may not have been finished till the 1120s. But it is probable that its scale was already conceived in Walkelin's time.

Its immense length is an extraordinary puzzle; and we do well to see it as a puzzle. The Saxon Old Minster was a massive structure of considerable length. It was outclassed by Walkelin's cathedral, but the contrast in architectural conception must have been more striking than in scale.[21] For Old Minster was essentially a Carolingian building: not a single great house, such as the large Romanesque churches of 11th-century Christendom had become, but a collection of houses, built up of cells small and large, of separate structures almost.[22] By the late Middle Ages Walkelin's cathedral had been divided by massive screens into a number of compartments once again—though the nave alone remained larger than most other churches in the island.[23] We cannot tell exactly how large or impenetrable were the original screens he and his masons designed. But there can be no doubt that his cathedral was conceived as a single building, so that a humble layman standing in the west of the nave, or an eminent bishop enthroned in the east, could see the full extent of it. This is the main contrast between Walkelin's cathedral and its predecessor, as it was between Walkelin's cathedral and Richard Fox's.[24] So far we are describing the normal fashion of the Romanesque world of the 11th century. Many a cathedral, like that at North Elmham, or in earlier days Bede's abbey churches at Monkwearmouth and Jarrow, had been relatively modest in size,[25] though in Rome and elsewhere one might see basilicas which could hold their own throughout the Middle Ages. But from the turn of the 10th and 11th centuries—starting with the white mantle of churches observed by Rodulfus Glaber about the millennium—the fashion for building on the grandest scale became ubiquitous.[26] The change is especially visible today in the abbey church of Reichenau, a great centre of cult and culture already in the 9th and 10th centuries; but it was at the turn of the 10th and 11th, when its wider influence was in decline, that the immense church we see today was built (Fig. 1.2). Similarly at Speyer, perhaps the largest of all the surviving (or partly surviving) German cathedrals of the age (Fig. 1.3), the scale of the church is due to the patronage of Walkelin's contemporary—Pope Gregory VII's chief enemy—the Emperor Henry IV.[27] One could multiply examples, especially in France, almost indefinitely. But apart from Cluny few competed with the Anglo-Norman cathedrals in length.

The full explanation is hidden from us: no contemporary text sets out at all precisely to explain what is most puzzling to us about these buildings. Yet something we can infer from an imaginative contemplation of their context and function. 'The immense size of the new church ...' wrote Biddle and Keene, 'was undoubtedly a response to the eminence of

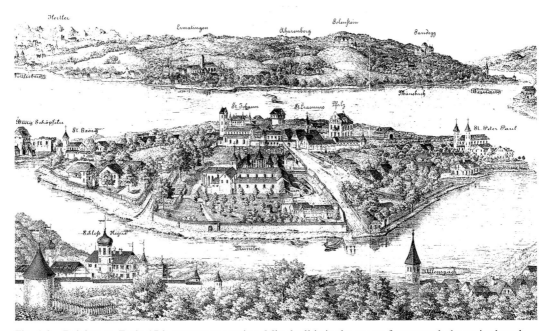

Fig. 1.2   Reichenau. Early 17th-century engraving. Mittelzell is in the centre foreground; the entire length of the church is visible behind it.

the city in royal and ecclesiastical affairs'.[28] By 1079 Walkelin could consider two models and two rivals, more or less complete. Edward the Confessor's Westminster Abbey had provided England with its first major Romanesque church, and Winchester with its first major rival as a royal chapel, the throne and burial place of kings.[29] Edward's shrine had canonised Westminster as the centre of a royal cult; by the mid-12th century Osbert of Clare and his team of expert forgers had established it as the unique home for royal coronations.[30] This was no more than a distant threat in Walkelin's time. Ironically, William Rufus, the king of Walkelin's later years—with whom, so far as we can tell, he was on good terms—was the last to be buried there (Fig. 1.4); and the chroniclers were to suggest, not that his body was claimed in triumph by the cathedral which had been the burial ground for so many earlier kings, but that it was noticeably reluctant to receive so notorious a sinner. The tower fell on his tomb not long after he was buried there, and William of Malmesbury, in a famous passage, indicated that he was not the

Fig. 1.3   The nave, Speyer Cathedral. *John Crook*

sort of man a self-respecting tower liked to have beneath it.[31] The chroniclers were prejudiced, and Rufus has had a better press from Frank Barlow than he had from William of Malmesbury.[32] It may well be that Walkelin hoped that Rufus and many of his successors would lie in his cathedral, and built a church worthy to be a royal palace.

Among the landed aristocracy, in the English countryside, the Normans and their continental allies rapidly came to oust their English predecessors. Not so in the towns;[33] and there the Norman cathedrals were an early and striking reminder that there was a new regime blessed (as the conquerors optimistically hoped) by divine approval. The new regime did not hide its light under a bushel: it was at first extremely insecure and needed propaganda as well as force to support it. The cathedrals were the major public buildings of the age, only a little less formidable and a great deal larger than early Norman castles. They were a constant reminder of God's blessing on the new rulers. This is dramatically revealed at Lincoln, where the first Norman bishop, Remigius of Fécamp, chose a hill-top site for his cathedral when he moved it from the further end of his huge diocese.[34] Even more striking, perhaps, is Durham (Fig. 1.5), where the natural fortress in the bend of the

Fig. 1.4   The so-called 'tomb of William Rufus' in the choir, Winchester Cathedral. It is probably the tomb of Bishop Henry of Blois (see pp. 40, 100). *John Crook*

river Wear had been chosen a while before by St Cuthbert's community as a home and fortress to protect his bones—and a base from which the saint could protect his people. But the impressive castle and the far more impressive cathedral were devised by the Normans; and the spectacular combination of beauty and strength which catches the eye of the beholder across the Wear is a memorial both to what was new and to what was already established in the years after the Norman Conquest.[35] New and old: they are strangely mingled in these buildings. At Durham the shrine of Cuthbert, his role in the life of church and community, and the site itself, were already established when the Normans came.[36] The great Romanesque cathedral, which by the 1120s was to bring this outpost of Christendom into the centre of the Romanesque world in the style and the technology of building, was new. At Norwich a new cathedral rose (apparently) on a new site at the turn of the 11th and 12th centuries; but in its heart, where the bishop sat enthroned behind the high altar, the Norman builders enshrined the traditional throne of the bishops of East Anglia brought (most probably) from North Elmham.[37] For St Albans Abbey Lanfranc and his Lombard nephew, Abbot Paul, provided a large, plain basilica, partly built of red brick in the manner of the Lombards.[38] But in the triforium of its transepts they set perfect replicas of Anglo-Saxon arcading. At Winchester one of the greatest churches of the land was completely rebuilt; the cathedral was entirely new. But at its centre lay still the relics of St Swithun; and after he had been translated there in 1093 the cathedral and priory of

St Peter and St Paul became generally known as St Swithun's.[39] As at Ely—though rarely elsewhere—the local saint ousted the prince of the apostles; in the cathedral which more than any other reflected the new fashions of the Normans, the Old English patron still ruled.

This illustrates a curious ambiguity in medieval popular cults. Cuthbert at Durham, Etheldreda at Ely and Swithun at Winchester were reckoned the special patrons of their communities because their relics had long been preserved in shrines there, and miracles had been performed or anyway reported. The patron saint was expected to perform works of mercy; but he or she was also a protector. From the days when St Martin of Tours took vengeance on those attacking his property in the 6th century, to the 14th century, when the armies of Siena marched under the protection of the Blessed Virgin Mary, this patronage was reckoned to be of a practical and sometimes warlike character.[40] Naturally the relics of local saints came to be immensely prized. The 10th-century tract on 'The saints and where they rest' is a remarkable guide to the treasure houses and pilgrim centres of the land; and the increasing popularity of pilgrimages far and near in the 10th, 11th and 12th centuries gave a special prestige to churches which could claim ample and successful relics.[41] Swithun could not compete with Jerusalem or Rome or St James at Compostela; and from the late 12th century he was outclassed by St Thomas of Canterbury. But his fame was firmly grounded already in the 10th and early 11th centuries, and his shrine remained a centre of pilgrimage, and received the offerings of the faithful, throughout the Middle Ages. As in most English cathedrals, the east end was extensively remodelled in the late 12th and early 13th centuries. But Walkelin's choir survived: what was added was a remarkable and extensive retrochoir, built to a much lower height—a kind of shelter, primarily designed, one must suppose, for visitors to the shrine.[42] Swithun himself remained behind the high altar, on high, with a clear view to the west till the reredos was built many generations later; his worshippers gathered at his feet, to the east.

The contrast between the single immense mansion of the Norman cathedral and the charming Gothic pavilion to its east underlines the fundamental ambiguity in the purpose of the building. It was God's house, dedicated

Fig. 1.5   Durham Cathedral, from across the Wear. *John Crook*

to the Trinity and the apostles of Rome; it was also the shrine of a great and active local saint, the home of the relics of St Swithun.[43] As so often with major Anglo-Saxon churches, there is much diversity in the evidence of its pre-Conquest dedication. The most constant theme is Peter and Paul, but fairly often the Holy Trinity is also invoked. Surviving evidence from the 7th and 8th centuries makes clear that St Peter's was the most popular dedication of that age in England, and that his name was often coupled with St Paul's.[44] This highlights the Roman origin of the English mission from which the province of Canterbury sprang, and Bede makes it clear that the original Winchester Cathedral was dedicated to Peter and Paul.[45] The church was first and foremost God's church; his the presence most constantly invoked. It therefore seems strange to us to have a special dedication to the Holy Trinity. But in the 10th and 11th centuries such dedications became common; and at the end of the Middle Ages the Trinity was one of the most popular of cults, as innumerable portrayals in late medieval art—and the dedication, for example, of two Cambridge colleges—make clear. In the 10th and 11th and especially the 12th centuries dedication to local saints, dedications which took note of local relics, became much commoner: the material and the immaterial saints flourished side by side. By immaterial one means in particular God himself; but also popular saints like Michael, who was an angel and could have no relics, or Mary, who was universally believed to have been assumed into heaven and left no relics behind.[46] Sacred images, even fragments of Mary's veil or Jesus' manger—and milk teeth—occasionally greet us in the more esoteric collections of relics. But in essence these cults were unconnected with earthly, material things; like many of the most popular of medieval cults, they dwelt only in heaven—or, as we might say, in the imagination. Peter and Paul lay between. Their shrines could be visited in Rome and fragments of their bones might circulate elsewhere. But in Winchester they were not material saints: they were living rulers of the Church, but living in heaven—members of the divine chapter, as powerful as ever, able to protect and guide their earthly flock, and visit them in the spirit. The study of liturgical and iconographical evidence, such as has been undertaken by Veronica Ortenberg, leaves no doubt that the leading apostles, especially Peter, flourished exceedingly all over western Europe in the central Middle Ages.[47] The study of dedications, as revealed in Alison Binns' *Dedications of Monastic Houses,* shows that Mary took the lead from Peter in the 12th century; in the dedications of religious houses she was overwhelmingly the most popular.[48] The immaterial and the universal saints headed all the polls in an age which has commonly been supposed—and with reason—to see the high-water mark of medieval devotion to relics. In Winchester Peter and Swithun presided side by side over the cathedral for the rest of the Middle Ages. In New Minster, after its removal to Hyde Abbey in or about 1110, a similar combination of Peter and Grimbald, the saintly founder of the church, enjoyed its dedication, even though for a time St Barnabas performed miracles there.[49] If we wish to know how the saints were viewed in the city in the central Middle Ages, the best evidence lies in the parish churches of Winchester, which were exceedingly numerous; most of them received their dedications, in all probability, between the 10th and the late 12th centuries. At their zenith in the 12th and 13th centuries, Mary came to number nine, Peter five, St Martin—the great French monk-bishop whose cult had flourished early in Britain—six; the other apostles had an occasional showing, including one for James. Michael had four; several of the saints popular in the 11th and 12th centuries had a church apiece: some associated with the French—Faith, Giles, Leonard—some with the crusades—Helen, George and Maurice, for example. Swithun had two churches, the Cornish Petroc one, but otherwise local saints were strikingly rare.[50]

Thus, the cathedral was the home of God the Holy Trinity, of Peter and Paul the apostles, and of St Swithun, bishop and confessor. It housed many other relics and its altars carried other dedications. The monumental scale of the building made it a fitting palace for God and his saints to sit cheek by jowl with the royal palace in this ancient royal city. But it was designed for many earthly inhabitants too. First and foremost, the liturgy of its altars and daily offices and masses were serviced by the community of monks. These were, in age, a cross-section of the male population, for doubtless at the Old Minster, as at the New, the majority came as boys in the 11th century, offered as 'oblates' by their parents;[51] the boy oblates gradually died out in the 12th century. They were trained up in the monastic school, served its altars, and learned the monastic Rule and the liturgy of the church. As they grew to man's estate they took solemn vows, and holy orders. From the 10th century it became the normal practice for monks to proceed to orders and become, in the end, priests; it also came to be the normal practice for a priest to celebrate a private mass every day.[52] The ancient and modern rite of concelebration was quite unknown in the central Middle Ages, and so a large and growing community of priests—even if they said their masses in relays—needed a very large number of altars. Thus a great church had (in the fashion of the day) to be both one room and many: to have a high altar and other main altars, and numberless small chapels besides. Some altars were gathered round the ambulatory or in the choir aisles, others in the transepts, perhaps also in the galleries.[53] But it is likely that in the long run a great many of the altars were against pillars in the nave, as can still be seen at St Albans and more rarely elsewhere.

Much of the nave was not built when Walkelin's church was dedicated in 1093. Nonetheless, the idea of the great nave may well have been already in his mind, and was soon put into practice.[54] The immense naves of these Romanesque churches are their most puzzling features and Winchester, as the longest, is the most puzzling of all. It clearly played a role in the religious sentiment and religious life of the city and the see, and it clearly had a political and economic significance too. It was presumably above all the home of the laity in the cathedral; and it is striking that in so clerical and monastic an age the laity nonetheless commanded, here and elsewhere, a predominant place in a sacred building.

William Giffard, Walkelin's successor (1100-29), tells us himself that he was the first bishop of Winchester to institute the Pentecostal processions, which were evidently introduced by the Norman bishops from the Continent. At the feast of Pentecost processions came from every parish to the cathedral and offerings were made, Pentecostal oblations; and Bishop William recorded his innovation in a charter granting the fruits to the cathedral.[55] Pentecostal processions, and the ensuing grants, are recorded from a number of English sees in the first third of the 12th century, precisely in the age when the enormous naves were being added to the Norman choirs in many of these churches: Ely, York, Lincoln and Winchester are striking examples. Doubtless the nave gave shelter to the vast numbers who came on special occasions: not only at Pentecost, but at the major feasts of the diocese, presumably on St Peter's day and surely on the feasts of St Swithun. This is the most tangible reason we can assign. But indeed the cathedral nave was the greatest public building of the city, and just as Westminster Abbey was frequently used for councils of the realm as well as of the church, so doubtless Walkelin and his successor intended the nave of Winchester Cathedral to serve a like purpose; its close proximity to the royal palace made it as suitable as Westminster.[56] Add to this the love of processions and the need for altars, and we are on the way to understanding how the idea of the great nave could be conceived.

But not, perhaps, so near understanding its execution. The concentration of resources and skills—the money, materials, labourers, and craftsmen—is extraordinary. It must have puzzled the wits of contemporaries too; and it may be that the relatively crude masonry of early Norman buildings, and their plainness, reflect in some measure a shortage of craftsmen of the highest skill due to the exceptional demands of the age.[57] Nor do we know how it was paid for. But it is evident enough that religious sentiment, economics and politics were closely united in the enterprise. A common purpose inspired English and Norman, clerical and lay, men and women alike. The see of Winchester was immensely rich, and the bishop may have paid for much of the building. We can hardly suppose he paid for it all; and a substantial building appeal, drawing in king and nobility and citizens, as well as pilgrims to the shrine, is highly probable. To the nave particularly we may suppose that Henry I contributed. Unlike Rufus, he was a generous benefactor of great religious enterprises.[58] He was one of the chief patrons of the third church at Cluny; it is likely that Romsey Abbey church was in part a thank-offering for the childhood of his first wife,[59] and it would be surprising if he did not help in Winchester itself. As for the labourers, they must have been numbered in hundreds; and we may conjecture that there was evident political advantage—as the pharaohs had found in building the pyramids—in occupying humble folk only partly employed outside the time of harvest, and in keeping their minds from riot and tumult. It is only too evident that all this is conjectural: the texts are silent. But along these lines we can, in imagination, understand some of of the significance of this great building. The stones themselves are extremely eloquent, even if we are not perfectly able to understand their language.

Notes

1. In preparing this chapter I have been very grateful for the kind help of John Crook. For general background see F. Barlow, *The English Church 1000-1066*, 2nd edn. (London, 1979) and, *idem, The English Church 1066-1154* (London, 1979); M. Brett, *The English Church under Henry I* (Oxford, 1975); D. Knowles, *The Monastic Order in England, 940-1216*, 2nd edn. (Cambridge, 1963); R. and C. Brooke, 'I vescovi di Inghilterra e Normandia nel secolo XI: contrasti', in *Le Istituzioni Ecclesiastiche della 'Societas Christiana' dei Secoli XI-XII*, Miscellanea del Centro di Studi Medioevali, 8 (Milan, 1977), pp. 536-45.
2. Barlow, *English Church I*, esp. pp. 302-10; cf. D. Knowles, C. N. L. Brooke and V. C. M. London (eds.), *Heads of Religious Houses, England and Wales, I, 940-1216* (Cambridge, 1972) p. 64, note 4.
3. D. Whitelock, M. Brett and C. N. L. Brooke (eds.), *Councils and Synods with Other Documents relating to the English Church, I* (Oxford, 1981), pt. 2, pp. 565, 569, 571-3.
4. D. E. Greenway (ed.), *John Le Neve, Fasti Ecclesiæ Anglicanæ 1066-1300, II, Monastic Cathedrals* (London, 1971), p. 85; B. Thorpe (ed.), *Florence of Worcester, Chronicon ex Chronicis*, English Historical Society, 2 vols. (London, 1848-9), ii, pp. 6-7; for Walkelin as canon of Rouen, see esp. D. Spear, 'Les chanoines de la cathédrale de Rouen pendant la période ducale', *Annales de Normandie* 41 (1991), p. 137.
5. '*Ecclesiam ... quam spatio septem annorum a fundamentis ferme totam perfectam reddidit*': M. Rule (ed.), *Eadmer, Historia Novorum in Anglia*, RS 81 (1884), p. 13. '*Ferme*' has been variously interpreted; it cannot mean that much was left to do.
6. Cf. esp Knowles, *Monastic Order*, chap. 36.
7. *Ibid.* See also (and for what follows) C. Brooke, *The Medieval Idea of Marriage* (Oxford, 1989), pp. 82-3. Worcester, Winchester and Canterbury were monastic before 1066; Rochester, Durham, Bath, Norwich, Coventry and Ely joined them as monastic cathedrals between 1066 and 1109.
8. Eadmer, *Historia Novorum*, 18-21. On Alexander III's letter '*Accepimus*' there is a considerable literature: see esp. V. H. Clover in *La Normandie Bénédictine au Temps de Guillaume le Conquérant* (Lille, 1967), pp. 417-42. For Lanfranc's acceptance of English saints cf. R. W. Southern (ed. and trans.), *The Life of St Anselm, Archbishop of Canterbury by Eadmer* (London, 1962), pp. 51-4; the extent of Norman hesitation about English saints has been much debated: see S. J. Ridyard, 'Condigna

Veneratio: Post-Conquest Attitudes to the Saints of the Anglo-Saxons', *Anglo-Norman Studies* 9 (1986), pp. 179-206.

9. Spear, 'Chanoines', p. 137.
10. From 1082-93: *Heads I*, p. 45.
11. C. Johnson, M. Brett, C. N. L. Brooke and M. Winterbottom (eds.), *Hugh the Chanter, The History of the Church of York, 1066-1127* (Oxford, 1990), p. 21, note 3 and refs. there cited; Janet Burton (ed.), *English Episcopal Acta, V, York 1070-1154* (London, 1988), pp. xxiv-xxv; D. Spear, 'Les dignitaires de la cathédrale de Rouen pendant la période ducale', *Annales de Normandie* 37 (1987), pp. 121-47, at pp. 122-3. Spear notes that Gerard's position as precentor depends on a single late mention by Robert of Torigni, and that there was a Gerard, archdeacon of Rouen, who occurs in 1091.
12. Spear, 'Chanoines', p. 137.
13. Brooke, *Marriage,* pp. 89-92.
14. See below, p. 125.
15. G. Zarnecki, in *English Romanesque Art 1066-1200,* Exhibition Catalogue, Hayward Gallery (London, 1984), p. 147, attributes the simplicity of early Norman building especially to a shortage of sculptors in relation to the scale of the Norman building campaign. This may well be part of the story (cf. note 57, below), but the absence of sculpture suggests also a more deliberate puritanism among the first generation of Norman patrons.
16. C. N. L. Brooke and G. Keir, *London 800-1216: The Shaping of a City* (London, 1975), p. 137 and pl. 42.
17. K. J. Conant, *Cluny: les Eglises et la Maison du Chef d'Ordre* (Mâcon, 1968), *passim; idem, Carolingian and Romanesque Architecture,* rev. edn. (Harmondsworth, 1978), pp. 167-75, pls. 122-5. On Lanfranc's cushion capitals see E. Fernie, 'The Effect of the Conquest on Norman Architectural Patronage', *Anglo-Norman Studies* 9 (1986), pp. 71-85, at p. 77: '... of a type ubiquitous in the Empire and North Italy, but unknown in Normandy until considerably later'. He comments on the scale of Walkelin's cathedral in the same passage.
18. For this and what follows see *Councils and Synods I,* pt. 2, pp. 586-616. For the primacy dispute see esp. Brett, in Johnson *et al., Hugh the Chanter,* pp. xxx-xlv.
19. *Winchester Studies 1,* p. 310 and note 3.
20. The Annals of Winchester survive in two closely related manuscripts: the earlier, Cambridge, Corpus Christi College, MS 339, fo. 22v, has under 1080: *'Walkelinus episcopus cepit a fundamentis reedificare Wintoniensem ecclesiam'* ; the slightly later manuscript, BL, Cotton. Domit. A.xiii, edited by H. R. Luard (*Annales Monastici, II: Winchester and Waverley,* RS 36 (1865), p. 32), has, *sub anno* 1079: *'Walkelinus episcopus a fundamentis Wintoniæ coepit reædificare ecclesiam.'* The entry relating to the events of 1093 is only in the Cotton manuscript, under 1093: *'Hoc anno in præsentia omnium fere episcoporum atque abbatum Angliæ cum maxima exultatione et gloria de veteri monasterio Wintoniæ ad novum venerunt monachi vi. id. Aprilis. Ad festum vero Sancti Swithuni, facta processione de novo monasterio ad vetus, tulerunt idem feretrum Sancti Swithuni et in novo honorifice collocaverunt.'* Next day they began, at Walkelin's orders, to demolish the old church, and the whole was destroyed that year except *portico uno et magno altari* (*Winchester Annals,* p. 37). This does not describe the meeting of 8 April as a dedication, but it is hard to imagine so great a gathering for any other purpose. On the manuscripts and history of the annals see J. T. Appleby, 'Richard of Devizes and the Annals of Winchester', *Bulletin of the Institute of Historical Research* 36 (1963), pp. 70-7. The surviving annals were edited by Richard of Devizes in the 1190s.
21. For this difference in conception see C. Brooke, *Medieval Church and Society* (London, 1971), pp. 167-75.
22. See below, pp. 13-20.
23. *Ibid.,* pp. 176-7.
24. See below, p. 177ff.
25. A. W. Clapham, *English Romanesque Architecture before the Conquest* (Oxford, 1930), pls. 6-8, fig. 22 (p. 89).
26. J. France (ed.), *Rodulfus Glaber, Historiarum Libri Quinque* (Oxford, 1989), pp. 126-7.
27. Conant, *Architecture,* pp. 131-5 and pls. 87-91; C. Brooke, *The Twelfth Century Renaissance* (London, 1969), p. 96, pl. 57. Speyer was partly destroyed in the late 17th century: much of what we now see is sympathetic reconstruction.
28. *Winchester Studies 1,* p. 310.

29. *Ibid.,* pp. 310-11; H. M. Colvin (ed.), *The History of the King's Works: The Middle Ages, I* (London, 1963), pp. 14-17; E. Fernie, *The Architecture of the Anglo-Saxons* (London, 1983), pp. 154-7, suggesting Jumièges as the model for Westminster Abbey.

30. On the forgeries, see P. Chaplais, 'The Original Charters of Herbert and Gervase, Abbots of Westminster (1121-1157)', in P. M. Barnes and C. F. Slade (eds.), *A Medieval Miscellany for Doris Mary Stenton,* Pipe Roll Society, 76 (1962 for 1960), pp. 89-110.

31. W. Stubbs (ed.), *William of Malmesbury, De Gestis Regum,* 2 vols., RS 90 (1887-9), ii, p. 379.

32. F. Barlow, *William Rufus* (London, 1983), esp. pp. 433-7.

33. Cf. Brooke and Keir, *London,* pp. 29, 99, 146, 342-3.

34. D. Owen, 'The Norman Cathedral at Lincoln', *Anglo-Norman Studies* 6 (1984), pp. 188-99.

35. It is most dramatically revealed in D. Knowles and J. K. S. St Joseph, *Monastic Sites from the Air* (Cambridge, 1952), p. 3.

36. C. F. Battiscombe (ed.), *The Relics of St Cuthbert* (Oxford, 1956).

37. Brooke, *Medieval Church,* p. 168 and note 15.

38. C. Brooke in R. K. Runcie (ed.), *Cathedral and City: St Albans Ancient and Modern* (London, 1977), p. 51; C. Brooke, 'The Normans as Cathedral Builders', in Willis, *Winchester Cathedral,* p. 90.

39. A. Binns, *Dedications of Monastic Houses in England and Wales, 1066-1216* (Woodbridge, 1989), p. 90.

40. Gregory of Tours, *History of the Franks*, e.g. vi.10, vii.42, trans. L. Thorpe (Harmondsworth, 1974), pp. 340-1, 426.

41. On these lists see esp. D. W. Rollason, 'Lists of Saints' Resting Places in Anglo-Saxon England', *Anglo-Saxon England* 7 (1978), pp. 61-93; for what follows, R. and C. Brooke, *Popular Religion in the Middle Ages* (London, 1984), pp. 22-6, 35-41, 159-60.

42. See below, pp. 61 and 179, and, for a different view, 247.

43. For this and what follows, see Binns, *Dedications,* p. 90.

44. W. Levison, *England and the Continent in the Eighth Century* (Oxford, 1946), pp. 259-65.

45. Bede, *Ecclesiastical History,* iii.7, ed. B. Colgrave and R. A. B. Mynors (Oxford, 1969), pp. 232-3.

46. Brooke and Brooke, *Popular Religion*, pp. 33-5.

47. V. Ortenberg, *The English Church and the Continent in the Tenth and Eleventh Centuries* (Oxford, 1992).

48. Binns, *Dedications,* pp. 18-38.

49. *Ibid.,* p. 90. For the date of the move to Hyde, see especially *Winchester Studies 1,* p. 317, note 5.

50. *Winchester Studies 2,* i, pp. 134-5.

51. For New Minster, there is an exceptional source of information in the lists of monks in the *Liber Vitæ* (BL, Stowe 944): W. de Gray Birch (ed.), *Liber Vitæ: Register and Martyrology of New Minster and Hyde Abbey Winchester,* HRSoc (1892); cf. C. Brooke and W. Swaan, *The Monastic World* (London, 1974), p. 88 and pls. 141-3.

52. See C. N. L. Brooke, 'Priest, Deacon and Layman, from St Peter Damian to St Francis', *Studies in Church History* 26 (1989), pp. 69-71.

53. At Winchester provision was made from the start for six altars at gallery level on the east side of the transept. See below, p. 34.

54. See below, p. 22.

55. Brett, *English Church,* pp. 162-4, and 164, note 1; a critical text of William Giffard's charter is published in M. J. Franklin (ed.), *English Episcopal Acta* 8 (London, 1993), No. 19.

56. *Councils and Synods I,* pt. 2, pp. 691, 709-16, etc.; Biddle and Keene, *Winchester Studies 1,* p. 311, note however, that 'the uses to which it was put reflect only the waning importance of Winchester as a royal centre'.

57. Brooke, 'Cathedral Builders', p. 96. Cf. the conclusion of Derek Phillips that the foundations of the Norman cathedral at York were specially designed so that good labourers, not skilled masons, could do much of the work: *The Cathedral of Archbishop Thomas of Bayeux: Excavations at York Minster, II,* Royal Commission on Historical Monuments (London, 1985), pp. 191-3.

58. For this and what follows, see C. N. L. Brooke, 'Princes and Kings as Patrons of Monasteries: Normandy and England', in *Il Monachesimo e la Riforma Ecclesiastica (1049-1122),* Miscellanea del Centro di Studi Medioevali, 6 (Milan, 1971), pp. 125-52.

59. *Heads I,* p. 219, corrected by Brett in *Councils and Synods I,* pt. 2, p. 661 and note 3. The evidence suggests, however, that she had been in both Romsey and Wilton.

OLD MINSTER, ST SWITHUN'S DAY 1093

Birthe Kjølbye-Biddle

By the summer of 1093 there stood in the south-east quarter of Winchester a remarkable complex of ancient and venerated buildings: the royal palace, perhaps going back to the 5th century; Old Minster, the cathedral, by now 445 years old; New Minster, constructed *c*.901-3, the church of Alfred's new *burh*; Nunnaminster, built about the same time; and the bishop's palace, in existence from the later 10th century. Something different, and alien, was the east end of the new Norman cathedral built by Bishop Walkelin in the years since 1079 (Fig. 2.1).

The transepts and east arm of the new church were fitted into the only available space, clear to the east of Old Minster. When they had been dedicated, and the reliquary of St Swithun translated from the old church into the new on St Swithun's day, 15 July 1093, Bishop Walkelin had Old Minster demolished so that the nave of the new cathedral could be constructed over the site of the old one. 'And it was all broken down in that year except for one *porticus* and the great altar'; next year 'relics of St Swithun and of many other saints were found under the altar of the old church'.[1]

The church so expeditiously demolished had been a creation of different architectural and religious impulses over the last 450 years, and was probably the finest building in England. Immediately to the north lay New Minster, a basilican church essentially of one period (Fig. 2.2). In style and historical development these two were like the present cathedrals of Winchester and Salisbury, the former composed of many parts and styles, the latter of one period. The impression would be as if those two lay side by side.

Old Minster achieved its final shape in around 993-94, exactly 100 years before it was demolished (Fig. 2.3f). The ancient core was a square-ended, cruciform church partly constructed of re-used Roman stone (Fig. 2.3a). This church was laid out in a module, which we shall call 'X', of 16.5 Long Roman feet, equivalent to 5.50 m. This foot is called Drusian in the late Roman period, and is basically the same as the foot used in the 8th and 9th centuries on the Continent, now sometimes called the Carolingian or Northern foot. This module (later to be replaced in this country by the shorter rod of 16.5 English feet) and the diagonal (R) of a square whose sides were equal to the length of the module (R = X $\sqrt{2}$ = 7.78 m.) remained in use until the last elements of Old Minster had been added in the late 10th century. By contrast, the English foot was used in the lay-out of New Minster *c*.901-3, and may well have been the foot generally in use from the early 10th century, but for Old Minster the module of the first church remained the overriding factor throughout its architectural development.

The 7th-century nave of Old Minster was 66 Long Roman feet (4X or 22 m.) in length and 33 feet (2X or 11 m.) wide. In around 993-4 the total length of Old Minster

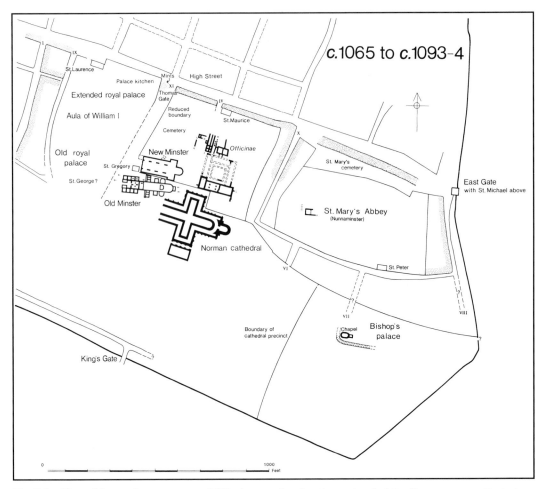

Fig. 2.1   Plan of the south-east quarter of Winchester, showing the east end of the Romanesque cathedral.
Winchester Research Unit

was 220.5 Long Roman feet (73.5 m.). The first alterations took place during the 8th century, when the square east end was changed into an apse with an external length equal to R (Fig. 2.3b). In the same century St Martin's tower was built free-standing axially to the west, with its west front five modules (5X) west of the west front of the 7th-century nave, and its width north-south (2X) equal to the width of the nave.

A path ran through St Martin's tower to the great west door of the nave. It was in the middle of this path that Bishop Swithun was buried in 862. He had been a successful bishop in a period of rising prosperity for both Winchester and Old Minster. This is reflected, albeit faintly, in the archaeology, with finds such as coloured window-glass, and fragments of painted scenes and sculpture. King Alfred (871-99) made Winchester into an urban place again in the late 9th century and seems to have taken the first steps towards the foundation of New Minster, probably as a church for the citizens of the revitalised town. Although King Alfred brought Grimbald from the monastery of Saint-Bertin at Saint-Omer to England, probably with the intention of entrusting the creation of the new church to his care, it was in

Fig. 2.2   Old Minster and New Minster from the north, as they were from *c*.993-94 to 1093. *Winchester Research Unit*

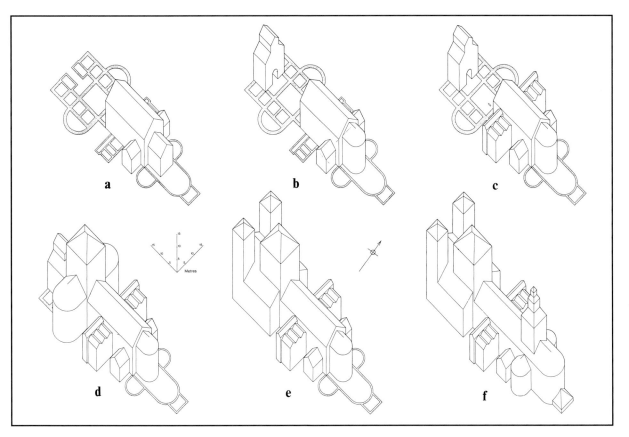

Fig. 2.3   Old Minster: structural development, *c*.648 to *c*.993-94. *Winchester Research Unit*

the event Alfred's son, Edward the Elder (899-924), who founded New Minster and saw to its construction c.901-3.

The Old Minster clergy cannot have been delighted to see this new church rise in the northern churchyard of their cathedral, so close, as is well known, that 'the voices of the two choirs confounded one another'.[2] The community responded at once, building a grand façade so that Old Minster would look the larger of the two churches when approached from the west.

During the reign of Bishop Ethelwold (963-84) and his successor, Ælfheah (984-1006), Old Minster reached its final form. First, a vast structure was built around and over the grave believed, probably with justice, to be that of Bishop Swithun. This building joined St Martin's Tower to the 7th-century nave by the construction of a great central tower, 91 Long Roman feet (30.33 m.) high, over the grave, flanked to north and south by apses each as wide as the ancient nave (Fig. 2.3d). The total span across the apses was 99 Long Roman feet (6X or 33 m.): larger, that is, than the diameter of Charlemagne's great octagon at Aachen. This centrally planned, quintessentially English, building did not last long. It is possible that the Rule of the monastic reform, *Regularis Concordia,* was signed in it c.971 or c.973, in the presence of Archbishop Dunstan of Canterbury, Bishop Oswald of Worcester, Bishop Ethelwold himself, and King Edgar (959-75).

On 15 July 971 the bones of Bishop Swithun, now sainted, were translated by order of King Edgar from the original grave outside Old Minster into the ancient nave.[3] Three years later, perhaps in 974, some of the bones were placed near the high altar, and others were enshrined in the great double-apsed *martyrium* which had by then been built around the site of the original grave.

A new sort of western structure was, however, now required, one in which the king could see and be seen in a distinctive setting. King Edgar had played an extraordinary role in the monastic reform, and his patronage was of exceptional importance. This is reflected in *Regularis Concordia,* where about 475 words out of the total of about 1,290 in the foreword are about the king himself (36 per cent), and where prayers are instructed to be said for the royal house, summer and winter, no fewer than seven times a day.[4] A new work was therefore built at the west end of the church (Fig. 2.3f) and dedicated in 980 in the presence of King Æthelred, Archbishop Dunstan of Canterbury, Bishop Ethelwold, and seven other monastic bishops, as well as nobles and thegns, including most of the English ealdormen. The ceremony was followed by a very good feast.

In this new westwork the king would have a seat high in the building, from which he would be able to see right to the east end of the church, and thus observe what was happening at the high altar (Fig. 2.4). The westwork was wrapped around St Martin's Tower and also around the central tower of the *martyrium* which had been built only a few years before above the saint's tomb. The new westwork was built in the standard module (X) with a square ground plan, each side the same length as the ancient nave, i.e. 66 Long Roman feet (4X or 22 m.). To the west there were two corner towers, each 90.5 Long Roman feet (30.17 m.) high, and to the east there were chapels on two floors. The archaeological remains of the western part of Old Minster, as they survived the Norman destruction, can thus be interpreted and at least its major elements can be described.

There were eight chapels at ground level, four to each side of the central area. The latter was itself divided into five distinct spaces from west to east: (i) the area below St Martin's Tower, from which stairs led to north and south into the corner towers; and (ii) a narrower area at the same level, probably with wide stairs leading north and south into chapels. An

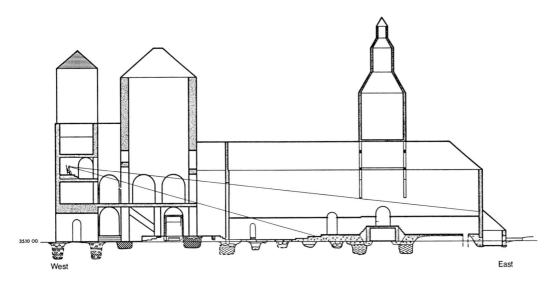

35.10 OD

West   East

Fig. 2.4a Old Minster
showing the king seated
in the westwork and his
line of sight. *Winchester
Research Unit*

Fig. 2.4b Artist's
impression of the view
east from the royal seat.
*Winchester Research
Unit*

Fig. 2.5   Block from a narrative frieze from Old Minster, possibly showing Sigmund in an episode from the Volsung saga. *John Crook*

arched opening led east into (iii) an area west of the saint's shrine, from which stairs led east into (iv) the saint's shrine, and also to north and south up to the first floor of the westwork. In relation to the main floor of the westwork the saint's chapel could be described as a 'crypt', meaning essentially a lower, stone-roofed space, even if at ground level rather than sunken. From the saint's chapel one could move west into (v), an area which lay immediately west of the 7th-century nave, serving almost like an ante-chamber or narthex. Here there were major tombs, including a built structure like that around the saint, but constructed for an unknown person.

Only now have we reached the ancient nave. The western structure, reconstructed in the previous paragraph from the archaeological evidence, is the work described by the Cantor Wulfstan before 1005 in his 'special letter' to Bishop Ælfheah. This letter precedes Wulfstan's poem on the miracles and translation of St Swithun, and describes the additions to Old Minster made by Ethelwold and Ælfheah. In the lines which follow Wulfstan describes Ethelwold's part of the work:

istius antiqui reparauit et atria templi,
moenibus excelsis, culminibusque nouis,
partibus hoc austri firmans et partibus arcti
porticibus solidis, arcubus et uariis.
addidit et plures sacris altaribus aedes,   45
quæ retinent dubium liminis introitum,
quisquis ut ignotis hæc deambulat atria plantis,
nesciat unde meat quoue pedem referat,
omni parte fores quia conspiciuntur apertæ,
nec patet ulla sibi semita certa uiæ;   50
huc illucque uagos stans circumducit ocellos,
Attica Dedalei tecta stupetque soli,
certior adueniat donec sibi ductor, et ipsum
ducat ad extremi limina uestibuli.
hic secum mirans cruce se consignat, et unde   55
exeat, attonito pectore scire nequit.[5]

The translation of this passage is difficult because so many of the specific words have today not one single meaning but several. Roger Quirk translated it thus:[6]

He [Ethelwold] also repaired the courts (*atria*) of this ancient temple with lofty walls and new roofs, strengthening it in its southern and northern parts with solid *porticus* and divers arches. He also added many chapels with sacred altars which keep the entry of the threshold doubtful, so that whoever walks in these courts (*atria*) with unfamiliar tread cannot tell whence he comes or whither to return, since open doors are seen on every hand, nor does any certain path of a way appear. Standing he turns his wandering gaze hither and thither and is amazed at the Attic roofs of the Daedalian floor, until a better informed guide appears and leads him to the threshold of the furthest vestibule. Here wondering in himself he crosses himself and cannot know in his astonished breast from what place he is to get out.

This contemporary account is a faithful, if flowery, description of the westwork revealed by archaeology nine centuries after it had been flattened to the ground.

Ælfheah continued the reconstruction after Ethelwold's death in 984. The façade added to Old Minster in response to the construction of New Minster still stood, with chapels, perhaps on two floors, added to the back. These chapels were approached from the west end of the ancient nave. Ælfheah now raised the floor of the nave, with a wide flight of steps leading to the high altar. These steps also led north and south into the 7th-century *porticus*. The northern of these had always been a baptistry, but it was completely remodelled in the late 10th century with a circular or perhaps octagonal sunken area, probably once marble-clad.

Ethelwold had probably been buried in a monolithic coffin placed immediately to the north of the high altar, which at the time of his death was still in its 7th-century position. Now the altar was moved so that it stood on a raised area above a crypt created in the old east *porticus*. Beyond this a long eastern apse, three times as long as its predecessor, was now built. On the central axis at the east end there was a deep stone-lined well, and an external crypt (an *Aussenkrypta*) was built beyond the furthest point of the apse. To the north and south of the new high altar area smaller north and south apses were

Fig. 2.6   The plan of Old Minster laid out on the ground north of the cathedral. *John Crook*

constructed, a memory of the much larger apses which had once flanked St Swithun's grave, where now the westwork stood. A five-staged tower was constructed. No certain traces of the foundations for this tower were found in the excavation, but the only place where it could reasonably have stood was above the new high altar. Here the tower would have been buttressed to north and south by the lateral apses. Reconstruction studies suggest that this tower was 105 Long Roman feet (35 m.) high. Ælfheah's completed works were dedicated in 993-94 (Fig. 2.2).

The works of Ethelwold and Ælfheah had enormously enlarged the floor area of Old Minster, probably by four to five times. The church now had four towers, three crypts (if one includes St Swithun's chapel), three apses, at least 24 smaller chapels, an elaborate baptistry, and a splendid nave which in large steps led the eye and person to an elevated high altar. This exciting building was embellished with coloured window-glass, painted walls, and elaborate stone reliefs, including, perhaps as a later addition, a narrative frieze which seems to have told the story of the Danish and English royal houses in a 'Bayeux Tapestry' of stone (Fig. 2.5). The floor of Old Minster was partly stone flagged, and partly laid with multicoloured relief tiles. A booming organ, said to have required 70 strong men to operate it, was placed in the new church, and bells were cast to ring from the tower. The five-staged tower was crowned by a weathercock which

> stands on its summit, adorned in gold, awe-inspiring to behold ... It holds the sceptre of rule in its proud talons and stands above the entire populace of Winchester ... Thus the weary wayfarer is carried along by his rapt gaze, and although he is still remote [from Old Minster] ... he is nonetheless fixed to it by virtue of his eyesight.[7]

This was the church that was demolished in 1093-94, to be resurrected by archaeological excavations almost a thousand years after its last dedication in 993-94 (Fig. 2.6).[8]

Notes

1. *Winchester Annals,* p. 37; text quoted by R. N. Quirk, 'Winchester Cathedral in the Tenth Century', *Arch. J.* 114 (1957), p. 61 note 1..
2. N. E. S. A. Hamilton (ed.), *Willelmi Malmesburiensis De Gestis Pontificum Anglorum,* RS 52 (1870), p. 174:'... *et erant ambæ ecclesiæ sic vicinæ parietibus contiguis ut voces canentium aliæ obstreperent aliis.'*
3. Lantfred, I. 3.24: E. P. Sauvage (ed.), 'Sancti Swithuni ... Translatio et Miracula auctore Lantfredo', *Analecta Bollandiana* 4 (1885), p. 31; A new edition and translation will be published in M. Lapidge, *The Cult of St Swithun,* Winchester Studies, 4.ii (forthcoming).
4. T. Symons (ed.), *Regularis Concordia: the Monastic Agreement of the Monks and Nuns of the English Nation* (London, 1953), pp. 1-9 and xliii-xliv.
5. A. Campbell (ed.), *Frithegodi Monachi Breviloquium vitæ Beati Wilfredi et Wulfstani Cantoris Narratio Metrica de Sancto Swithuno* (Zurich, 1950), p. 66, lines 41-56; also to be published in *Winchester Studies 4.ii.*
6. Quirk, 'Winchester Cathedral', p. 44.
7. Wulfstan, *Narratio Metrica,* p. 71, lines 189-206; translation kindly supplied by Michael Lapidge, from *Winchester Studies 4.ii,* forthcoming.
8. The excavations and associated research will be published as *The Anglo-Saxon Minsters of Winchester*: M. Biddle and B. Kjølbye-Biddle, *The Anglo-Saxon Minsters,* Winchester Studies, 4.i; M. Lapidge, *The Cult of St Swithun,* Winchester Studies, 4.ii; A. R. Rumble, *Anglo-Saxon and Early Norman Charters Relating to the Topography of Winchester,* Winchester Studies, 4.iii (Oxford, forthcoming).

BISHOP WALKELIN'S CATHEDRAL

John Crook

Within half a century of Archbishop Lanfranc's Council of London (1075) every cathedral church in England had been built anew: a phenomenon which has aptly been called 'an ecclesiastical building explosion'.[1] Several cathedrals were transferred to more populous towns or rich abbeys: North Elmham to Norwich (via Thetford); Sherborne to Old Sarum; Selsey to Chichester; Dorchester-on-Thames to Lincoln; Lichfield to Coventry (via Chester); and Wells, for a time, to Bath. A new cathedral was made out of the abbey of Ely in 1109.[2] Where appropriate, other cathedrals were rebuilt on the same site: Lanfranc began to reconstruct Christ Church, Canterbury in 1070, the year of his consecration, and Hereford, Worcester and Durham followed not long after.

Winchester was already a thriving major city, and there were compelling reasons why the new cathedral should occupy the same site as its Anglo-Saxon predecessor. Firstly, there was an active pilgrimage cult associated with the grave and relics of St Swithun.[3] It was not the Conqueror's policy to suppress the memory of Saxon saints, or indeed Saxon kings; after all, William wished to be regarded as the legitimate successor of the Confessor.[4] The remains both of saints and kings, preserved in Winchester Cathedral to this day, bear witness to this aspect of Saxo-Norman continuity.[5] Secondly, the Anglo-Saxon cathedral was just one part of a royal and ecclesiastical complex comprising Old Minster, the royal palace immediately opposite the west end of that church, New Minster (the royal foundation of Alfred and Edward the Elder), Nunnaminster (founded by Alfred's queen, Ealhswith), and Wolvesey Palace.

There was at the same time a need for the religious life of St Swithun's Priory to continue: the *Opus Dei* and the attendant functions of the cathedral church could not be interrupted while the new church was under construction.[6] Consequently the first parts of the Romanesque cathedral to be built—the east arm containing the monastic choir, the transepts, and perhaps three bays of the nave—were erected immediately south-east of Old Minster, allowing that building to remain standing until its replacement was ready for use. The Romanesque north transept stood just clear of the east end of the Anglo-Saxon church (Fig. 2.1).

Such matters must have been carefully considered by Bishop Walkelin and his master mason before the outline of the foundations was pegged out on site. Unfortunately the documentary evidence for the building campaign is confined to the annals compiled by the Winchester monk, Richard of Devizes, over a century later.[7] No contemporary chronicler, such as Canterbury's Eadmer, has left an account of the construction process. Richard's annals provide merely a basic framework of dates: the start of work in 1079,[8] a dubious reference to the provision of timber (presumably for the roof) in 1086, and the implied first consecration in 1093. No names are given apart from Walkelin's. But the erection of a major cathedral would have demanded a well-organised secretariat, probably drawn from the monks of St Swithun's Priory, as well as a large labour-force. One Hugh *cœmentarius* held two ploughlands from Walkelin on the monastery's Chilcomb estate, and it has been suggested that this Hugh—about whom nothing else is known—was the master mason involved in overseeing the construction project.[9]

One can only guess at the feelings of the monks of St Swithun's when the lines of the foundations of the new church were marked out, partly on the site of their cemetery. Meanwhile a suitable supply of stone was obtained from the newly-opened quarry near Fishbourne on the Isle of Wight.[10] The annalist's vivid but improbable account of the total destruction of the Conqueror's 'delectable wood' of Hempage in order to provide timber may have some basis in truth, implying that building materials were assured by the cathedral's royal patron.[11]

Despite extensive later additions and alterations, the plan of Winchester Cathedral remains largely as conceived in the late 1070s. The changes disguise, rather than obliterate, the Romanesque lay-out: even in the east arm, completely rebuilt above pavement level between about 1200 and 1520, the original plan survives in the crypt.

The most obvious feature of the Romanesque cathedral is its great length—164 m. (534 ft.)—far surpassing anything hitherto built in Normandy, and longer than any other English cathedral built by the Normans.[12] Various theories have been advanced to explain the exceptional length of Walkelin's cathedral, particularly its 12-bay nave. It has been noted, for example, that the length and width of the Winchester nave almost exactly match certain equivalent dimensions of Constantine's church of St Peter in Rome, suggesting that Bishop Walkelin may have wished to emulate that influential early Christian basilica.[13] However, a simpler explanation of the length of the nave is that it resulted from the demands of the site. Martin Biddle has argued that it was intended that the west front should occupy the same position as its Anglo-Saxon predecessor.[14] Secondly, because Old Minster remained standing during the first 14 years of building work, the north transept had to be built on the clear ground east of the earlier church. These two constraints, determining the position of the west front at one end and the crossing at the other, may in turn have determined the length of the nave and its orientation. Other factors may, however, have played their part, not least, the intention of king and bishop that the royal church should be a powerful symbol of the new, Norman version of the Church Militant on earth.

Walkelin's church was cruciform, with transepts extending by three bays beyond the nave aisles. The choir was located in the crossing, beneath a lantern tower, and extended as a platform by one bay into the nave. Beyond the crossing, the original east arm, raised 2 m. (6 ft. 6 ins.) above nave floor level on a crypt, consisted of a presbytery of four straight bays terminating in an apse, around which the aisles continued as an ambulatory (Fig. 3.1).[15] Leading off the ambulatory was an unusually long axial chapel, also apsidal, and this was flanked by a pair of chapels at the ends of the presbytery aisles. These chapels were square on plan, and must have concealed the apsidal design of the presbytery from outside the church, at least at lower level.

The traditional idea that the apse-and-ambulatory scheme in this country was imported from the Touraine via the abbey church at Battle must now be abandoned:[16] there can be little doubt that the formula was introduced to post-Conquest England directly from Normandy, particularly from a small but significant group of churches in the lower Seine valley. The Romanesque cathedral of Rouen, dedicated by Archbishop Maurilius in 1063, appears to

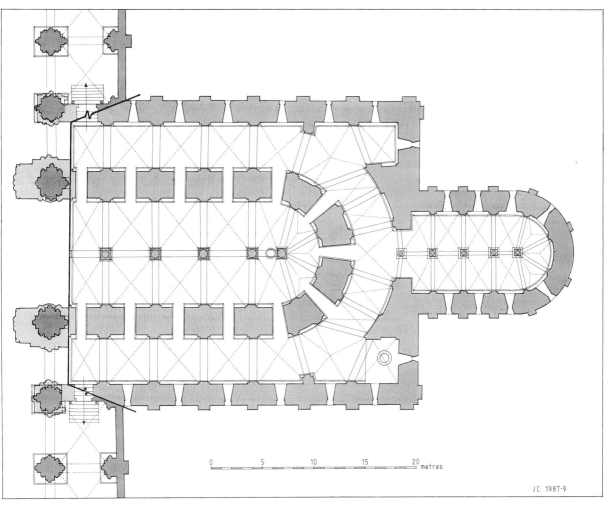

Fig. 3.1   Winchester Cathedral. Plan of the Romanesque crypt. *John Crook*

have been particularly influential in this regard, and this may reflect Walkelin's Rouen origins.[17] As at Winchester, the design of Rouen's original east end is known only from its crypt, which was rediscovered in the late 19th century, having been forgotten since the Middle Ages.

Although some of the features of the Rouen crypt are found at Winchester, a more immediate source had been built at St Augustine's Abbey, Canterbury by Abbot Scotland, shortly after his appointment in 1070 (Fig. 3.2). It is likely that the Winchester master mason was aware of the important architectural developments taking place at Canterbury; and the plan of Winchester's crypt and east arm should perhaps be regarded as a synthesis of the liturgical requirements and architectural preconceptions of the patron, Walkelin, and the practical experience of his master mason.

The plan of the Romanesque east arm of Winchester Cathedral differed fundamentally from contemporary continental work in its treatment of the three chapels at the east end. The

Fig. 3.2   Canterbury. St Augustine's Abbey. Remains of the crypt. *John Crook*

axial chapel is unusual in its length, but otherwise finds a counterpart at Rouen and elsewhere. Without parallel in Normandy, however, are the pair of square chapels terminating the aisles. Continental apse-and-ambulatory churches favoured chapels radiating from the ambulatory: there were two such chapels at Rouen as well as the axial chapel, and the great pilgrimage churches had five radial chapels. Radial chapels could not be correctly oriented, however, and in England, where there seems to have been a preference for chapels which faced east, this problem was solved in various ways. At Norwich, the radial chapels, already apsidal, have secondary apses on their eastern sides; while at Worcester the chapels were polygonal, allowing the altars to be placed against walls facing approximately east. The problem did not arise in churches of 'apse-échelon' type, where the flanking chapels lay parallel to the central one; and the Winchester side-chapels should perhaps be regarded as an idiosyncratic fusion of the two major traditions: apse-and-ambulatory and apse-échelon.

The plan of the transepts was equally ambitious. They have aisles both on the east and the west sides: an arrangement without known parallel in Normandy, but one which would later be followed at Ely—perhaps owing to the influence of Walkelin's brother, Simeon, who was abbot there from 1082 to 1093—and also at Old St Paul's, London. In addition the Winchester aisles continue around the end of the transepts, providing a complete processional circuit similar to that found in several of the great pilgrimage churches of similar date, such as Santiago de Compostela (*c*.1078) and Saint-Sernin, Toulouse (*c*.1080).

The design of the Romanesque west front of Winchester Cathedral is disputed. The footings have been partially excavated on several occasions,[18] and a substantial portion of the core of the south wall still stands above ground level. It is clear that an important western *massif* dominated this end of the cathedral until it was demolished in the mid-14th century, an operation which shortened the church by about 15 m. (45 ft.).

Two interpretations of the limited evidence are possible: the west end consisted either of a central tower with flanking transepts, or of twin towers flanking a central structure at the end of the nave. Supporters of the transept theory cite the extant example of Ely, regarding the feature as another manifestation of Abbot Simeon's influence there.[19] However, the balance of evidence seems to indicate twin towers.[20] The relative thicknesses of the three cells of the foundation are consistent with this notion. More compelling still is the comparative evidence. Twin towers, flanking a balcony, possibly for royal ceremonial, were a feature of the westwork of Old Minster, built by Bishop Ethelwold between 974-80;[21] if the Romanesque west front was designed with the same function in mind, a similar arrangement might be expected. Furthermore, flanking towers were a feature, either planned or actually built, of all the other extremities of the cathedral, even though the transept towers were an afterthought.[22] Walkelin's eventual idea may have been that Winchester should boast nine towers in all (including the central one) as shown in our conjectural reconstruction (Fig. 3.3); this formula may be traced back to Carolingian prototypes. The Norman abbey church at Jumièges (1042-67) provides a somewhat earlier continental parallel for a church with flanking towers and a central balcony at the west end, open to the nave (Fig. 3.4), though the towers there, being smaller on plan, do not project beyond the aisle walls. Closer still may have been the original western tower-porch

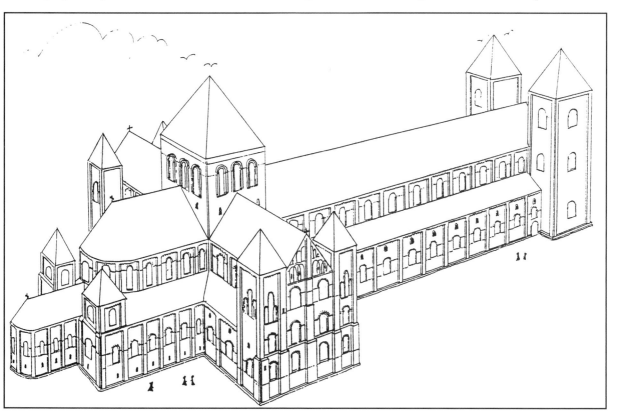

Fig. 3.3   Conjectural view of Winchester Cathedral as it might have appeared *c.*1120 had all the planned elements (including the abortive transept corner towers) been completed. *John Crook*

Fig. 3.4   Jumièges. Interior view of west end. *John Crook*

of Sainte-Trinité, Caen, begun in 1062 under the patronage of Queen Matilda (Fig. 3.5).[23] In our view, the probable arrangement at Winchester consisted of a tribune at gallery level, supported on two arches below, continuing the main arcade of the nave (an arrangement similar to the transept ends but two bays deep).

So far we have considered mainly the plan of Winchester cathedral, as Bishop Walkelin and his master mason might have discussed it before a single stone was laid. The first work consisted of the excavation of the crypt. In a superficial way it echoes its Anglo-Saxon predecessor, raising the eastern limb by 2 m. (6 ft. 6 ins.) above the rest of the church. The Romanesque crypt was excavated to a depth of about 2.15 m. (7 ft.) below ground level. It was lit by splayed windows slanting down through the walls; these are all now either blocked or altered. There were entrances from the eastern aisle of each transept and an external entrance on the south side.

Walkelin's crypt is rightly regarded as an outstanding example of late 11th-century religious architecture (Fig. 3.6). Its authenticity is the happy result of the fact that a tendency to flood has prevented it from being turned to any useful or profit-making purpose. Even though four out of the five straight bays of the central chamber were blocked off at an early date, the essential atmosphere of this place has been preserved.

The groined vaulting of the central chamber is supported by a single row of massive cylindrical piers. These are the earliest piers in the cathedral, and they appear primitive because they lack a true capital: the pier itself is of sufficiently large diameter to permit the abacus to rest directly on it. The piers of the axial chapel are slender by comparison, and have conventional cushion capitals.

The well in the central chamber never ceases to intrigue visitors. It is located almost exactly on the focus of the apse, and seems to have been sunk before the adjacent piers were constructed, even though it is unlikely to be of Anglo-Saxon origin. The well is a potent symbol of the living water of the Christian gospel, and it is entirely appropriate that it should have echoed the position of the most sacred part of the church: the high altar was placed immediately above it. Wells in crypts are not uncommon: Rouen had one, placed in the ambulatory on the central axis of the building, and so did Old Minster, in a position analogous to the well in Walkelin's crypt. There is a second well in the south-eastern chapel of the Romanesque crypt, possibly also of 11th- or 12th-century date.

Fig. 3.5   Caen. Sainte-Trinité. West front. *John Crook*

The crypt now floods regularly most winters with the seasonal rise in the water-table. It is inconceivable that this was originally intended, and the crypt floor must have been safely above the water-level when its level was determined.[24] Possibly the rise in Winchester's water-table, apparent since Roman times, was still in progress in the late 11th century, or perhaps the cathedral was built during a dry period in the cyclical variation of the English climate. By the time the Lady Chapel crypt was added 125 years later its floor was set 300 mm. above the Romanesque crypt floor level, which might provide a clue to the prevailing water-table at that date.

The original purpose of the crypt remains obscure. One function of crypts on the Continent, and in Anglo-Saxon England, was as a place for saintly burials, a tradition

Fig. 3.6   Winchester Cathedral. The crypt. *John Crook*

recently revived at the abbey of Fleury at Saint-Benoît-sur-Loire, where the bones of St Benedict are now enshrined within the crypt, beneath the high altar, perhaps echoing the original arrangement (Fig. 3.7). Relics in post-Conquest England were usually displayed in the body of the church, however, and there is no evidence for burials in the crypt of Walkelin's cathedral.[25]

Crypts also provided space for altars. At Christ Church, Canterbury, for example, Archbishop Lanfranc enjoined in his *Constitutions* that the monastic roundsmen known as *circas* should examine all the altars in the crypts in case any of the brethren should be sleeping there.[26] The Winchester crypt could have provided space for four altars—one in the central chamber and three in the chapels—though the south-east chapel is encumbered by the well. However, there are no clear signs of the expected altar step in these locations.[27]

It would have been possible for processions to pass around the crypt. The entrances were rebuilt in the early 12th century, and the original entry arrangement is unclear, but it seems likely that the 11th-century entrances were also through doors in the ends of the east aisles of the transepts, an arrangement which survives, despite remodelling, in the present entrance on the north side.[28]

In short, the evidence for the use of the crypt is inconclusive. It may well be that within a short time of its construction the rising water-table caused it to be abandoned for liturgical purposes. Thus it was never floored with anything more substantial than a grey plaster screed.

The foundations of the walls of the Romanesque cathedral go only a little deeper than the crypt floor. In this part of Winchester the chalky deposits of the Itchen valley conceal a layer of peat, some 1 m. to 1.75 m. (3 to 5 ft.) thick, overlying a bed of gravel about 6 m. (20 ft.) below the surface. This firm gravel would have provided an excellent foundation, but the builders were hampered by the high water-table and were able to dig down only as far as the top of the peat. They resorted to filling their foundation trenches with loose flints and chalk until they were able to build in the dry; in places they supplemented these rough-and-ready foundations with short vertical oak piles driven down, not always successfully, towards the gravel. Such foundations were far less sophisticated than the timber *grillage* devised by Archbishop Thomas of Bayeux' master mason at York Minster.[29]

Upon these foundations the Anglo-Norman builders began to construct the walls and piers of the cathedral. The footings consist of massive walls, up to 4 m. (12 ft.) thick, of flint and rubble in a pinkish lime mortar, enclosing a thick concrete raft. Above ground level the walls are correspond-

Fig. 3.7 Saint-Benoît-sur-Loire. Altar and reliquary of St Benedict in the crypt. *John Crook*

ingly massive. Courses of almost square blocks of Quarr limestone, with rough diagonal tooling, provide a regular face to a thick rubble core. The wide jointing of this 11th-century work is crude when compared with that of the following century, but it would have been a building method ideally suited to a large workforce of mainly unskilled labour.[30]

The elevations of the transepts, which fortunately escaped the late Gothic transformation of the rest of the cathedral, are broadly typical of the Romanesque design of the entire church. To enter the north transept from the Gothic nave is a powerful experience: one steps back in architectural time by nearly three centuries (Fig. 3.8). Here one enjoys a glimpse of the austere, original Romanesque building: tall and mysterious, its cliff-like elevations pierced with dark, brooding caves.

In fact the transept elevations are not as consistent as at first appears: their actual form is the result of compromise and rebuilding. Nevertheless, the original design is recoverable.[31] There were the usual three storeys—main arcade, gallery,[32] and clerestory—and all three were of approximately equal height between floor levels.[33] This is a design feature which links Winchester with the Conqueror's abbey church of Saint-Etienne, Caen, as well as the important, but later, church of Cerisy. At Saint-Etienne the gallery arches are open (Fig. 3.9); at Cerisy they have paired sub-arches, exactly as at Winchester (Fig. 3.10). In view of Walkelin's Rouen connection, one would dearly love to know the design of the elevations there, but no evidence survives.

The bays are defined by rectangular dosserets, supporting mast-like half-shafts, rising through the full elevation. These strong vertical elements perform an important aesthetic function, reducing the tendency for the elevation to appear as three separate levels stacked one upon the other. They formerly gave partial support, too, to the great tie-beams of the original open timber roof, of which no part certainly survives. The elevations are also articulated horizontally, by string courses at clerestory level and at the springing of the main clerestory arches.

The capitals are mostly of the plain cushion type already encountered in the axial chapel of the crypt.[34] Cushion capitals do not occur in 11th-century Normandy, and the Normans appear to have introduced them to England from the Ottonian Empire; they occur, for example, in the crypt at Speyer, started c.1030 (Fig. 3.11). When compared with contemporary churches on the Continent, the design of Winchester Cathedral seems austere; decoration is limited to architectural elements, including the blind arcading of the outer walls of the aisles on the west sides and the ends of the transepts and, presumably, throughout the nave. But we should not imagine that Walkelin's cathedral was undecorated; wall-painting may well have compensated in some measure for the lack of sculptural decoration.[35]

Before the transept elevations had reached the clerestory a decision had been taken to add flanking towers at the end of each transept. At ground level the piers in the corner of the transepts were enlarged to take the weight of the towers, and in the east and west galleries transverse arches were built over the aisles to sustain the unsupported wall of each tower. But the most radical modifications occurred at clerestory level. Here, the original design, with a tall central arch flanked by two shorter ones in each bay, was modified; the two outer bays were now linked by relieving arches enclosing paired sub-arches, giving a double-bay system. In the outermost bay large arches were to open into third-storey chambers within the towers themselves. Vestiges of the springing of a groin-vault in the corner bay at clerestory level,

Fig. 3.8   Winchester Cathedral. North transept. *John Crook*

Fig. 3.9   *(above)* Caen. Saint-Etienne. Nave
elevation. *John Crook*

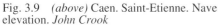

Fig. 3.10   *(right)* Cerisy-la-Forêt (Manche). Nave
elevation. *John Crook*

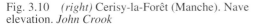

and a fragment of external decorative arcading on the north wall of the north transept,
suggest that the north-east tower was probably completed; the others had progressed less
far when it was realised that the inadequate foundations simply would not take their
weight. The towers were discontinued and the transept corners were completed in a rough-
and-ready way. All this work, with its changes of intention, must have taken place before
the dedication of the cathedral in 1093, for it is unlikely that the monks would have
moved into the new church until building work in the transepts had been completed.

The clerestory double-bay system, first worked out as a compromise connected with
the introduction of corner towers,[36] seems to have been considered a design improvement
and was used in the second phase of the construction of the nave, after 1093.[37] Otherwise,
the surviving elements of the Romanesque nave visible in the roof spaces confirm that the
nave elevations were essentially similar to those of the transepts.

One other feature of the transepts may be noted at this point: the wide platforms
extending over the whole terminal bay. Such platforms were found in several contemporary
churches in Normandy: notably Saint-Etienne (Fig. 3.12) and Saint-Martin (both at Caen),
Jumièges, and Cerisy. Evidence has been found for similar platforms at Bayeux Cathedral.
At Winchester, with its double transept aisles, the platforms linked the east and west

galleries, permitting circulation right round the cathedral at this level; the core of the stairs leading up to the higher gallery of the east arm may still be seen.

The elevations of the east arm were different from those of the transepts and nave, at least at main arcade level. All the piers seem to have been set on a low stylobate wall separating the ambulatory from the presbytery. The main arcade consisted of alternate cylindrical and compound piers, and the piers of the apse were all cylindrical.[38] The main arcade was the same height as in the rest of the church; the gallery storey was lower to take account of the raised floor level of the east arm.[39] The clerestory, however, remained at the same level throughout the building: it was possible to make a complete circuit of the church at this level in order to maintain the windows which lit the building.

So what did Winchester Cathedral look like when in April 1093 the monks moved into their new church? By then the entire east arm, the transepts and three bays of the nave had been completed; this was the part of the church reserved to the monks. Only when Old Minster had been demolished, in 1093-94, was it possible to continue westwards. Work seems to have proceeded quickly; there is little progression either of style or masonry technique even at the west end of the nave—in contrast with the distinctive masonry and capitals of the central tower and its associated bays, rebuilt after the collapse of 1107.[40]

Fig. 3.11   Speyer Cathedral. The crypt, facing north-east. *John Crook*

Fig. 3.12 Caen. Saint-Etienne. Platform at end of south transept. *John Crook*

The most important part of the church was the monastic choir, situated, as we have seen, below the lantern tower. The high altar stood on the chord of the main apse, on a platform some 0.50 m. above the level of the ambulatory: approximately the same relationship between floor levels as today.[41] We speculate that St Swithun's shrine was, even at this early date, situated immediately behind the high altar; the episcopal throne may also have been located at the head of the apse. In the later Middle Ages—certainly by the time the 14th-century choir-stalls were built—the choir was enclosed to the west by a stone pulpitum, but the detail of the Romanesque masonry which has survived in this part of the cathedral, being shielded by the pulpitum during the remodelling of *c*.1400, shows that there was no integral Romanesque structure here originally. It is likely that some sort of screen, perhaps of timber, closed the west end of the choir, at the top of the steps leading up from the nave to the higher level of the choir platform. There were also lateral entrances to the choir, in line with the western aisles of the transepts; the monks could have processed out of these, around the transept aisles, and possibly down into the crypt.

The eight services of the monastic day were sung in the choir. So was the daily High Mass; only one mass each day could take place at the high altar,[42] and an altar outside the choir, perhaps in the axial chapel, was used for the Morrow Mass. Furthermore, altars had to be provided elsewhere, where monks who had been ordained priest could say their own, private masses.[43] There was room for many such altars, including three against the east wall of each transept, both at ground and gallery levels.[44] In the east galleries of the transepts some of the round-headed niches may still be seen where oriented altars were formerly placed. Once the nave had been completed, additional altars may have been added against the piers: tradition holds that the Wykeham chantry chapel was built on the spot where, as a boy, the future bishop used to observe the daily mass said by the Winchester monk, Richard Pekis.

By the 12th century one of the windows lighting the terminal aisle of the south transept had been altered to serve as a door leading from the monastic buildings. This transept was reserved for the monks; the north transept seems to have been used for the reception of pilgrims, who could enter through a contemporary 'pilgrims' door' in the angle of the transept and nave aisle. They then made their way around the ambulatory, from where they could glimpse St Swithun's reliquary on the high altar platform, an arrangement which was considerably improved during the following century.[45]

The annalist's laconic account of the events of 1093 conceals the emotion which the Winchester brethren must surely have felt as they left Old Minster, the church which Wulfstan the Cantor—himself a monk—had praised so highly, less than a century previously. Were there those amongst them who, like another Wulfstan, the Anglo-Saxon bishop of Worcester, regretted the passing of the old order? 'We poor wretches have destroyed the work of saints that we may get praise for ourselves,' he had lamented.[46] Three months later the monks of Winchester returned to Old Minster for the last time to collect the reliquary of St Swithun. The very next day Bishop Walkelin gave orders for Old Minster to be destroyed, and, says the annalist, within a year almost all of the great Anglo-Saxon church had been taken down. The site was clear for the completion of Walkelin's cathedral.

Notes

1. See above, p. 3.
2. D. Whitelock, M. Brett and C. N. L. Brooke (eds.), *Councils and Synods with Other Documents relating to the English Church, 1* (Oxford, 1981) pt. 2, pp. 607-16.
3. M. Lapidge, *The Cult of St Swithun,* Winchester Studies, 4.ii (forthcoming).
4. In his *Vita Anselmi* Eadmer comments, however, that Lanfranc was at first 'somewhat green as an Englishman' (*'quasi rudus Anglus'*) and quotes his initial reservations about English saints: 'These Englishmen amongst whom we dwell have set up for themselves certain saints whom they revere. But sometimes, when I turn over in my mind their own accounts of who they were, I cannot help having doubts about the quality of their sanctity': R. W. Southern (ed.), *The Life of St Anselm, Archbishop of Canterbury by Eadmer* (London, 1962), p. 51. But the main point of the anecdote was to illustrate Anselm's skill in persuading Lanfranc of Ælfheah's sanctity, and it should probably not be regarded as indicative of the archbishop's attitude (still less, that of the Conqueror) towards all Anglo-Saxon saints, many of whom remained even in the Canterbury calendar.
5. J. Crook, 'The Bones of King Cnut', in A. Rumble (ed.), *The Reign of Cnut,* forthcoming.
6. Immediately after Walkelin's consecration he attempted to dissolve the monastery and replace the monks by secular canons, but the monks appealed to Lanfranc and to the Pope, Alexander II, who upheld their complaint: N. E. S. A. Hamilton (ed.), *Willelmi Malmesburiensis De Gestis Pontificum Anglorum,* RS 52 (1870), pp. 71-2. See above, p. 2.
7. For this ascription, see J. T. Appleby, 'Richard of Devizes and the Annals of Winchester', *Bulletin of the Institute of Historical Research* 36 (1963), pp. 70-7.

8. The earliest manuscript of the *Annals* has 1080 (Cambridge, Corpus Christi College, MS 339, fo. 22v). The 1079 date occurs in BL, Cotton. Domit. A.xiii, which Luard transcribed for the post-Conquest period in his edition (*Winchester Annals*). See above, p. 11, note 20.

9. J. H. Harvey, *The English Mediæval Architect* (London, 1972), p. 61; *VCH Hants,* i, p. 464.

10. See below, p. 37.

11. *Winchester Annals,* pp. 34-5.

12. As planned, Winchester was the longest Romanesque cathedral in Christendom, but it was quickly overtaken by Abbot Hugh's church at Cluny, built 1086-1109 (187 m.).

13. R. Gem, 'The Romanesque Cathedral of Winchester: Patron and Design in the Eleventh Century', *BAA Winchester,* pp. 3-4.

14. M. Biddle (ed.), *Winchester in the Early Middle Ages,* Winchester Studies, 1 (Oxford, 1976), p. 310.

15. J. Crook, 'The Romanesque East Arm and Crypt of Winchester Cathedral', *JBAA* 142 (1989), pp. 1-36, *passim.*

16. Eleanor Searle's work on the history of Battle Abbey suggests that the earliest date for the Conqueror's vow to build a church on the site of the battle was 1070; it does not therefore pre-date St Augustine's Canterbury: E. Searle (ed.), *The Chronicle of Battle Abbey* (Oxford, 1980), pp. 20-1.

17. See above, p. 2

18. See below, pp. 228-9, note 15.

19. The western towers at Jumièges bear a superficial resemblance on plan to the footings at Winchester, but do not project beyond the aisles. Closer still is the west front of La Trinité, Caen, but there the original ground-level scheme appears to have consisted of an open, transversal porch. For the west front of this church, see M. Baylé, 'Sainte Trinité de Caen', *Congrès Archéologique de France* 132 (Paris, 1978), pp. 22-58 and *eadem, La Trinité de Caen; sa Place dans l'Histoire de l'Architecture et du Décor Romans* (Geneva, 1979), pp. 40-41, 49-51, 54, 56-8, 68. Both churches featured a western tribune at gallery level; such a gallery at Winchester might have been used for royal ceremonial.

    The surviving footings at Winchester indicate solid flanking towers rather than a porch. The alternative view is that Winchester's Romanesque west front comprised a western transept, similar to that found at Ely Cathedral, a building influenced by Winchester. Adherents of this view include C. R. Peers and H. Brakspear, (*VCH Hants,* v, p. 52) and A. W. Clapham (*English Romanesque Architecture after the Conquest* (Oxford, 1934), p. 31). Twin towers are postulated by M. Biddle (*Winchester Studies 1,* p. 310), while for Richard Gem, 'twin towers might be ... more expected' ('The Romanesque Cathedral of Winchester: Patron and Design in the Eleventh Century', *BAA Winchester,* p. 8). Together with the crossing tower, the eastern turrets, and the ad-hoc attempt to add four towers at the transept terminals (J. Crook and Y. Kusaba, 'The Transepts of Winchester Cathedral', *Journal of the Society of Architectural Historians* 50 (1991), pp. 293-310), two western towers would have given a nine-tower scheme. The western towers need not have been carried up to an excessive height; they could have terminated at the same level as, or slightly above, the roof of the nave.

20. This conclusion has also been reached by P. McAleer, *HFC Proc.,* forthcoming.

21. See above, p. 16.

22. Crook and Kusaba, 'Transepts', pp. 300-5.

23. The west front of La Trinité was remodelled early in the 12th century, and the original scheme is known only from archaeological evidence discovered by Ruprich-Robert in the 19th century: Baylé, *La Trinité de Caen,* p. 49.

24. The earliest Romanesque plaster floor, investigated in the summer of 1992 by the author, was, most unusually, set almost level with the top of the chamfered plinth, suggesting that the builders were already aware of the problem by the time the floor was laid.

25. We argue, however, that the *locus indecens* from which Bishop Henry of Blois translated relics of pre-Conquest bishops and monarchs in 1158 was the 'memorial court' established around the original grave of St Swithun soon after the completion of the Romanesque nave (see below, pp. 60-1).

26. D. Knowles (ed.), *The Monastic Constitutions of Lanfranc* (London, 1951), p. 79.

27. The platform in the south-eastern chapel appears to be contemporary with the well.

28. The entrance was remodelled in the early 14th century (date of the inner doorway) and again in the early 19th century when the 'Romanesque' doorway from the transept was constructed.

29. D. Phillips, *The Cathedral of Archbishop Thomas of Bayeux at York: Excavations at York Minster, II,* Royal Commission on Historical Monuments (London, 1985), pp. 61-90. The foundation wall was 3.4-3.7 m. thick in the York transepts, and up to 6.4 m. wide in the east arm (*ibid.,* p. 84).

30. See above, p. 10.

31. Crook and Kusaba, 'Transepts', *passim.*

32. The term 'gallery' is employed in preference to 'triforium', which is more appropriate for Gothic elevations. Inexplicably, at Winchester the latter term is used to denote the platforms at the end of the transepts: the ambiguous name 'Triforium Gallery' (literally a 'gallery gallery') by which the cathedral museum is known compounds the problem.

33. The heights between the floor and the gallery sill, and between the gallery and clerestory sills, reduce slightly: pavement to original gallery floor level, 8.03 m.; gallery floor to clerestory passage, 7.98 m.; clerestory passage to head of wall, 7.70 m.

34. The massive piers supporting the platform at the transept ends do not need a capital, and the masonry merely swells out slightly immediately below the abacus.

35. But see David Park's findings on this matter, below p. 125.

36. Crook and Kusaba, 'Transepts', pp. 304-5.

37. The evidence consists of the alternating wall-shafts, many of which are visible in the roof space over the high vault.

38. Evidence for the alternating system was discovered when the north presbytery aisle floor was renewed in 1969; the cylindrical piers of the apse are evidenced by the surviving stump of one such pier, complete with its base, within the Gardiner chantry chapel.

39. This is evident from the surviving arches at the west end of the presbytery galleries, which overlook the transepts.

40. For M. Biddle, *Winchester Studies 1,* p. 309 and note 3, however, the nave may not have been completed until *c.*1121.

41. A small area of *opus signinum* floor has recently been discovered in the feretory, immediately behind the high altar.

42. J. A. Jungmann, *The Mass of the Roman Rite,* rev., Eng. edn. (London, 1959), p. 162: 'It was the practice to celebrate but one mass each day at any one altar' (the period 9th/12th century is implied).

43. From the 10th century priests were expected to say mass every day: C. N. L. Brooke, 'Priest, Deacon and Layman, from St Peter Damian to St Francis', *Studies in Church History* 26 (1989), pp. 70-1.

44. The question of the position of altars in Winchester Cathedral was addressed by Arnold Klukas in two papers: 'The Continuity of Anglo-Saxon Liturgical Tradition in Post-Conquest England as Evident in the Architecture of Winchester, Ely and Canterbury Cathedrals', *Les Mutations Socio-Culturelles au tournant des XIe-XIIe Siècles,* Proceedings of the Colloques Internationaux du Centre National de la Recherche Scientifique (Paris, 1984), pp. 111-23; and 'The Architectural Implications of the Decreta Lanfranci', *Anglo-Norman Studies* 6, p. 152. There must have been great demand for altars at which to celebrate. Rodolphus Glaber observed that at Cluny Mass was celebrated without interruption from day-break to dinner-time: *Historiarum Libri Quinque,* ed. J. France (Oxford, 1989), pp. 236-7.

45. See below, pp. 59-61.

46. *Gesta Pontificum,* p. 283.

BUILDING STONES OF WINCHESTER CATHEDRAL

Tim Tatton-Brown

When Bishop Walkelin began to rebuild the cathedral 'from the foundations' in 1079, he used two main types of stone for the facing masonry of the walls (the core of the walls was of flint rubble). These were Quarr stone from the Isle of Wight, and an oolitic limestone from the Bath area. The source of stone in the Isle of Wight is well documented in an important charter of King William Rufus granting Walkelin:

> ... half a hide of land in the Isle of Wight for the building of his church, just as my father at his death had granted it to him for the good of his soul. Reserving my rents, I have given him licence to dig for stone not only there but also throughout my land on the island, in open country, and in woodland, that is if the woodland is so small that the horns of a stag can be seen going through it.[1]

Quarr stone came from quarries at Binstead, near Ryde, in the north-east corner of the island; the name comes directly from the medieval Latin *quarria* or *quadraria* (hence our word quarry), a place where rectangular blocks of stone were cut. Quarr Abbey (not founded until 1132) took its name from the quarries nearby, though it never owned them. Quarr stone is a very shelly ('bioclastic') limestone with an unusual texture (Fig. 4.1a). It was originally a mass of tiny arcuate shell fragments, sometimes showing characteristic whorls caused by the movements of marine animals—the process known as 'bioturbation' (Fig. 4.1b). These fragments exist now as only empty moulds, their calcium carbonate having been redeposited as crystalline calcite in what originally were interstitial spaces between the fragments. Quarry men have accurately termed it 'featherbed stone'. It occurs as a lens in the Bembridge Limestone of Tertiary age,[2] and can be found as rough, diagonally-tooled blocks throughout the earlier Romanesque walls of the cathedral. It was also used for carved work, and until the 13th century was by far the commonest type of stone used in the building. However, right from the beginning, a second type of stone was occasionally used (Fig. 4.1c). This is an oolitic limestone which also contains many tiny fragments of broken fossils, and often shows cross-bedding. The stone must come from the Great Oolite formation in the area south and east of Bath.[3] It can be seen occasionally as plain blocks (for example on the outside of the south wall of the nave, formerly the north cloister wall), but it is most commonly used for the blocks in the Romanesque compound piers in the nave. As Professor Willis showed, nearly a century and a half ago, most of the piers of the south side of the nave (the seven western bays) are Romanesque and were merely pared back in the 14th century.[4] On the north side most of the piers were refaced using Beer stone. The Romanesque work can easily be distinguished, however, as it still displays very thick mortar joints. Virtually all the original rounded ashlar visible from ground level on the south side, is of oolitic limestone; only very occasionally is Quarr stone seen.

Fig. 4.1   Stone types from Winchester Cathedral: (a) Close-up of Quarr limestone showing flaky texture (cm. scale), (b) Quarr limestone showing bioturbation, (c) Close-up of oolitic limestone with characteristic 'aero bar' texture and some fossil fragments, (d) 15th-century Bembridge limestone showing characteristic cavities, together with a modern block of Portland. *John Crook*

In the crypt all the visible Romanesque masonry is of Quarr stone except the cushion capitals and drum blocks, which are of oolite. It is odd to record that in the Romanesque transepts much more Quarr than oolite is used in the drum blocks of the piers. Without a detailed study of all the masonry, however, it is not possible at this stage to discern any real pattern in the use of oolite. An initial theory that much more oolite was used inside the western two-thirds of the nave (i.e. after the demolition of Old Minster) is not yet sustainable. It would be nice to suggest that the major source of the oolitic limestone was the old cathedral,[5] but though this may be the case, it is also highly likely that new stone was also being quarried and transported to Winchester from the Bath area. So far no documentary evidence for this has been found, though it is worth noting that in 1222 Hazlebury stone (from the Box area north-east of Bath) was being brought to Winchester for building the large buttresses of the new great hall at Winchester Castle.[6]

When the central tower fell in 1107, it was rebuilt almost immediately, and the ashlar is better jointed, and of noticeably higher quality than in the earlier work (Fig. 4.2). The stone used is mostly Quarr, but a fair amount of randomly used oolite is also visible.[7] Similarly the decorative, mid 12th-century infilling into the earlier arcade on the west side of the south transept, forming Henry of Blois' treasury, is also largely of Quarr with some oolite. Perhaps the best place to compare the two types of stone, however, is in the eroded western arcade of the ruined chapter house, at the end of the south transept (Fig. 11.2). Here there are four very large monolithic shafts: three are clearly made of a very shelly oolite with calcite veining, while the fourth is the largest single piece of Quarr stone known to me. On the other hand, three of the large bases are of Quarr and only one is of oolite.

As is well known, Bishop Henry of Blois (1129-71) was interested in the use of coloured marble for architectural decoration, and on one occasion, while staying in Rome, he purchased antique statues.[8] The introduction of coloured marbles (i.e. stones that could take a high polish) to England for the first time since the Roman period is seen at several places at exactly this period. For example, at Canterbury and Rochester Cathedrals, Tournai marble and onyx marble were first used for monolithic shafts in the mid-12th century,[9] and at the same time Purbeck marble was also first brought in by sea for use in decorative capitals, columns and bases.[10] At Winchester the most obvious example of Bishop Henry's patronage is the magnificent Tournai marble font (Fig. 9.1),[11] which must have been brought to the city, along with others for churches in his diocese, in the mid-12th century.

Fig. 4.2　High-quality 12th-century Quarr limestone masonry in the present bell-chamber of the central tower. *John Crook*

No early use of Purbeck marble has been found at Winchester Cathedral, but nearby at Henry of Blois' own palace at Wolvesey it was certainly being used for mid 12th-century decoration.[12] Purbeck marble is also used for the large slab covering the tomb (Fig. 1.4), supposedly of William Rufus (d.1100), now under the crossing, but originally placed further to the east. As Professor Zarnecki has pointed out, this tomb is much more likely to have been that of the bishop himself.[13]

Another type of stone which first makes its appearance at the cathedral in the middle of the 12th century is Caen stone, from Normandy. This stone was first used in south-east England (at the White Tower in London, for example) in the late 11th century, but it does not appear to have been used in the Hampshire Basin until somewhat later, no doubt because of the plentiful supply of Quarr stone from the Isle of Wight.[14] By the later 12th century, however, good quality Quarr stone was becoming more difficult to find, which probably led to the use of Caen stone.

Caen stone can also be carved much more delicately than Quarr.[15] In the Holy Sepulchre Chapel, on the north side of the monks' choir, both Quarr and Caen stone can be seen, but all the earliest work (of c.1160), including the capitals and arches, appears to be of Caen. This chapel was rebuilt c.1210, and in the central pier-buttress on the north, which is

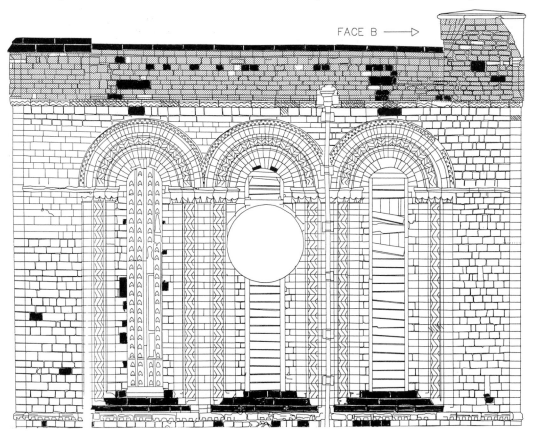

Fig. 4.3   Stone types of the 12th-century tower. Unshaded: Quarr limestone. Shaded: 13th-century Caen addition. Black: modern Portland repairs and parapet coping. *John Crook*

Fig. 4.4   Detail of the 13th-century dorter door (see also Fig. 11.2) with Purbeck marble jambs and Caen arch over, both now very eroded. *John Crook*

probably of this later date, both Quarr and Caen stone are used. Caen stone also seems to have been used when the top of the tower was raised by a few courses *c.*1200 (Fig. 4.3).[16]

At the beginning of the 13th century, work started on a large new east arm, first under Bishop de Lucy (1189-1204), and then (presumably after the end of the Interdict) under Bishop Peter des Roches (1205-38). Most of the outer wall face for this incomplete structure is of Quarr stone. The moulded plinth and much of the internal walling is, however, of Caen, and it is in the magnificent interior of the new east arm that we first find Purbeck marble being used in the cathedral on a large scale (Fig. 13.4). All the capitals, bases, shaft rings and moulded string-courses are in Purbeck, but so too are the tall slender shafts used *en délit*.[17] We even find that the flat panels set within the quatrefoils of the outer wall arcade are of Purbeck marble. The retrochoir must have been very striking before the area was filled up with the very large late medieval and Tudor chantry chapels. Among other tombs in Purbeck marble, mostly moved to the east arm by Prebendary Nott in the early 19th century,[18] are those of Bishops de Lucy (1204) and des Roches (1238), Prior William Basing (1295), Sir Arnaud de Gaveston (1302), and the heart-burial of Bishop Aymer de Valence (1260).[19] Another large-scale use of Purbeck marble of the early 13th century is in the magnificent, but now very worn, dormitory doorway (Fig. 4.4). Note particularly the huge tympanum slab and the large moulded Purbeck jamb-stones.

Fig. 4.5   The presbytery and Great Screen. *John Crook*

The presbytery was rebuilt in the early 14th century, and it is in the piers of the presbytery arcade that we find the last major use of Purbeck marble in the cathedral (Fig. 4.5). Here the compound columns used drums not monoliths, and the Purbeck is not polished.[20] Interestingly the contemporary half-piers used at the west end of the presbytery (against the eastern crossing piers) are of Caen stone not Purbeck marble, but were from the start painted grey to look like Purbeck. The retrochoir screen of c.1310-20, with its exquisitely carved canopies, is made of Caen stone with some, perhaps re-used, Quarr in the plain walling.[21] Just before the Black Death, work started, under Bishop Edington, on the rebuilding of the nave. The two western towers were demolished, and a new porch and west front with a vast new great west window were built.[22] Externally this west front has been restored in many places with plastic stone, and it is difficult to make out the type of stone of the original masonry.[23] It appears, however, that the main material was Caen stone.[24]

When Bishop William of Wykeham (1367-1404) resumed the rebuilding of the nave in 1394, he used much Caen stone and, internally for both the refacing and the vaults, Beer stone, a hard form of chalk. This latter stone was brought from quarries on the coast near the Devon-Dorset border. Beer stone was widely used in the 14th century. It is frequently documented for royal building work in London as well as at Rochester, Porchester and Winchester Castles at this time,[25] but there does not appear to be any documentary evidence for its use at the cathedral. Both the chantry chapels in the nave (of Bishops Wykeham and Edington) are of Caen stone. The tombs themselves are made of Purbeck marble with alabaster effigies. On the south side of the nave south aisle, two new doorways into the cloister (both now blocked) were inserted into the late 11th-century nave wall in Wykeham's time. These are certainly of Caen stone, though there are also a few blocks of Upper Greensand (perhaps a later repair) immediately to the west of the western of these doorways. These blocks are probably of Selborne stone rather than 'Green Ventnor' stone from the Isle of Wight, which is discussed below.

The other areas of large-scale rebuilding of the cathedral at a later date are the east bay of the Lady Chapel and Bishop Fox's new presbytery of 1503-25. The Lady Chapel is of early 13th-century date, but externally work of this period survives only on the north side, up to a level corresponding to the top of the crypt vaulting. The projecting east bay appears to have been rebuilt first in the 14th century, and the clasping buttresses at the north-east and south-east corners are of this period.[26] They contain many Upper Greensand blocks.[27] Around 1500 the walls of this bay were again rebuilt (or at least refaced) between the buttresses, and again Upper Greensand blocks, mixed with Caen stone, are found. At the same time the north-facing buttress at the north-east corner was thickened on its west side; oolitic limestone blocks, perhaps re-used, are found here, as well as in the 15th-century walling throughout.

The Upper Greensand blocks, as already stated, only occur in the cathedral from the 14th to early 16th centuries, and are therefore characteristic of the latest work in the building. The stone was probably quarried at Selborne (nearly twenty miles east of Winchester) rather than on the south side of the Isle of Wight,[28] where it is usually called 'Green Ventnor' or 'Bonchurch' stone after the places from which it was obtained. It would have been cheaper to transport it by road direct from Selborne, rather than by sea from Ventnor to Southampton, and then overland to Winchester. At Winchester College, Upper Greensand was occasionally used in the original buildings, but it was used much more extensively for later work such as Fromond's Chantry.[29]

The outer aisle walls and buttresses of Bishop Fox's new presbytery are mostly of Caen stone. However, on the north side of the cathedral, it is possible to see blocks of what is probably Bembridge stone used at the base of the walls below the plinth. By this date, Quarr stone had been worked out, but a coarser form of Bembridge limestone was still being used (Fig. 4.1d). At Porchester Castle, for example in 1397 and 1399, Bonchurch stone from 'South Wight' as well as 'ragplatenerston from the quarry of Bynnebrigge beside St Helens' is documented.[30]

Inside the presbytery, the walls are all of fine quality Caen stone, as are Beaufort's Great Screen and Fox's side screen walls. Three of the four great chantry chapels, of Waynflete (d.1486), Fox (d.1528) and Gardiner (d.1555), are also of Caen stone. Cardinal Beaufort's (d.1447) magnificent chantry chapel is, however, mostly made of superbly carved Purbeck marble, while Bishop Langton's (d.1501) chantry in the south-east chapel of the retrochoir is a refurnishing in beautifully carved timber. Much of the floor of the east arm, where it is not covered in medieval tiles, is also of Purbeck marble. Most of this must be medieval as well, though there are many later repairs.[31]

The masonry of the many restorations that have been carried out on the cathedral since the Reformation tells a story in its own way and, once this is known, it is often possible to suggest the date of the new masonry by the type of stone used. For example, when Bishop Curle's new passage was created on the south side of the nave at the west end in the early 17th century, Portland stone was used. The old doorhead, dated 1632 and now set in the south wall, is of this stone, as is the refacing of the extreme south-west corner of the cathedral, where another doorway was cut through. William Garbett, on the other hand, used quite a lot of Bath stone in the 1820s. This can be seen, for example, in the area around the Townsend memorial on the north side of the south transept. He also used a stone which is full of holes (in the shape of fossil gastropods) for an area around the new door leading from the north transept down into the crypt.[32] This is almost certainly another stone that came from the Bembridge limestone on the north and north-east coast of the Isle of Wight.[33] A small amount of artificial Coade 'stone' was even introduced by Nash in the 1830s. Then at the beginning of this century Sir Thomas Jackson used mostly concrete for his well-known underpinning of the cathedral.[34] He also used Portland for his 'long stones' to bridge across the cracks in the transepts and east arm, and Doulting for repairs to the east end.[35] When he was about to erect new flying buttresses on the south side of the nave in 1910, Jackson pointed out that if Clipsham stone was used, it would cost £665 per buttress, while Weldon stone would only cost £560.[36] The cheaper stone was chosen.

The surveyor to the fabric (and later architect) to the Dean and Chapter from 1936 until 1973 was Wilfrid Carpenter Turner, successor to T. D. Atkinson. Among several new building stones that he introduced for repairs were Ketton for the outside of the nave clerestory and Richemont for the infilling of the north aisle window in the north wall of the old consistory court (at the extreme west end of the north aisle). He also used Purbeck stone for the floor. For the repairs to the western porches he used plastic stone and Ancaster 'hard white', and in the repairs to six piers in the nave, Lepine or Richemont.

The most favoured stone for the last two decades has been Besace or Courteraie, which are considered good replacements for Caen.[37] However, when work started on the nave north aisle at its eastern end, Beer stone was used to replace old Beer. Unfortunately the supply of good Beer could not be kept up, so Richemont was used for the lower part of the easternmost window.

In the recent programme of restoration work on the tower Clipsham has been used as a replacement for the original Quarr and Beer stone for the parapet. Chicksgrove is being used for the parapets of the north aisle.[38]

Acknowledgements

I am extremely grateful to Mrs. Corinne Bennett, Dr. Derek Keene and John Crook for their most helpful comments on an earlier draft of this essay; also to my two geologist friends, Bernard Worssam and Professor Desmond Donovan who, over a number of years, have greatly increased my knowledge of building stones in Southern England. Bernard Worssam was also kind enough to read and comment on an earlier draft of this paper. For the final section I have relied heavily on notes provided by Corinne Bennett (*née* Wilson), Surveyor and Architect to the Dean and Chapter 1974-89 and, for the most recent work, on comments kindly provided by her successor, Peter Bird.

Notes

1. V. H. Galbraith, 'Royal Charters to Winchester', *EHR* 35 (1920), pp. 382-400.
2. F. W. Anderson and R. N. Quirk, 'Note on the Quarr Stone', in E. H. Jope, 'The Saxon Building Stone Industry in Southern and Midland England', *Medieval Archaeology* 8 (1964), pp. 115-17.
3. Professor Desmond Donovan, in a report to John Crook (after a visit on 17 June 1991), suggests that the oolitic limestone in the early 12th century tower might have come from the Ancliffe Oolite in the Upper Rags. See also G. W. Green and D. T. Donovan, 'The Great Oolite of the Bath area', *Bulletin of the Geological Survey of Great Britain* 30 (1969), pp. 1-64.
4. Willis, *Winchester Cathedral*, pp. 68-9.
5. I am grateful to Bernard Worssam for the information that a large amount of the carved stone from the Winchester Research Unit's excavations of the Anglo-Saxon minsters in Winchester is Bath stone.
6. H. M. Colvin (ed.), *Building Accounts of King Henry III* (Oxford, 1971), pp. 124-31.
7. I am grateful to John Crook for showing me this in 1991 on the scaffolding outside the tower, and for allowing me to see his marked-up elevations showing stone types and Professor Donovan's report.
8. See below, p. 70.
9. T. Tatton-Brown, 'Building Stone in Canterbury *c.*1070-1525', in D. Parsons (ed.), *Stone: Quarrying and Building in England A.D. 43-1525* (Chichester, 1990), pp. 70-82, at p. 74.
10. Recent studies of Purbeck marble include R. Leach, *An Investigation into the Use of Purbeck Marble in Medieval England* (Hartlepool, 1975), and J. Blair, 'Purbeck Marble', in J. Blair and N. Ramsay (eds.), *English Medieval Industries* (London, 1991), pp. 41-56.
11. See below, p. 98.
12. M. Biddle, *Wolvesey: The Old Bishop's Palace, Winchester, Hampshire*, English Heritage Handbook (London, 1986), p. 11; see also below, p. 71.
13. G. Zarnecki, 'Henry of Blois as a Patron of Sculpture', in S. Macready and F. H. Thompson (eds.), *Art and Patronage in the English Romanesque* (London, 1986), pp. 159-72, at p. 164.
14. At Chichester Cathedral, for example, Caen stone is also first used only in the mid-12th century.
15. See, for example, the magnificent mid 12th-century sculptural fragments in Caen from Wolvesey Palace: Biddle, *Wolvesey*, p. 8.
16. J. Crook, 'New Findings on the Tower of Winchester Cathedral', *WCR* 61 (1992), pp. 15-17.
17. The term refers to detached shafts where the stone is not set in its original horizontal bedding-plane, but vertically: J. Bony, 'Les origines des piles gothiques à fûts en délit', *Gedenkschrift Ernst Gall* (Berlin and Munich, 1965), pp. 95-122.
18. See below, pp. 102-6.
19. N. Pevsner and P. Metcalf, *The Cathedrals of England: Southern England* (Harmondsworth, 1985), pp. 337-41.
20. Polished shafts and unpolished drums in Purbeck marble, used together, are seen best at Salisbury Cathedral.

21. It is, however, worth noting that 675 stones (at 10s. the hundred) were purchased in 1294 at Southampton for Winchester Castle. This was almost certainly Quarr/Binstead stone: L. F. Salzman, *Building in England down to 1540* (Oxford, 1952), p. 121.

22. For the building sequence, see below, pp. 215-21.

23. On the south-west buttress of the west front there are some blocks of the fine-grained oolitic limestone from Ancaster. There is also much refacing of all the buttresses with Portland stone. The Portland is probably late 18th-century, while the Ancaster 'hard white' and the plastic stone was put in recently in Wilfrid Carpenter Turner's time. Some Portland was also used in the early 17th century (see below).

24. The original statue of a bishop from the top of the west front gable (now in the Lady Chapel crypt) is in Caen stone.

25. Salzman, *Building in England,* p. 132. Corinne Bennett kindly tells me that Quarr/Binstead stone was sometimes used outside as well (for the rose window in the north transept, for example). This was probably re-used stone.

26. A forthcoming paper by John Crook on the Lady Chapel crypt will include details of this previously un-noticed 14th-century campaign, first detected above ground level by Peter Welford of the Courtauld Institute (see below, pp. 132-3).

27. The plinth mouldings, and the coursing also distinguishes the two phases of work.

28. However, it is worth noting that for work at Winchester Castle in 1222, both 'Isle of Wight' and Selborne stone were used. The stone quarried at Selborne is also Upper Greensand, and it is hard to distinguish from 'Green Ventnor': Colvin, *Henry III,* p. 103. See also *Winchester Studies 2,* p. 70. Corinne Bennett tells me that the north nave aisle parapets were of Upper Greensand until their recent replacement by Courteraie. It is also worth noting that Bishop Waynflete dissolved the Augustinian Priory at Selborne in 1484, and gave the manor to Magdalen College, Oxford; this was during a period when the stone was enjoying its maximum use.

29. J. H. Harvey, 'Winchester College', *JBAA* 27 (1965), p. 113. See also *idem,* 'The Buildings of Winchester College', in R. Custance (ed.), *Winchester College Sixth Centenary Essays* (Oxford, 1982), pp. 77-128.

30. Salzman, *Building in England,* p. 133. St Helens is on the north side of Bembridge (Brading) harbour on the east side of the Isle of Wight, and the 'ragplatnerston' can still be seen on the Bembridge ledges on either side of the harbour entrance. Stone purchased from the prior of St Helen's was also used in the construction of Winchester College. In 1395, for example, 355 tons of 'burres', 30 tons of greensand and 13 tons of 'platens' were brought by boat to St Denys and then by road to Winchester for the second phase of the construction of Winchester College: J. H. Harvey, 'The Buildings of Winchester College', in R. Custance (ed.), *Winchester College Sixth Centenary Essays* (Oxford, 1982), pp. 88-9, citing Winchester College Muniments, 73.

31. In the central aisle of the Lady Chapel the newer paving is probably of Sussex marble.

32. Corinne Bennett and John Crook also tell me that this stone was used for repairs *c*.1820 in other places such as the piers of the Epiphany Chapel, and the transept clerestory.

33. It has been identified by Professor Donovan as Bembridge limestone ('Second Geological Report' for the Dean and Chapter of Winchester, dated 21 April 1992).

34. I. T. Henderson and J. Crook, *The Winchester Diver, the Saving of a Great Cathedral* (Winchester, 1984). The work was carried out by the well-known firm, John Thompson of Peterborough.

35. In the great finials of the high east gable stair turrets and for the central niche and parapet (dated 1914). Parts of the Lady Chapel are now also in Doulting, which, as Mrs. Bennett points out, looks like 'plastic stone'.

36. Jackson Collection C, MS, WCL, p. 102.

37. It is imported from near Bar-le-Duc in France by the Cathedral Works Organisation of Chichester. Corinne Bennett comments: 'The Besace, a finer grain than Courteraie, has not been available for at least six years, but the Courteraie has served well'. Some Purbeck stone was also used on the copings of the high transept gables. The various types of new stone used this century for restoration at nearby Winchester College, and the reasons for their use, are well documented in Harvey, 'Winchester College', pp. 113-4.

38. This is a form of Chilmark stone from the Portland beds that is now being quarried two miles south-west of the Chilmark quarries.

LITURGY AND THE FABRIC

Kenneth Stevenson

Nine hundred years is a long time in the life of an ecclesiastical building, especially when the worship offered there has undergone significant stages of evolution. And yet in its main architectural elements the cathedral dedicated in 1093 is the building we know today. It is a combination of three functional uses of space: a processional nave that can also hold a large crowd; a choir area for the capitular and singing body; and, all round, in various smaller spaces, room for side-altars. This is the essential conception of the use of liturgical space that dominates the western cathedral tradition.

Winchester's conformity to what was going on in the rest of western liturgy is testified in the life of the previous cathedral by a late 11th-century manuscript from Old Minster containing part of the Romano-Germanic pontifical,[1] a liturgical tradition formulated *c.*950 at St Alban's Abbey, Mainz, which spread virtually all over western Europe.[2] Even though Winchester's new cathedral monastic use was less 'Normanised' than Canterbury, and therefore kept its Anglo-Saxon saints in the calendar, this made little difference to the way in which the building was used for the liturgy.[3]

In this study we shall concentrate on certain key periods, when the building and the liturgy changed, and at each stage consider the motivations and the effects of such changes. The survey is inevitably restricted, but the stages seem to the author—rector of a parish formerly in the great diocese of Winchester, but since 1927 in that of Guildford—to be the most significant to date in the life of this building. Finally, a few suggestions are offered as to how the building might adapt further to the needs of the contemporary Church.

Bishop Walkelin's Cathedral

A visitor to the cathedral towards the end of the 11th century would have entered through the west door and gazed up a nave devoid of seating.[4] The length of Winchester's nave is rightly regarded as unusual (Fig. 5.1). A long nave has the obvious advantage of making processions more impressive, not least in the processional hymn on festivals and the litany before Sunday capitular High Mass, which were important points in the round of monastic worship.[5] The 12th-century black Tournai marble font had yet to be installed, but since the font was an important part of the Church's liturgical life, especially at the great Easter vigil, a large stone font would have had its position near the main door. As Christopher Brooke has explained, in the original scheme it would have been possible to look along the entire length of the building, as far as the apse behind the high altar where the bishop's throne presumably stood.[6]

At a later date, the cathedral would be divided by two screens: a rood-screen three bays west of the crossing tower, with lateral doorways either side of a nave altar, and, one

Fig. 5.1   The nave, Winchester Cathedral. *John Crook*

bay further east, a large, stone pulpitum separating the nave from the monastic choir, the area still occupied by the clergy and choir today. Here the monastic body met for the daily offices, some of them, like Mattins and Vespers, elaborate, and on Sundays and festivals ornamented with vestments and ceremonial such as lights and incense, though a formal liturgical colour scheme had yet to be worked out.[7] On the east side of the transepts, the only part of the present cathedral not to have been substantially reworked in subsequent centuries, were up to twelve side-altars, six at main level and six in the gallery, and at these altars ordained monks said private masses. The lay-out reflects the mixture of the corporate monastic offices and individual masses.

Let us try to picture the scene. Each monk would enter clad in the by now conventional eucharistic garments: an amice (a collar around the neck), a long white alb, girded at the waist, a long narrow stole, a maniple on the left wrist, and an ample, draping chasuble. The whole building would breathe activity, the activity of the church at prayer. If the visitor was lucky, it might be the time for some special ceremony, such as the Candlemas celebration (2 February), with the blessing and distribution of candles before the mass commemorating Our Lord's Presentation in the Temple, the chants being repeated as ever larger numbers of people came forward to receive their light.[8] It could be that High Mass had just been celebrated at the high altar by the bishop, at which one of the special blessings in such a book as the Benedictional of St Ethelwold was used just before communion,[9] a rich quarry of liturgical prayers which varied according to the occasion and which developed as a kind of substitute for receiving communion as lay reception of the sacrament declined.

The building was a sort of grandiose space for people to move around in, a far cry from the pew-confinement of later liturgical fashions. Like many churches of the Eastern traditions today, worshippers stood, and moved hither and thither. It was a combination of the *mobile* and the *static,* expressed by the posture both of monks and other worshippers. The mobile character was the processional element, the static was the monastic office and the low mass. In short, it must have been an enjoyable, if overwhelming, place to experience the worship of God.

1490: The Great Screen Completed

By 1490 the cathedral's remodelling was virtually complete. The liturgy had not undergone any drastic changes, but it had evolved nonetheless. During this century controversies about and heightening piety towards the Eucharist caused some changes to the way mass was celebrated.[10] It was at this time that the priest began to elevate first the consecrated host, and then the chalice, at the words in the eucharistic prayer which record those of Christ at the Last Supper. Such elevations were partly for the worshippers to see (they could not hear what was going on), and partly to increase the sense of adoration of this virtually untouchable mystery that was the Eucharist. When worshippers did communicate, they did not do so from a particle of unleavened cake, as in earlier times, but received a small round wafer,[11] deliberately shaped like a coin in order that communion might resemble a reward for the effort of going to private confession beforehand, mandatory practice since the Fourth Lateran Council of 1215.[12]

Such an intensified understanding of the Eucharist had many results. One of these was the need to display the consecrated bread, the reserved sacrament, outside the actual service. It also enhanced the dramatic ambience of the altar. These are two of the reasons for the erection of the Great Screen between 1470-90. Here was depicted the crucified Christ, surrounded by his apostles and other saints of the Church, and atop was suspended a hanging pyx, a small box containing the consecrated bread, covered in a rich-coloured cloth.[13] There could be no more powerful statement of the Real Presence of Christ in the Eucharist, the commemoration of his death, than this sight of the reserved sacrament so close to the figure of Christ on the Cross.

Such screens, however, were by no means exceptional at the time.[14] In much later Catholicism, of course, they became the norm. It could be argued that they do not change substantially the building which they occupy. But they do change the visual and liturgical focus. Impressive as they are, when as vast as the Great Screen at Winchester they have the effect of dwarfing the liturgical action, unless that, too, is equally bold and impressive. I cannot think of Winchester's new 15th-century screen without imagining a festival High Mass going on underneath it, with the bishop as celebrant, clad in full pontificals, and surrounded by assistant clergy, perhaps even seven deacons and subdeacons, all wearing the garments in what were now the recognised and established liturgical colours:[15] gold for festivals, red for martyrs and certain saints, blue for Advent, sackcloth for Lent, and green or some ordinary colour for occasions when no special colour is appointed. With billows

Fig. 5.2   The retrochoir in the early 19th century, showing the chantry chapels of Bishops Beaufort, Waynflete and Gardiner. Engraving by John le Keux from a drawing by Edward Blore (Britton, *Winchester Cathedral*, plate XVIII)

of incense-fumes puffing out of a large thurible, what went on under the screen must have appeared almost a match for the splendour of the screen above.

Side-altars begin to get their reredoses too, depicting their patron saint or some feature appropriate to the chapel in question. Low masses offered at side-altars at this time included requiems for the departed; hence the increasing use, from the 14th century, of chantry chapels, where priestly stipends were endowed for masses offered for the repose of great souls (Fig. 5.2).

The creation of the Great Screen, of course, had one other notable result, namely the rehousing of the relics of St Swithun in precisely the space which the screen could demarcate: the retrochoir. This set the final seal on the area as a large-scale reliquary and processional ambulatory.

The Reformation

It is almost impossible for us to imagine the contrast between the pre-Reformation and post-Reformation cathedral. The dissolution of the priory of St Swithun affected not only the running of the cathedral, where a dean and canons replaced the prior and monastic community, but the whole character of its worship. The 1549 Book of Common Prayer was a bold, though conservative, synthesis of what was going on in European Reformation liturgy and of older Catholic practice.[16] The liturgy was drastically changed, nonetheless. Instead of seven daily offices, and the other extra offices, such as those of Our Lady and the Dead, there were now only two: Morning and Evening Prayer. And these were deliberately written in a more substantial form, and therefore in the mother-tongue, with long passages of the Bible read for the edification of the congregation. Instead of the monks beginning the first office of the day with *Pater Noster* and *Domine, labia mea aperies,* the (yet more radical) 1552 Prayer Book has a beautiful didactic exhortation: 'Dearly beloved, the Scripture moveth us in sundry places to acknowledge and confess our sins ... yet ought we most chiefly so to do when we assemble and meet together...'. All the other services were changed, the marriage rite perhaps the least.

Possibly the most drastic change for buildings like Winchester and their former occupants involved the Eucharist. All the Prayer Books (1549, 1552, and 1559 through to 1662) insisted that Holy Communion should be celebrated only when there were a sufficient number to communicate with the priest. Such a direction could not fail to reduce by an unprecedented degree the number of Eucharists celebrated. Formerly the building had been a kind of eucharistic house, with masses offered in many places all through the morning, in the presence of congregations or not, including laity, who were accustomed to communicate only three or four times a year. Now the Holy Communion was probably celebrated only on Sundays and on the (now greatly reduced) holy days. The Anglican Reformation strategy was to scoop all communicants into a single celebration. Such a celebration would have taken place at the high altar, before the Great Screen, now deprived of its statuary, and with the Litany, the latter chanted in choir rather than sung processionally round the nave. The service was a simplification of the capitular High Mass, with three clergy, the old priest, deacon and subdeacon trio, either in some of the old eucharistic vestments or else in copes.[17] There is a strongly collegiate feel to the Prayer Book directions all through the Eucharist, for it keeps referring to the other clergy and clerks (singers) who might be present.

Whether it was at the Dissolution, during the reign of Edward VI, or at the start of Elizabeth I's, or a combination, Winchester Cathedral's interior fittings were altered; not beyond recognition, for the shell remained, but side-altars, statues and reliquaries all disappeared, including those in the various chantry chapels where requiem mass had been celebrated. Although Catholicism gained a brief respite during the reign of Mary Tudor, the national tide was clearly for the bold reaction against Catholic worship.

Robert Horne, a native of Guildford, was bishop of Winchester from 1561-80 and was of the Reformed party. He had spent the time of Mary's reign in Zurich, where the more extreme Protestants had their centre. His visitation articles for Winchester Cathedral in 1562 and 1571 are revealing.[18] They emphasise order in worship, the need for sound (Protestant) teaching, a weekly Eucharist, and a proper moral conduct for all ministers and cathedral employees. In 1571 the Eucharist is still to be weekly, and the dean must be the celebrant four times a year. The communion is to be administered 'in a plain cope without any images'. While there is nothing exceptional in the general tone of these regulations, they reflect nonetheless a rather different function of the worship of Winchester Cathedral from its previous use. They have the feel of the much more static type of worship typified by the Reformation. Much of the old ceremonial has gone. The priest celebrates at the altar, now a wooden table, and preaches from the pulpit, now a much more important piece of furniture. The congregation have to sit and listen. The choir offices, previously in the hands of the monks, are now to be sung (in cathedrals and collegiate churches) by lay choirs specially appointed. Even this latter practice becomes suspect to the Reforming party.

Vicissitudes followed, not least the Commonwealth, when the cathedral was without a dean and chapter. The episcopate of George Morley (1662-84), however, was not without

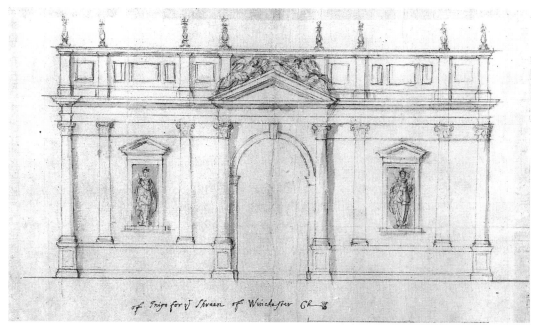

Fig. 5.3   The design by Inigo Jones for the choir-screen of 1638. *British Architectural Library, RIBA, London*

significance. Although we do not have details of his cathedral visitation articles, it is clear from those for the parish churches that he was very much a Caroline high churchman, insisting on episcopal ordination and the comely conduct of worship.[19] By this time the Eucharist was celebrated by a priest at the north side of the altar, a practice whose precise origins are obscure, but which persisted in cathedrals until the Tractarian Movement altered liturgical customs gradually in the later 19th century.

Earlier in the century, in 1638, the rood-screen some way down the nave had been dismantled, and adapted as the new choir-screen designed by Inigo Jones (Fig. 5.3), part of an earlier Caroline churchmanship, and a prelude to the destruction wrought by the Commonwealth troops. But the fact that the choir-screen was replaced merely serves to underline that, while the moderate Protestantism of the Anglican settlement had won the day, it was adapting rather than radically reordering the basic lay-out of the building.

The Modern Era

So much has happened over the last two centuries in church life that it is impossible to do more than highlight the changes here, insofar as they affect the life of a cathedral. The two choir-screens of the 1820s and 1875 and the revival of interest in choral music, and the concomitant interest in the organ as a liturgical instrument, have all left their mark on the way the building has been used. The Tractarian Movement made its own gentle influence felt on cathedrals, which led to the gradual refurnishing of some of the medieval chapels. One example will suffice: Arthur Valpy, after some indefatigable years (1885-95) as rector of Holy Trinity and St Mary's, Guildford, which saw, among other things, the extension of the east end of Holy Trinity, became a residentiary canon of Winchester Cathedral and created and furnished the Epiphany Chapel, making it the important oasis of private prayer that it now is (Fig. 5.4).

The early 20th century saw, too, the experimental beginnings of an evening 'nave service' on Sundays, which opened the cathedral to a wider clientele than previously, heralding those large Sunday congregations that it probably had not seen for several centuries. With that concern for both dignity and popular appeal, the later 19th century helped to bring the cathedral back to something of what it was like when it was first built. Worship remained faithful to the Prayer Book of 1662, but increasingly adapted to such developments as the renewed concern for fine choral

Fig. 5.4   The Epiphany Chapel. *John Crook*

music and congregational hymn-singing. Cathedral worship was becoming less static, more mobile.

Another new development that was in a sense not quite new was the setting up of an altar in front of the choir-screen; this nave altar was installed for the Anglo-Catholic conference in 1925 and allowed to remain. A mid-20th century fashion, it reaches back in fact to the Middle Ages, when most cathedrals had in front of the rood-screen an altar of the Holy Cross. The worship of the cathedral has over the years set increasing importance on the Eucharist, celebrated with simple, bold and visible ceremonial at that altar (Fig. 5.5), both on major feast-days and those larger diocesan occasions at which the bishop

Fig. 5.5   Eucharist at the nave altar, Easter Day 1989. *John Crook*

presides, such as ordinations or the Blessing of the Oils on Maundy Thursday. As one reflects on these changes, one glimpses medieval practice returning in a new way, as modern worshippers, whether at these services or at the many special services for various organisations, come to a modern cathedral and are faced with a deeply traditional building where they feel at home in a way that they do not in many parish churches.

What of the present? A priest from what is now another diocese, who loves this building from a distance, hesitates to be specific, but there are perhaps three areas that are worth exploring, all of them adaptations of tradition.

First, one of the gems of Anglican cathedral liturgical tradition is daily Evensong. But it is an office exclusively celebrated in the choir-stalls, and one to which many visitors would like to have access, both physical and spiritual. One of the ways in which liturgies have varied down the ages is the context in which they begin.[20] It is, in fact, one of the weaknesses of many modern services, too. There may be a way in which, for example during the summer months, when visitors abound, the vestry prayer could be expanded into some kind of 'gathering rite' at the west door, after which choir, clergy and congregation could process up the nave into the stalls.

Secondly, while the last hundred years have seen the revival of the use of some of the medieval side-chapels, including the Holy Sepulchre Chapel, and the Venerable Chapel, it might be possible to refurbish yet more, so that each one was used, on an appropriate day, for the celebration of the Eucharist. That would have the advantage of opening out more of the building and extending more of the praying space.

Thirdly, the arrangement of choir-stalls and altar in front of the choir-screen has undoubtedly brought many advantages, visual, musical and other. But from a distance the clergy and altar seem to be dominated by the choir. A next step might be to extend the dais into the nave and provide more space for the altar. At a stroke, history would turn full circle and produce an effect not dissimilar to the old basilical arrangement, giving architectural expression to that ancient synthesis of Eucharist as both awesome and intimate, which later medieval and Reformation conceptions perhaps exaggerated in different directions.[21] Buildings which express genius of design have a habit of producing their own inherently appropriate solutions to new problems and possibilities, as the people of God move on into new centuries.[22]

Notes

1. BL, Cotton. Vitellius E.xii.
2. W. H. Frere, *Pontifical Services Illustrated from Miniatures of the XVth and XVIth Centuries*, Alcuin Club Collections, 3 (London, 1901), p. 97. For the full text, see C. Vogel, R. Elze (eds.), *Le Pontifical Romano-Germanique du Dixième Siècle*, II, Studi e Testi, 227 (Vatican City, 1963), pp. cvii, 1-14. See also *Winchester Studies 1*, pp. 268-70, for a discussion of the processional character of festivals. There is also a full discussion of the influence of *Regularis Concordia* on the liturgy in O. B. Hardison Jr., *Christian Rite and Christian Drama in the Middle Ages* (Baltimore, 1965), p. 178ff.
3. A. Klukas, 'The Continuity of Anglo-Saxon Liturgical Tradition in Post-Conquest England as Evident in the Architecture of Winchester, Ely, and Canterbury Cathedrals', *Les Mutations Socio-Culturelles au Tournant des XIᵉ-XIIᵉ Siècles,* Proceedings of the Colloques Internationaux du Centre National de la Recherche Scientifique (Paris, 1984), pp. 111-23. Klukas makes important observations about Anglo-Saxon survival, notably in the lay-out of the side-altars. However, this does not significantly affect the *principle* of the side-altar mass at this time.
4. For the completion date of the nave, see above, p. 32.
5. T. Klauser, *A Short History of the Western Liturgy* (London, 1969).
6. See above, p. 33.
7. W. St. John Hope and E. G. Cuthbert Atchley, *English Liturgical Colours* (London, 1918) remains the standard work.
8. For this rite, see K. Stevenson, 'The Origins and Development of Candlemas: a Struggle for Identity and Coherence?', *Ephemerides Liturgicæ* 102 (1988), pp. 316-46, reprinted in J. N. Alexander, *Time and Community*, N.P.M. Studies in Church Music and Liturgy (Washington, 1990), pp. 43-76. See also K. Stevenson, 'The Ceremonies of Light—Their Shape and Function in the Paschal Vigil liturgy', *Ephemerides Liturgicæ* 99 (1985), pp. 170-85, and reprinted in K. Stevenson, *Worship— Wonderful and Sacred Mystery* (Washington, 1992), pp. 189-210.

 9. For the origins and development of the pre-Communion episcopal blessing and their texts, see E. Moeller (ed.), *Corpus Benedictionum Pontificalium,* Corpus Christianorum, Series Latina, 162, 162A, 162B, 162C (Turnhout, 1971-9).

10. Klauser, *Liturgy;* K. Stevenson, *Eucharist and Offering* (New York, 1986).

11. R. M. Woolley, *The Bread of the Eucharist,* Alcuin Club Tracts, 10 (London, 1913). Although the practice of 'intinction' (dipping the bread in the wine) at communion was adopted in some places in the 12th century, it died out in the 13th, from which time emerged the general practice of communicating everyone but the priest with bread only. It was a symptom of infrequent lay communion; witness the revival of the chalice in 20th-century Catholicism, where lay communion is frequent.

12. This was the council which defined 'transubstantiation' as the official way to describe Christ's presence in the bread and wine of the Mass.

13. W. H. Freestone, *The Sacrament Reserved,* Alcuin Club Collections, 21 (London, 1917), still the standard history of the practice of reservation, along with A. A. King, *Eucharistic Reservation in the Western Church* (London, 1965). The 'hanging pyx' for public reservation purposes is a derivation of the ordinary pyx used for taking the sacrament to someone's home; early examples of the latter, going back to the 6th century and earlier, were often of ivory and other precious substances.

14. In 1479 a painted wooden screen of similar proportions was completed in Aarhus Cathedral, Denmark, by the famous Lübeck craftsman Bernt Notke, whose work is well known across the Baltic.

15. Hope and Atchley, *Colours*; see also W. H. St. John Hope, *English Altars,* Alcuin Club Collections, 1 (London, 1899), for illustrations of later medieval ceremonial.

16. G. J. Cuming, *A History of Anglican Liturgy,* 2nd edn. (London, 1982), p. 45ff. On the sources for Morning Prayer, see F. E. Brightman, *The English Rite,* 2 vols. (London, 1915), i, p. 126ff.

17. The cope was a ceremonial rather than a sacramental garment in the previous era, sometimes worn by laymen, and was therefore less unacceptable to those of the Reformed persuasion who were critical of vestments.

18. W. H. Frere (ed.), *Visitation Articles and Injunctions of the Period of the Reformation,* Alcuin Club Collections, 16 (London, 1910), pp. 134-9, 318-23. Horne's injunctions of 1562 and 1571 have been re-edited by Sarah Lewin, 'The Visitation Injunctions of Bishop Horne', *WCR* 60 (1991), pp. 24-41.

19. *Articles of Visitation and Enquiry* (London, 1662 and 1665), *passim.* Morley wrote on various doctrinal matters, including the Eucharist, from the standpoint of a high Caroline theologian. These and other works are to be found in his library in Winchester Cathedral.

20. Gabriel Bertonière, *The Historical Development of the Easter Vigil and Related Services in the Greek Church,* Orientalia Christiana Analecta, 193 (Rome, 1972), discusses the evolution of this interesting rite, including its various ways of beginning.

21. See G. W. O. Addleshaw and F. Etchells, *The Architectural Setting of Anglican Worship* (London, 1948) for a general discussion of the lay-out of Anglican churches since the Reformation.

22. On the changing role of the cathedral, see Roger Lloyd, *The Church of England, 1900-1965* (London, 1966), pp. 386-402. The concept of the 'visitor' crept back into the cathedral story some time in the late 19th century. The astonishing factor is that the ministry of cathedrals has grown yet further since this book was written. Lloyd, by a happy coincidence, was a canon residentiary of Winchester.

ST SWITHUN OF WINCHESTER

John Crook

The cult of St Swithun at Winchester was closely linked with the monastic reforms of the late 10th century.[1] On 15 July 971, a rainy day, his relics had been ceremonially exhumed from the grave between Old Minster and St Martin's tower,[2] and carried into the cathedral; by 974 the major part of the relics were enshrined in a splendid reliquary of silver and gold, adorned with jewels and decorated with scenes showing Christ's Passion, Resurrection and Ascension, the gift of King Edgar to the monastery. This magnificent Anglo-Saxon artefact may have survived until it was melted down in 1451.[3] The reliquary was probably displayed on an altar situated in the middle of the westwork of Old Minster,[4] over the site of Swithun's original grave.

According to the late 12th-century Winchester monk, Richard of Devizes,[5] the brethren returned to Old Minster for the last time on the feast of St Swithun,[6] 1093 and carried St Swithun's *feretrum*—presumably the reliquary given by Edgar—into the new church. The very next day Bishop Walkelin ordered that Old Minster should be demolished, and within a year everything had been taken down, except for the high altar and one *porticus*. However, Swithun's original grave remained a potent focus of his cult until the Reformation. The excavations of the 1960s showed that soon after Old Minster had been demolished, an area which Martin Biddle and Birthe Kjølbye-Biddle have called a 'memorial court' was formed around the grave.[7] Several important tombs remained *in situ* in

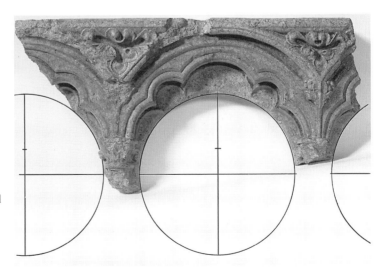

Fig. 6.1   Purbeck marble panel (showing geometry) thought to have come from the 13th-century 'tomb-shrine' over Swithun's original grave. *John Crook*

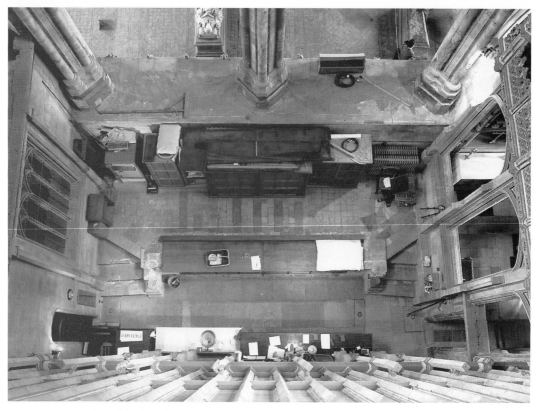

Fig. 6.2   The feretory platform from the top of the Great Screen. *John Crook*

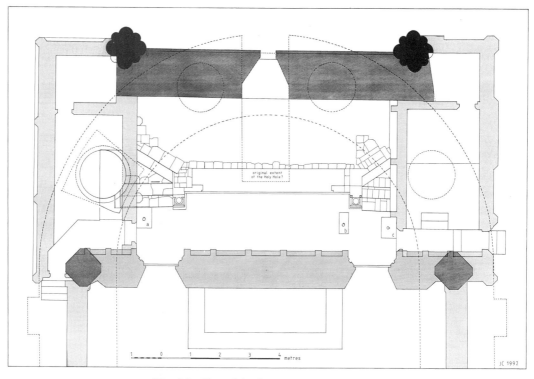

Fig. 6.3   Plan of the feretory area. *John Crook*

this area; these are thought to have contained the mortal remains of pre-Conquest kings and bishops who had been buried *ad sanctum*—near to the saint.[8] The central feature of the court was a chapel enclosing a monument over Swithun's empty grave. Both the monument and the chapel were rebuilt more than once. The latest monument has been shown to date, on archaeological evidence, from the mid-13th century;[9] and a fragment of that monument has now been identified (Fig. 6.1).[10] It was of the type we have called a 'tomb-shrine': a rectangular, tomb-like structure whose sides were pierced with large apertures through which pilgrims could put their heads and shoulders in order to touch or kiss the site of the empty grave.[11] This monument survived the rebuilding of the chapel in the mid-14th century, an operation contemporary with the remodelling of the west front,[12] but both the monument and the chapel were demolished at the Reformation. Thus at Winchester, as elsewhere—York, for example—the patron saint was venerated both at a grave and at a shrine containing his relics. The particular placing of Swithun's shrine behind the high altar, an area to which only the monks had access, meant that for the pilgrim a more accessible focus of the saintly power was the empty grave, scene of the miracles described at such length by the Old Minster monks Lantfred and Wulfstan. The author of the 15th-century *Liber Historialis* drew particular attention to the 'modest chapel' built over the grave, emphasising that it was there that many miracles had taken place through the action of the saint.[13]

The annalist does not recount where the *feretrum* was placed in 1093, but later developments point to the area behind the high altar as the most likely site. In the mid-12th century new arrangements were made for the veneration of St Swithun and other relics in the cathedral. A platform was constructed within the apex of the Romanesque apse, surrounded by a retaining wall, in which the four cylindrical piers of the apse arcade were perhaps half embedded (Figs. 6.2 and 6.3). An intriguing feature of this arrangement was a tunnel-vaulted passage extending from the ambulatory westwards under the platform: the tunnel was retained in the subsequent

Fig. 6.4   The Holy Hole. Early 14th-century arch, with 12th-century masonry visible in the tunnel behind. *John Crook*

Fig. 6.5   Reconstruction of wall painting, possibly showing the translation of St Swithun, concealed behind bookshelves in the Morley Library. *John Crook*

remodelling of the area, and became known as the 'Holy Hole' (Fig. 6.4). In our view, its purpose was to allow pilgrims to crawl, in a suitably humble posture, beneath the reliquary of St Swithun in order to benefit from the healing powers of the saint. The high altar and the reliquary of St Swithun appear to be illustrated in a wall painting dating from the turn of the 12th/13th centuries (Fig. 6.5),[14] possibly indicating an increased interest in the saint's cult resulting from the new arrangements for his veneration.

Our interpretation is supported by a *memorandum* from the following century, which explains how Bishop Henry of Blois translated the bodies of kings and bishops from 'an unworthy place' (*locus indecens*) in 1158, raising them up in lead coffins around the high altar.[15] This documentary account is neatly confirmed by physical evidence: blocks of masonry from the retaining wall have been discovered (Fig. 6.6), bearing inscriptions relating to the pre-Conquest monarchs and prelates within the mortuary coffers.[16] Although the 'unworthy place' from which the bodies were removed is not identified, the most likely site is the memorial court, which was falling into disrepair in the mid-12th century. Some

Fig. 6.6   Inscribed stones from the 12th-century retaining wall to Bishop Henry of Blois' raised feretory platform. *John Crook*

of the bodies may have been housed in a surviving fragment of Old Minster forming a possible charnel chapel on the east side of the court.[17] The move from the court to the feretory area behind the altar and near the shrine thus placed the remains once again under the protection of Winchester's most powerful saint, replicating in effect the earlier arrangement in Old Minster.

The east arm of the cathedral was remodelled in around 1200-35.[18] The traditional interpretation of the retrochoir attributed to Bishop Godfrey de Lucy is that it was intended as a suitably vast setting for the reception of large numbers of pilgrims to St Swithun's shrine, supposed to have been located within the 13th-century extension. In our view, however, Swithun's reliquary remained on the feretory platform behind the high altar until as late as 1476. Indeed, there are clear indications that the feretory platform was remod-

Fig. 6.7   The feretory platform at the beginning of the 20th century, showing remains of the long reliquary cupboard (from a postcard:*Wykeham Series,* No. 24)

elled in the mid-13th century precisely with relic cults in mind: a long recess, fronted by a metal grille, was inserted on the west side of the platform (Fig. 6.7). This presumably held relics of secondary importance, which would have derived additional sanctity from being near the principal saint.

However, the main changes to this area were undertaken early in the 14th century, when the remodelling of the east arm was resumed after a pause of some seventy years.

Fig. 6.8   The early 14th-century feretory screen. *John Crook*

The Romanesque apse was replaced by the present straight Decorated screen at the west end of the retrochoir, with two open arches supporting the east choir gable above (Fig. 6.8).[19] Behind this screen the feretory platform survived, as did the Holy Hole, whose entrance was remodelled with a pointed arch.[20] The lead mortuary chests were placed on top of the Decorated screen, over the Holy Hole, or on beams flanking the feretory. There they were seen by the author of a 15th-century 'Chronicle of Winchester Priory', who noted, for example, that the bones of a certain Edmund (then identified as an infant son of Alfred the Great) were placed *In quoddam sarcofagum locatum supra locum nominatum The Holy Place Hoole.*[21]

In the Romanesque arrangement the occupants of the lead coffers of Henry of Blois (insofar as they could be certainly identified)[22] had been made known by the inscriptions on the face of the retaining wall. The 14th-century scheme showed a greater integration of function and decoration. The screen was adorned with a series of paired niches which, until the Reformation, contained statuettes representing the supposed occupants of the mortuary chests, together with the Blessed Virgin Mary and her Son. Although not a single piece of statuary survives,[23] the missing figures are identified by *tituli* under the niches: the central pair, *Sancta Maria* and *Dominus Iesus*, were flanked by those pre-Conquest kings and bishops who were recognised as the principal benefactors of the cathedral and whose supposed remains still survive in the six mortuary chests on top of Bishop Fox's presbytery screens.

The relationship between the statuettes and the mortuary chests is clarified by the inscription which runs along the face of the screen:

> *Corpora sanctorum hic sunt in pace sepulta*
> *Ex meritis quorum fulgant miracula multa.*[24]

Furthermore, the author of the 15th-century 'Chronicle of Winchester Priory' provides a confirmatory list of the royal and episcopal remains which were placed around the presbytery. He states for example that the remains of Cynegils (*Kinewaldus*) and Æthelwulf (*Adulphus*) reposed 'in a lead coffer on the south side of the high altar'.[25] The coffer containing the bones of Egbert and Cynewulf, who did not figure amongst the screen statuary, stood rather further to the west, 'above the heart-burial tomb of Nicholas of Ely'.[26]

It will be noted that the evidence so far presented for the location of the reliquary of Swithun behind the high altar is entirely circumstantial. It might be argued, for example, that the feature which attracted the royal and episcopal relics was not the shrine of St Swithun but the high altar itself. Fortunately the author of the early 15th-century 'Chronicle of Winchester Priory' precisely described the position of St Swithun's reliquary. The passage occurs in his discussion of the gifts of King Edgar:

> He caused the relics of St Swithun, patron of this church, to be translated, and had them placed within a great reliquary, marvellously and skilfully made of silver, gold and precious stones, which shrine is situated at and joined to the high altar.[27]

This single documentary reference to the site of the shrine before the changes of the mid-15th century confirms our view that the focus of interest behind the high altar—one which determined the development of the feretory platform and its associated royal and episcopal relics—was indeed the major reliquary of St Swithun. This long-standing arrangement was dramatically changed following the death in 1447 of Cardinal Beaufort, bishop of Winchester, when three mutually dependent projects were initiated: the construction of the Great Screen, the creation of a new shrine-base and reliquary in the middle of the retrochoir, and the erection of Beaufort's own chantry chapel. The moving of the shrine to the retrochoir appears to have been a consequence of the construction of the Great Screen, which blocked the former view of the feretory platform from the choir. The feretory, now an enclosed space between the two screens, was adapted as the 'minor' or 'capitular' altar.[28] That Beaufort envisaged the new shrine position is indicated by the fact that he chose a site for his chantry chapel that would be immediately next to the new shrine, on the favoured south side (Fig. 6.9).[29]

The operation is partially documented in the cathedral's *Register of the Common Seal*.[30] Beaufort had left a large number of items of gold and silver to the prior and convent; they resolved to employ part of the bequest in the creation of the 'new shrine' of St Swithun and the silver-gilt *retablo* which was to be the centrepiece of the Great Screen. The 'Old Shrine' (*antiquum feretrum*) was melted down in 1451, yielding 47 lb. 7¼ oz. of silver.

During this operation, the relics were placed in a temporary, ivory reliquary. The architectural part of the Great Screen took some twenty-five years to complete; the major building work appears on stylistic evidence to have been completed by the 1470s.[31] The construction of the Beaufort chantry chapel, which shares stylistic features with the screen, was contemporary with it.

The inauguration of the new shrine is described in full in a *memorandum* in the archiepiscopal register of Cardinal Morton.[32] On St Swithun's eve, 14 July 1476, the 'ivory coffer' was placed on the high altar.[33] Bishop Waynflete presided at Vespers; then all the monks retired to bed, apart from two or three who kept watch over the relics. Next morning a solemn procession was formed; the relics were placed on a bier and carried around the greater part of the city of Winchester. When they had returned to the choir of the cathedral, mass was said; then the relics were carried to the retrochoir,

> ... where a marble tomb had been constructed to the glorious saint, upon which a silver and
> gilt reliquary had previously been placed. Those of the clergy who were capable of doing
> so climbed up a ladder which had been erected from the ground to the reliquary on the east
> side, and on top of the monument the bishop of Winchester and the prior inserted the coffer
> containing the glorious relics into the reliquary through a certain hatch that had been made
> for this purpose on the east side of the reliquary. Then the bishop of Winchester got into
> the reliquary and, having kissed [the relics] with great devotion came out again, as did all
> the other prelates, one after another, as well as certain lords. After this the hatch was closed
> and the ladder taken away, and all those who were there withdrew, with outpourings and
> prayers to God and his glorious saint, blessed Swithun.

The relics of Swithun remained in their final location for just 62 years. When in 1538-48 the *Liber Historialis* was again updated, the author of the new passages describing the burial of Cardinal Beaufort and Bishop Waynflete was able to relate their chantry chapels to the nearby shrine. Beaufort was said to have been buried

> *in ecclesia sua ante altare Beatæ Mariæ inter duas columbas ex australi parte in capella
> propria iuxta feretrum Sancti Swythuni.*[34]

> ... in his own church before the altar of Blessed Mary between two columns on the south
> side next to the shrine of St Swithun.

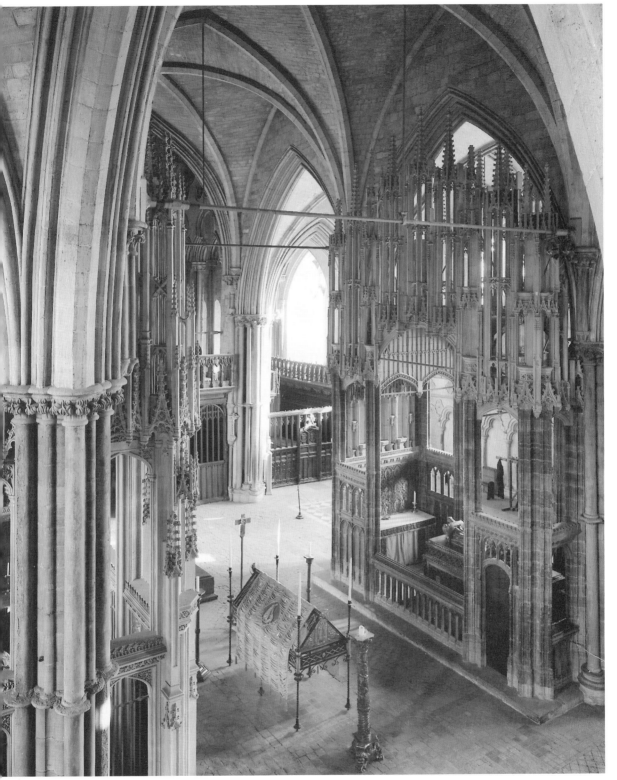

Fig. 6.9   The retrochoir, showing the modern memorial erected on the final site of St Swithun's shrine, with Cardinal Beaufort's chantry chapel to the south. *John Crook*

Fig. 6.10   Iron bracket in the retrochoir roof space, thought to have supported the wooden cover over the 15th-century shrine of St Swithun. *John Crook*

The site of Waynflete's chantry chapel was similarly described, with the substitution of 'north' for 'south'.

There is some physical evidence for the final shrine: the remains of an iron pulley have survived, attached to a tie-beam of the 15th-century roof above the vaulting (Fig. 6.10). This formerly supported the wooden cover of the reliquary. In the crypt a block of flint masonry was inserted to take the weight of the shrine-base, similar to adjacent blocks supporting the chantry chapels of Beaufort and Waynflete. The 'flint solid' was removed by Dean Kitchin in 1886, who identified it at the time as the support for St Swithun's shrine.[35]

Shortly before the dissolution of St Swithun's Priory an inventory of the monastery's valuables was made, and the appraisers noted, 'behynd the hyghe awter Sancte Swithins Schrine beynge of plate selvar and gilte & garnishid with stones'.[36]

In a famous letter to Thomas Cromwell, his commissioner Thomas Wriothesley reported the events of the night of 21-22 September 1538:

> About three o'clock this Saturday morning we made an end of the shrine here at Winchester. There was no gold, nor ring, nor true stone in it, but all great counterfeits; but the silver alone will amount to 2,000 marks.[37]

The fate of Swithun's relics is not known. According to a contemporary account dated 1539,

> St. Swithan and other reliques whereabout abuse of ipocrasy was be layde save, and not, as it is untruely surmitted, brent, but according to reason collocate secretely, wher ther shal be no cause of superstition given by them; as some say that for the like cause, the body of Moyses was hyden lest the Jues shuld fall to idolatry.[38]

Notes

1. The development of the cult of St Swithun will be fully discussed in M. Lapidge, *The Cult of St Swithun*, Winchester Studies 4.ii, (forthcoming).
2. See above, p. 14.
3. J. Crook, 'King Edgar's Reliquary of St Swithun', *Anglo-Saxon England* 21 (1992), pp. 177-202.
4. The westwork in its final form was dedicated in 980. The ceremony is described in the *epistola specialis* which opens Wulfstan's *Narratio de Sancto Swithuno*: A. Campbell (ed.), *Frithegodi monachi breviloquium vitæ beati Wilfredi et Wulfstani Cantoris Narratio Metrica de Sancto Swithuno* (Zurich 1950), pp. 66-8 (lines 41-118). A new edition and translation by Michael Lapidge of the *Narratio Metrica* will be published in *Winchester Studies 4.ii.*
5. *Winchester Annals,* p. 37. For Richard of Devizes, see above, p. 11, note 20.
6. This was presumably the *translatio,* 15 July, which by the late 11th century had replaced the *obit,* 2 July, as the major feast of Swithun.
7. M. Biddle, 'Excavations at Winchester 1966', *Antiq. J.* 47 (1967), pp. 270-1; *idem,* 'Excavations at Winchester 1967', *Antiq. J.* 48 (1968), pp. 274-5, 278; *idem,* 'Excavations at Winchester 1968', *Antiq. J.* 49 (1969), pp. 321-2.
8. Or, more accurately, the place made holy by the saint's former presence.
9. M. Biddle, 'Excavations at Winchester 1967', *Antiq. J.* 48 (1968), p. 278: 'The second monument was probably ... not later than the thirteenth century'; B. Kjølbye-Biddle, *pers. comm.*
10. J. Crook, 'The Typology of Early Medieval Shrines—a Previously Misidentified "Tomb-Shrine" Panel from Winchester Cathedral', *Antiq. J.* 70 (1990), pp. 49-64.
11. Extant examples of such structures are found at Jerusalem (Tomb of the Virgin, at Gethsemane); Salisbury (St Osmund); Whitchurch Canonicorum, Dorset (St Wita); Ilam, Staffs. (St Bertelin); the prototype may have been the marble slab installed to protect the empty tomb of Christ in the Church of the Holy Sepulchre.
12. See below, p. 223.
13. '... *sepultus est extra portam borialem navis ecclesie, qui locus tunc indecens erat; modo vero ibidem pulchra capella in eius honore constructa est, ubi crebra, Deo operante per eum, ostensa sunt miracula.'* BL, Cotton. Galba A.xv, fos. 62v-75; Oxford, All Souls College, MS 114, fo. 4. An edition of the *Liber Historialis* is in preparation: J. Crook (ed.), *Monastic Chroniclers of St Swithun's Priory,* forthcoming.
14. Crook, 'King Edgar's Reliquary'.
15. Winchester Cathedral Cartulary, MS, WCL, item 4, published by A. W. Goodman (ed.), *Chartulary of Winchester Cathedral* (Winchester, 1927), p. 3.
16. The lettering style of the inscriptions suggests that they were cut into the blocks *in situ,* at a somewhat later date, perhaps *c.*1200.
17. M. Biddle and B. Kjølbye-Biddle, *pers. comm.* Our interpretation of the *locus indecens* as the memorial court, rather than, for example, the Romanesque crypt, finds possible support in the fact that the phrase *locus indecens* was used by the author of the 15th-century *Liber Historialis* to denote the same area: '*sepultus est extra portam borealem navis ecclesie qui locus tunc indecens erat'* (Oxford, All Souls College, MS 114, fo. 4).
18. The start of this work is usually dated to 1202 on the basis of an entry in the *Winchester Annals* referring to the establishment of a 'confraternity for the repair of the church'. There is, however, physical evidence for a late 12th-century scheme to extend the east arm of the church (J. Crook, forthcoming article). The 13th-century retrochoir shows many changes in design, and on stylistic grounds work may have continued until the third decade of that century; see below, p. 178.
19. See below, p. 183.
20. The opening is of course very much smaller than its Romanesque predecessor; it is difficult to imagine that it was now intended that pilgrims should enter here.
21. 'In a certain sarcophagus over the place called The Holy Place Hole.' Cambridge, Corpus Christi College, MS 110, p. 327. We hope to publish this text in Crook, *Monastic Chroniclers.* A parallel passage occurs in the *Historia Major* attributed to Thomas Rudborne, in H. Wharton (ed.), *Anglia Sacra sive Collectio Historiarum,* 2 vols. (London, 1691), i, p. 207.
22. The author of the All Souls version of the *Liber Historialis* (see note 13, above) states that the bones

of pre-Conquest monarchs were translated 'from the eastern crypt' by Henry of Blois, 'and because it was not known which were kings and which were bishops, and because there were no inscriptions on their monuments, the aforesaid Henry mixed bishops with kings and kings with bishops all together in lead coffers' (Cambridge, All Souls College, MS 114, fo. 5v). Other passages in the same document make it clear that the 'eastern crypt' referred to was that of Old Minster (which the monks believed to be one and the same with the present cathedral); this had been demolished over half a century before the translation of 1158. The clear archaeological evidence for prestigious burials within the memorial court outweighs, in our view, any suggestion that the 'lowly place' might have been the crypt of the present cathedral; the passage is most plausibly interpreted as an explanation of the manner in which the royal and episcopal relics were by the 15th century grouped several to a box.

23. In contrast with the good survival of statuary from the Great Screen, Fox's chantry, and other locations within the cathedral. Phillip Lindley (*pers. comm.*) has suggested that the statuettes may have been of another material than stone.

24. 'The bodies of saints are here buried in peace, through whose merits many miracles shine forth.' Similar lines occur in Wulfstan's *Narratio Metrica de Sancto Swithuno*, lines 309-10: '*Corpora sanctorum sunt hic in pace sepulta/et vivunt eorum nomina in æternum*'. This passage is a metrical recasting of *Ecclesiasticus*, 44:14: '*Corpora ipsorum in pace sepulta sunt/et nomen eorum vivet in generationes et generationes*'.

25. Cambridge, Corpus Christi College, MS 110, p. 318:' *modo ossa ipsius [Kingilsi] in locello plumbeo ex australi parte eiusdem altaris supra ostium meridionalis cryptæ cum ossibus Athulphi regis ...*'

26. Cambridge, Corpus Christi College, MS 110, p. 320: '*modo vero in plumbeo locello ossa [Kinewlphi] reconduntur ex eadem plaga super sepulturam ubi cor Nicholai episcopi reponitur. Cum Egberto rege ponuntur enim ossa amborum regum in uno sarcofago ...*'

27. Cambridge, Corpus Christi College, MS 110, p. 336.

28. A 16th-century copy of the *Liber Historialis,* BL, Cotton. Vespasian D.ix, fo. 24, states that Bishop Fox (d.1528) was buried *in ecclesia sua in capella propria iuxta summum altare in parte australi minoris altaris.*

29. The will states simply that Beaufort was to be buried '*in eo videlicet loco quem pro sepulture mei elegi et assignavi*': N. H. Nicolas (ed.), *Testamenta Vetusta* (London, 1826), p. 249. In our view the place was chosen precisely because the chantry chapel would eventually stand beside the new shrine of Swithun, on the favoured south side. The fact that Beaufort does not mention the shrine as a reference point is additional (albeit negative) evidence that at the time he made his will (20 January 1445/6) the reliquary of Swithun was located elsewhere.

30. J. Greatrex (ed.), *The Register of the Common Seal of the Priory of St Swithun, Winchester, 1345-1497,* Hampshire Record Series, 2 (Winchester, 1978), items 320-22.

31. P. Lindley, 'The Great Screen of Winchester Cathedral, I', *Burlington Magazine* 131 (1989), pp. 604-15.

32. Published in C. Harper-Bill (ed.), *The Register of John Morton, Archbishop of Canterbury*, 2 vols., Canterbury and York Society (1987-91), i, pp. 52-3 (item 184).

33. Harper-Bill (*ibid.*) incorrectly translates *eburnea* as 'ebony'.

34. BL, Cotton. Vespasian D.ix, fo. 23v.

35. G. W. Kitchin, 'The Crypts of Winchester Cathedral', *Hampshire Chronicle,* 17 April 1886. The position of the 'flint solid' is shown in a plan of the crypt by John Colson Sr., dated 8 January 1869: Society of Antiquaries of London, 'Brown Portfolio' 6 (Hampshire).

36. BL, Harley 358, fo. 17v.

37. PRO, State Papers, 1.621, printed in W. de Gray Birch (ed.), *Letters and Papers of Henry VIII*, xiii.ii (London, 1893), p. 155 (item 401).

38. From a draft sermon, in hand of Thomas Derby, clerk of the Privy Council, printed in full by J. Collier, *An Ecclesiastical History of Great Britain, Chiefly of England ...* 2 vols. (London, 1708-14), Appendix ('A Collection of Records'), pp. 36-40, item xlvii. The text was discussed and corrected by H. S. Milman, 'The Vanished Memorials of St Thomas of Canterbury', *Archaeologia* 53 (1892), pp. 211-28. It should be noted that the 'other relics' mentioned were not necessarily Winchester ones, and the passage, taken in context, seems to refer to relics of St Swithun at Canterbury.

HENRY OF BLOIS, WINCHESTER, AND THE 12TH-CENTURY RENAISSANCE

Yoshio Kusaba

It is a well-known fact that Henry of Blois, bishop of Winchester (1129-71) and abbot of Glastonbury (1126-71), was instrumental in forging the artistic activities of Winchester in particular and England in a broader sense. However, no systematic study concentrates on

the complexities of the artistic atmosphere at Winchester in the time of Bishop Henry, relating it to the historical circumstances, his political activities, and his artistic contacts, including medieval and 'antique' sources. This paper is presented not as an exhaustive study, but as part of a working set of ideas for understanding Henry of Blois as a patron of art and architecture, and focuses mainly on some of the classicising expressions that can be associated with him.[1]

Henry of Blois and the 12th-Century Renaissance

Bishop Henry's physical appearance is known only from the enamel plaques now at the British Museum, one of which shows him as a crouching, humble, bearded cleric, holding a crozier and a decorated tablet,[2] and from the image shown on his episcopal seal (Fig. 7.1). The exact year of his birth is unknown, but Henry was not the youngest of the children his mother, Adela, daughter of the Conqueror, had by Stephen Henry Count of Blois (d.1102), so Henry must have been born by around 1100 at the latest. This means that when he became bishop of Winchester in 1129,

Fig. 7.1   Seal of Henry of Blois. *John Crook/Warden and Scholars of Winchester College*

69

Henry was about thirty years old. His aristocratic stature and taste resulted from his illustrious family background and monastic upbringing. A grandson of William the Conqueror and younger brother of King Stephen, trained as a monk at the premier abbey of Cluny at the time when its impressive third church was being constructed, Henry of Blois had both royal wealth and intellectual sophistication.[3] In addition he possessed practical administrative skills, for example, in straightening property rights and restoring the endowments of his diocese,[4] and in the financial affairs of his mother abbey at Cluny. Such gifts of birth and intellect were put to good use in providing Winchester Cathedral and Glastonbury Abbey with a rich fabric of artistic ideas. His generous gifts to Winchester Cathedral have been documented, including an astonishing number and range of artistic objects, such as gold and silver liturgical items.[5] He was as much a vital part of the 'twelfth-century Renaissance' as, for example, Abbot Suger of Saint-Denis.[6] He travelled widely, including several visits to Rome, where he purchased antique statues and had them shipped to Winchester.[7]

The date and circumstances of Bishop Henry's visit to Rome and purchase of antique statues are by no means certain.[8] He seems to have purchased the statues as a consolation, either when he had failed to persuade Pope Celestine II (1143-44) to remove him from the jurisdiction of the archbishop of Canterbury by elevating Winchester into a metropolitan see of Wessex with Henry as archbishop,[9] or after he had received absolution from Pope Eugenius III (1145-53) relating to allegations against him, especially his non-attendance at the Council of Reims in 1148.[10] Nevertheless, his act may be regarded as a learned, aesthetic appreciation of the image of the classical past, a humanistic attitude as the foundation of a renaissance.[11]

In addition, it is likely that Bishop Henry saw many of the remains of classical Rome identified in the *Mirabilia Urbis Romæ* written *c.*1143 by Benedict, a canon of St Peter's.[12] Benedict's description includes not only Christian monuments, but also classical ones— arches, pyramids, theatres, baths, circuses, sacred sites, palaces and temples—still visible in the 12th century.[13] Henry of Blois and Canon Benedict were not alone in their concern with the antiquity of Rome and appreciation of classical monuments. This is demonstrated in the *Narratio de Mirabilibus Urbis Romæ* of Magister Gregory, an Englishman who was so enamoured by a statue of Venus that he went back 'three times to look at it ...'; he was also informed enough to be able to identify the image as

> made from Parian marble with such wonderful and intricate skill that she seems more like a living creature than a statue; indeed she seems to blush in her nakedness, a reddish tinge colouring her face, and it appears to those who take a close look that blood flows in her snowy complexion.[14]

There is no way of telling whether the *veteres statuæ* were Greek originals, Roman copies, or Roman originals. The fact that Bishop Henry had them shipped to Winchester might imply that they were quite large figures.[15] Unfortunately, none has survived; nor do we know where he wanted to keep them.[16] But his interest in classical antiquity and his multi-regional contacts are manifested in subtle ways in Winchester, no more so than in the remains of his own palace of Wolvesey—the *domus quasi palatium* emulating the Palatine Palace in Rome—with its impressive capitals now in the possession of Winchester Cathedral and the City Museum. In examining these, it is important to remember that Henry's interest in classical forms was integrated with other stylistic factors which have tended to obscure his role as an active antiquarian and patron.

Introduction and Use of Purbeck and Tournai Marbles

Henry of Blois' affinity with the classical past was not limited to the antique statues he purchased in Rome. Equally important was his interest in marble. Because of its cost and capacity to take high polish, marble was always associated with the dignity of the past, and was used as a means of giving visual expression to the power and taste both of ecclesiastical and secular builders.

Purbeck Marble

William of Sens, who was responsible for rebuilding the choir of Canterbury Cathedral after the fire of 1174, has generally been credited for the beginning of the popular use of colourful Purbeck 'marble' in England;[17] the stone subsequently became the hallmark of English Gothic architecture and sculpture in the 13th and 14th centuries, as, for example, at Salisbury Cathedral and Westminster Abbey. But recent studies clearly show that Bishop Henry was responsible for its first use, during the construction of Wolvesey Palace. According to the new dates assigned by Martin Biddle to the various parts of the palace built and enlarged by Bishop Henry, carved Purbeck marble details were already being employed in those parts of the east hall which were built soon after the siege of Winchester in 1141 but before Bishop Henry's exile at Cluny (1154-58).[18] While the lower parts of the walls of the hall are

of earlier date (*c*.1135-38), the clerestory level was built *c*.1141-54; a Purbeck marble respond capital remains *in situ* just above a later inserted corbel head (Fig. 7.2). Other Purbeck marble capitals and bases were found during the excavations of 1962-71, most likely belonging to *c*.1158-71, although their original locations are difficult to ascertain. Judging from the five-shafted capitals in Purbeck (Fig. 7.3), the northern extension (Woodman's Gate), built in the post-1158 period, must have been of a sumptuous character. These capitals and bases are stylistically echoed at Bishop's Waltham Palace, repaired or enlarged by Bishop Henry between 1158 and 1171.

Furthermore, it appears that Hyde Abbey and Bishop Henry's foundation at St Cross Hospital also benefited from his interest in the use of Purbeck marble, perhaps involving the same carvers. The bases and capitals from Hyde are datable to the 1160s on stylistic grounds, and appear to be closely related to those at Wolvesey.[19] At St

Fig. 7.2   Wolvesey Palace. Purbeck marble respond capital at north-east corner of East Hall. *John Crook*

Fig. 7.3   Five-shafted Purbeck marble capital with downward curving volutes, excavated from Wolvesey Palace. *Yoshio Kusaba*

Cross, the two piers in the choir, finished by 1171, when Bishop Henry died, were originally of Purbeck.[20] Their socle bases, still visible above the floor, clearly indicate a design consisting of a cylindrical core surrounded by four *en délit* shafts.[21] These piers represent one of the earliest, if not the earliest, examples of Purbeck marble used in a major, weight-supporting role, followed in southern England by those in the retrochoir at Chichester Cathedral after the fire of 1186.[22] These examples from Wolvesey, Hyde Abbey and St Cross suggest a wider application of Purbeck marble by the early 1160s. A similar Purbeck capital (Fig. 7.4), closely associated with those from Winchester, was found at St Saviour's Abbey, Faversham (Kent), a royal foundation of 1148, established by King Stephen and his queen, Matilda of Boulogne (d.1152), as the tomb-place for themselves and their son Eustace (d.1153), and initially colonised by Cluniac monks from Bermondsey. A date as early as 1148 would be difficult to assign to this capital on stylistic grounds. Although we do not know its exact original context, the evidence of masonry vaults found during excavations in 1965 suggests that this capital belonged to the choir or its aisle,[23] and thus a date in the 1150s is possible.[24] Henry of Blois was a witness when King Stephen granted the foundation of Faversham Abbey in 1147,[25] and may have been particularly interested in the construction of the abbey founded by his brother.

Tournai marble
Until the local substitute, Purbeck marble, became available, Henry of Blois relied on the more expensive imported Tournai marble for architectural projects (such as the colonnettes with spiral decoration now in the City Museum), and for liturgical objects such as fonts, the best of which is now found in the nave of Winchester Cathedral (Fig. 9.1).[26] Henry's interest in imported Tournai marble carved objects is further indicated by permission granted to the Tournai trade guild, La Charité Saint-Christophe, to carry on business at Winchester in the 1160s.[27]

Fig. 7.4 Faversham Abbey, Purbeck marble capital. *Ann Zielinsky*

These examples datable to the 1150s and '60s clearly indicate Henry's interest and taste in using Tournai marble and its local substitute, Purbeck, in his architectural enterprises in Winchester and elsewhere. His interest in the highly polished quality of marble may have resulted from his exposure to the remains of the grand classical buildings, such as the Baths of Diocletian, that he saw in Rome.

Problems of the Stylistic Sources of Capitals and Other Fragments

The introduction of Purbeck marble for architectural details raises the question of the skills involved in carving them, since the stone requires special handling.[28] For Winchester, this need could have been satisfied by the presence of the Tournai marble guild in the 1160s, and Bishop Henry may have enlisted some of the Tournai carvers. However, the question of whether the Tournai marble works were carved before shipment or at their intended destination remains disputed.[29] The relatively homogeneous styles found on the Tournai fonts and tomb-slabs seem to favour production before shipment. But the fonts must have been assembled at their intended sites, which would involve the skilled carvers from Tournai working in a supervisory capacity. In addition, architectural members (bases and capitals) could not be easily prefabricated, unlike the fonts. This naturally argues for involvement of Tournai or skilled marble carvers at Winchester and elsewhere.

Marble Capitals and Fragments

If this is the case, we can now explain one possible source of the stylistic features apparent in the Purbeck marble bases, shafts and capitals at Winchester. The similarity in style between the Purbeck capitals at Faversham and St Cross in Winchester has already been alluded to,[30] both of whose foliate decorations are of decidedly English character. Further comparisons strengthen the stylistic ties between Winchester and Tournai resulting from the influence of Tournai carvers. Waterleaf capitals, with or without inward and outward curving volutes, and bases with scallop foliage spur decorations as at Wolvesey are also found in the nave and transepts of Tournai Cathedral, datable to *c*.1140-60, similar to ones excavated from Wolvesey (Figs. 7.5 and 7.6).[31] It is true that such decorative motifs are not exclusive to Tournai or Winchester.[32] But the critical factors at Winchester are that the motifs (the

Fig. 7.5   Single-shafted Purbeck marble capital excavated from Wolvesey Palace, with upward-curling volutes.
Yoshio Kusaba

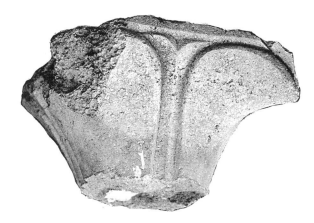

Fig. 7.6   Single-shafted Purbeck marble capital excavated from Wolvesey Palace, with waterleaf decoration.
Yoshio Kusaba

scalloped foliage on bases, as in the Triforium Gallery example), are used both on Tournai and Purbeck marbles, and that the quality of the waterleaf work is quite superb in the Winchester capitals, suggesting that they were not just mass-produced. The conclusion seems to be that, in the absence of experienced sculptors for newly-introduced Purbeck, the Tournai marblers could have worked in close association with the Winchester workshop operating under Bishop Henry's organisation.

The Ex-Situ Capitals

About eight well-preserved limestone capitals are displayed in the Triforium Gallery, Winchester Cathedral.[33] They include figurative motifs, single and trefoiled geometric patterns, scallops, and even a modified 'palm-tree'. They cannot all belong to one group. The best-known (Fig. 7.7) shows a centaur fighting a basilisk, and another killing a griffin (Fig. 9.3), and is datable to 1150-55.[34] The griffins bear a superficial resemblance to those on the Hyde Abbey capitals, but the cathedral capital has gained volume and plastic quality in its overall treatment. A clue to dating this capital even slightly later than 1150-55 is the sharp edge of angle leaf curling downwards, similar to the Purbeck waterleaf, five-shafted capital from Wolvesey, probably belonging, as mentioned above, to the period after 1158. The griffin was popular as a decorative feature in Romanesque Europe, and occurs on the borders of the Bayeux Tapestry, in the crypt at Canterbury, *c.*1100, and in early 12th-century France in the abacus details of a capital in the cloister at Moissac.[35] But its association with a rigorous, stately treatment of the centaur motif (also familiar throughout the medieval period) might suggest a classical influence not only as part of the 12th-century Renaissance, but more specifically linked to Henry's purchase of antique statuary in Rome. While we do not know what these antique figures were, a hint of how some of them might have appeared can be found in such examples as the statue of a young centaur at the J. Paul Getty Museum in Malibu (late 1st century A.D.), the two Ferietti centaurs at the Capitoline Museum, Rome, or the centaur with cupids at the

Louvre; or from mosaics, such as the floor mosaic depicting the battle of centaurs and wild beasts from Hadrian's villa at Tivoli (*c.*135 A.D.), or the one with sea-monsters from the Neptune Baths at Ostia (mid-2nd century).[36]

Since the Norman cathedral at Winchester was finished well before Henry became bishop in 1129, none of the *ex situ* capitals could belong to the cathedral itself. The only securely datable addition Henry made to the cathedral fabric is the so-called treasury in the south transept, created in the late 1150s, with its classically-influenced fluted pilasters.[37] The 12th-century monastic buildings at Winchester await full analysis, but some 12th-century details are still visible in the dorter range, to the south of the chapter house. The infirmary cloister, later known as the 'Little Cloister', is another possibility (Fig. 11.1).

What makes the study of the stylistic background complex at Winchester is the fact that there must have been diverse strands of contacts and sources available to the artists working during Henry of Blois' long episcopate. The Tournai connection has already been mentioned. In addition to the Byzantinising contacts, as seen in the two full-page illustrations from the life of the Virgin in the Winchester Psalter,[38] and classical influences and sources attributable to Henry's interest, stylistic diversity can be demonstrated by other remains. One of these is a capital found in the High Street, Winchester, datable to about 1140 (Fig. 7.8).[39]

Fig. 7.7   Capital showing combat of centaur and basilisk. *John Crook*

Fig. 7.8   Capital with seated, haloed figures. *John Crook*

The capital may be associated with the cathedral, though St Mary's Abbey, damaged in the siege of 1141 along with Hyde Abbey, is another possible provenance. It shows eight haloed, seated figures framed in arches, two on each face, each holding a book. A close examination of the drapery style indicates that these seated figures do not rely on the usual, damp-fold style commonly used in English manuscripts, but employ plate drapery instead. The area from Burgundy to Languedoc in the first half of the 12th century was the region where this style was popular.[40] In view of Henry's association with Cluny, a Burgundian connection is not so surprising. As for Languedoc, we know that Bishop Henry visited Compostela during a return journey from one of his trips to Rome,[41] so a stylistic link with Toulouse is also plausible. A more striking variant is found in yet another example from St Bartholomew's, Hyde, now at the City Museum (Fig. 7.9). It is a stoup, possibly a re-used capital, with a grotesque mask. Its date is probably post-1141, and it closely compares with a capital from the entry into the bell-tower of Saint-Martin at Périgné (Deux-Sèvres) in Aquitaine.[42] Both have large eyes and prominent pointed ears emerging from foliage or a scalloped background.

Lastly, a palm-tree motif issuing from a grotesque mask and flanked by acrobats is seen on the capital now in the Triforium Gallery, dating from 1130-40 (Fig. 7.10).[43] The palm-tree of this capital may be regarded as a medieval translation of the classical Corinthian motif, such as the splendid pilaster capitals from the temple of Mars Ultor in the Forum of Augustus, in Rome, derived through Romanesque intermediaries such as the capitals at the third church at Cluny; and the acrobats can also be identified as an imaginative adaptation of many gesticulating figures on capitals and façades seen in Burgundian and south-west French Romanesque works of the first half of the 12th century.

Conclusions

In conclusion, it is quite clear that a great deal of work is still ahead of us, such as the question of workshops under Bishop Henry's control, which he employed for his projects, and of the actual modes of transmission of various styles. The length and nature of this essay have not permitted detailed discussion of Hyde Abbey and Glastonbury, both of which are equally important in relation to Henry of Blois. The connection with Saint-Denis proposed by George Zarnecki is similarly critical,[44] but its examination must be a different study. Also, no systematic discussion of Henry's architectural achievements has been included, nor the relationships between the well-known mid-century Winchester manuscripts and sculpture, including ivory and other minor arts. Nevertheless, the diverse and rich artistic activities found in Winchester and so far discussed must be attributed to the aristocratic and efficient patron, Henry of Blois. His royal connections and monastic training at Cluny, as well as his several visits to Rome, must all have contributed to the multi-faceted artistic atmosphere of Winchester in the 12th century.

Acknowledgements

I would like sincerely to thank John Crook, my colleague and friend, for his energetic transactions concerning this paper, and for the knowledge about Winchester he has generously shared with me in working on various aspects of the architectural and artistic history of Winchester Cathedral. Similarly, my thanks are due to Martin Biddle, for his continued interest in my work, and for sharing with me more recently his latest interpretations regarding Wolvesey Palace and other aspects of 12th-century Winchester. I extend my appreciation to John Hardacre, Curator at the cathedral, who graciously shared his busy time with me at short notice to discuss the 12th-century works shortly before their display in the Triforium Gallery. I would like to thank Elizabeth Lewis, Curator, Winchester City Museums, for sharing her knowledge, especially of Hyde Abbey, and kindly letting me examine the fragments in the City Museum.

Fig. 7.9   Stoup, probably a re-used capital, with a grotesque mask. *John Crook*

Fig. 7.10   Capital with palm-tree and acrobats. *John Crook*

Notes

1. Various aspects of ideas discussed here have been presented in three conference papers: at the Sixteenth Annual Conference of the Association of Art Historians (Great Britain), at Trinity College, Dublin (March 1990); during a 'Symposium on Medieval Visions of Antiquity' at the Center for Medieval Studies, California State University at Northridge (February 1989); and at the 23rd International Congress on Medieval Studies at the Medieval Institute, Western Michigan University (May 1988). My larger study on Henry of Blois as a 12th-century patron, especially of architecture, is forthcoming. For a bibliography of the principal studies of Henry of Blois and his period, see the footnotes to Y. Kusaba, 'The Function, Date and Stylistic Sources of the Treasury of Henry of Blois in the South Transept of Winchester Cathedral', *WCR* 57 (1988), pp. 38-49.

2. For a recent study of the enamel plaques, now attributed to a Mosan workshop, see N. Stratford, 'The Henry of Blois Plaques', *BAA Winchester,* pp. 28-37. Abbot Suger of Saint-Denis is depicted in a similar crouching position in the Annunciation panel from the stained glass of the Infancy of Christ window in the Lady Chapel of his church, *c.*1144.

3. The best study of Bishop Henry's career remains L. Voss, *Heinrich von Blois, Bischof von Winchester (1129-1171)* (Berlin, 1932).

4. A. R. Rumble, 'The Purpose of the Codex Wintoniensis', *Anglo-Norman Studies* 3 (1981), pp. 153-232.

5. E. Bishop, 'Gifts of Bishop Henry of Blois, Abbot of Glastonbury, to Winchester Cathedral', *Downside Review* 3 (1884), pp. 33-44.

6. For the 12th-century Renaissance, see C. H. Haskins, *The Renaissance of the Twelfth Century* (Cambridge, Mass., 1927); R. W. Southern, 'The Place of England in the Twelfth Century Renaissance', *History* 45 (1960), pp. 201-16; C. Brooke, *The Twelfth Century Renaissance* (New York, 1969), esp. pp. 144-54. For a recent and unique historical perspective, see K. F. Morrison, *History as a Visual Art in the Twelfth-Century Renaissance* (Princeton, N.J., 1990).

7. For the purchase of antique statues, see M. Chibnall (ed.), *The Historia Pontificalis of John of Salisbury,* rev. edn. (Oxford, 1986), p. 79. The relevant passage reads: *'Cum vero episcopus preter absolutionem se nichil optinere posse videret, accepta licentia rediens veteres statuas emit Rome, quas Wintoniam deferri fecit.'*

8. For Bishop Henry's itinerary and visits to Rome, see Chibnall, *Historia Pontificalis,* pp. 91-4; also M. Colish, 'A Twelfth-Century Problem', *Apollo,* July 1968, pp. 36-41, at p. 39 and note 48.

9. *Winchester Annals,* s.a. 1143.

10. *Winchester Annals,* pp. 54-5 records under the year 1151 that Henry of Blois was summoned to Rome by Pope Eugenius III to clarify allegations brought against him by Bernard of Clairvaux, the monks of Hyde Abbey, and 'many others', and that matters were satisfactorily resolved and Henry was restored to his full powers.

11. Cf. M. Camille, *The Gothic Idol: Ideology and Image-Making in Medieval Art* (Cambridge, 1989), pp. 77-87. Many of the classical works of the Vatican Collection survive because of papal interest in preserving antiquity.

12. E. Gardiner (ed.), *The Marvels of Rome: Mirabilia Urbis Romæ,* 2nd edn. (New York, 1986).

13. Among the monuments identified are the Forum, the Temple of Mars Ultor, the Colosseum, Trajan's Column, the Pantheon, the Baths of Diocletian, and the Arch of Constantine.

14. J. Osborne (trans.), *Master Gregorius: The Marvels of Rome* (Toronto, 1987), p. 27. The text may date from early in the 13th century. The figure is identified as the Capitoline Venus, now in the Capitoline Museum.

15. However, E. Bishop, 'Henry of Blois', p. 38, note 1, speculates that Bishop Henry's gifts to the cathedral included a few items he bought in Rome. Bishop identifies two silver candlesticks *in effigie hominis,* a silver vessel *in modo hominis,* a great cameo, and one other jewel (*anulus*). For the cameo, see also *ibid.,* p. 42 and note 2.

16. The most likely place would be Wolvesey Palace. For a recent study on the survival of Roman artefacts in the medieval period, see M. Greenhalph, *The Survival of Roman Antiquities in the Middle Ages* (London, 1989).

17. For the stone types, see above, pp. 39-40.

18. M. Biddle, *Wolvesey: The Old Bishop's Palace, Winchester, Hampshire,* English Heritage Handbook (London, 1986), p. 11.

19. The 12th-century building sequence at Hyde Abbey is the subject of a forthcoming article as one of my Winchester-related studies.

20. The piers were restored in the mid-19th century by William Butterfield, who released them from the late 14th-century octagonal encasing by Master John de Campeden.

21. Y. Kusaba, 'The Architectural History of the Church of the Hospital of St Cross in Winchester and its Place in the Development of English Gothic Architecture', Ph.D. dissertation, Indiana University, 1983, publ. University Microfilms International (Ann Arbor, Michigan, 1984), pp. 163-212.

22. The Purbeck marble clustered columns of the round nave of the Temple Church in London (probably finished by 1161) must be roughly contemporary with Bishop Henry's work at St Cross.

23. B. Philp, *Excavations at Faversham, 1965: The Royal Abbey, Roman Villa and Belgic Farmstead* (Kent Archaeological Research Group, 1968), esp. p. 10 for the nave and pp. 14-17 for the choir and royal chapel, where the stone vaults are discussed. The capital was found before the 1965 excavations.

24. The capital shares with the continuous capital decorations of the north side of the north aisle entrance at St Cross a foliage pattern consisting of long stems and leaf-ends with rhythmic twists.

25. W. Telfer, 'Faversham Abbey Reconsidered', *Archaeologia Cantiana* 80 (1965), p. 215.

26. Three other similar fonts are found in Hampshire alone—at the churches of St Michael in South-ampton, All Saints in East Meon, and St Peter at St Mary Bourne—all of which date from *c*.1140. and can be associated with Bishop Henry: C. H. Eden, *Black Tournai Fonts in England* (London, 1909), and G. Zarnecki, 'Henry of Blois as a Patron of Sculpture', in S. Macready and F. H. Thompson (eds.), *Art and Patronage in the English Romanesque* (London, 1986), pp. 159-72.

27. L. Stone, *Sculpture in Britain: The Middle Ages* (Harmondsworth, 1972), p. 89 and note 28. On the popularity of Tournai marble in the 11th and 12th centuries, see P. Rolland, 'L'expansion tournaisienne aux XIe et XIIe siècles: art et commerce de la pierre', *Annales de l'Académie Royale d'Archéologie de Belgique* 71 (1924), pp. 175-219, and on the guild, esp. pp. 206-8.

28. For the problems of carving, see J. Blair, 'Purbeck Marble', in J. Blair and N. Ramsay (eds.), *English Medieval Industries* (London, 1991), pp. 41-56.

29. Rolland, 'L'expansion tournaisienne', pp. 188-210, believed that the pieces had been worked at Tournai before shipment. One exception, as indicated by G. Zarnecki, 'Henry of Blois', p. 167, is the tomb-slab (now at St John the Baptist's, Southover, Lewes) of Gundrada, wife of William de Warenne, founder of Lewes Priory.

30. See note 24, above.

31. A well-preserved Tournai marble double-column base of *c*.1160 is on display in the Triforium Gallery, Winchester Cathedral. For the architectural sculpture at Tournai, see V. Scaff, *La Sculpture Romane de la Cathédrale Notre-Dame de Tournai* (Tournai, 1971).

32. Similar waterleaf Purbeck capitals have been found at Battle Abbey, Shaftesbury Abbey, and at the priory of St Nicholas, Exeter, and are common among the Cistercian foundations in England (e.g. Fountains, Roche and Kirkstall Abbeys) and in France, especially in Burgundy (e.g. Paray-le-Monial (transept clerestory), Pontigny Abbey (nave and narthex)).

33. J. Hardacre, *Winchester Cathedral: Triforium Gallery*, Catalogue (Winchester, 1989), items 1-3, 7, 8-11.

34. See below, p. 99; G. Zarnecki, in G. Zarnecki, J. Holt and T. Holland (eds.), *English Romanesque Art 1066-1200*, Exhibition Catalogue, Hayward Gallery (London, 1984), item 151.

35. Illustrated in M. Durliat, *L'Art Roman* (Paris, 1982).

36. For the Getty centaur, see *Handbook of the Collection*, J. Paul Getty Museum, 2nd edn. (Malibu, CA, 1988), p. 37; for the Capitoline and Louvre centaurs, F. Haskell and N. Penny, *Taste and the Antique: the Lure of Classical Sculpture 1500-1900* (New Haven and London, 1981), catalogue Nos. 21-2 respectively; for the mosaics from Hadrian's villa and Ostia, N. H. Ramage and A. Ramage, *Roman Art: Romulus to Constantine* (Englewood Cliffs, N.J., 1991), figs. 7.7 and 7.8 respectively.

37. Kusaba, 'Treasury of Henry of Blois', *passim.*

38. BL, Cotton. Nero C.IV, fos. 29-30.

39. Winchester City Museum, Acc. No. 834. Zarnecki, in *English Romanesque Art*, item 119, gives a date between 1130-40 and suggests its association with the cathedral.

40. For example, in a double capital with scenes of Salome offering the head of St John the Baptist from the cloister of Saint-Etienne Cathedral, Toulouse, now at the Musée des Augustins there: illustrated in Durliat, *Art Roman*, fig. 50.

41. Colish, 'Twelfth-Century Problem', p. 40 and note 57, analysing John of Salisbury's *Historia Pontificalis.*

42. L. Seidel, *Songs of Glory: The Romanesque Façades of Aquitaine* (Chicago and London, 1981), fig. 36.

43. Hardacre, *Catalogue*, item 2.

44. Zarnecki in *English Romanesque Art*, items 147a-c.

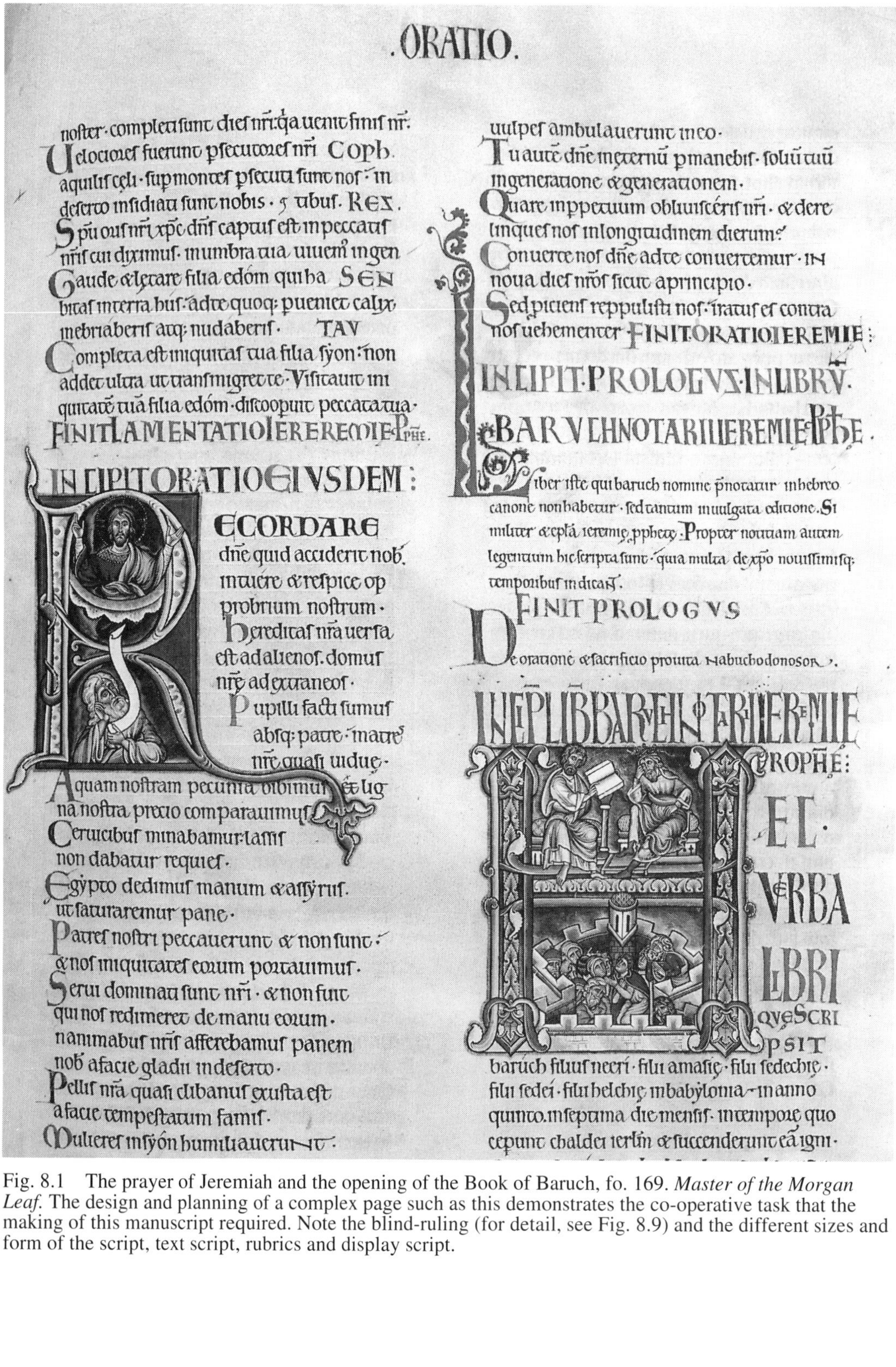

Fig. 8.1   The prayer of Jeremiah and the opening of the Book of Baruch, fo. 169. *Master of the Morgan Leaf.* The design and planning of a complex page such as this demonstrates the co-operative task that the making of this manuscript required. Note the blind-ruling (for detail, see Fig. 8.9) and the different sizes and form of the script, text script, rubrics and display script.

THE WINCHESTER BIBLE

Claire Donovan

The Winchester Bible, a massive heap of calf-skin leaves encased in great oak boards is, like the cathedral in which it has been housed for almost its whole existence, a compendium of the scholarship and art of its time. In its size and complexity it matches the cathedral. It is now bound in four volumes and, with folios measuring nearly two feet by one foot (583 mm. x 396 mm.), the original two volumes would have been monumental. The very act of turning a page becomes ceremonial with a book so big (Fig. 8.1).

Lectern bibles of proportions approaching these had accompanied the building of the great monastic cathedrals of the new dioceses of Norman Britain; they were part of the fabric, as essential as a magnificent shrine for the relics of the local saint. As would be expected, such projects followed the building itself. Although Winchester Cathedral's consecration in 1093 was among the first of this wave of new cathedrals, its bible was not undertaken until approximately 1160.[1] Both in decoration and illustration the Winchester Bible follows in the wake of earlier great bibles, such as that of Bury St Edmunds (*c.*1135), the Dover Bible from Christ Church, Canterbury (*c.*1150), and the Lambeth Bible of *c.*1140-50, which may have belonged to the other great foundation in Canterbury, St Augustine's Abbey.[2]

The 12th century saw considerable development in the extensive libraries of these foundations—it was a great century for scholarship, for copying texts and compiling books. In Winchester the writing of manuscripts had long been an established part of monastic life. Traditions of fine script and a calligraphic drawing style went back well before the Conquest, with a particularly rich period of manuscript illumination in the time of Bishop Ethelwold (963-84), a vigorous reformer of monastic life. By the mid-12th century the monastic library was evidently well stocked with some hundreds of volumes, only some of which were illuminated or decorated.[3]

Although the text of the great bible drew on the biblical scholarship of the time, its major function was not related either to scholarly or to private reading. The stately script is carefully corrected throughout, and its text is marked to assist it to be read aloud fluently to the monastic community and perhaps to the larger community of the diocese. The illuminated initials which stand at the start of most of the biblical books and many of their prologues gloss the text with imagery drawn from the words and contribute to its theological wholeness. Although the detail of the imagery was available to the reader alone, its presence would symbolically have affirmed the Word of God to all, the weight of the words reinforced through the rich gold and colours of its illuminations.

Like the cathedral, the bible was under construction over many years, and its decoration and illustration was ultimately left incomplete. But the design of the bible—all 468 folios of it—was undertaken as a single enterprise, although not without changes of plan. The preparation of the folios was completed, each folio blind-ruled with a sharp point to guide the scribe, and the text itself was finished, written in pale brown ink in a clear and even script, to all appearances the work of a single scribe. Later it was thoroughly checked over and corrections were made by at least two individual hands, adding and altering words and phrases in the margin of the text.[4]

Spaces for the illuminated initials were set into the text, each space specific to the letter that it was to contain and graded as to size and complexity. Display script headings were painted, above or alongside the main initial space, and the initials were set out, drawn, gilded and painted, according to the specification of the design. However, this decorative process was not fully completed throughout the volumes. Some of these initials remain entirely blank, some have been left as a drawing only, some prepared for gilding, some gilded but not painted. It is plain that the design process of the illumination was not undertaken as a linear progression, in which the design of the initials kept pace some steps behind the writing of the text, or where the designer worked through book by book, quire by quire. Although the final volume contains a larger proportion of unfinished initials— and the Gospel initials are all left only at the drawn stage—the programme of illumination

Fig. 8.2   The Book of Ecclesiastes, fo. 268. *Master of the Leaping Figures.* Drawn and gilded.

The main designer of the bible sets out the form of the illustration—the king rejecting all vanities offered by his court—in line, initially sketched lightly (maybe in graphite pencil) then overdrawn in pen. The linear rhythm contrasts with the solemnity of expression.

was evidently not tackled from the top, starting with Genesis. Certain entirely blank spaces appear, as with the initial to Job, where it is only the shape left by the script which defines the initial—no outline, no design, nothing. And there is also evidence of fundamental change in the illustrative plan. The decision to include some more elaborate illustration, and to prefix some sections of text with whole-page miniatures, was made after the opening of the Book of Kings had been completed, where a miniature page was inserted which, later removed, survives now as a single magnificent double-sided miniature in the Pierpont Morgan Library.[5] Further additions may have been planned although none has survived, but two full-page miniatures prefixing Judith (fo. 331v) and Maccabees (fo. 350v) were included, drawn but not painted, that for Maccabees within the quire structure of the manuscript, on a leaf left blank by the scribe. This must have been determined while the formulation of the text lay-out and writing was still in progress.

The production of this bible presented a massive undertaking, and the fact that it was in the making over a period during which artistic style was fundamentally modified by new influences makes this history that much more complex. Walter Oakeshott, in his major study of the bible, identified five or six separate artists who worked both as

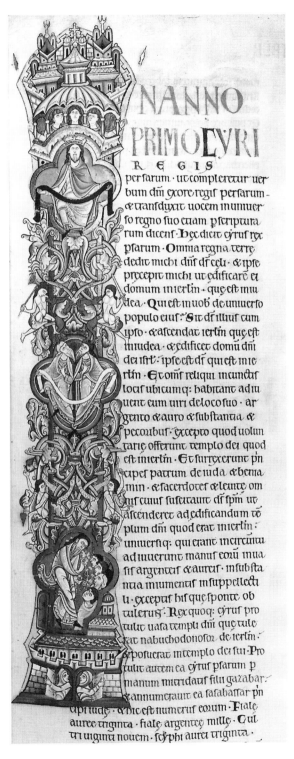

Fig. 8.3   The Book of Ezra, fo. 342. *Master of the Apocrypha Drawings.*

The book opens with a proclamation, 'throughout all his kingdom and in writing also', that a house be built for the Lord in Jerusalem. The Apocrypha Master constructs a vertical kingdom, the multiple roofs and balconies and the tanglewood in which wild creatures cavort framing the figures of King Cyrus and the disseminators of the proclamation, both in writing and by word.

Fig. 8.4   The Epistle of St Peter, fo. 430v. *Master of the Leaping Figures.* Drawn and gilded.

St Peter is enthroned, holding his key. Four messengers come to receive the epistle, shown as a bound volume, and, according to the gesture of the front figure, make ready to disperse to pass it on to the strangers to whom this epistle is addressed.

Fig. 8.5   The Book of Judith, fo. 331v. *Master of the Apocrypha Drawings.* Drawn.

This detail of the huge full-page miniature shows the top register of three in which the cowardly servants of Holofernes tie Achior to a tree. These full-page miniatures summarise the whole narrative of the books they prefix.

Fig. 8.6 The Book of Exodus, fo. 21v. *Master of the Leaping Figures.*

Illustrating Exodus, 2, the Egyptian is seen striking the Hebrew, one of the people of Moses. The lower register of the initial shows the young and vengeful Moses killing the Egyptian in retribution.

Fig. 8.7   The Gospel of St Mark, fo. 387v. *Master of the Leaping Figures.* Drawn.

The initial illustrates the text as closely as possible. Topped by the beast-headed Evangelist portrait, the baptism of Christ is illustrated immediately opposite the narrative in the text, as is the temptation by Satan at the base.

painters and as designers.[6] These artists worked in fundamentally different styles, to the extent that, were these distinctive hands not all found bound within the same manuscript, they would have been said to have worked at very varied dates and locations. As it is, the bible provides evidence of a remarkable level of co-operation between artists, although the way this worked—over a period of ten or more years—is still to be fully explained. Walter Oakeshott's detailed analysis provides the outline template, through his identification of the hands involved in each element of the bible's illumination, in some case relating those with artists working in other manuscripts. As he showed, the historiation of some sections of the bible was completed by a single hand, but there are many initials which were worked on by two artists—one to design and draw, the other to complete the painting. Although the painting of another artist's drawing might suggest that the draughtsman was no longer available to complete the work, here this may also reflect a complex form of collaboration, which included both painting another's design and designing for others to paint.[7]

The variety of artistic styles, in these two-artist initials and in the illumination as a whole, provides evidence of a rich interchange between different artistic traditions, deriving from very different visual experiences in design and figure drawing. These same varied influences are evident in the selection and design of iconographies to illustrate the various biblical books, their prologues and other texts. And, just as the design and style of the illumination is subject to the ideas and the imagination of a number of individual artists, working within varied stylistic traditions, so the imagery draws on different iconographic traditions and works in different ways to illustrate the texts.

Moving through the books of the bible, each illustration fulfils a number of functions. Each section of text has a historiated or decorative initial fitting to the importance of the section, and the size and scale of these illuminated initials, accompanied by the display

Fig. 8.8   The Book of
Ezechiel, fo. 172.
*Master of the Morgan
Leaf.*

The vision of Ezechiel
described in the first
chapter is of the four-
headed beast and the
four wheels. These
images recur as the
prophecy unfolds.
Many-eyed wheels
and cherubim amidst
the glory of the Lord
frame the revelation
of Ezechiel here
shown asleep by the
river Chebar, which
flows from vessel to
vessel, like that of a
classical river god.

script of the rubric and the opening words of the text, establishes the hierarchy of texts and forms an effective book-marking system (Fig. 8.1).

The complex imagery has much to do with the traditions of bible iconography that had developed in the 12th century, but the design of this programme of illustration was far from a simply eclectic process. The way in which the illustration interacts with the text in the 51 historiated initials varies throughout the bible, and depends on the nature of the text illustrated, whether a narrative tale, a prophetic or proverbial text, words of prayer or praise, letters of exhortation. But the type of illustration also depends upon the approach of the designing artist. Thus the imagery may be purely narrative, depicting the events described, as is the case (among many others) for the Exodus initial, fo. 21v (Fig. 8.6),

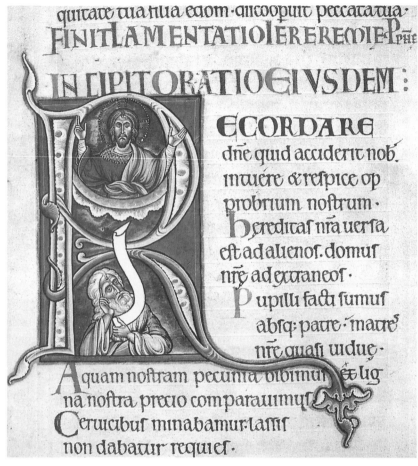

Fig. 8.9   The Prayer of Jeremiah, fo. 169. *Master of the Morgan Leaf.*

The gloomy Jeremiah reaches the Christ Pantocrator with his prayer, the scroll successfully rising up to the upper level where, his arms stretched in solemn blessing, the image of Christ equals the solemnity of a Byzantine apse mosaic.

and the design for the initial of the Gospel of St Mark, fo. 387v (Fig. 8.7), which links the images depicted in the vertical series of roundels precisely with the place in the text where the scene is described. A symbolic allegory woven in partnership with the text, as for example in the description of the vision of Ezechiel (fo. 172), creates the beast-headed evangelists and the many-eyed wheels, hinting at theological expositions to enrich the text. The image accompanying Ecclesiastes (fo. 268) works through the development of the theme of the text, personifying ideas as the king rejects the *vanitas vanitatum* offered to him. And a constant theme of the bible's illustration is the conveying of knowledge. This is shown as preaching in Hosea, fo. 198 and St Peter, fo. 430v; the passing of tablets in the fourth roundel of the Genesis initial, fo. 5 (Fig. 8.15), where the tablets of the law are being passed to Moses, with an accompanying conversation via the scroll; the passage of a scroll as supplication in the prayer of Jeremiah, fo. 169 (Fig. 8.9), in St James, fo. 429 (Fig. 8.10) and Ezra, fo. 342; and as the giving and acknowledging of a vow, as in I Kings, fo. 88, below Elkanah's feast, showing Anna's prayer to the Lord, and the hand of God in response. Speech, argument and disputation are constantly depicted through the vigorous use of gesture, both in the course of narrative and didactic illustration; for example I Kings, Elkanah's feast, fo. 88; Exodus, fo. 21v; the Song of Songs, fo. 270v (Fig. 8.11).

In whatever way the text/image link is made, the image develops the understanding of the words: making connections, both visual and conceptual; developing philosophical debates through focusing on and extrapolating from the truths revealed in the Bible; and making reference to contemporary events much as the chroniclers referred to biblical precedents to make sense of their present. At the very beginning, the illustration to the book of Genesis sets down a marker for the rest of the bible (Fig. 8.12). Usually described as a Creation cycle (the expected illustration of Genesis), the Genesis initial in the Winchester Bible brings together a sequence of roundels which focuses quite directly on key episodes to demonstrate that ultimately redemption could only be achieved through the sacrifice of Christ. The first roundel, the creation of Eve (Fig. 8.13), shows the creation of the woman whose transgression was to lead to original sin. To wash away this sin, the flood emphasises the role of the dove in delivering the olive branch to Noah, a sign of forgiveness, as was the rainbow. The sacrifice of Isaac (Fig. 8.14) similarly is both an image of atonement and of reprieve; Abraham's sword is restrained by the angel, his body twisted into a *contrapposto* of enquiry. Moses given the tablets of the Law (Fig. 8.15), and the young David anointed as king (Fig. 8.16), both lead to the birth of Christ (Fig. 8.17). It is not a joyful birth. The Child is laid out sacrificially on a raised crib, half altar, half sarcophagus. Deep in contemplation, heads sunk in hands, Mary and Joseph consider the sacrifice awaiting the Child. In the last of this sequence of images (Fig. 8.18), the crucified Christ doubles as Christ the Judge and both anticipates and summarises the whole message of the Bible in the image of the Last Judgement. The crucified Christ, who displays his wounds and is seated on a double rainbow (symbol of forgiveness given by God after the flood), holds between his knees the Cross of his sacrifice, the Cross in the form of a roughly hewn tree-trunk, green and branching, in the guise of the Tree of Life.[8] The design of this roundel recalls an image of the Trinity: Christ on the Cross held between the knees of God the Father with the

Fig. 8.10   The Epistle of St James the Apostle, fo. 429. *Master of the Leaping Figures*. Drawn.

The epistle is to the 12 tribes, scattered abroad, and St James conveys it through the long scroll and the pointing finger. The finished quality of the drawing shows the drapery design, so characteristic of this master.

Fig. 8.11   The Song of Songs, fo. 270v. *Master of the Leaping Figures.*

Whereas Christ with *Ecclesia* is often the illustration for this text, interpreting the focus of the love song as the Church of Christ, this artist provides a narrative interpretation. King Solomon, the author of the poem, exchanges words of love with his queen, the Queen of Sheba.

Dove of the Holy Spirit hovering between them. Conflating these in the mind of the observer, both judgement and salvation are offered through the sacrifice of Christ, Son of God, to the souls who emerge from the graves in the spandrels of the initial.

This whole statement in imagery is abbreviated but clearly expounded, a theological sermon in pictures. Iconographically so complex, it is as if the design of this key first initial functions as a summary of the iconography of the remainder of the bible; in the beginning is the overture—hints of all the best tunes.

Yet its design is not that of the artist credited with the major role in laying out the historiation, Oakeshott's Master of the Leaping Figures. It is the work of one of the later generation of artists, who paints in a dramatic style but with heavily modelled and robust solid figures. Oakeshott named him the Genesis Master. Although in many initials the curvilinear patterning hand of the Leaping Figures Master is evident in the design and the underdrawing beneath the painting of another artist, the Genesis initial shows no such signs. It is characteristic of the Genesis Master in composition, figure form, and in the laying on of the paint in thick swathes of colour.[9] Whoever it was who determined the subjects of the roundels, however, drawn from whatever sources written or visual, this opening statement serves both to introduce and to sum up the theology of the Bible, and bind it into a single statement. As such it echoes the work of the biblical scholars in their constant setting together of prophecy and fulfilment, type and antitype, and it sets the theme for the illustration of the rest of the bible.

The themes develop out of Genesis as does the narrative of the Old Testament. In contrast to this theological setting, the second book of the bible, the Book of Exodus, fo. 21v, opens with a double register of narrative, framed within the upper and lower registers of the initial 'H' (Fig. 8.6). Both designed and painted by the Master of the Leaping Figures, these two events of the second chapter of Exodus show Moses aligning himself with the Hebrews, people of his birth, as he takes revenge upon the Egyptian. Typical of the designs of this artist, the figures are in conflict, twisting and leaping, their richly coloured draperies flying. Narrative scenes are characteristic of his work, often creating a double scene from a single initial to carry a story from one episode to another. He does this again illustrating Psalm 51.

Fig. 8.12 The Book of Genesis, fo. 5. *Master of the Genesis Initial.*

The importance of this initial is conveyed by its huge scale, the complexity of its iconography and the incredible detail, both decorative and iconographic, such as the souls emerging from their tombs on either side of Christ of the Last Judgement.

Fig. 8.13   The Book of Genesis, fo. 5. *Master of the Genesis Initial.*

Genesis, 8. The creation of Eve, drawn from Adam's side by God, opens the cycle of Fall to Redemption, the theme of this initial. Noah's salvation, confirmed for him by the arrival of the dove, contrasts with the drowned figures sunk beneath the water.

Fig. 8.14   The Book of Genesis, fo. 5. *Master of the Genesis Initial.*

Genesis, 22. Abraham's readiness to sacrifice his son Isaac parallels the Crucifixion, sacrifice of the Son of God.

The Winchester Bible includes not just one set of psalms but two, written in parallel in the two columns setting the Gallican next to St Jerome's translation from the Hebrew, and for the illustrated psalms this means two historiated initials together. In illustrating Psalm 51, *Quid glorias,* fo. 232 the Master of the Leaping Figures sets out two roundels of narrative (Fig. 8.19), containing two episodes of the story of the betrayal of David by Doeg and the killing of the priests.[10] Doeg stands before the enthroned Saul, the figure of Doeg in mid-action as, having betrayed Achimelech and all the priests, no-one is willing to slay them but Doeg himself. He whirls around, eagerly moving away from Saul, his right hand raised in a gesture of acquiescence, his left hand reaching towards the priests, so eager to begin that his hand is about to burst the bounds of the initial frame. Within the second initial, Doeg raises his sword for the third time, with the second severed head still in his hand, and two headless corpses in mid-fall. Delicate swinging bodies, jewel-like colours enclosed in gilded frames, belie the gruesome murder that is taking place.

Fig. 8.15   The Book of Genesis, fo. 5. *Master of the Genesis Initial.*

Exodus, 31:18, 'The Lord gave to Moses two stone tables of testimony, written with the finger of God'. The lengthy instructions God gave to Moses (Exodus, 20-31) are represented in the long scroll God passes down to him, supplementing the tablets.

Fig. 8.16   The Book of Genesis, fo. 5. *Master of the Genesis Initial.*

I Samuel, 16. The young David is anointed by Samuel, 'in the midst of his brethren'. The vertical form suggests the line of David, which leads from this anointing to the birth of Christ.

Fig. 8.17   The Book of Genesis, fo. 5. *Master of the Genesis Initial.*

Luke, 2. The Nativity is the culmination of the line of David. Through the sacrificial aspect of the Nativity—Christ in a sarcophagus-crib—this image reminds the viewer of the Redemption of the birth and the ultimate sacrifice of the Crucifixion.

Fig. 8.18   The Book of Genesis, fo. 5. *Master of the Genesis Initial.*

Christ of the Last Judgement seated on the double rainbow, the Cross supported by angels, who hold instruments of the Passion. Below, the dead rise from their opened graves.

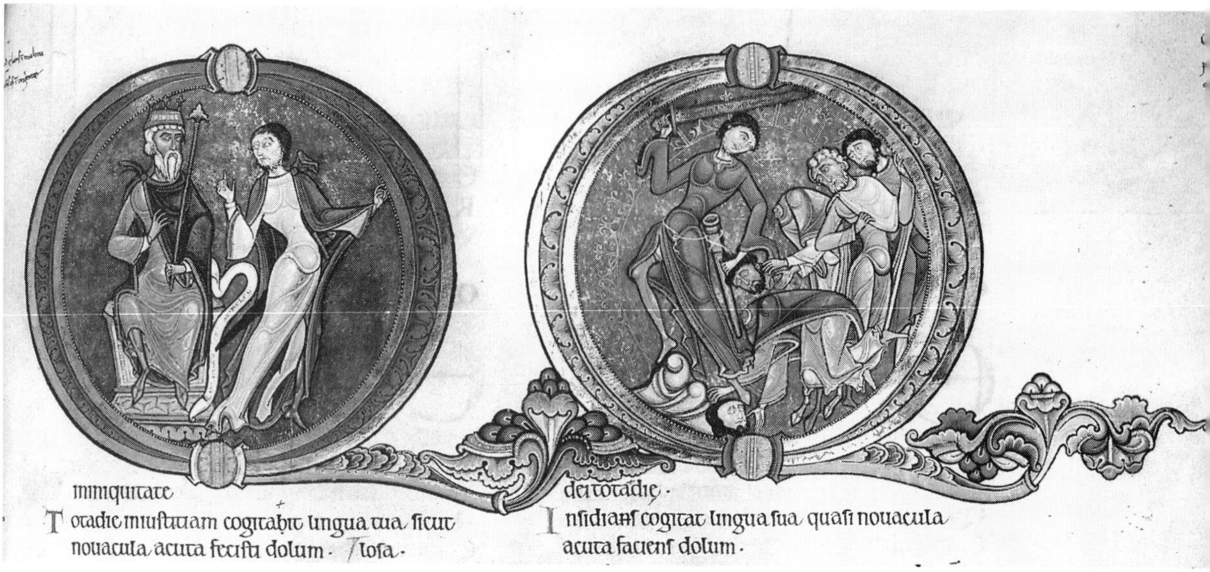
miniquitate
T otadie iniustitiam cogitabit lingua tua sicut
nouacula acuta fecisti dolum ·
dei tota die ·
I nsidians cogitat lingua sua quasi nouacula
acuta faciens dolum ·

Fig. 8.19 Psalm 51, fo. 232. *Master of the Leaping Figures.*
The parallel texts of the Psalms—the Gallican and Jerome's translation from the Hebrew—are illustrated only at Psalms 1, 51, 101 and 109, but each time with a double initial, heading each text. Two episodes (I Samuel, 22) depict the narrative of Doeg, who betrayed Achimelech to Saul and then, at Saul's command, killed Achimelech and the priests who were faithful to David.

The major narrative sequences of illustration are those of the full-page miniatures, including the Morgan Leaf, each designed by the Apocrypha Master and added to the scheme of illustration after the completion of at least the first volume.[11] He is able to develop a long narrative, passing from episode to episode, from the top register to the lowest. The page prefacing the Book of Judith, fo. 331v (Fig. 8.5) tells the whole tale. Holofernes commands Achior to be delivered to Israel, but his servants tie him to a tree rather than face the Hebrews themselves. Judith feasts with Holofernes in his tent, and then severs his head with his own sword as he lies asleep. She shows the head to the gathering of the Israelites, who are inspired to rout the Assyrian horde, which by now is intimidated by the loss of its leader, Holofernes. The design is clear, the settings and the essential props fully depicted—the trees, the scabbard of Holofernes' sword hung on his death-bed, the city walls. The text elaborates every part of this story, describing circumstance, discussing the character of the protagonists. But the role of the illustration is to highlight the story in imagery, and create a visual memory to complement or even to substitute for the words.

For whatever purposes the bible's text was read out, whether in the context of ceremony, the sections prescribed for the liturgy of the divine office or the mass or, less formal but more sustained, readings for instruction, these miniatures and the many historiated initials would set a visual context which developed the words for the reader and his hearers. To elaborate the illustration with these full-page miniatures (and maybe more were planned) provided a quite different view of illustration from the didactic sequence of the Genesis initial, or indeed from the vision of Isaiah. Like the design of the cathedral, it is not the product of one person. The scale of the project, the variety of style, the varied iconographic imaginations, the changes of plan, involved a considerable number of highly skilled craftsmen. But it would also have depended on a patron.

Henry of Blois, bishop of Winchester from 1129 until his death in 1171, was the wealthiest churchman in England and among the most active patrons of the arts of this period. He built and collected, and imported works for his building, including antique statuary and Tournai fonts, the grandest of which stands in Winchester Cathedral.[12] There seems little doubt that the Winchester Bible depended upon his enthusiasm and financial support, and that the stylistic and iconographic richness was, to some extent at least, inspired by the imagination of Henry, who, through his travels, could draw upon the widest experience of the styles and iconographies of European art.

Acknowledgements

It has been a great pleasure to contribute to this commemorative volume, and my first thanks must go to its editor, John Crook, who also took the excellent photographs of the bible. My thanks also go to the Dean and Chapter of the cathedral, in particular to the librarian, Canon Keith Walker, who allowed me access to the bible. John Hardacre, as curator, generously provided that access, and I thank him for those many hours of company, often accompanied by intermittent discussion of a thorny problem, as he watched over the bible. My thanks, too, for help on specific matters to Dr. Alan Piper, Leonard Boyle, O.P., Professor Yoshio Kusaba, and Michael Gullick.

Notes

1. Although the dating of the bible has been much debated, there is general agreement that the main text script is of the mid-century, for example N. R. Ker, *English Manuscripts in the Century after the Norman Conquest* (Oxford, 1960), pp. 35, 48, 51ff, and C. M. Kauffmann, *Romanesque Manuscripts 1066-1190,* Survey of Manuscripts Illuminated in the British Isles, III (London, 1975), No. 83, pp. 108-11. Michael Kauffmann suggests a date of *c.*1155-85 in his entry for the bible in G. Zarnecki, J. Holt and T. Holland (eds.), *English Romanesque Art 1066-1200* (London, 1984), the catalogue for the exhibition in which three volumes were displayed, together with the Morgan Leaf. The other lectern bible to be considered a Winchester product of much the same time, Oxford, Bodleian Library, Auct.E.inf.1 and 2, was also displayed there (Nos. 63 and 63a). Ker (*English Manuscripts,* p. 52) identified the correcting hand of the Winchester Bible also in the Bodleian Auct. bible, establishing their close textual association.
2. Bury St Edmunds Bible: Cambridge, Corpus Christi College, MS 2, whose origins at Bury are supported both by a press-mark and through its attribution to Master Hugo in the contemporary *Gesta Sacristarium Monasterii Sancti Edmundi* (Kauffmann, *Romanesque MSS,* No. 56); Dover Bible: Cambridge, Corpus Christi College, MS 304 (Kauffmann, *ibid.,* No. 69); Lambeth Bible: Lambeth Palace Library, MS 3 and Maidstone Museum (Kauffmann, *ibid.,* No. 70). C. R. Dodwell, *The Great Lambeth Bible* (London, 1959), argued a St Augustine's, Canterbury provenance for this great manuscript, the nearest in size to the Winchester Bible at 518 mm. x 353 mm.
3. N. R. Ker, *Medieval Libraries of Great Britain; a List of Surviving Books* (London, 1964); F. Bussby, *Winchester Cathedral Manuscripts* (Winchester, 1959). A key manuscript to survive from Bishop Ethelwold's episcopate is his Benedictional, now BL, Add. MS 49598; F. Wormald, *The Benedictional of St Ethelwold* (London, 1959).
4. The later corrector used black ink and a thicker point to his pen, and his work stands out clearly. The addition of two cognate folios in this later hand includes the opening of Isaiah, whose initial is illuminated by the latest artist to work on the manuscript initials, the so-called Gothic Majesty Master (see below, note 6). For a description of the processes of creating a manuscript, see C. de Hamel, *Scribes and Illumination,* British Museum Publications (London, 1992).

5. New York, Pierpont Morgan Library, MS 619, illustrated in *English Romanesque Art,* pl. 65. For discussion of these additions, see W. Oakeshott, *The Two Winchester Bibles* (Oxford, 1981), pp. 18-21.

6. He originally identified and named these artists in 1945: W. Oakeshott, *The Artists of the Winchester Bible* (London, 1945), and his analysis was widely accepted. He did not substantially revise the identifications in his later *Two Winchester Bibles.*

7. Oakeshott first thought (*Artists,* pp. 4-7) that this complexity resulted from a very long period of construction, from 1160 to 1225. The distribution of the hands suggests a closer collaboration than this, and a revision of understanding of artistic style has now compressed the period. In the discussion by Larry Ayres, 'Collaborative Enterprise in Romanesque Manuscript Illumination', *BAA Winchester,* pp. 20-7, he suggests a parallel with other examples of collaboration at this period. Notes related to the illustration in the margins survive next to some of the initials (not always descriptive of the image that occurs) as 'instructions' to the illuminator. These, together with designs left at all stages of completion, provide undisputed evidence of collaboration, although it remains to be explained how this was organised. For further discussion, see Claire Donovan, *The Winchester Bible* (London, 1993).

8. A group of examples of this form of crucifix from the mid-11th century in the context of an iconic crucifixion, not otherwise identified with the Trinity iconography, derives also from Winchester, e.g. BL, Cotton. Tiberius C.VI, *c.*1050 and BL, Arundel 60, *c.*1060, reproduced and discussed in E. Temple, *Anglo-Saxon Manuscripts, 900-1066,* Survey of Manuscripts Illuminated in the British Isles, II (London, 1976), Nos. 98 and 103; also in Nos. 93 and 104. This motif was occasionally used at a later date also (e.g. London, Society of Antiquaries, MS 59, fo. 35v, *c.*1220).

9. Seen under a microscope, the facial modelling of, for example, Christ the Judge, is laid on as if it were wall-painting, mosaic, or the *impasto* of oil colour. A block of parallel brush-strikes, each bearing different hues— brown, white, yellow ochre, green—models the robust bone structure of the face as it appears seen with the naked eye.

10. Told in the Book of Samuel (I Kings, 22).

11. The lay-out and writing were already complete, although further decoration and illustration was finished after this stage. See note 5, above.

12. See Yoshio Kusaba's article, above, pp. 69-79.

THE MEDIEVAL SCULPTURE OF WINCHESTER CATHEDRAL

Phillip Lindley

Introduction

It may be a surprise to some of Winchester Cathedral's visitors to learn that the cathedral houses one of the largest, finest, and widest collections of medieval figure-sculpture in the country outside Westminster Abbey. Sadly, very few of the sculptures remain in their original position or condition. Today the major schemes of free-standing imagery—those of the Great Screen or of Bishop William of Wykeham's chantry chapel for instance—are not medieval at all but are examples of the great late 19th- and early 20th-century drive to 'repopulate' empty medieval screens and monuments.[1] The havoc and destruction caused by iconoclasts in the 16th and 17th centuries is central to any understanding of Winchester's sculpture; indeed, to that of all medieval figure-sculpture in England. For it was one of the consequences of the Reformation in England that religious imagery was violently destroyed, a destruction so severe that, on one authority's estimate, less than one-tenth of the country's medieval figure-sculpture survives today.[2] A visitor to Winchester at the end of the 16th century would probably have seen little evidence of the imagery which 60 years earlier had been deployed on screens and altars, chantry chapels and reredoses throughout the building. A visitor a century later would have found even less.[3] Fortunately stone sculptures are quite difficult to destroy entirely and, through a series of chance discoveries, a number of the damaged and defaced medieval images have been rescued from their ignominious role as building materials in walls separating gardens in the Cathedral Close, or in blocked door-ways and windows. The exhibition of some of the finest sculptures, following careful conservation and study, in the cathedral's Triforium Gallery, can help us form a reasonably accurate picture of some of the many programmes of stone sculpture produced for the cathedral in the Middle Ages. On the other hand, sculpture in precious materials, the work of goldsmiths and silversmiths, has disappeared completely, leaving a terrible void in our knowledge; almost all the wooden sculptures have disappeared too, although important survivals are to be found in the 14th-century choir-stalls and their misericords.

Besides the damaged stone sculptures, few of which are in their original locations, two other main categories of sculpture survive: the first is a type of figure and foliage sculpture which is generally considered 'marginal', although the term as used here reflects its positioning rather than its actual importance. The chief works to consider here are vault bosses, the corbel-table of the nave, and the corbel sculptures of the interior and exterior of the cathedral. The other class of sculpture comprises tomb effigies. Monumental effigies constitute the one category of figure-sculpture in England to have survived iconoclasm without severe destruction. Although tomb effigies in dissolved monastic churches or their

97

ancillary buildings have certainly suffered, particularly of course if the church did not continue in use but was pillaged for building materials (e.g. Titchfield Abbey, Hants), the majority of medieval effigies survived; they were very rarely a primary target of social revolutionaries as were, for instance, their French counterparts in the late 18th century.[4] Winchester's tomb effigies include a number of examples of national importance and, in the case of the late medieval chantry chapels, sometimes constitute virtually the only intact figure-sculpture left from the large original programmes. All three categories of sculpture will be considered together in this essay, which is arranged roughly chronologically to provide an indication of the range of the cathedral's sculpture, and to make comparisons or contrasts from different categories of imagery. An important point will also emerge, one which is not, perhaps, itself without significance in understanding the reformers' attitudes towards religious imagery: the sheer number of images increased dramatically in the later Middle Ages, until, by the dissolution of the monastery, the church housed several hundred sculptures. It will be my aim here to repopulate for the reader, mentally at least, some of the still empty niches, and to outline some of the major areas awaiting future research.

The Romanesque Period
The earliest significant sculptures to survive in the cathedral date from the second quarter of the 12th century. It is no accident that the fine Romanesque sculptures can be associated with the episcopate of Henry of Blois (1129-71), one of the greatest patrons of the period. Bishop Henry, enriched by the huge revenues of the bishopric (and by those of the abbacy of Glastonbury, which he retained in plurality), had a particular interest in sculpture, as a tantalising reference in the *Historia Pontificalis* reveals: when Henry was in Rome he bought pagan (classical) statues.[5] Sadly, we know nothing more about these images, but we can deduce something of Henry's range of interests from surviving sculpture in the cathedral. The Tournai marble font (Fig. 9.1) undoubtedly belongs to his patronage, which was so important in introducing the taste for this dark 'marble' to England; the font, usually dated to the 1150s or '60s, and a key work in the dating of the whole group of nine or ten in England, is the finest in the country.[6] It was imported, ready worked, from Tournai. On the east side are three beaded roundels showing pairs of doves and bunches of grapes (reminiscent of Byzantine textile design) or foliage; on the north side are three roundels (one of which is partially beaded) with single doves and a salamander in the centre. The southern and western sides have figural scenes from the legend of St Nicholas. The south side shows the saint giving dowries for the poor nobleman's daughters; rather confused scenes showing the miracles in which St Nicholas restored the murdered boys to life and the nobleman's journey to offer up a gold cup to the saint are found on the west side. The top of the font has in the spandrels doves drinking from cups, which are surmounted by a cross, alternating with foliage.[7]

Unlike Anglo-Saxon imagery, which is generally treated virtually as *appliqué* ornament to buildings, most Romanesque sculpture plays an architectonic function in its architectural environment. Much of the finest surviving Romanesque sculpture therefore adorns features such as capitals or corbels, doorway jambs, lintels and tympana. An exquisite fragment of a stone head (Fig. 9.2) from Wolvesey Palace, dated by Professor Zarnecki to 1140-50, is possibly a fragment of a column figure, and may reflect Henry of Blois' knowledge of the developments in Abbot Suger's church of Saint-Denis, where the Gothic sculptured portal first appeared.[8] The fragmentary Wolvesey head, and door-jambs from

Fig. 9.1 The Tournai marble font. South side: St Nicholas gives dowries. *John Crook*

the same palace, reveal a confluence of influences from Saint-Denis on the one hand, and, on the other, from the flourishing school of manuscript illumination and ivory carving often termed the 'Winchester School', providing convincing evidence of stylistic continuity from Winchester's great Anglo-Saxon past. Similar sources underlie some of the *ex situ* capitals in the gallery, notably the extremely fine limestone example showing centaurs in combat with other hybrid monsters (Fig. 9.3), or the more weathered specimen with tumblers at the corners.[9] A Purbeck marble double capital and a Tournai marble double base may come from a cloister arcade: however, another surviving double capital, this time carved from limestone, and showing entwining stalks of bead-enriched foliage is also a candidate for this location. A very weathered carved panel of an architectural frieze from an unknown location may belong to Bishop Henry's episcopate: it has recently been assigned, surely correctly, to *c.*1150-75, on stylistic grounds.[10] With the destruction of so many of the important monastic buildings and with the denudation of most of Wolvesey Palace, it is difficult to evaluate accurately the full range of Bishop Henry's magnificent

Fig. 9.2   Mid 12th-century column figure from Wolvesey Palace. *John Crook*

Fig. 9.3   12th-century capital showing a hybrid monster, assigned to the patronage of Bishop Henry of Blois. *John Crook*

patronage. However, Professor Kusaba has analysed the architecture of the treasury housed in the western side of the cathedral's south transept.[11] The heavily decorated northern bay shows architectural embellishment with decorative sculpture of great richness, including chevron mouldings and multi-scalloped capitals (similar to those in the Holy Sepulchre Chapel, whose construction must also be assigned to the bishop), appropriate for the function of this part of the building as a treasury to house the bishop's gifts. By the end of his stormy life he had given away all his possessions and devoted himself to prayer and acts of penitence. To the end, however, he seems to have retained his fondness for dark stones: his tomb was marked by a simple coped gravecover with no ornament or inscription but carved from polished Purbeck marble (Fig. 1.4).[12]

The 13th Century

Although it is now headless, rather weathered, and has lost its lower arms, the figure usually identified as representing *Ecclesia* (Fig. 9.4), a personification of the church, often paired with *Synagoga* (as in the Judgement Porch, Lincoln Cathedral) is the finest piece of figure-sculpture from the 13th century on show in the cathedral (it is now housed at the east end of the south retrochoir aisle).[13] The sweeping, tightly pleated folds of the drapery and *mouvementée* pose, developing ideas found in some of the sculpture from Wells Cathedral, place it among the most accomplished pieces of sculpture of its date (*c.*1230-35).[14] There are holes for metal fixings, indicating that the image possessed a rich brooch and belt; other holes may indicate that she carried a sword or pennant. Such use of metalwork accessories, which would have greatly increased the figure's cost, suggests that it came from an important location and, judging from the weathering of the image, probably an exterior position:[15] T. D. Atkinson's argument that the figure came from one of the niches of the buttresses on the front of the prior's house was based on a comparison between the measurements of the figure and the shape of its base with these now empty niches, and seems convincing.[16] A slightly later *ex situ* work, a vault boss showing two dragons in combat springing out of foliage is probably from the cathedral itself. It has been suggested by Dr. Tudor-Craig that the boss resembles the very deeply undercut, foliate, central boss in the Guardian Angels Chapel;[17] it more closely resembles her other suggestion, the corbels and bosses of the Holy Sepulchre Chapel, and the stiff-leaf foliage and sportive dragons seem characteristic of the period *c.*1240. The boss may have come from the vault of the eastern bay of the Lady Chapel or the centre of Bishop Langton's Chapel, both of which were revaulted in the late Middle Ages.[18]

Another *ex situ* fragment should be mentioned here: a head corbel identified by Dr. Tudor-Craig as stylistically close to the corbel still in place at the entrance to the Lady Chapel, on the south side.[19] The damaged corbel shows a balding man with swept-back curly hair wearing a garment buttoned at the shoulder. Corbel heads of mid 13th-century date, at Salisbury Cathedral and Westminster Abbey, for example, show a striking interest in realistic depiction, and this Winchester head, whose grimacing expression is particularly suited to the corbel's load-bearing position, is comparable with

Fig. 9.4 13th-century statue of *Ecclesia*, probably from a niche outside the Deanery porch. *John Crook*

one of the finest of the period, the corbel from Clarendon Palace, carved by a sculptor who also worked at Westminster Abbey.[20]

The superb quality Purbeck marble heart-tomb of Bishop Aymer de Valence (d.1260) (Fig. 9.5)[21] bears witness to the increasing popularity amongst royalty, the nobility and ecclesiastics, of the separate burial of the heart from the corpse.[22] The heart of Bishop Aymer, whose body lay in Paris, was buried in a golden cup close to the high altar, where his effigy doubtless surmounted the burial until the time of Bishop Fox, whose 1525 screens displaced several monuments.[23] The monument shows the bishop at half-length within a trefoil-lobed niche with a crocketed canopy supported by splendidly curved columns, housed within a mandorla adorned with sprigs of foliage. Aymer de Valence was half-brother to King Henry III and to Richard of Cornwall, whose shields are found in the upper spandrels of the monument; the bishop's own arms occupy the base of the mandorla. This early employment of heraldic arms on a Purbeck monument, like the crisp carving (except where damaged) and the new sharp-fold draperies, suggests a London origin.[24] The effigy was placed in its present position at the east end of the north aisle of the retrochoir in 1818, but was then incomplete: a horizontal line across the block, running through the bishop's mitre, shows where it had been sawn in half, and the top section was not rediscovered until 1911, when a workman, digging the foundation for one of the new buttresses on the south side of of the cathedral, found the missing section six feet below the surface. The charmingly anachronistic ogee top provided by William Garbett in 1818 was then replaced.[25]

Another Purbeck marble episcopal effigy, generally identified as that of Bishop Peter des Roches (d.1238) (Fig. 9.6) certainly precedes Aymer's.[26] The bearded bishop, with a book in his left hand and his right hand resting on his lower chest (there is no sign of his episcopal crozier), is housed under a canopy, the sides of which have plate tracery in the pinnacles. The front surfaces of the canopy have been broken off. The whole monument is, indeed, in rather poor condition, and the feet and foot-rest (a simple flat base), together with the foliate sprigs running down the sides of the monument, have also been broken. In spite of the cushion on which the bishop's head rests, there is a characteristic tension between the recumbency of the effigy and the verticality implied by the canopy, the handling of the draperies and the conception of the figure. Peter des Roches' effigy was probably moved, when the presbytery screens were built, to the north aisle of the nave; it was again moved by Prebendary Nott to the north retrochoir aisle.[27] The much earlier style of this effigy compared to that of Aymer suggests that it was commissioned before 1238.

The Purbeck marble episcopal effigy in the north presbytery aisle, by contrast, postdates Bishop Aymer's figure, as its style testifies. The damaged, headless figure had his right hand raised in blessing and held his crozier in his left hand. The figure is dressed in chasuble, stole, maniple, amice and alb, with the remains of the pastoral staff on the left shoulder. This effigy can be identified as the 'old bishop in marble' seen by Lieutenant Hammond before the Civil War; perhaps, as Quirk suggests, it then retained its head.[28] The effigy was then located, together with Prior Basing's tomb, in the south transept just outside the Venerable Chapel, beside the steps up to the south presbytery aisle. It was moved by 1818 to the floor of the north retrochoir aisle, when it was separated from the stone base now wedged between the arches of the Holy Sepulchre Chapel. The base is now surmounted by an earlier slab with relief sculpture of a foliate cross.[29] The flat, sharp-fold style of the effigy suggests that it is one of a number executed c.1265-90, though further analysis of effigies from the period is certainly necessary. The identity of the individual is difficult to establish: Bishop John of Exeter, *alias* Gervais, (d.1268) was buried in Italy and Nicholas of Ely (d.1280) at Waverley; the tomb of his successor, John of Pontoise (d.1304), still lies on the north side of the presbytery under Fox's screen.[30] The likeliest candidate appears to be John of Exeter, though the style of the effigy marks a considerable

Fig. 9.5   Purbeck marble heart-burial slab of Bishop Aymer de Valence (d.1260). *John Crook*

Fig. 9.6   Purbeck marble tomb effigy of Bishop Peter des Roches (d.1238). *John Crook*

departure from that of his predecessor; it is just possible that the tomb commemorates Bishop Nicholas of Ely, whose heart was buried in Winchester, and who may have commissioned the effigy before his death. It is also possible that it represents not a bishop but a prior: Winchester's priors had the right to episcopal vestments from 1254.[31]

The tomb of Prior Basing (d.1295) with his incised mitred head, keys and sword and floriated cross poses no such problems of identification: an inscription in Lombardic lettering identifies Basing. The Purbeck marble slab has unfortunately flaked badly since it was drawn in the 18th century.[32] The tomb was moved by Nott from a position in the south transept just outside the Venerable Chapel, to its present position in the retrochoir, between the chapels of Beaufort and Fox. Incised monuments are a very common form of memorial, widely available to different social classes because of their relative cheapness and sometimes, as in this instance, of quite high quality.[33] The fact that the inscription runs round only three sides implies that the tomb was probably originally placed against a wall.

What was, in many ways, the central monument of 13th-century sculpture in Purbeck marble at Winchester, the shrine of St Swithun, was smashed in September 1538. The (paper) reconstruction of the shrine by J. D. Le Couteur and D. H. M. Carter in 1924 has been shown to be seriously flawed. An important paper by Pamela Tudor-Craig and Laurence Keen published in 1983 showed that the head of a monk, incorporated into a frieze in the earlier reconstruction, could be reunited with his body and could be shown to be a spandrel relief, carved on both sides; in addition, they published another double-sided spandrel relief, this time carved with figures of bishops (Fig. 9.7), and proposed that these spandrels belonged to a screen which preceded the 14th-century feretory screen.[34] More recently, John Crook has further undermined the 1924 reconstruction of the shrine, showing that the authors misidentified 'arcading' sections: he has proposed a new reconstruction, identifying it as a tomb-shrine, a more complex example of a type well known from the shrine of St Osmund in Salisbury Cathedral.[35]

Fig. 9.7   Purbeck marble spandrel relief (*c*.1270) of a bishop holding a book. *John Crook*

The evidence for what was evidently a dramatic assemblage of Purbeck marble elements remains confused and confusing: there was a later 15th-century shrine and the precise relationship of this shrine to the 13th-century one remains extremely unclear. Matters have not been helped by the inclusion, in one account of the 13th-

Fig. 9.8   Inserted doorway in south retrochoir aisle (detail). *John Crook*

century fragments, of what is self-evidently some of the 15th-century material. The dating of the earlier work also remains controversial:[36] the style of the spandrel reliefs probably postdates that of Bishop Aymer's effigy and would suit a date in the later 1260s or early 1270s; berries are found together with the stiff-leaf, as they were in the south retrochoir doorway (Fig. 9.8), with which there are also architectural design features in common.

The 14th Century

The only medieval effigy of a layman to survive in the cathedral is the partially restored Purbeck marble figure of Arnaud de Gaveston (d.1302) (Fig. 9.9), the father of Edward II's catamite, Piers. It is almost certainly datable to between 1302 and 1312, the latter year being the date of Piers Gaveston's execution. Purbeck marble effigies of knights became popular in the early 13th century and this effigy is a late example of the type, for by the end of the century Purbeck had been all but superseded by freestone as the dominant material for effigial sculpture. Sculpted effigies were increasingly densely painted, with the result that the material could barely be seen: there was therefore little point in using a material which was so difficult to work. The effigy is of a knight wearing chain-mail; his right hand grasps the hilt of a sword and on the left arm is his shield. The remains of ailettes, rather unusual

Fig. 9.9   Purbeck marble tomb effigy of Sir Arnaud de Gaveston (d.1302). *John Crook*

on effigies, can be seen on his shoulders. His head rests on two pillows formerly supported by angels, the bodies of which remain. The legs from the knees down are restored, but enough survives to show the accuracy of the restoration: the legs are crossed and his feet rest on a lion, a typical foot-rest for military effigies. Stylistically, the effigy would have resembled a lost brass from Peterborough Abbey.[37] The heraldic arms borne by the effigy, identified by W. S. Walford, can also be seen on one of the shields suspended from foliage housed under ogee-headed niches with diagonal pinnacles, carved on a marble slab now housed in the Guardian Angels Chapel: this was doubtless the front face of the tomb-chest.[38] The effigy was moved from the north transept, behind the choir-stalls, to the centre of the retrochoir, in the rearrangements of monuments under Prebendary Nott and Dean Rennell; it was moved again in 1936 to its present position.[39] It cannot, apparently, have been housed in the recess in the end wall of the north transept, where the north window had perhaps been replaced at the same time and where the vault, judging by the bubbly foliage of the central boss, had also been rebuilt, because it is too wide.[40]

The other 14th-century sculpture from Winchester poses a number of problems. The figures from the stalls and their misericords (see pp. 193-205) constitute perhaps the only securely datable imagery. The well-known and much studied choir-stalls were the work of William Lyngwode, a carpenter from Blofield in Norfolk who is known to have been employed by Bishop Henry Woodlock in 1307-8.[41] The close stylistic correspondence between one of the corbels, located on the south side of the eastern bay of the presbytery arcade, and one of the 'Green Men' on the stalls, suggests that at least one local sculptor was employed, unless the masonry corbel was the product of an East Anglian sculptor who remained at Winchester.[42] Interestingly there are also close parallels between the stalls (and the related Norwich sculptures) and the *marginalia* of some of the 'Fenland' group of manuscripts, suggesting that the artists of the latter did indeed originate in East Anglia.[43] The unprogrammatic and often amusing nature of the misericord imagery and of the sculpture decorating the architecture strongly appeals to modern taste, but these sculptures were once supplemented in the upper area of the stalls by a large programme of imagery from the Old and New Testaments, seen and described by Lieutenant Hammond before its destruction at the hands of Waller's troopers in 1642. It is unlikely that this was a Marian

Fig. 9.10   Early 14th-century head corbel portraying a young king. *John Crook*

Fig. 9.11   Freestone head of Christ wearing the Crown of Thorns. *John Crook*

or 17th-century cycle and it seems that these Old and New Testament subjects had escaped the 16th-century iconoclasts only to fall to their 17th-century successors.[44]

An *ex situ* head corbel (Fig. 9.10) can be confidently dated to the early 14th century both by the style of the architectural mouldings and by that of the head.[45] This head of a young king with wavy hair and smiling face has been plausibly attributed to the conversion of one of the transept chapels, a rolling programme of modernisation which took place in the first decades of the 14th century.[46]

Three *ex situ* heads pose serious problems of dating and attribution: a head of Christ wearing the Crown of Thorns (Fig. 9.11), and two young sainted (?) queens, correctly grouped by Lawrence Stone on the basis of their style, though dated by him to the second or third quarter of the 15th century.[47] They are evidently not corbels or similar architectural sculptures, since they have no mouldings attached to them: it is clear, then, that they are from dismembered figure-sculpture. To date these heads, as with some of the earlier images, the historian is forced to rely on stylistic analysis and on the evidence of provenance. However, 14th-century sculpture is notoriously difficult to date stylistically, particularly since much late imagery seems stylistically rather conservative.[48] Since the bodies of the figures are missing, we do not even have the evidence of drapery style, which is generally a key diagnostic tool. A general point may conveniently be raised here, that assigning imagery to a precise date on the basis of style alone is likely to be unreliable:

we could hypothesise that a single sculptor with a working life of three decades might retain the style in which he was trained, whilst younger contemporaries experimented in new directions. The evidence of provenance is not unproblematic either. Clearly the heads are much too large to have come from the retrochoir screen imagery, which probably dates from the second decade of the 14th century and from which some small-scale figure sculpture survives.[49] One possible location would be Bishop William of Wykeham's chantry chapel of c.1399-1403.[50] Although the heads would be surprisingly conservative compared with the imagery adorning Wykeham's Winchester College gateways, fragments of greater than life-sized imagery in a closely related style, which could also have originated in the bishop's chapel, tend to support this hypothesis. A central problem, though, is that, on purely stylistic grounds, the sculpture seems to fit a date in the 1320s or early 1330s more satisfactorily than the 1390s. Although there are several stylistic similarities, none of the images has the furrowed brows of the vault bosses from the nave aisles, unequivocally from the late 14th century:[51] the crown shape also seems to favour an early dating. A possible alternative location for the imagery should perhaps be sought in the decoration of the conversion of the chapels in the first half of the 14th century. Two large ogee-headed niches with fine foliate finials, and now housing 18th- or 19th-century monuments, are set into the piers flanking the central north transept chapel and this might be a possible location for two of the images, though no other niches remain: could a figure of Christ wearing the Crown of Thorns inside the chapel, perhaps located above the altar, have been flanked by two female saints in niches?

Four corbel sculptures still in place inside the chapel formed part of a campaign to revault this chapel (note the fine foliate boss) and seem, on the basis of the differences between the mouldings of the niches and of the corbels, to come from a separate, later, campaign. Two music-playing angels flanking the east window face a young man wearing a hood and holding a money-bag, die and chess-board (Fig. 9.12), enticing a bearded man with hood and curly hair opposite him to play, a clear temptation to vice. In these corbels, a simple moral contrast is being made between the behaviour of gamblers on the west side of the chapel, and angels, on the east side, flanking the altar and perhaps co-ordinated with imagery in the lost stained glass or even, if the suggestion above is correct, with a sculpted image of Christ.[52] The smooth, slick draperies of the angels, the complicated poses and the style of the curly ringlets of hair and beard suggest a date from the 1320s to the early 1340s.[53] Such a date would be appropriate for the tracery of the window, one of a trio of windows with reticulated tracery.[54]

A free-standing headless image may also have originated in one of these chapels renovated in the 14th century. This figure, now about 0.70 m. tall, is carved in the round, which suggests that it stood either on an altar or in an open screen. The figure carried an attribute in the left hand; the cloak sweeps round from the right shoulder and is draped over both arms. The style of the draperies suggests a date in the second quarter of the 14th century.[55]

The western side of the north transept, set aside as the Epiphany Chapel, also features 14th-century sculpture and, although it is very oddly placed and of low stylistic quality, it is of considerable interest. According to T. D. Atkinson the shafts of the wall-arcade were removed in the 1320s or 1330s to gain a little extra space in the chapel, and the plain cushion capitals were carved with heads to give them the appearance of corbels. Two half-shafts against the north-east pier were similarly treated to give space for the piscina; likewise those opposite for more cupboards. In the 19th century, however, all these shafts were replaced in a restoration, resulting in the present very odd effect.[56]

Two further episcopal effigies should be mentioned here. They are both of alabaster, a material which became popular for effigies in the third decade of the 14th century and which remained a common choice of material for tomb sculptures until the end of the Middle Ages. It is an easily worked material, whose colour was prized, and which took a polish. The use of alabaster probably marks a reaction against the lavishly textured and polychromed effigies of the late 13th and early 14th centuries, and it seems likely that alabaster effigies were generally only partially polychromed.[57] The earlier effigy at Winchester is that of Bishop Edington (d.1366) (Fig. 9.13) and is contained in the first surviving chantry chapel in the cathedral; the effigy is somewhat damaged and the angels at the head, and animals which serve both as foot supports and as metaphors for vice, are headless. The effigy is placed on a free-standing Purbeck marble base, ornamented with alternating sexfoils and trefoil-headed panels. Bishop Wykeham's (d.1404) effigy is a product of the London workshop which supplied the effigy of Archbishop Courtenay at Canterbury:[58] Lawrence Stone has pointed out that the angels at the bishop's head are treated in the familiar London manner, though the three (very heavily restored) clerks, representing his chantry chapel monks, show an unusual iconographic intervention which must have been specified by the bishop. The chapel and tomb had been constructed by the time Wykeham wrote his will in 1403.[59] The tomb-chest's empty niches are now filled by 19th-century paintings (1894-97) of Wykeham's coat-of-arms. The monument is housed in the bishop's gigantic chantry chapel, which was once heavily encrusted with sculpture. Three niches (two over the doors) at each of the canted ends of the chapel housed standing images, and the reredos had two tiers of five niches; the west wall also has space for five images.

The vault bosses and corbel-table of the nave are difficult to date precisely, and further work is certainly required to sort out the stylistic sequence; work on reconstructing the nave had been put in hand under Bishop Edington and was resumed by Wykeham. He may have been preparing to resume work in 1371, when materials were stolen from the churchyard, but work only actually resumed, after he had founded his Oxford and Winchester Colleges, in 1394.[60] The

Fig. 9.12   14th-century capital in north transept. *John Crook*

south side of the nave clearly preceded the north but at the time of the bishop's death neither was fully finished, as we learn from the fact that he left the very considerable sum of 2,500 marks to complete it.[61] Evidently the nave vault postdates Wykeham's death, although the south and north aisle bosses can be ascribed to his patronage. The style of the corbels at the west end of the nave strongly supports Crook and Kusaba's argument that the break between Edington and Wykeham's work occurs at the head of the panelling below; the style of the head of a king and his flanking angels (Fig. 16.4) is identical to some of the vault bosses. The stylistic preoccupations of Wykeham's carvers with physiognomic expression and the often slightly coarse quality of the work have been viewed as manifesting a tendency towards an increasingly secular treatment of religious art, and certainly the preoccupation with heraldry is remarkable.[62]

The 15th Century

Dating is also a problem with a number of *ex situ* images which can, however, be shown to have come from a reredos in the Guardian Angels Chapel.[63] By 1840 at the latest, the area behind the Great Screen was used as a repository for miscellaneous pieces of sculpture collected together from round the cathedral (there is some evidence that fragmentary sculptures from the Great Screen itself may have been placed there, and floored over, immedi-

Fig. 9.13   Alabaster effigy of Bishop Edington. *John Crook*

ately after their defacement).[64] This group of fragments has been reunited using a mixture of stylistic analysis and the evidence left by the 16th-century iconoclasts. When the images were taken down from their niches, the figures' shoulders were sawn at an angle of 45 degrees from the back, and the bases were cut at the same angle in the opposite direction, probably so that they could be re-used as double cornerstones in a wall.[65] Four headless figures (Fig. 9.14) could be reunited following this clue and to them could be added a small upper section of a fifth figure, whose shoulders had also been sawn at the same angle, a treatment apparently reserved for images from this one programme. Although neither the shoulders nor the base of a very damaged torso of an image of the Risen Christ survive, the figure can be added to this group primarily on the basis of its material, style, and scale.[66] With slightly less certainty, the lower half of a fine female head, still complete when it was photographed by 1936, can also be included.[67] The diaphanous draperies and swaying poses of these images closely align them with alabaster imagery, as a number of scholars have recognised: both the image of St John the Baptist and that of the Risen Christ can be paralleled in late medieval alabaster panels. In view of the very considerable difficulties in dating the related alabaster panels, the date of these figures is likely to remain controversial.[68] However, the dimensions of the figures, which are tall, flat and wide, tend to show that if they came from an extant screen or monument, there is only one possible location for them: the reredos in the Guardian Angels Chapel, the architecture of which suits the sculptural style of the images. The niches seem to be comparable, in a number of details, with the smaller lower niches of the reredos inside Cardinal Beaufort's (d.1447) chantry chapel. Neither his chapel nor that of Bishop Waynflete (d.1486), nor the niches in the Langton Chapel, would have room for such large images in their interior or exterior niches. The reredos has space for seven large images, one niche to the north being larger than the others, alternating with groups of four small images in niches, above a frieze of shields with instruments of the Passion and foliage fleurons, above two-light blind tracery enclosed in panels.

Hardly anything appears to survive from the sculptural programme of Cardinal Beaufort's Chapel; the effigy itself, seen by Lieutenant Hammond in 1635, was destroyed in 1642.[69] He described it as carved from wood, a surprisingly cheap material in view of the lavishness of the chantry chapel and its furnishings and also in view of Beaufort's enormous wealth. As Quirk suggested, the wooden effigy may originally have been covered with gilt plates, as was that of King Henry V in Westminster Abbey.[70] The present effigy must postdate the Civil War and probably belongs to c.1660-65. The only medieval figure-sculpture still *in situ* is the angel holding Beaufort's arms in the centre of the splendid fan-vaulting of the chapel and the frieze of angels holding coats-of-arms beneath the reredos.

Bishop Waynflete's chantry chapel contains, in addition to the prelate's restored effigy of polychromed freestone with its unusual foot-rest of an angel holding his coat-of-arms, a considerable amount of small-scale sculpture, of decidedly low quality but considerable iconographic interest, set below niche bases and below the foliage brattishing running round the interior.[71] Two damaged statues can also be connected with Waynflete's chapel: these, a monk (Fig. 9.15) and a nun, are, like the minor sculpture, of rather poor quality. Sir William St. John Hope argued that the three eastern niches of the chapel's reredos housed images of St Mary Magdalen and SS. Peter and Paul, and that the western niche held an image of the Virgin and Child: it is difficult, though, to accommodate the two surviving figures to this

Fig. 9.14   Figure of St John the Baptist from the reredos of the Guardian Angels Chapel. *John Crook*
Fig. 9.15   Figure of a monk attributed to Bishop Waynflete's chantry chapel. *John Crook*

iconography.[72] The tomb-base has large foiled shapes enclosing Waynflete's lily and scrolls. At the angles are twisted Purbeck marble columns, reminiscent of those of a shrine, and the sub-base is of the same material. The chantry chapel is closely modelled on that of Cardinal Beaufort and the centre of the vaulting also features an angel, rather round-shouldered and of lesser quality, holding the prelate's arms. The foliage sculpture set in the doorway spandrels is of considerable interest. The left hand spandrel parallels, in its fastidious naturalism of detail, contemporary Flemish manuscript illumination (Fig. 9.16a). It shows a rose-bush springing from long grass with three daisies at the base. Two of the roses are seen frontally, one from the side and three buds from the side. A large snail crawls up the rose-tree's stem. As I have pointed out elsewhere, this foliage can be very closely paralleled in one of the spandrel sculptures of the Great Screen (Fig. 9.16b) and forms one of the reasons for connecting the latter with Bishop Waynflete, a munificent patron of architecture and the arts.[73]

The low quality of the sculpture from Waynflete's chantry chapel might suggest that one should not anticipate better quality imagery on the Great Screen. Here, there is still some surviving figure-sculpture in place, in the doorway spandrels on the east front of the screen, where the Annunciation and the Visitation (Fig. 9.17) are depicted: the quality of the sculpture is, indeed, directly comparable with that of the chantry chapel, although the details are blurred by coats of whitewash, through which considerable traces of the original polychromy can be seen. However, there is good reason to believe that, when the screen was being furnished with imagery, Waynflete had access to sculptors who were amongst the best of their period working in England. The evidence for this statement is provided by a large number of sculptural fragments which can be identified as coming from the screen; many of them could be seen grouped together against the western face of the feretory screen in early 20th-century photographs (Fig. 22.2).[74] Some of the figures, most of which had been sawn into three pieces by the 16th-century iconoclasts for re-use as building blocks in the Close walls, had already been reunited in the late 19th or earlier 20th century. Recently, after further study, several more figures have been pieced back together. The sculptures, many of which are currently on display in the Triforium Gallery, seem to fall into two stylistic groups: the first comprises some large heads, the bodies of which have not yet been rediscovered, and a group of generally headless bodies from the smaller niches, as well as the famous 'Winchester Madonna' and 'God the Father' (Fig. 9.18). One important 'missing link' was seen in a photograph of c.1907 (Fig. 22.2) but has since disappeared: this is the head of a young king, the same scale as the headless bodies but stylistically identical to some of the larger heads. I still have not given up hope that this head will be rediscovered for the second time. This first group is strongly Netherlandish in character (Fig. 9.19). The second group, a series of five scowling heads of approximately the same size (Fig. 9.20) as the large heads in the first group, is easier to relate to native sculpture, and is both stylistically and iconographically distinct, although it appears also to come from the Great Screen.[75]

In 1476 the relics of St Swithun were ceremonially placed by Bishop Waynflete in a new reliquary, made with a legacy from Cardinal Beaufort, his predecessor. John Crook has argued that a new shrine-base for St Swithun's reliquary had been constructed by this date and that the shrine was then moved from its previous position, on the feretory platform, to the centre of the retrochoir.[76] It can hardly be doubted that the Purbeck marble material misidentified by Tudor-Craig and Keen as dating from the 13th century actually came from the new shrine-base constructed during Waynflete's episcopate and completed by 1476: these remains are part of one of the largest and latest surviving shrine-bases in

Fig. 9.16   Spandrel reliefs (a) from the entrance door to Bishop Waynflete's chantry chapel and (b) from the east side of the north door in Great Screen. *John Crook*

the country.[77] In the account of the translation ceremony, it is stated that the relics had been in storage for about twenty years: it seems highly probable that the reason for this was the construction of the Great Screen and the consequent disruption to the area behind the High Altar. This argument strongly implies that the Great Screen was also complete, structurally at least, by 1476, and that the sculptures may have been put in place very shortly afterwards: there is nothing in the style of the sculptural fragments to contradict such a belief. Evidently, by the time that the screen was fully furnished with imagery, a new shrine-base, possibly incorporating much of its 13th-century predecessor, had been set up, flanked by the great chantry chapels of Beaufort and Waynflete.[78]

Later in the 15th century, the Lady Chapel was reconstructed and furnished with a series of wall paintings: the work on the chapel begun during the priorate of Prior Hunton (1470-98) was completed only under his successor Prior Silkstede (d.1524), as can be seen from the vaulting bosses: the central bosses show Our Lord in Judgement and the Assumption of the Virgin, whilst subsidiary bosses include those of bishops from Beaufort to Langton (d.1501) but not Fox (1501-28), and the rebuses of Hunton and Silkstede. Bishop Langton's rebus can be seen in the vaulting of his chapel, on the south side of the Lady Chapel, and in the cornice which surmounted the altar wall until its removal in 1818.[79] The ghostly outlines of the lost sculptures can be seen in the paintwork of the reredos below.

The 16th Century
The last great building campaigns at Winchester Cathedral date from the episcopate of Richard Fox. The high vault of the presbytery was constructed of wood, presumably because the presbytery walls, reconstructed in the 14th century, would not have borne the weight of a masonry vault. The wooden vault bosses (Fig. 9.21) are of three types, the most sacred towards the east: emblems of the Passion (the *Arma Christi*); royal arms and

emblems; and arms connected with Bishop Fox and the sees he successively occupied.[80] The evidence of the arms suggests a date of c.1503-9 for the bosses: one shows the arms of the Prince of Wales, another those of Katherine of Aragon, and on a third the conjoined initials **HK**. As Cave points out, this seems to indicate that the arms date between 1503, when Henry became Prince of Wales on the death of his elder brother, and the pope granted him a dispensation to marry Katherine, and 1509, when he became king.[81] There has been general agreement that the bosses were added to a pre-existing vault: the debate has centred on whether the vault antedated Fox's episcopate or

Fig. 9.17   Spandrel relief showing the Angel Gabriel from the west side of the south door in the Great Screen. *John Crook*

not. In fact, the basic premises of this debate are unsound. Two points have to be considered. First, the vault is supported by stone corbels of angels holding coats-of-arms whose iconography is directly linked to the vaulting bosses, and which unequivocally date to Fox's episcopate (Fig. 9.22): this very strongly suggests that the vault also does.[82] The extreme unlikelihood that scaffolding would again be erected in the presbytery, with all the consequent disruption to services, no more than seven years after the vaulting had been put in place, and the difficulty of viewing the vaulting as in any sense complete *without* the coats-of-arms in place must rule out any theory that, a few years after the vault had been erected, Fox decided to have bosses with coats-of-arms added. It is surely much more probable that the arms were carved from separate pieces of timber, by specialist sculptors, but that they were always an integral part of the design.

Bishop Fox's chantry chapel, which houses his *transi* image in the south side, visible from the aisle, was constructed in the next most prestigious part of the church after the spaces occupied by Beaufort's and Waynflete's chapels, just to the east of the Great Screen, on the south side. The chapel was complete by 1518 and its position, at least, had been fixed by 1513, when an indenture was drawn up between Fox and the prior and convent.[83] Very little remains of the chantry chapel's original sculptural programme besides some of the heraldic carvings, the vault bosses, and the frieze of angels with the arms of the Passion below the empty reredos with its intricate niches. A few fragments of the small figure-sculptures have been gathered together, enough to show that they were of excellent quality, as one might expect from a patron of Fox's importance, and from the excellence of the remaining sculpture *in situ*.[84] (Just possibly, an early 16th-century fragment of an annunciate Gabriel, retaining much of its extremely complex polychromy, may belong to his patronage too.)[85] An interesting indication of future stylistic developments at Winchester is provided by the classical volutes of the chapel's interior.[86] By the time of the 1525 presbytery screens, Renaissance ornament starts to play a decisive role in the decoration.[87]

Fig. 9.18 *(above left)* Head of (?) God the Father from the Great Screen. Polychromed freestone. *John Crook*

Fig. 9.19 *(above right)* Head of a bishop. Polychromed freestone. *John Crook*

Fig. 9.20 *(left)* Scowling head from the Great Screen. Polychromed freestone. (This head is from the second group). *John Crook*

The 1513 indenture mentioned above specified that any money left over after the completion of Fox's Oxford college was to be spent on

> the makinge of a new vaulte of stone over St Swithune his shrine & of the new makinge & vaultinge with stone of two Ilis upon the side of ye said Church & the vaulting of the Cross-Ile in ye sayd Cathedrall Church of Winchester with stone after the manner & forme of the vaultinge of ye sayd Cathedrall Church.[88]

The interpretation of this document seems, at first sight, clear: it was Fox's intention to revault the retrochoir, in which St Swithun's shrine was located, and to rebuild and revault the presbytery aisles and the transepts. Of this work, only the re-building and revaulting of the presbytery aisles was ever completed, though a start was made on the tran-septs: work *in situ*, including one fine label-stop of a bishop's head, shows that the eastern aisles of the Roman-esque transepts were to be removed.[89] This straightforward interpretation is complicated by the fact that the Prince of Wales' feathers appear in the aisle vault bosses, suggesting a pre-1509 date (when Henry VIII became king) should apply to them. This would then imply that the aisles indicated in the indenture are not those of the presbytery but the retrochoir aisles, flanking the shrine of St Swithun in the central vessel; on this interpreta-tion the rebuilding and revaulting of the presbytery aisles would already have been completed.[90]

This alternative reading of the evidence places a great deal of weight on the dating significance of the Prince of Wales' three ostrich feath-ers in the aisle bosses, which may be unwise given that there are errors in

Fig. 9. 21   Bosses in Bishop Fox's presbytery vaulting (1503-9). Royal coat-of-arms, ciphers and devices to the east (at top); Fox's arms and those of the sees he occupied, further west. *John Crook*

the heraldry of the high vault (and in the 1525 presbytery screens). If their inclusion is significant, however, they could be intended to show that the aisle vaults and high vault of the presbytery are to be viewed as part of the same programme, conceived before 1509, rather than an indication of the date the vaulting was actually completed. The design of the presbytery aisle vaults is, of course, remarkably similar to that of the high vault, and the bosses include, in common with it the *Arma Christi,* Tudor devices, and Fox's arms held by angels, as well as the Prince of Wales' feathers. They could also, conceivably, commemorate a donation by the king when Prince of Wales. The fact that the same

Fig. 9.22   Presbytery. Angel corbel holding Veronica.
John Crook

sculptor was responsible for some of the aisle bosses and for those of the vaulting of Fox's chantry chapel tends to suggest a closely related dating, but it would be unwise to argue that this rules out a pre-1509 date for the aisle bosses. Either interpretation of the documents is possible, and both help to stress Fox's concentration on the presbytery, which housed the high altar and Great Screen, with the bishop's own chantry chapel to the east. It may be that the bishop's post-1513 concern with the enlargement of Corpus Christi College prevented his turning his attention to the shrine area or the transepts of the cathedral; instead, he confined his attention to the construction of his chantry chapel and a reconstruction of the presbytery screens. Whatever the date of the aisle vaults, their style and that of the high vault are interesting because of Fox's express concern to ensure stylistic congruity with the earlier vaults of the nave. The same concern with ensuring visual continuity animates the final chantry chapel, Bishop Gardiner's, which postdates the Reformation. It is interesting because its form and function closely echo that of Fox's chapel, though in a Renaissance idiom.[91] Its imagery is greatly reduced in quantity and is now confined to the interior, but it also features the bishop's *transi* image, built into the aisle elevation. Stylistically up to date, the chapel nevertheless, Janus-faced, looks back to Winchester's great medieval past.

Acknowledgements

I suspect that none, or very little, of my work at Winchester Cathedral, which has been progressing, slowly and rather intermittently, over the past eight years, would have ever been concluded without the constant help and advice, hospitality and encouragement of John Hardacre. John Crook has been an exemplary editor and Pat Pottinger has helped in many ways. S. F. Baylis, S. J. Gunn, Martin Biddle and Nicholas Rogers have each contributed helpful comments. For the faults that remain, the equivocations and uncertainties, I should alone be held responsible.

Notes

1. The Wykeham chantry chapel sculptures by Frampton date from the end of the 19th century. For the Great Screen restoration see G. W. Kitchin, *The Great Screen of Winchester Cathedral,* 2nd. edn. (Winchester, 1891), and below, pp. 321-5.
2. L. Stone, *Sculpture in Britain: The Middle Ages* (Harmondsworth, 1972), p. 2.
3. For iconoclasm in England, see J. Phillips, *The Reformation of Images* (Berkeley, 1973); for an account of the cathedral by a 17th-century visitor, see L. G. Wickham Legg, ' "A Relation of a Short Survey made of the Western Counties" Made by a Lieutenant of the Military Company in Norwich in 1635', *Camden Miscellany* 16, Camden Society, 3rd ser., 52 (1936), pp. 44-9.
4. For French tombs, see J. Adhémar, 'Les tombeaux de la Collection Gaignières', *Gazette des Beaux-Arts* 84 (1974), pp. 5-192 and 88 (1976), pp. 3-128. In England, effigies of brass and precious materials, such as the silver and silver plate employed for Henry V's tomb at Westminster Abbey, were victims of cupidity rather than religious fanaticism, although auxiliary imagery was often attacked.
5. M. Chibnall (ed.), *The Historia Pontificalis of John of Salisbury,* rev. edn. (Oxford, 1986), p. 79. See also Professor Kusaba's paper, above, p. 70.
6. For the font see, C. H. Eden, *Black Tournai Fonts in England* (London, 1909), pp. 12-16; Stone, *Sculpture,* pp. 88-9, and, most recently, G. Zarnecki, 'Henry of Blois as a Patron of Sculpture', in S. Macready and F. H. Thompson (eds.), *Art and Patronage in the English Romanesque* (London, 1986), pp. 159-72. A font at Boulge, eight miles north-east of Ipswich, is added to the list of fonts by J. Blatchly and B. Hayward, *The Tournai Font in St Peter's, Ipswich* (Ipswich Historic Churches Trust, 1983); they also view the font at Iffley as being of Tournai marble.
7. Milner, *Winchester Cathedral,* ii, pp. 76-83, was the first to see that the subjects of the font were derived from the legend of St Nicholas, though he misinterpreted part of the west side. There is still considerable confusion in the literature about the identification of the central figure on the south side and the western scenes are also puzzling; it would be helpful to have some account of possible manuscript sources for the iconography.
8. Zarnecki, 'Henry of Blois', pp. 161-2. See also M. Biddle, *Wolvesey: The Old Bishop's Palace, Winchester, Hampshire,* English Heritage Handbook (London, 1986).
9. J. Hardacre, *Winchester Cathedral: Triforium Gallery* Catalogue (Winchester, 1989) item 2
10. This fragment was dated for the Triforium Gallery catalogue by Dr. Jeffrey West (Hardacre, *Catalogue*, item 13) though his argument has not yet been published.
11. Y. L. Kusaba, 'The Function, Date and Stylistic Sources of the Treasury of Henry of Blois in the South Transept of Winchester Cathedral', *WCR* 57 (1988), pp. 38-49. Milner, *Winchester Cathedral,* ii, p. 30, was the first to identify the function of the treasury.
12. The suggestion that this was the tomb of William Rufus has been convincingly refuted by Zarnecki, 'Henry of Blois', pp. 168-9.
13. The aisles themselves seem once to have contained small figure-sculptures in the quatrefoils above the arcading.
14. For this figure, see Stone, *Sculpture,* pp. 112-13. The classicism of its style may have been influenced by Henry of Blois' classical sculptures, if these survived, though 'classicism' is a strong stylistic current in early 13th-century European art.
15. The Winchester *Ecclesia* can be compared with the Virgin and Child from the central portal of Wells Cathedral: there is copious evidence for the use of metal decorations there.
16. T. D. Atkinson, 'Medieval Figure Sculpture in Winchester Cathedral', *Archaeologia* 85 (1936), pp. 161-2. In the summer of 1938 members of the Hampshire Field Club and Archaeological Society visited the Deanery and were shown the supposed site of the discovery: Dean Selwyn told them that 'the beautiful headless statue which was at present in the Cathedral was found under the lawn where, he expected other treasures might be discovered if excavation work were tried': *Hampshire Chronicle,* 2 July 1938. I am grateful to Mrs. Brenda Kipling, who supplied this reference. For a more sceptical view of its original provenance, see P. Williamson in J. Alexander and P. Binski (eds.), *Age of Chivalry: Art in Plantagenet England 1200-1400,* Catalogue, Royal Academy Exhibition (London, 1987), p. 301.
17. P. Tudor-Craig in *Age of Chivalry,* pp. 301-2.

18. Tudor-Craig's suggestion is endorsed by Hardacre, *Catalogue,* item 27. For the imagery, see also a misericord at Christchurch Priory: *Age of Chivalry,* p. 304.

19. P. Tudor-Craig and L. Keen, 'A Recently Discovered Purbeck Marble Sculptured Screen of the Thirteenth Century and the Shrine of St Swithun', *BAA Winchester,* p. 65. This corbel, however, seems too large to have come from the northern side of the chapel: it measures approximately 250 mm. by 200 mm.; the *in situ* corbel is 170 mm. wide and 160 mm. high.

20. S. Whittingham, *A Thirteenth Century Portrait Gallery at Salisbury Cathedral* (Salisbury, 1979) and Stone, *Sculpture,* p. 118.

21. Vaughan, *Winchester Cathedral,* p. 34-5.

22. C. A. Bradford, *Heart Burial* (London, 1933) and P. Brieger, *English Art 1216-1307* (Oxford, 1968), p. 103.

23. Vaughan, *Winchester Cathedral,* p. 36, relates how the golden cup was uncovered during the Commonwealth period, when the altar steps were levelled. The heart must have been buried close to where Bishop Fox's inscription to Aymer can be read (see below, pp. 263-7).

24. M. E. Roberts, 'The Tomb of Giles de Bridport in Salisbury Cathedral', *Art Bulletin* 61 (1983), p. 568 sees Aymer's effigy as perhaps 'the earliest surviving example of the new style' of heavy, broad-fold draperies in Purbeck effigies. The very close relationship between this effigy and that of Giles de Bridport raises the question whether Salisbury workshops produced Purbeck marble effigies (see Whittingham, *Portrait Gallery,* p. 8) or whether both these effigies originated in a London workshop. See also E. S. Prior and A. Gardner, *An Account of Medieval Figure-Sculpture in England* (Cambridge, 1912), pp. 597-8. Roberts is non-committal on this matter.

25. See I. T. Henderson and J. Crook, *The Winchester Diver* (Crawley, 1984), pp. 109-13 for this episode (including plate of Garbett's addition).

26. His predecessor Godfrey de Lucy (d.1204), is another possible candidate; his successor, William de Raleigh (d.1250) was apparently buried in St Martin's, Tours (H. R. Luard (ed.), *Annales Monastici, II* (Winchester and Waverley), RS 36 (1865), p. 92; but cf. H. Wharton (ed.), *Anglia Sacra,* 2 vols. (London, 1691), i, p. 307 (from BL, Cotton. MS Domitian A.9), which states that he was buried at Pontigny.

27. R. N. Quirk, 'The Monuments of Prior Basing and the "Old Bishop in Marble"', *WCR* 23 (1954), pp. 12-21, at p. 15.

28. *Ibid.,* p. 13.

29. *Ibid.,* p. 16.

30. *Ibid.,* p. 19. For the location in the 15th century of the burials of John of Pontoise and Henry Woodlock, see the *Historia Major* attributed to Thomas Rudborne in *Anglia Sacra,* i, p. 286. For the burial of John of Exeter *alias* Gervais at Viterbo, see *Winchester Annals,* p. 106; and for that of the body of Nicholas of Ely at Waverley see *ibid.,* pp. 54 and 393 (Waverley Annals).

31. Milner, *Winchester Cathedral,* i, p. 247; *VCH Hants.,* ii, p. 109.

32. Quirk, 'Prior Basing', pp. 13-14. F. A. Greenhill, *Incised Effigial Slabs; A Study of Engraved Stone Memorials in Latin Christendom, c.1100 to c.1700,* 2 vols. (London, 1976), i, p. 11, cites evidence from continental sources for slabs being incised at the quarry but slabs could also be engraved elsewhere. Cf. also the lost brass of Bishop Thomas Bitton (d.1307), accounted for in 1310; *Monumental Brass Society Bulletin* 27 (1981), pp. 7-9.

33. Greenhill, *Incised Effigial Slabs,* i, pp. 16ff.

34. J. D. Le Couteur and D. H. M. Carter, 'Notes on the Shrine of St Swithun formerly in Winchester Cathedral', *Antiq. J.* 4 (1924), pp. 360-70; Tudor-Craig and Keen, 'Screen'; see also J. Crook, 'The Thirteenth-Century Shrine and Screen of St Swithun at Winchester', *JBAA* 138 (1985), pp. 125-31, pl. XXIII.

35. J. Crook, 'The Typology of Early Medieval Shrines—a Previously Misidentified "Tomb-Shrine" Panel from Winchester Cathedral', *Antiq. J.* 70 (1990), pp. 49-64; and above, p. 59.

36. Cf. Tudor-Craig and Keen, 'Screen', p. 69.

37. M. Norris, *Monumental Brasses: The Craft* (London, 1978), fig. 123.

38. W. S. Walford, 'Remarks on an Effigy of a Knight in Winchester Cathedral', *Arch. J.* 15 (1858), pp. 125-36. F. J. Baigent discovered the words 'Petrus Gavston' twice incised on the slab. It is possible to see the use of shields suspended from their guiges, rather than weepers in the niches, as an updating of Queen Eleanor of Castile's tomb-chest in Westminster Abbey.

39. Quirk, 'Prior Basing', p. 18; Wickham Legg, 'Survey', p. 48.

40. G. Russell, 'Decorated Tracery in Winchester Cathedral', *BAA Winchester,* p. 94. The window is her N.IV (pl. XXVA). The suggestion that Gaveston's tomb belonged here was made by A. Rannie, 'Decorated Architecture in the Cathedral', *WCR* 35 (1966), p. 21, following J. R. Planché.

41. The evidence for this is contained in A. W. Goodman, 'The Choir Stalls, Winchester Cathedral', *Arch. J.* 34 (1927), pp. 125-6; Rannie, 'Decorated Architecture', pp. 15-16; S. Jervis, *Woodwork of Winchester Cathedral* (Winchester, 1976), pp. 19-21, provides an excellent analysis of the stalls, for which see also see Dr. Tracy's essay in this volume.

42. Cf. C. Tracy, *English Gothic Choir-Stalls 1200-1400* (Woodbridge, 1987), p. 21.

43. L. F. Sandler, *The Peterborough Psalter in Brussels and other Fenland Manuscripts* (London, 1974), pp. 133-5; see the important review by A. Bennett in *Art Bulletin* 64 (1982), pp. 502-8, which has started the process of bringing other media into comparison with manuscript illuminations.

44. F. Warren, 'The Lost Panels of the Choir Stalls', *WCR* 4 (1935), pp. 12-16.

45. Hardacre, *Catalogue,* item 29.

46. For the modernisation programme, see Russell, 'Decorated Tracery'.

47. Stone, *Sculpture,* pp. 225-6.

48. See the points made in R. Didier and R. Recht, 'Paris, Prague, Cologne et la sculpture de la seconde moitié du xive siècle', *Bulletin Monumental* 138 (1980), pp. 173-219. This problem is implicitly recognised in the very wide dating bracket (*c.*1340-80) given by Dawton (*Age of Chivalry,* Nos. 699-701) to the Flawford alabasters. It is evident that sculpture of the second half of the 14th century needs more study before fundamental questions of dating and attribution can be answered.

49. Russell, 'Decorated Tracery', p. 94, views the retrochoir screen as slightly earlier than 1317; Draper and Morris favour a date of *c.*1310-15 (see below, pp. 182-3 and note 29). A Coronation of the Virgin (?) group on the south side of the screen was incorporated in Fox's chantry chapel: their outlines have been left in the paintwork (see below pp. 131-2).

50. For this suggestion, advanced very tentatively, see P. Lindley, 'Figure Sculpture at Winchester in the Fifteenth Century: A New Chronology', in D. Williams (ed.), *England in the Fifteenth Century* (Woodbridge, 1987), pp. 158-9.

51. Lindley, 'Figure Sculpture', p. 159.

52. Compare the position and general style of the bearded man with the corbel at Winchelsea illustrated in Tracy, *Choir-Stalls 1200-1400,* fig. 43.

53. Compare the later work in the de Lisle Psalter (that of the 'Majesty Master') or the Ely Cathedral misericords of *c.*1338-42: P. G. Lindley, 'The Monastic Cathedral at Ely, *circa* 1320 to *circa* 1350: Art and Patronage in Medieval East Anglia', unpubl. Ph.D. thesis, University of Cambridge, 1985, pp. 177-8.

54. North transept 2 and 3, south transept 1 following Russell's numbering.

55. Lindley, 'Figure Sculpture', p. 163, dating it *c.*1320-50.

56. T. D. Atkinson, 'The Epiphany Chapel', *WCR* 6 (1937), pp. 14-15. The arcading on the west side of the chapel looks original to me.

57. A. Gardner, *Alabaster Tombs of the Pre-Reformation Period in England* (Cambridge, 1940), remains the only general survey.

58. Stone, *Sculpture,* p. 197.

59. Lindley, 'Figure Sculpture', p. 158; R. Lowth, *The Life of William Wykeham, Bishop of Winchester,* 2nd edn. (London, 1777), Appendix XVII, p. xxxv.

60. T. F. Kirby (ed.), *Wykeham's Register,* 2 vols., HRSoc (1896-9), ii, p. 127; for an alternative interpretation of the events of 1371, see below, p. 227.

61. Willis, *Winchester Cathedral,* p. 57.

62. Stone, *Sculpture,* p. 188. See also C. J. P. Cave, 'Corbels of the Nave', *WCR* 4 (1935), pp. 7ff and *idem, The Roof Bosses of Winchester Cathedral* (Winchester, 1935).

63. Lindley, 'Figure Sculpture', pp.164-5.

64. The third edition of Milner's *Winchester Cathedral* (Winchester, 1839), ii, p. 86, refers to sculpture as gathered in this location.

65. Atkinson, 'Figure Sculpture', p. 160.

66. P. G. Lindley, 'Sculptural Discoveries at Winchester Cathedral', *HFC Proc.* 46 (1990), pp. 101-11, at pp. 102-3.

67. Lindley, 'Figure Sculpture', p. 164.
68. Lindley, 'Sculptural Discoveries', pp. 104-6.
69. Wickham Legg, 'Survey', p. 47; R. N. Quirk, 'The Tomb of Cardinal Beaufort', *WCR* 23 (1954), pp. 6-10. The tantalising possibility that the wooden effigy might have been Beaufort's funeral effigy is rendered improbable by the fact that the chapel and its furnishings were so rich and the cardinal left so considerable a fortune. His chapel was doubtless provided with a splendid tomb effigy.
70. Quirk, 'Cardinal Beaufort', p. 8. The figure of Henry V, though, had a solid silver head: Lieutenant Hammond does not mention that Beaufort's figure was headless, so it may have been covered in plate rather than solid.
71. Lindley, 'Figure Sculpture', p. 166.
72. Lindley, 'Figure Sculpture', pp. 165-6; W. H. St. J. Hope, *Report on Bishop Waynflete's Chapel in Winchester Cathedral* (London, 1898), p. 5.
73. P. G. Lindley, 'The Great Screen of Winchester Cathedral, II', *Burlington Magazine* (forthcoming). See also V. Davis, *William Waynflete: Bishop and Educationalist* (Woodbridge, 1993).
74. P. G. Lindley, 'The Great Screen of Winchester Cathedral, I', *Burlington Magazine* 131 (1989), pp. 604-15 (fig. 4). For the date when these figures had been gathered together, see Lindley, 'Great Screen, II' and *idem*, 'Figure Sculpture', pp. 164-5.
75. Lindley, 'Great Screen, I'.
76. J. Crook, 'Excavating the Holy Hole', *WCR* 58 (1989), pp. 34-42 for the crucial evidence of the 1476 dating, and above, pp. 63-4.
77. Cf. C. Wilson, *The Shrines of St William of York* (York, 1977), pp. 19-21, for the principal shrine of St William, completed by 1472.
78. Crook, 'Holy Hole', pp. 34-42.
79. For the cornice, see Hardacre, *Catalogue,* item 73. For the interpretation of the various rebuses, see below, pp. 257-8.
80. For the vault bosses, see W. J. Carpenter Turner, 'The Presbytery', *WCR* 19 (1950), pp. 4-8; C. J. P. Cave, 'The Bosses on the Vault of the Quire at Winchester Cathedral', *Archaeologia* 76 (1927), pp. 161-78 and *idem, Roof Bosses,* pp. 19-26. See also A. J. Smith, 'The Life and Building Activities of Richard Fox, *c.*1448-1528', Unpubl. dissertation, University of London (1988), pp. 159-184.
81. Cave, 'Quire Bosses', pp. 162-3. The arms and ostrich feathers of the Prince of Wales are most unlikely to refer to Prince Henry, born on New Year's Day 1511 and dead by or on 22 February, so Cave's argument seems substantially correct. Professor Biddle suggests to me that the heraldry, which lays some stress on the Prince of Wales' arms, may be connected with the prince's visit to Winchester, in January 1506, to meet Philip of Burgundy.
82. J. Munby and J. Fletcher ('Carpentry in the Cathedral and Close at Winchester', *BAA Winchester,* pp. 101-11, at p. 107) favour a date in Fox's episcopate for the roof and vault.
83. A. Smith, 'The Chantry Chapel of Bishop Fox', *WCR* 57 (1988), p. 32 note 12, where a phrase is unfortunately omitted from the quotation.
84. P. G. Lindley, 'The Sculptural Programme of Bishop Fox's Chantry Chapel', *WCR* 57 (1988), pp. 33-7.
85. Hardacre, *Catalogue,* item 64.
86. I was under the impression that I was the first to notice these volutes, but they are also mentioned by C. Peers and H. Brakspear in *VCH Hants.,* v, p. 56.
87. See Professor Biddle's paper, below, pp. 257-304.
88. Corpus Christi College, Oxford, MS 'Twyne Transcripts', vol. i, p. 25.
89. Willis, *Winchester Cathedral,* pp. 47-8.
90. I owe this suggestion to Martin Biddle and John Crook.
91. See Martin Biddle's analysis of the chantry chapel, below, pp. 281-7.

THE MEDIEVAL POLYCHROMY OF WINCHESTER CATHEDRAL

David Park and Peter Welford

Few cathedrals are as celebrated for their medieval paintings as Winchester: in particular, those in the Holy Sepulchre Chapel are the finest of their date in England. Yet it is remarkable how much painting, or evidence of painting, has remained virtually unknown.[1]

Amongst these 'forgotten' paintings is that on the west wall of the south transept, hidden by canopied seats erected *c*.1520, but partly visible from a ladder. It includes two figures surely to be identified as the Virgin and Child (Fig. 10.1), and, since the Virgin is reclining and the Child faces her,[2] is presumably part of a Nativity rather than an Adoration. Other elements of the painting remain mysterious, however, such as the identity of a bearded figure peering out from behind a colonnade. Fully evident, though, is the superb quality of this painting and its early 14th-century date. Temporary removal of the seats when conservation work is undertaken will no doubt resolve the remaining questions concerning the iconography.

Fig. 10.1   South transept, west wall: detail of Virgin and Child, *c*.1320, hidden behind early 16th-century woodwork. *Conservation of Wall Painting Department, Courtauld Institute of Art*

Other painting survives in the eastern aisle of the transept, including, on the altar wall of the Venerable Chapel, part of a tiny male head and an ogee-headed canopy bearing an inscription. The style of the canopy indicates that the painting is contemporary with the large windows inserted in the east walls of both transepts in the early 14th century. The original appearance and function of these paintings is apparent from the more considerable

Fig. 10.2 Silkstede Chapel, east wall: watercolour by F. J. Baigent of Christ calling SS. Peter and Andrew, uncovered in 1846 (no longer visible). *Dean and Chapter of Winchester/John Crook*

evidence surviving on the same wall of the adjoining Silkstede Chapel. Although little is now visible here except incised guidelines for the canopies, a description was made by Professor Tristram of the paintings visible earlier this century, and there are also copies of one scene by both Tristram and the Winchester antiquary F. J. Baigent, who uncovered the paintings in 1846.[3] Comparing these copies it is evident that Baigent's is more accurate (Fig. 10.2). Far from holding a piece of cloth as Tristram suggested, the central figure was grasping the prow of a boat, with a pennon flying from the mast behind, and with Christ standing to the right. The subject, therefore, was Christ calling SS. Peter and Andrew, as indicated even by the respective ages of the bearded Peter and clean-shaven Andrew.[4] This naturally casts doubt on Tristram's description of the other six scenes, four of which apparently included the figure of Christ, though Tristram also thought he could discern a number of monks (one nimbed) and 'possibly a nun'.

Identification of the subject matter would be easier if we knew the dedication of the altar erected here c.1320. Clearly, the remodelling of the eastern aisle of both transepts was associated with the installation of new altars, lit by the large window inserted in the east wall of each chapel.[5] The paintings in the Silkstede and Venerable Chapels functioned as a reredos to their respective altars, with the rows of canopies imitating the kind of carved reredos still surviving from this period elsewhere.[6] The chapels must have been completely redecorated at this time, as is evident from the foliate scrollwork surviving on the window splays, and chevron pattern on a pier in the Venerable Chapel. Although much less painting of this period now survives in the north transept, the figure of a crowned male saint still exists high up in the north-east corner, now virtually invisible under a darkened 'preservative' coating.[7]

The decoration of the transepts c.1320 is by no means the first time that they had been painted. Surprisingly, however, recent examination of the late 11th-century masonry has revealed no trace of original painting. In keeping with the severity of the architecture, a decorative effect was achieved simply by the thick white pointing of the masonry itself. Although elements such as the capitals may have been painted, it appears that, as in the 14th century, figure subjects must have been wholly or largely confined to important areas such as altars.[8] In the crypt the same type of white pointing survives,[9] as well as much of the original plastering of the vault, possibly the most extensive survival of early Romanesque plasterwork in England. Particularly interesting is the deliberate ridging of the plastering at the edges of the groins, solely for aesthetic effect, and anticipating the much more pronounced relief achieved in the rib vaults introduced at Durham Cathedral in the 1090s. Is it conceivable that actual rib vaults may have existed in some part of Bishop Walkelin's cathedral?

The only known Romanesque paintings in the cathedral, other than in the Holy Sepulchre Chapel, are two life-size figures of prophets uncovered by Schnebbelie in 1788 and drawn by him before their destruction.[10] Set within the blind arcading of the north transept, they presumably formed part of a more extensive series; even from Schnebbelie's copy it is clear that they were very close stylistically to the 12th-century paintings in the Holy Sepulchre Chapel, and, indeed, very likely by the same hand.[11] The transept seems to have been entirely redecorated, however, in about 1220 and, although only fragments of this scheme survive, we again have records by Tristram and earlier antiquarians.[12] A reconstruction drawing by Tristram shows the piers horizontally banded, and though little of that decoration survives, foliate and other patterns still exist on some of the main arches at the north end. One soffit was decorated with a series of roundels, their frames incised with a compass before painting. The lowest roundel on the west side appears to enclose the bust of a male figure holding a scroll.[13] Very likely, therefore, a series of prophets was represented in this transept, as previously in the late 12th century. The ornament includes a repetitive lozenge pattern, of which a similar example survives on the soffit of the arch leading from the south transept to the presbytery aisle,[14] so it is also possible that substantial painting was undertaken on the south side of the cathedral in the same period.

A fascinating painting was discovered in 1907 behind the 17th-century bookshelves against the north wall of the Morley Library, located over the Slype between the south transept and the chapter house. It shows a cut-away view of the east end of a church, a chalice and reliquary on the altar and a lamp suspended above; to the right of the church, and on a much larger scale, is a Benedictine monk supporting a recumbent nimbed figure. John Crook has recently interpreted the subject as the translation of St Swithun in 971-74, showing the precious new reliquary provided then by King Edgar. Presumably it formed part of a series of scenes, and there were evidently imitation draperies below.[15] In an alteration probably made during the original painting the head of the monk was redrawn on a new limewash ground, and the rather weak linear style suggests a dating of c.1210-20. Much finer is another painting of a Benedictine monk, set within the Romanesque arcading at the south end of the south transept, though unfortunately it has deteriorated dramatically since its discovery in 1927.[16] This nimbed figure is perhaps intended for St Benedict himself, and his pose—holding up his quill to check its point—derives ultimately from early medieval author portraits. Stylistically, the painting, with its characteristic 'pear-shaped' head reminiscent of court painting such as the Westminster Retable, would seem to be of c.1260-80.

Certainly the most important 13th-century paintings surviving in the cathedral are those in the Holy Sepulchre Chapel, datable on stylistic grounds to c.1220. Until the 1960s virtually all the painting visible here was of this date, though part of an earlier scheme could be glimpsed on the east wall. The decision was taken to detach the 13th-century painting from this wall, and as a result the finest of all late Romanesque wall paintings in England was revealed.[17] The subject matter of both phases of painting on this wall is almost identical: a Deposition above, and Entombment and Marys at the Sepulchre below, though the 12th-century painting also includes the Harrowing of Hell. The motivation for the redecoration was clearly provided by the architectural alterations made at the time, including the insertion of a rib vault; in the new scheme, the composition of the Deposition was altered to fit the triangular field that resulted. Such redecoration, necessitated by architectural alterations, was paralleled not long after at Winchester Castle, where Henry III ordered new windows for the Painted Chamber in 1233, stipulating, however, that it was to be repainted with 'the same pictures and stories' as before.[18]

In the revised scheme in the chapel, the Harrowing of Hell was painted at the east end of the south wall, together with the Entry into Jerusalem, Raising of Lazarus, and Noli me tangere. The upper scenes here were also detached in the 1960s, and underneath them a unique preliminary drawing was discovered for part of the Romanesque scheme, apparently showing scenes of Christ before the high priest and Pilate, though only the head of the priest was recovered from the final paint layer.[19] The vault of this bay is painted with Infancy scenes in roundels and busts of prophets set in scrollwork, but the western vault of the chapel was destroyed in the 19th century by the insertion of a staircase to the organ above. A 12th-century Resurrection of the Dead survives, however, at the west end of the south wall, and in Tristram's period this was still partially covered by a 13th-century scene within a roundel, apparently of a soul accompanied by a devil, showing that here the roundels scheme of the vault extended lower down.[20] Tiny 13th-century scenes of St Catherine remain in the recess below, and other subjects were recorded on the west wall in the 19th century.[21]

Recent scientific examination has shown the technique of the Romanesque paintings to be no less sophisticated than their style. For instance, red lead was employed for the decorative motifs on the Magdalen's robe in the Deposition, and must have been applied in an organic medium; clearly, the paintings were executed in a 'mixed media' technique including organic binders.[22] Stylistically, the paintings are very close to the latest illumination in the Winchester Bible, especially that by the Master of the Morgan Leaf. They share the same relatively naturalistic draperies, green modelled flesh, 'billowing' grounds and red and blue panelled backgrounds, though there are sufficient small dissimilarities to suggest a different hand. This late Romanesque style is strongly influenced by Byzantine art, and similar influences are evident in the iconography—indeed, the Entombment (Fig. 10.3) provides a unique opportunity to observe an artist changing from a western to an eastern model during the painting, while also making adaptations of his own. Originally, the figure with the broad-brimmed hat was shown anointing Christ's torso rather than legs (as in the Winchester Psalter, c.1150);[23] traces of his hat are still discernible to the left of the Virgin. The painter then changed to an eastern model, which must have included the Lamentation elements of the Virgin embracing Christ and St John kissing his raised hand,

Fig. 10.3   Holy Sepulchre Chapel, east wall: the Entombment, c.1170-80. *John Crook*

though—perhaps through lack of space—he eliminated John and instead showed the Virgin kissing Christ's hand.[24] Most likely the Pantocrator on the eastern vault in the 13th-century scheme (Fig. 10.4) was modelled on an example in the original paintings, itself perhaps derived directly from one of the mosaic programmes of Norman Sicily.

The Morgan Master's work in the bible probably dates from c.1170-80, but, given the likelihood that monumental painting was often slightly more 'advanced' than small-scale illumination, the question arises as to whether the Holy Sepulchre Chapel paintings might belong to the period of Bishop Henry of Blois (1129-71), celebrated for his artistic patronage.[25] Interesting evidence in this respect is provided by the paintings at Petit-Quevilly in Normandy; it has been argued recently that they are by an English-trained artist working in the 1160s for Henry II, in a style particularly close to the Winchester Psalter.[26] Although similar in many respects, these paintings are however less naturalistic (in their drapery folds, for example) than those of the Holy Sepulchre Chapel, which are in fact much closer to another series of wall paintings on the Continent—those in the chapter house at Sigena (Aragon) of c.1200, and convincingly attributed to an English artist, very likely from Winchester.[27] Overall, therefore, a dating not earlier than the 1170s for the first scheme in the Holy Sepulchre Chapel still seems most plausible.

Although the earliest reference to the chapel as that of the Holy Sepulchre is only 18th-century, there can be little doubt that it was used—like similar chapels in Germany and elsewhere—for liturgical ceremonies at Easter: the Entombment would be re-enacted in a ceremony on Good Friday, and the Resurrection on Easter Sunday.[28] Nor can there be much doubt that the crusades of the period provided part of the inspiration. Indeed, a likely explanation of the 13th-century remodelling and decoration rests in the fact that one of the leaders of the English crusaders at this time was none other than Peter des Roches, bishop of Winchester (1205-38), who took the cross in 1221 after the fall of Damietta.[29] Such an explanation would also account for the presence of the earliest surviving cycle in England of the martyrdom of St Catherine of Alexandria, a saint popularised through the crusades, while a parallel in Winchester itself would be provided by the decoration of Rosamund's chamber in Winchester Castle, ordered by Henry III to be painted with the 'history of Antioch' in 1251, the year following his own vow to go on crusade.[30]

Fig. 10.4   Holy Sepulchre Chapel, east end: 12th-century Deposition on the east wall and 13th-century painting on the vault. *Conservation of Wall Painting Department, Courtauld Institute of Art*

By far the most important alteration to the cathedral in the early 13th century was the rebuilding of the entire east end in the chaste Early English style, seen elsewhere at Salisbury Cathedral and in the Great Hall of Winchester Castle. Particularly striking in these buildings is the contrast of the limestone and the polished Purbeck marble columns, and some have been dubbed 'a kind of black-and-white architecture',[31] but it is clear that this contrast was to some extent tempered—and the buildings articulated—by carefully selective painting. In the Castle Hall, subject-paintings—such as the Wheel of Fortune—appeared, and traces of the plain masonry pattern used elsewhere may still be seen; likewise, Salisbury Cathedral is characterised by very simple decoration in the nave, with more elaborate painting, including figure subjects on the vaults, reserved for the liturgically more important eastern parts. A similarly restrained approach to painted decoration can be observed in the 13th-century parts of Winchester Cathedral, where only decorative painting survives on the arcading at the east end, and the only figure subjects are in the north-eastern chapel, known from the 20 angel busts on its vault as the Guardian Angels Chapel (Fig. 10.5).[32] These angels are strikingly similar in some respects to the Salisbury vault figures, now replaced by 19th-century copies but known from earlier drawings by Schnebbelie. The Salisbury scheme included 48 angel busts over the eastern transepts, and it may well be that this slightly later programme—like its architectural context—was influenced by Winchester.[33]

Aspects of the figure style in the Guardian Angels Chapel are still very Byzantinising, and the angels can therefore hardly be dated later than c.1230, corresponding to the approximate completion date of the chapel. Close examination of the vault, however, shows that it has been partially repainted. In the first scheme, large- and medium-sized roundels with angel busts were regularly distributed across the vault and the intervening spaces filled with smaller plain roundels. When the foliate scrollwork was painted, the small roundels were partly painted out, and partly embellished with blue backgrounds and gilt attachments of stars and rosettes (Fig. 10.6). However, from holes in the original small roundels it is clear that they too contained attachments, though it is uncertain whether these were re-used or replaced by new examples at the time of the repainting. In fact, most of the present attachments are reproductions dating from the 1950s, when the vault was restored,[34] but from comparison with two originals kept in the cathedral's reserve collections, it does appear that some are medieval. Such attachments are very characteristic of expensive 13th-century schemes—a number have been recovered, for instance, from Henry III's Antioch Chamber at Clarendon Palace[35]—but the Winchester examples are possibly unique in being of wood rather than metal. Although it has been thought that the heavy black outlines added in places to the vault formed part of the medieval renovation,[36] they are rather crudely painted and extend into losses, so must be modern. Copies of the vault by Baigent survive in the library, and one of these—the only one in full scale—is so similar to one of the angel medallions as to suggest the latter may be largely or entirely his work.

When was the medieval repainting undertaken? In general, the foliate scrollwork is highly stylised, but it incorporates a single naturalistic leaf spray that can hardly be earlier than c.1260-70. Similar naturalistic foliage survives on the dado arcade, so presumably the chapel underwent general renovation in the second half of the 13th century, like various royal schemes at this time.[37] Other decorative painting (surviving or recorded) at the east end of the cathedral probably formed part of the original decoration: for example, fictive marbling, painted voussoirs, and black masonry pattern on the arches between the Lady Chapel and the

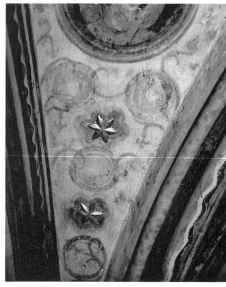

Fig. 10.5 *(left)* Guardian Angels Chapel: vault paintings of *c*.1225-30, partially repainted *c*.1260-80. *Royal Commission on the Historical Monuments of England*

Fig. 10.6 *(above)* Guardian Angels Chapel: detail of vault, showing overpainting with foliate scrollwork of original small roundels. *Conservation of Wall Painting Department, Courtauld Institute of Art*

adjoining Guardian Angels and Langton Chapels. There seems to be no evidence of naturalistic foliage surviving elsewhere than in the Guardian Angels Chapel, so it is unclear whether the whole east end was repainted in the second half of the century; if it was, however, this renovation might well have been contemporary with the new tiled floor laid in the retrochoir *c*.1260-80.[38]

Both the earlier and later elements of the Guardian Angels Chapel painting have at different times been attributed to Master William of Westminster, appointed painter for life to the priory of St Swithun by Henry III in 1239.[39] Perhaps it is more likely that he undertook the repair of a picture *(tabula)* over the high altar, for which Henry III gave 100 shillings in 1251,[40] and possibly he was also responsible for another panel painting, which survives in an extremely fragmentary state, though fortunately a copy was made shortly after its discovery in 1924 (Fig. 10.7).[41] The design was of two roundels with intervening stylised foliage, both roundels containing a horse; on the left, the head of the rider could be seen looking back. Stylistically, the panel is datable to *c*.1240-50, and though no other panel painting of this type survives from such an early date in England,[42] close parallels are provided by English-influenced altar frontals in Norway. One of the frontals from Tingelstad (of *c*.1260-1300, now known as 'Tingelstad II') is especially close, with similar foliage and bosses clasping the roundels.[43] Although the Norwegian frontals are larger and contain more scenes, it seems most likely that the Winchester panel was also an altarpiece, perhaps a retable showing scenes from a saint's life, though further study is needed to ascertain whether it may have been cut down from a larger panel.[44] It was found within an aumbry behind 16th-century panelling in the Langton Chapel, together with an indulgence of 1254 referring to the 'altar of the blessed Birinus'; but there is no obvious connection with the iconography of this 7th-century 'Apostle of Wessex', who became the first bishop of Dorchester in Oxfordshire.[45]

It has already been seen that the early 14th century was a period of considerable activity in the transepts at Winchester, though even more significant was the remodelling of the presbytery, including the installation of the superb new choir-stalls. Circumstantial

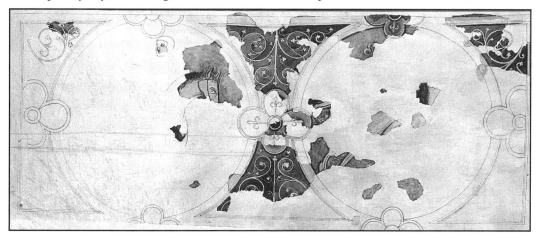

Fig. 10.7   Panel painting, *c*.1240-50. Watercolour by T. D. Atkinson. *Dean and Chapter of Winchester/ John Crook*

evidence of corresponding painting activity at this time is provided by the purchase for the new works at Exeter Cathedral of gold foils, lead white and red lead from Winchester in 1321; the master mason there, Thomas of Witney, had also been in charge at Winchester, and it has been suggested that he was profiting from these connections.[46] Part of the work at Winchester was the construction of the feretory screen *c*.1315, with its images (now lost) of Anglo-Saxon benefactors of Winchester, and a central Christ and the Virgin. Sufficient traces survive for the original polychromy to be almost entirely reconstructed. The backs of the niches containing the images were painted alternately red and green—a favourite colour scheme of the period—and the trefoils of the canopies above with an opposite red/ green alternation, while the walls behind the canopies were alternately red and blue. The exquisite polychromy of the carved angel at the head of the central niche survives almost intact, including blue wings and a black collar. Further important evidence for the screen's polychromy survives in the continuation of the scheme on the contemporary pier on the south side, now enclosed within the 'vestry' of Fox's chantry chapel. Here there is a large canopied niche with evidence for two smaller niches below, now contained within a 16th-century cupboard. Although the lower niches are now obscured, two damaged canopy-tops, again showing traces of red and green polychromy, testify to their existence. The back of the upper niche, originally red, was limewashed in Fox's time to provide a white background for two carved figures kneeling on shields.[47]

An extremely fine 14th-century painting was discovered when Bishop Fox's tomb was opened in 1820 and, though once again little now survives, a splendid copy was made in 1848 by the 18-year-old Baigent (Fig. 10.8).[48] The painting, on a slab of Purbeck marble, shows the Coronation of the Virgin flanked by a pair of censing angels standing on unusual 'bifid' pedestals; the figure style and ogee cusps of the frame around the Coronation scene point to a date of *c*.1310-20. Presumably the fragment formed part of an altarpiece, and Tristram suggested that it was the frontal of the Lady Altar.[49] This theory is supported by previously unnoticed evidence that the Lady Chapel was remodelled at this period. Although it has been assumed that the eastern bay was entirely rebuilt *c*.1500, various evidence suggests that the fabric is essentially a 14th-century rebuilding of 13th-century work, with the *c*.1500 elements being merely additions. The bays of the crypt

Fig. 10.8   Purbeck slab painted with the Coronation of the Virgin, flanked by censing angels. Watercolour by F. J. Baigent, 1848. *Dean and Chapter of Winchester/John Crook*

beneath the east end of the Lady Chapel are basically 13th-century, with clear evidence of 14th-century remodelling.[50] Externally, the buttresses are of typical 14th-century type with ogee canopies; they are of full height and are not coursed into the walls. Taken together these observations indicate that the *c.*1500 arcading and great windows of the eastern bay were respectively applied to and inserted in the pre-existing fabric. A less plausible alternative is that the panel may have come from the high altar itself—very close to Fox's chantry chapel—even though the cathedral was dedicated not to the Virgin, but to St Peter and St Paul. Thus at Exeter Cathedral in the 1320s SS. Peter and Paul were shown on either side of the Virgin *in frontispicio magni Altaris,* though here the Virgin *was* included in the dedication of both altar and cathedral.[51]

It is indeed extraordinary how much evidence the cathedral provides of medieval altarpieces, since yet another example survives from the 14th century: the so-called 'Lillebon panel'.[52] This wooden panel, painted with the Crucifixion, Virgin and Child, angels, and various saints, probably formed the lid of a portable altar, similar to the late 13th-century example at Newport, Essex.[53] The panel bears the arms of Sir William de Lillebon, of Lilbourne in Wiltshire, who undertook a pilgrimage to Compostela in 1313, which may account for the inclusion of St James among the saints. William himself, and his wife Anastasia, are portrayed as kneeling donors, so the panel must date from before the annulment of their marriage in 1320.[54]

Little or no painting survives in the nave of the cathedral as remodelled by Bishop William of Wykeham in the late 14th century, and doubtless the polychromy was always selectively applied to particular features such as ribs and bosses. Traces of such decoration were found during restoration of the vault of the chapel of Winchester College, founded by Wykeham in 1382,[55] but, as in the college, the most striking colour element in the cathedral nave must have been provided by the stained glass. The college chapel still retains some of its glazing in the 'International Style' of *c.*1400, closely related to contemporary painting in Germany. In this respect it is noteworthy that a payment is recorded for a painter named Herebright to travel between the bishop's palaces of Esher and Farnham in 1393; presumably he is to be identified with the Herebright of Cologne contracted to paint an image in St Paul's Cathedral in 1398.[56] Although it has been speculated that Herebright designed the college windows, there is unfortunately no direct evidence that he ever worked in Winchester.

From the 15th century, the most important surviving polychromy is undoubtedly that of the Great Screen behind the high altar, erected probably in the 1470s during the time of Bishop Waynflete, and with its serried ranks of sculptures completed by *c.*1490. These images were almost all broken at the Reformation, but many impressive fragments still survive with extensive remains of painting. Some have recently been subjected to scientific examination, with azurite, red lead and vermilion among the pigments identified, as well as gilding.[57] Original polychromy also survives on the doorways of the screen, including colour and gilding on the exquisite small-scale sculptures of the Annunciation and Visitation in the spandrels (Fig. 9.17).

One last major scheme of wall painting was to be executed in the cathedral: that in the Lady Chapel, whose eastern bay, as we have seen, was remodelled rather than substantially rebuilt in the years around 1500. The side walls of this bay are painted with a series of miracles of the Virgin, and include a representation of Prior Silkstede (1498-1524) with an inscription recording that he caused these 'polished stones' to be decorated. A dating of *c.*1510-20 is confirmed by details of costume. The paintings have been little studied—and in fact what the visitor now sees is reconstructions on panels placed over the paintings by Tristram in the 1930s—but the remaining parts of the originals are of very high quality (Fig. 10.9).[58] The same applies to the many tiny figures painted in a row about the main scenes on each wall, and set beneath a cornice decorated with gilt metal star attachments. Perhaps the most interesting aspect of these paintings is their close dependence on those in the chapel of Eton College, of *c.*1479-87, and the most important of all surviving late medieval paintings in England. The Eton scheme likewise comprised two registers of Virgin miracles, painted in semi-grisaille; some of the scenes and inscriptions are nearly identical, though in a number of cases the compositions are reversed. The Eton influences are easily explained by its close connections with Winchester; not only was it modelled on Wykeham's Winchester College, but for many years Bishop Waynflete was in charge

Fig. 10.9   Lady Chapel, south wall: detail of the Miracle of Mont-Saint-Michel, showing a mother, miraculously protected by the Virgin from the incoming tide during her labour, with her newborn child. *Conservation of Wall Painting Department, Courtauld Institute of Art*

of the building works there.[59] Whereas the Eton paintings were whitewashed by the college barber at the Reformation, their counterparts at Winchester show actual evidence of iconoclastic damage at the west end of the south wall, where faces and inscriptions have been deliberately scored out.[60]

Italian Renaissance influences are evident in much of the work undertaken in the cathedral by Bishop Fox in the first decades of the 16th century,[61] including sculptured friezes surmounting the presbytery screens,[62] and the mortuary chests, which have been described as 'unique documents of the high quality of early renaissance painted furniture in this country'.[63] It has been argued that these influences are due to an Anglo-French decorative sculpture workshop operating at Winchester,[64] and assumed that the reredos in the Langton Chapel is wholly of this date. This retains its splendid polychromy and gilding largely intact, dating from the time that the chapel was converted to a chantry for Bishop Langton (d.1501), but again close examination suggests that the reredos itself is essentially of much earlier date. Its ogee-headed canopies are of 14th-century type, and their crockets and pinnacles have been carefully cut off for attachment of the purely Renaissance-style cornice now preserved in the Triforium Gallery. The rather similar reredos in the Guardian Angels Chapel—the corresponding chapel to the north of the Lady Chapel—is certainly of late 14th-century date,[65] and it appears that the Perpendicular windows in both chapels are also attributable to this period. In fact, the Langton Chapel reredos may date from slightly earlier in the 14th century, since it is partly covered by the blind arcading of the north wall, which appears to be coeval with the windows. Curiously, the last of the chantry chapels built before the Reformation, that for Bishop Fox himself (d.1528), contains almost no Renaissance elements. But of all the chantry chapels for which the cathedral is so justly celebrated, it retains its original polychromy most completely—the last major scheme of painting before the Reformation.

Notes

1. The cathedral's polychromy has however now been subjected to careful examination in a survey undertaken by the Courtauld Institute's Conservation of Wall Painting Department in April 1992, supported by a grant from the Dean and Chapter; much of the present article is based on the new findings. I am grateful, for many original observations, to Adrian Heritage, Ioanna Kakoulli, Tracy Manning, Silke Mellin, Robyn Pender, Alison Sawdy, Lisa Shekede, Christoph Tinzl and Jun Zheng. Much help was also kindly provided by Peter Bird, Sharon Cather, John Crook and John Hardacre.
2. The Virgin holds a small round object—an orb?—while the Child touches her wrist.
3. E. W. Tristram, *English Wall Painting of the Fourteenth Century* (London, 1955), pp. 266-7. Tristram's watercolour is in the Victoria and Albert Museum; Baigent's is in the cathedral library.
4. A note on the back of Baigent's watercolour identifies the scene as 'Christ calling Peter'.
5. For these alterations, see G. Russell, 'Decorated Tracery in Winchester Cathedral', *BAA Winchester,* pp. 94-100; and for associated tiled floors in the north transept, E. C. Norton, 'The Medieval Tile Pavements of Winchester Cathedral', *BAA Winchester,* pp. 85-7.
6. E.g. at Sutton Benger (Wilts.), see C. Wilson, 'The Neville Screen', *Medieval Art and Architecture at Durham Cathedral,* British Archaeological Association Conference Transactions for 1977 (London, 1980), p. 93; and F. Bond, *The Chancel of English Churches* (Oxford, 1916), pp. 73-83.
7. E. W. Tristram, *English Medieval Wall Painting: The Thirteenth Century,* (Oxford, 1950), pp. 163, 612, suppl. pl. 31a. The letters '**DVS**' survive from an inscription on the capital above, and it has been suggested that St Edward and the Pilgrim were represented (Tristram, unpubl. notes, Courtauld Institute). Other paintings formerly existing in the north transept, of St Christopher and the Adoration of the Magi, were very likely of this date, and Tristram also recorded decorative painting on the western arch of the central chapel in the north aisle. In the Epiphany Chapel, on the west side of the transept, traces of red remain on the lips of one of the carved heads of kings added in the early 14th century.
8. Cf. the painting executed above the main altar of St Albans Abbey, between 1077 and 1093: C. R. Dodwell, *Anglo-Saxon Art: A New Perspective* (Manchester, 1982), p. 227. According to C. A. Hewett, *English Cathedral and Monastic Carpentry* (Chichester, 1985), p. 228, fig. 270, a wooden column with a cushion capital, fixed to the gable of the south transept at Winchester 'was, apparently, disguised with paint and painted ashlar-markings, to resemble part of the masonry', but this column is, in fact, modern.
9. As too on the exterior of the south transept and chapter house, showing that the outside of the cathedral was similarly treated. Reliance solely on white pointing for any decorative effect might seem more appropriate to the austere Cistercians than to the richest see in England, but recent research has shown that the interior of Chartres Cathedral was decorated simply with white masonry pattern (imitating pointing) on an ochre ground; J. Michler, 'La Cathédrale Notre-Dame de Chartres: reconstitution de la polychromie originale de l'intérieur', *Bulletin Monumental* 147 (1989), pp. 177-31.
10. J. Milner, 'An Account of Some Paintings Discovered in Winchester Cathedral', in J. Schnebbelie, *The Antiquaries Museum ...* (London, 1791), pp. 1-3, pl. III.
11. D. Park, 'The Wall Paintings of the Holy Sepulchre Chapel', *BAA Winchester,* pp. 52-3.
12. P. Gélis-Didot and H. Lafillée, *La Peinture Décorative en France du XIe au XVIe Siècle* (Paris, 1889), pl. 29; V. Ruprich-Robert, *L'Architecture Normande* (Paris, 1884-9), p. 225, pls. LVIII,

CLXVI; E. W. Tristram, *English Medieval Wall Painting: The Twelfth Century* (Oxford, 1944), pp. 42, 155; Tristram, *Thirteenth Century,* pp. 162-3, 611-12, pl. 43, suppl. pl. 21b.

13. Tristram, *Thirteenth Century,* pl. 43d, interprets this figure as seated.

14. Tristram, *Thirteenth Century,* p. 612, pl. 43f. Tristram erroneously shows the accompanying ornament as a row of circles rather than continuous scrollwork. Both this arch and the corresponding arch at the entrance to the north presbytery aisle show evidence of attached fittings; might they once have framed sculptures, such as subsidiary roods?

15. F. N. Nisbett, 'Winchester Cathedral', *Winchester Diocesan Chronicle,* July 1909, p. 122; J. Crook, 'King Edgar's Reliquary of St Swithun', *Anglo-Saxon England* 21 (1992), pp. 177-202.

16. See W. G. Constable, 'The Paintings in the Chapel of the Guardian Angels, Winchester', *Connoisseur* 84 (1929), pl. VII, which shows the head intact. Traces of another monk in the arch to the west are recorded by Tristram, *Thirteenth Century,* p. 612.

17. The 13th-century layer was transferred to a new support at the other end of the chapel. For a full account of both schemes, see Park, 'Holy Sepulchre Chapel'.

18. H. M. Colvin (ed.), *The History of the King's Works: The Middle Ages, II* (London, 1963), p. 861.

19. These fragments were transferred to the opposite wall, and the later painting replaced *in situ.*

20. Tristram, *Thirteenth Century,* p. 614, pl. 40c.

21. Park, 'Holy Sepulchre Chapel', p. 42.

22. S. Hluvko, 'Red Pigments in English Medieval Wall Painting', unpubl. diploma dissertation, Courtauld Institute of Art, 1991, p. 27, pls. 20-21. A comprehensive study of the original technique and condition of the chapel's paintings, with some necessary conservation treatment, will be undertaken by the Courtauld Institute in 1992-5, funded by the Skaggs Foundation.

23. BL, Cotton. Nero C.iv, fo. 23; F. Wormald, *The Winchester Psalter* (London, 1973), illus. 26.

24. This alteration, which meant that the censer swung by the angel above was blocked out by the Virgin's head, was evidently found unsatisfactory in the 13th-century repainting, when the composition was adjusted so that the whole of the censer could once more be seen.

25. G. Zarnecki, 'Henry of Blois as a Patron of Sculpture', in S. Macready and F. H. Thompson (eds.), *Art and Patronage in the English Romanesque* (London, 1986), pp. 159-72; see also above, pp. 69-79. Original polychromy survives on a carved head from Henry's rebuilding of Wolvesey Palace (*ibid.,* pl. XLIVa).

26. N. Stratford, forthcoming article in *Medieval Art and Architecture at Rouen* (British Archaeological Association Conference Transactions for 1989).

27. O. Pächt, 'A Cycle of English Frescoes in Spain', *Burlington Magazine* 103 (1961), pp. 166-75; W. Oakeshott, *Sigena: Romanesque Painting in Spain and the Winchester Bible Artists* (London, 1972).

28. Park, 'Holy Sepulchre Chapel', p. 50.

29. Tristram, *Thirteenth Century,* p. 166; C. Tyerman, *England and the Crusades* (Chicago and London, 1988), pp. 93, 98-101. Peter fulfilled his vow six years later, and together with the bishop of Exeter has been described as 'the central figure in the 1227 crusade' (*ibid.,* p. 100).

30. See S. Lloyd, 'King Henry III, the Crusade and the Mediterranean', in M. Jones and M. Vale (eds.), *England and her Neighbours, 1066-1453: Essays in Honour of Pierre Chaplais* (London and Ronceverte, 1989), pp. 102-3, for this and three other Antioch Chambers which Henry ordered to be painted in 1251.

31. V. Jansen, 'Lambeth Palace Chapel, the Temple Choir, and Southern English Gothic Architecture', in W. M. Ormrod (ed.), *England in the Thirteenth Century,* Proceedings of the 1984 Harlaxton Symposium (Grantham, 1985), p. 96; though see p. 97 and note 8 for her comments on the Winchester retrochoir.

32. Tristram, *Thirteenth Century,* pp. 168-71, 615-16, pls. 44-50, suppl. pl. 19. Slight traces also survive of a large subject on the upper part of the south wall of the chapel, perhaps originally showing large angels flanking a central figure, rather than 'painted arcading' as described by Tristram (*ibid.,* p. 615).

33. For the Salisbury paintings, see F. R. Horlbeck, 'The Vault Paintings of Salisbury Cathedral', *Arch. J.* 117 (1960), pp. 116-30, and D. Park, forthcoming article in *Medieval Art and Architecture at Salisbury,* British Archaeological Association Conference Transactions for 1991.

34. R. W. Baker and E. Baker, 'An Account of the Conservation of the Painted Vault in the Chapel of the Guardian Angels, Winchester Cathedral', *Conservator* 1 (1977), p. 21.

35. T. B. James and B. Knight, 'Lead and Lead-Alloy Objects', in T. B. James and A. M. Robinson, *Clarendon Palace: The History and Archaeology of a Medieval Palace and Hunting Lodge near Salisbury, Wiltshire* (London, 1988), p. 226, fig. 85, pl. LIX. The same 13th-century love of attachments is seen in the fine carved female figure (*c.*1230-35) now at the east end of the south retrochoir aisle: 'the carved surface would have been enlivened with metal fittings, the positions of which are indicated by pinholes: a belt at the waist, the end of which hung down at the front to the ground, jewellery at the neck and possibly a metal object held in the left hand': J. Alexander and P. Binski (eds.), *Age of Chivalry: Art in Plantagenet England 1200-1400*, Catalogue, Royal Academy Exhibition (London, 1987), p. 301. Traces of polychromy also survive in the drapery folds of this figure.

36. For previous discussion of the repainting, see Tristram, *Thirteenth Century,* pp. 169-70, 616; and F. R. Horlbeck, 'Decorative Painting in English Medieval Architecture', unpubl. Ph.D. thesis, University of London, 1957, pp. 72-3.

37. See, e.g. P. Binski, *The Painted Chamber at Westminster* (London, 1986), pp. 15-21.

38. Norton, 'Medieval Pavements', pp. 80-84, and below, pp. 167-70. Lengthy descriptions of the painted decoration at the east end are provided by Tristram, *Thirteenth Century,* pp. 169-70, and Horlbeck, 'Decorative Painting', pp. 74-7, both authors assuming that much of it was added in the late 13th century; see also Tristram, *ibid.,* pl. 51, for an attempted reconstruction of the decoration of the dado arcade.

39. See Tristram, *Thirteenth Century,* pp. 161, 169, 445; P. Tudor-Craig and L. Keen, 'A Recently Discovered Purbeck Marble Sculptured Screen and the Shrine of St Swithun', in *BAA Winchester,* p. 65.

40. Tristram, *Thirteenth Century,* pp. 162, 616-17.

41. Copy by T. D. Atkinson, now in the cathedral library. See also Tristram, *Thirteenth Century,* pp. 132, 171, 182, 616.

42. A problematic altarpiece of *c.*1250-60(?), now at Forth Worth, Texas, may possibly be English, but this is very doubtful; see J. Fletcher, 'The Barnabas Altarpiece: a Possible Link with Southern France, St Louis and Cyprus', *Antiq. J.* 64 (1984), pp. 43-52; and C. Norton, D. Park and P. Binski, *Dominican Painting in East Anglia: The Thornham Parva Retable and the Musée de Cluny Frontal* (Woodbridge, 1987), pp. 33 and 57, note 1.

43. L. E. Plahter, E. Skaug and U. Plahter, *Gothic Painted Altar Frontals from the Church of Tingelstad* (Oslo, 1974), pp. 43-61, pl. II. For the Norwegian panel paintings see also A. Lindblom, *La Peinture Gothique en Suède et en Norvège* (Stockholm, 1916), and H. Fett, *Norges Malerkunst i Middelalderen* (Kristiana, 1917).

44. Tristram, *Thirteenth Century,* p. 171, suggests the subjects may have been Virtues and Vices, or 'perhaps drawn from romance', but there is no reason to suppose, simply because of the horses, that this was a secular piece.

45. J. Crook, 'The Typology of Early Medieval Shrines—a Previously Misidentified "Tomb-Shrine" Panel from Winchester Cathedral', *Antiq. J.* 70 (1990), p. 58; for the iconography of St Birinus, see P. A. Newton, *The County of Oxford,* Corpus Vitrearum Medii Aevi, Great Britain, I (London, 1979), p. 80.

46. A. M. Erskine (ed.), *The Accounts of the Fabric of Exeter Cathedral, 1279-1353,* Devon and Cornwall Record Soc., new ser., 24, 26, pt. 1 (1981), p. 131; pt. 2 (1983), pp. xvii-xviii.

47. This painting in the vestry is unpublished; the cupboard appears to be an original fitting of the chapel, though it is regarded as 19th-century by S. Jervis, *Woodwork of Winchester Cathedral* (Winchester, 1976), p. 33. Presumably the feretory screen originally supported the relics of the Anglo-Saxon bishops and kings represented below, which were later transferred to the mortuary chests on the presbytery walls (see John Crook, above, pp. 61-3). A somewhat comparable arrangement existed slightly later at Ely Cathedral, where in the mid-14th century a series of painted figures of Anglo-Saxon benefactors, set beneath canopies, was executed on the north choir wall above arches enclosing their relics; see P. Lindley, 'The Imagery of the Octagon at Ely', *JBAA* 139 (1986), pp. 85-7, pl. XXX.

48. For the discovery of the painting, see Vaughan, *Winchester Cathedral,* pp. 62-3; also Tristram, *Thirteenth Century,* pp. 171, 616, pl. 54.

49. Tristram, *Thirteenth Century,* p. 618.

50. Other evidence of the 13th-century work still survives externally on the north side of the east bay,

comprising two windows (the western one largely destroyed by the insertion of a doorway) resting on a plinth which also carries, at the western corner, two bases of typical Early English character, for applied shafts, now lost.

51. See P. Binski, 'What was the Westminster Retable?', *JBAA* 140 (1987), p. 158 and note 46, though Binski states that the cathedral was dedicated to St Peter alone.

52. A. R. Green, 'Painted Lid of a Reliquary Chest or Altar Chest now Preserved in the North Aisle of the Presbytery, Winchester Cathedral', *HFC Proc.* 10 (1926-30), pp. 220-3; R. N. Quirk, 'Sir William de Lillebon, the Lady Anastasia and their Painted Panel', *WCR* 24 (1955), pp. 17-23. The panel was found in 1861, according to Baigent, in a 'lumber room near the singing school' in the south transept; he describes how 'My attention was called to it not long after its discovery by one of the officials of the cathedral, who informed me that when it was found one of the canons directed him to wash off the dirt with a bucket of water and a brush, that he might see what it was' (quoted by Quirk, *ibid.,* p. 18).

53. *Age of Chivalry,* p. 347. It has alternatively been suggested that the Winchester panel formed the cover of a silver altar frontal donated by Lillebon and broken up *c.*1440-1: Jervis, *Woodwork,* p. 30.

54. The background decoration, of five-dot flower motifs, is similar to that on the windows of the south transept. Traces of polychromy from this period also survive on the effigy of Sir Arnaud de Gaveston, father of Edward II's notorious favourite, Piers Gaveston. Doubtless the choir-stalls were also painted; the carvings of Old and New Testament scenes, at the top of the stall-backs, which were destroyed in 1642, were described as 'beautified with colours', though constructional details suggest these panels may have been secondary. The stalls were repainted at various times after the Middle Ages, and the present gilt lead stars are relatively modern; see Jervis, *Woodwork,* pp. 19-20.

55. J. H. Harvey, 'Winchester College', *JBAA* 28 (1965), pp. 118-9.

56. J. H. Harvey, 'The Wilton Diptych—a Re-examination', *Archaeologia* 92 (1961), p. 11, note 1.

57. See A. Brodrick and J. Darrah, 'A Description of the Polychromy on the Fragments of Limestone Figure-Sculpture from the Great Screen at Winchester Cathedral', *Burlington Magazine* 131 (1989), pp. 615-17; and, for the screen itself, P. Lindley, 'The Great Screen of Winchester Cathedral, I', *ibid.,* pp. 604-15.

58. The paintings were fully drawn by J. Carter, *Specimens of the Ancient Sculpture and Paintings now Remaining in the Kingdom from the Earliest Period to the Reign of Henry VIII,* I (London, 1780-86). The main study remains M. R. James and E. W. Tristram, 'The Wall Paintings in Eton College Chapel and in the Lady Chapel of Winchester Cathedral', *Walpole Society* 17 (1928-9), pp. 1-43.

59. H. M. Colvin (ed.), *The History of the King's Works: The Middle Ages, I* (London, 1963), pp. 279, 287, 290-1.

60. Other paintings possibly associated with Prior Silkstede survive in the chamber above the Guardian Angels Chapel, and on the entrance screen to the Venerable Chapel in the south transept. One wall of the chamber is decorated with stencilled rosettes, and a large wreath-like roundel enclosing a typical Tudor knot device. There are also traces of a brocade(?) pattern on the splay of the south window, and of foliate ornament on the main beam of the ceiling; originally there must have been a painted ceiling above, as part of the overall decoration of the room. Its function is unclear—possibly an office? On the Venerable Chapel screen is the 'ghost' of painted brocade pattern and foliate ornament, probably contemporary with the installation of the canopied seats (bearing Silkstede's initials) in the south-west corner of the transept *c.*1520. However, the painted ceilings of the transepts, sometimes assumed to be Tudor, were designed in 1819 by Dr. Nott, the canon who in the following year was to open Fox's tomb and discover the 14th-century Coronation of the Virgin painting.

61. For the Renaissance in Winchester Cathedral see Martin Biddle's full survey, below, pp. 257-304.

62. These friezes fit uncomfortably on the screens and have a curious tacked-on appearance. Although the vocabulary is Italianate, the syntax—a frieze without a surmounting cornice—is not. Moreover, the blocks of stone are thin, the upper edges and many of the ends unfinished, and the repeated motifs—which vary considerably on the north and south—do not fit the spaces between the piers. Could this be an adaptation similar to that noted below for the reredos of the Langton Chapel?

63. Jervis, *Woodwork,* p. 29. They have, however, been repainted at later dates. Two earlier mortuary chests, one of *c.*1425 (painted with heads, etc.) and the other of *c.*1500 (with inscribed scrolls and foliage), were discovered inside two of Fox's chests in 1874 (*ibid.,* pp. 31-2).

64. A. Blunt, 'L'influence française sur l'architecture et la sculpture décorative en Angleterre pendant la première moitié du XVIᵉ siècle', *Revue de l'Art* 4 (1969), pp. 21-3.

65. It still retains traces of its original polychromy; see P. Lindley, 'Figure-Sculpture at Winchester in the Fifteenth Century: a New Chronology', in D. Williams (ed.), *England in the Fifteenth Century,* Proceedings of the 1986 Harlaxton Symposium (Woodbridge, 1987), p. 165.

ST SWITHUN'S PRIORY IN THE LATER MIDDLE AGES

Joan Greatrex

Introduction and Historical Survey

Winchester Cathedral was in the continuous care of Benedictine monks for almost five centuries. The monastic chapter, which was introduced by Bishop Ethelwold in A.D. 964,[1] and ejected by Henry VIII in 1539, became the model for eight other cathedral monasteries within fifty years of the Norman Conquest.[2] William the Conqueror's choice for the primatial see of Canterbury was the Italian-born Lanfranc, abbot of Caen and a gifted teacher and administrator, who, although unfamiliar with monastic cathedrals, came to accept his new role as both diocesan and abbot. A product as well as a leader of a monastic revival then at its peak on the Continent, he compiled his *Monastic Constitutions* for the Canterbury community in order to institute reforms in liturgy and regular observance.[3] His aim was to re-invigorate English monastic life and restore it to the high standards that had been inspired by the 10th-century reform movement in which Ethelwold and Lanfranc's predecessor, Dunstan, had played a prominent part. These constitutions bore some resemblance to the earlier English customs set forth in the *Regularis Concordia* of the preceding century and, like the latter, were soon adopted by many Benedictine houses, including the cathedral priories of Rochester, Worcester and, probably, also Winchester.[4]

The Conqueror's promotion of Walkelin, a secular canon of Rouen and a royal chaplain, to Winchester in 1070 preceded that of Lanfranc to Canterbury by only a few months, and his arrival at Winchester proved to be a strain both for the new bishop and the cathedral community. Not surprisingly, he was unsympathetic to a monastic chapter and especially to one whose discipline had grown lax; and the monks were on the defensive, if not actually hostile in their reaction to the foreign conqueror and his episcopal nominee. However, after some initial hesitation, relations soon improved; Walkelin's brother, Simeon, a monk of Saint-Ouen, was installed as prior, and mutual toleration and respect ensued. Indeed, Walkelin proved to be a competent administrator, and his ambitious building programme for the cathedral and monastery must have earned the monks' lasting gratitude.[5]

The co-existence of a bishop and a monastic community in charge of the administration of the cathedral church was, with few exceptions, peculiar to the English medieval ecclesiastical scene.[6] The resulting relationship often proved difficult for both parties, owing to conflicting rights and interests which came to the fore during the performance of their separate but at times overlapping spheres of responsibility and jurisdiction. These tensions were not lessened by Lanfranc's instruction that the bishop was to rule as abbot and live among his monks; the two roles were incompatible for several reasons which soon became apparent. Indeed, the frequent and for the most part unsuccessful attempts to disentangle the strands of episcopal authority and jurisdiction from those of the prior and chapter recur as a constant theme through the next four centuries.

For the monks also there was a dual sphere of responsibility, which involved the faithful observance of their Rule and the general supervision, not simply of their own monastery church, but of the mother church of the see to which the bishop by tradition was espoused. St Benedict had instituted for his disciples what he modestly described as a 'school of the Lord's service', that is, a way of life and faith rather than a strict rule regulating every waking hour.[7] The essential components were three: the daily round of liturgical prayer (or *Opus Dei*), reading and study, and manual work, all of which were intended to take place within the monastic enclosure. In the five centuries that had elapsed between St Benedict's death and the Norman Conquest, monasteries had gradually lost their original characteristic of desert-like self-sufficiency, and had, through the acquisition of property by gifts and purchase, become visible participants in urban as well as rural affairs. From time to time certain modifications in the Rule had been introduced which reflected the changing conception of monastic life and the changing attitudes to its function in society, but none of these was regarded as intrinsic or fundamental. Gifts of land, for example, by lay and ecclesiastical patrons and benefactors were seen as an exchange which brought benefits to both parties: the monk recipients were provided with income in cash and kind to sustain their bodily needs and maintain their buildings, and the donors and their families were assured of spiritual blessings both during their lives and after death. Nonetheless, the introduction of monastic chapters at Winchester and other cathedrals, thereby necessitating the monks' constant and increased involvement in diocesan and secular affairs, may seem to us, in retrospect, to be no less than a fundamental contradiction of the Rule. But if so, where did this begin? The fact that the judgement of Ethelwold, Lanfranc and their colleagues differs from ours should furnish an important insight into their perception of the contemporary scene and of the spiritual needs of their time, as well as of their understanding and interpretation of the Rule; and it behoves the historian to strive for a view of the past through the contemporaries' eyes rather than through his own.

The decision to allow the cathedral-based monks to be exposed to worldly pressures and temptations was founded on the belief that the English Church as a whole would be influenced in the direction of much needed reform by means of the monastic example, and would be thereby infused with renewed Christian fervour. Thus, it may be seen as an attempt to extend the monastic reform programme to a wider sphere, where it might serve as a practical remedy for immediate needs. These monastic bishops must have believed that for society at large, whether clerical or lay, reform on the monastic model—the attempt to monasticise the laity, as it were—was an attainable goal. They could not have foreseen that, before the end of the 12th century, Benedictine influence would be on the wane and large numbers of clergy and laity would be looking to other religious orders for spiritual guidance.[8] Nevertheless, it would be a grave mistake to conclude that the remaining three and a half centuries of monastic life in England present a picture of unrelieved decline. The history of St Swithun's during this period, in common with that of the other cathedral priories, reveals a community continuing to fulfil its monastic and capitular duties within the cloister while at the same time still carrying out its required functions in the local community, in the diocese and in the wider realm of church and kingdom. These are the two broad themes on which this account of St Swithun's Priory will be constructed.

In addition, there is good reason to divide the four centuries under consideration into two approximately equal periods based in part on the kind and quantity of historical records at our disposal in each case. For the 12th and 13th centuries we are on the whole dependent on a relatively small number of annals, chronicles, loose deeds and charters; by contrast, in the 14th and 15th centuries there is an abundance of more diversified source materials, including both monastic and episcopal act books or registers, correspondence, financial reports and central government records. But the medieval historian must constantly be aware that his understanding of the past is limited and often distorted, as much by the fortunate and frequently chance survival of some records as by the unfortunate and sometimes wilful destruction of unknown quantities of others.

One early difficulty which troubled the internal life of the cathedral priories was the need to arrive at a mutually satisfactory division of the financial resources of the church or see when the bishop and chapter had ceased to share a common life. At Winchester Walkelin had arranged for a division in which both parties received a half share of the estates, but later he re-acquired some of the property which he had assigned to the monks; their complaints seem to have been fairly restrained as long as the diverted funds were put into the building expense account.[9] William Giffard, Walkelin's successor, also appropriated income from many of the churches belonging to the monks' portion on the strength of his need to meet the expenses of his large episcopal household; but after he had been persuaded, perhaps by a monastic protest march, to restore at least some of them to Prior Ingulph, bishop and monks become such close friends that in his final hours Giffard received the Benedictine habit and died in the monastic infirmary.[10]

The method by which the priors of St Swithun's were chosen in the years before the agreement of 1284 is rarely recorded; most of them would have been appointed by the bishop himself, asserting his right as patron or abbot, and probably after some consultation with the convent, as in 1111, when Giffard named Geoffrey II.[11] These early priors are shadowy figures about whom little is known. Some may have been transferred from other monasteries, as a number of Winchester priors went on to serve as heads of other important Benedictine establishments such as Westminster, Abingdon and Glastonbury.[12] When Prior Robert II was elected abbot of Glastonbury in 1173 he succeeded to the office which had previously been occupied by his former bishop, Henry of Blois, who had held concurrently the see of Winchester and the abbatial dignity.

Bishop Henry's relations with St Swithun's spanned an eventful period of over forty years (1129-71) during which the entire country suffered from a lengthy civil war between his elder brother, King Stephen, and his cousin, Matilda, who claimed the throne as the sole surviving heir of her father, Henry I. His early training as a monk of Cluny in no way hindered his ambitions in the realms of both church and state;[13] but it is the visible remains of his patronage of art and architecture at Winchester which have ensured for him a succession of admirers from his day to our own and which are the subject of other articles in the present volume.[14] The few extant charters concerned with his episcopate reveal that he fulfilled his responsibilities towards his chapter by confirming the priory in the possession of its lands and churches and by confirming and augmenting other sources of income, such as the monks' share of the revenues of St Giles' fair, which were assigned to the maintenance and repair of the cathedral fabric, and of the oblations of clergy and laity throughout the diocese during the week of Pentecost.[15] There is also some evidence of his personal concern for the welfare of the monastic community in his urging the priors to be

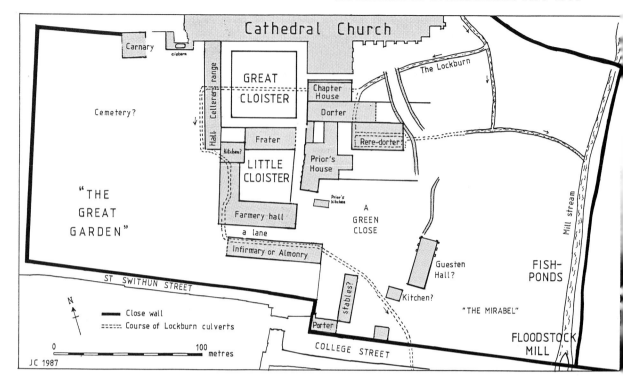

Fig. 11.1   Conjectural plan of the monastic buildings of St Swithun's Priory. *John Crook*

gentle and considerate in their treatment of their monks and in his guaranteeing asylum for
them at Cluny or any of its dependencies should the need arise.[16]

Despite the fact that contemporary chronicles describe most of the episcopal appoint-
ments to Winchester as though they were elections, it may be assumed that there was
usually royal and often papal intervention. Winchester was the one cathedral priory to be
situated in a town that was not only the site of a favoured royal residence but also one of
the centres of royal government under the Norman and Angevin rulers; consequently the
monks probably suffered more than they benefited from the king's frequent presence and
his influence on their affairs.[17] While the king's concern to name one of his trusted officials
and advisers to this, the wealthiest and most important of the medieval sees, seems reasonable in the light of prevailing government policy and practice, it must often have
appeared to the chapter as undue interference. The compromise of 1107 between Henry I
and Archbishop Anselm, in which the king admitted the right of free election by cathedral
chapters, with the proviso that the election must take place in the royal presence in
accordance with custom, guaranteed only the formality. A century later Pope Innocent III's
confirmation to Winchester of all the priory's privileges and possessions and of the chapter's right of free election of bishops did nothing to alter current practice, but it may have
stiffened the monks' resistance. By his reference in this bull to consultation with the
archdeacons as part of the election procedure, the pope may or may not have been aware
that archdeacons were not everywhere considered to be members of monastic as well as
of secular chapters.[18] The archdeacons at Durham, for example, were deprived of their right

to participate in episcopal elections before the end of the 12th century and at Canterbury even earlier; Winchester is the only cathedral priory where they were allowed to continue to exercise this right as late as the 15th century.

When the monks succeeded in holding out against the king, as they did after incurring the royal displeasure by postulating William Ralegh in 1240,[19] they paid a heavy price; and in this case there was a prolonged controversy, which was brought to an end only by papal diplomacy. During the four years of dispute Henry III declared the see vacant, took the priory into his own hands, appointed priors and ordered all the city gates of Winchester to be shut against the bishop-elect.[20] Again, when a contemporary chronicler and monk of St Albans noted that in 1250 the prior and convent were compelled to accept the king's half-brother, Aymer de Valence (or de Lusignan), as their bishop, it is not surprising to find that this proved the beginning of what developed into another prolonged period of intermittent conflict.[21] Part of the disagreement was centred on the forced resignation of the prior, William of Taunton, and the dismissal of obedientiaries, followed by the bishop's appointment of Andrew of London as prior in William's stead; these arbitrary and high-handed actions in their turn were the cause of internal dissension and division within the community for over twenty years. At the same time the constantly shifting fortunes in the king's struggle with the barons increased an already complex situation, as did the bishop's death in exile in 1260. In this vacancy the chapter's vulnerability was exposed by its failure to agree between the two candidates proposed, the votes being divided between the two above-mentioned priors.[22] Papal provision of the next two incumbents of the see may have resolved the episcopal problem, but it only led to a deepening crisis in the monastic community in the course of which the priors and other officials, who continued to be appointed and dismissed by the bishop, appealed to Rome.[23] The papal appointment of 1282 was also preceded by conflict and by a renewed but unsuccessful attempt of the chapter to assert its right of free choice of bishop. At the time of John of Pontoise's arrival in the diocese it is doubtful that any of the monks predicted an era of reconciliation and peace; nevertheless the chapter wrote at once to the bishop to inform him of their problems and financial straits, and he responded by paying them a visit within the week.[24] The resulting composition of 1284 effected a final settlement of the major issues relating to the internal organisation of St Swithun's: henceforth, on receipt of an episcopal licence, the monks were to be free to elect their own prior; the prior, after taking counsel with his brethren, was to have full control over the administration of the convent, and the appointment and dismissal of both monastic and lay officials as well as the admission of clerks to the community were to be decided by the prior and his advisory council. In return the chapter relinquished certain manors, and both sides settled their respective claims with regard to churches, manors, lands, rents, pensions, rights and services, all of which are specified in a series of charters and legal instruments.[25] Their underlying significance in terms of the future relationship between bishop and monks was that the former remained as patron but renounced all his rights as abbot except for that of receiving the profession of monks.

Pontoise's is the earliest extant episcopal register at Winchester and marks the beginning of an almost unbroken series of registers from this time until the Reformation. In addition, from approximately the same period come the earliest annual financial reports of those monk officials of St Swithun's who were required to render accounts, although unfortunately they are few in number compared with those remaining at Norwich and

Worcester.[26] A further source of information is available in the form of manorial records, including both rolls of accounts and of court proceedings of some of the priory estates.[27] When all of these sources have been studied and other relevant information tracked down and examined, there is a sufficient body of evidence with which to reconstruct some of the details of the daily life and organisation of St Swithun's in the two centuries between 1300 and 1500: to this reconstruction we shall now turn.

Internal Organisation and Monastic Routine

A survey of the administrative routine and discipline within any Benedictine establishment, whether it be medieval or more recent, cannot be undertaken without frequent resort to the Rule of the founder. St Benedict himself named only a few of the officials who are to be found holding authority in the later Middle Ages: he appointed a cellarer to be in charge of the general administration of the house, and he prescribed the duties of the guestmaster (or hostiller), infirmarian and kitchener. Lanfranc's *Constitutions* outlined the responsibilities of an additional four—the cantor (or precentor), sacrist, chamberlain and almoner—but fail to make clear whether or not these were innovations brought over from the Continent, as Professor Knowles thought most probable. However, there were precentors at Winchester in Ethelwold's day, one of whom wrote a treatise on music.[28] Thus the English origins of what is often called the 'obedientiary system'—the division of administration into departments or obediences to which monks were assigned 'under obedience'—remains uncertain. To define an obedientiary as one who held an endowed office for which he was required to render an annual account seems unnecessarily restrictive and was probably not the sense in which the monks themselves employed the term; but the gifts of land, which were often allocated by the donors to specific functions, like the feeding or clothing of the monks or the upkeep of the church fabric, must have encouraged the trend towards the separation of endowments. It is clear that Lanfranc still regarded the cellarer as in charge of the entire income, so that the shift from central control to devolution probably took place during the 12th century. Changing economic and feudal conditions also played a part in this transition, as the monk-landlords found it necessary to leave the monastery in order to supervise their large and scattered properties, and they required clerical and lay staff to assist them.

Little has appeared in print about the Winchester obedientiaries and their conventual life since Dean Kitchin's expansive introductory survey in his edition of the obedientiary rolls in 1892. However, within the last fifty years, scholars, like W. A. Pantin and M. D. Knowles and many of their students, have made impressive contributions in the field of English ecclesiastical and monastic studies; and it is now time to revise and re-assess the place of St Swithun's within this newly expanded historical landscape. The dictum that every generation must write its own history is a salutary reminder that the contemporary historian's approach differs from that of his predecessors because his perspectives have changed and, for this reason, so have the questions which he asks of the sources.

The Winchester community numbered over sixty in 1261 at the abortive election of William of Taunton to the bishopric, and the total was again over sixty in 1325. Although few statistics are available for the years immediately following the Black Death, it seems clear that for some unknown reason St Swithun's was not as successful as, for example, Canterbury and Norwich cathedral priories in coming close to a recovery of its former size. At the end of the 14th century Bishop Wykeham reprimanded the chapter because there were only 46 brethren; but for most of the 15th century numbers fluctuated between about

Fig. 11.2   The chapter house arcade. *John Crook*

forty and forty-five. However, despite the foreboding signs which appeared in the last decade before the Dissolution, there were still 45 monks as late as 1532-33.[29] Since there were about eighteen obedientiaries excluding their deputies, of whom there would have been at least seven or eight, as well as a few other positions like those of the prior's chaplain or chaplains and the novice master, it is almost certain that at least half the monks were holding office at any one time.

A conducted tour of St Swithun's at the beginning of the 14th century would have impressed the observant visitor by the complex network of functions performed by a number of separately run departments which, nevertheless, were interconnected and which co-operated at every level in order to ensure the smooth and efficient running of a large house. It will prove helpful to follow Kitchin in dividing these departments into four main groups according to the kind of services with which they were concerned: first, the prior, with his chief advisers and assistants, on whose shoulders the burden of financial and overall respon-sibility lay; secondly, the several obedientiaries whose attention was directed to the church, that is, to the liturgical services and to the building itself and its furnishings; thirdly, the largest group of obedientiaries, whose concern was the financial administration of the house and the provision of food, clothing and other necessities; and finally, those whose assignment was to provide care for all categories of outsiders who came to the monastery.[30]

The prior of a cathedral monastery was constantly reminded of the fact that his was a shared dignity, and at Winchester in the later Middle Ages the balance was heavily weighted on the episcopal side. Pontoise's immediate successor, Henry Woodlock de

Merewell (1304-16), was, however, an exception in that he was a member of the monastic community and the only monk of St Swithun's whose election to the see was approved and confirmed by both king and pope. On at least three later occasions the chapter valiantly tried to promote one of their brethren but had to yield to the pressure of papal mandates and royal commands.[31] One means of enhancing the prior's independence and also of compensating for his lack of abbatial status and consecration was afforded through the papal grant of *pontificalia*, that is, of the right to assume pontifical regalia, including mitre, ring and pastoral staff, and to give first tonsure and confer minor orders. This privilege was obtained by the otherwise unfortunate Prior William of Taunton, who went to Rome in 1254 to present the chapter's case against Bishop Aymer de Valence.[32] More cordial relations between bishop and community in the 1330s led to the former's petition for papal confirmation of this grant on the priory's behalf, a prudent move in the interests of both parties as the bishop was able to add his own request that the prior should refrain from bearing his staff in the episcopal presence.[33]

Despite the prescripts of the Rule the prior, like other religious superiors, had gradually acquired a separate household and staff. At Winchester, a prior's lodging on the site of the present Deanery was probably in existence in the mid-13th century (Fig. 11.3); a recently discovered account roll for the year 1280/1 refers to his chamber, and to his hall, where he entertained the visiting royal justices. Under the heading 'stipends of the *famuli* of the Lord Prior' there is a list of officials and servants which includes his valet and his

Fig. 11.3   The 13th-century porch to the prior's house, and the 15th-century Prior's Hall. Engraving by John Le Keux, after a drawing by Owen Carter (Milner, *Winchester,* 3rd edn. (1839), i, facing p. 33)

armiger.[34] Half a century later the receiver (or treasurer) was paying out at least £40 on the prior's clothing, medicine, gifts and travelling expenses.[35] Some of the supplies for the prior and his hospice, wine and spices for example, were probably purchased by his chaplain, a monk of many functions practical as well as spiritual: he acted as the prior's secretary and keeper of his seal, he distributed gifts and alms on the prior's behalf, and accompanied him on his manorial visits. There is some truth in Dean Kitchin's portrayal of the prior bearing himself as a noble lord, ruling over the large community attached to the cathedral and owner of considerable estates with their tenants and manorial staff; however, this requires qualification.[36] The role of a medieval prelate was defined in terms of lordship by the society of which he was a part; there was no alternative to this model, to which both ecclesiastical and secular authority conformed. The lands and revenues that provided the monasteries with the necessities of life, in the form of income and supplies, had come into their possession as donations 'in free alms' given by their lay owners in exchange for the spiritual services of prayer and intercession on behalf of the benefactors; thus, monks and donors regarded themselves as held, in perpetuity, by a bond of mutual service. In managing their properties the monastic landlords experienced the vicissitudes of success and failure, of wealth and poverty; however, the argument that no monk had any individual possessions and that everything was held in common for the good of the whole community did little to temper periodic accusations of worldliness and self-indulgence or incompetence and malversation. Moreover, before we in our turn assume the judge's role, we need to be reminded that a large number of clerical and lay personnel earned a livelihood in monastic service, either in and around the cloister or on the manors; and in the case of the prior and convent of St Swithun's the evidence reveals that as employers they were just in exacting their dues but also reasonable and even considerate.[37]

Kitchin went on to give a more balanced and discerning appraisal of the prior's responsibilities and routine within the cloister, where he presided at services in the cathedral, at chapter meetings, and at his council of senior monks. In these and other duties he was assisted by several deputies, first of whom was the subprior, followed by a third and sometimes a fourth prior. Although the subprior was the president of the chapter in the prior's absence, at Winchester and at some of the other cathedral priories he rarely emerges from the background. His responsibilities were chiefly concerned with the internal discipline of the house, which included instruction of the brethren and hearing their confessions.[38] His own accounts were not subject to audit, for only small sums were involved, but he had charge of the chest in which the money bequeathed to the priory by Bishop Edington was kept and to which obedientiaries in financial difficulties resorted for a loan.[39]

The group of obedientiaries whose duties centred on the cathedral church, that is, on the daily round of services and on the maintenance and repair of the fabric, were the precentor, sacrist, master of the works (*custos operum*), keeper of the Lady Altar, and the anniversarian. The liturgical chant performed daily at the divine office and at mass was under the direction of the precentor in his role as choirmaster of the community. His, too, was the care of the liturgical books, and of all the other volumes which belonged to the house, in his role as librarian and master of the scriptorium.[40] At all the cathedral priories the sacrist was responsible for the care of the many chapels and altars in the cathedral, and of the equipment and supplies necessary for their maintenance, including vestments, altar linen, lighting, and the sacred vessels and plate. At Ely and Canterbury, however, he was also master of the works; Winchester is unique in having a separate series of account rolls for this charge, for which the manors of Nursling and Millbrook were the major source of income before the Reformation. The two surviving accounts provide details of the constant attention and supervision required by the monk *custos* in a repair and renovation programme which also included the domestic buildings within the enclosure. In addition to his personal servants or *famuli* his workforce comprised many local artisans and craftsmen, several of whom were probably employed on a regular basis.[41] The sacrist was assisted by one or two subsacrists, who were, of course, monks; and in the 16th century there were also three monk *custodes* of the holy relics, as well as a paid servant who guarded the shrine of St Swithun.[42] In addition the sacrist's department included four *servientes in ecclesia*, two watchmen, a launderer (or laundress) and a clock keeper, all of whom received annual stipends. Kitchin's suggestion that the sacrist's dwelling was in the southernmost bay of the south transept at gallery level and directly over his office has received partial confirmation by Professor Kusaba, who locates the sacristy and treasury in the time of Henry of Blois in the three western bays of the south transept.[43] At an unknown date the sacrist was relieved of his responsibility for the Lady Chapel, which had been built originally by Bishop de Lucy as the central section of the eastern extension of the cathedral;[44] the earliest reference to the keeper of this chapel (*custos altaris beate Marie*) is in 1390, when he was named as John Bromle.[45] Another charge which, like that of the care of the Lady Chapel, would have been less demanding than the major offices of precentor and sacrist was that of anniversarian. The latter was required to keep record of the annual commemoration days of the patrons and benefactors of St Swithun's, and on these occasions to make distributions to the poor and give pittances or 'treats' in cash or kind to the brethren. Revenues from the manor of Bishopstone (Wilts.), provided the small income required for these duties, and its supervision was his other main concern.[46]

The third group of obedientiaries was responsible for the domestic economy of the house. This included the financial administration headed by the receivers and treasurers, whose control over income and expenditure was never complete because some of the other obedientiaries had sizeable incomes attached to their offices. These others were occupied with the provision of food supplies for the kitchen, with its adjuncts of granary, bakehouse and brewhouse, of clothing for monks and servants, of bedding for dormitory and infirmary, of table linen, crockery and other utensils for the refectory, of provender and other necessities for the stables and their many occupants. All but five fragments and one complete account of the receiver have perished; but these, along with other evidence, inform us of his regular visits to the manors; and they list his payments of fees and pensions to attorneys and other officials, his expenses in courts of law and negotiations on behalf of the house, and his costly outlays for the prior's requirements and for *marescalcia*, which included horses, riding equipment, waggons and carts.[47] The hordarian, an obedientiary unique to Winchester, seems to have been second in importance in terms of the size of the income under his control. He paid large sums to the monk kitcheners: in 1326/7 it was over £277 at the daily rate of 12s. 4d., a sum which by 1381/2 had been reduced to £190 based on 10s. per day, but the latter rate then remained unchanged for the next century.[48] Thus, the kitchen was dependent on the hordarian, and may not have been an accounting office, apart from the record on the so-called diet rolls, which list only some of the daily purchases, mainly meat and fish.[49] The cooks in the main kitchen of the convent and in the kitchens of the prior and infirmary were hired employees, as were many others like the refectorer's valet and the usher in the monks' dining hall. Regulations for the latter are summarised in a 14th-century roll entitled *Consuetudines in Refectoria.* This interesting document illustrates the complexity of the organisation within one department, for it defines the obligations and the privileges of the prior and other obedientiaries which concern the refectory or frater; the monk gardener, for instance, was to provide specified quantities of apples for the prior and obedientiaries in Advent and Lent, and was himself to receive a specified amount of bread in return.[50]

The cellarer at Winchester was of less importance than he was at other cathedral priories like Worcester because he too, like the kitchener, was subordinate to the hordarian (Fig. 11.4). It appears that the cellarer's responsibilities were similar to those of the subcellarer at Worcester, as both obedientiaries are frequently found visiting the manors to arrange for supplies of grain and stock to be sent to the priory kitchens. The few remaining accounts at Winchester are ascribed to both the curtarian and the cellarer as though the two offices were held by the same monk; the evidence suggests that this was indeed the case and that the curtarian's specific concern was to procure supplies for the prior, from whom he received the exact amounts of money needed to pay for the prior's essential purchases and other related expenses. Thus, we may assume that he was in charge of the prior's hospice, and was therefore the equivalent of the monk at Ely who was known as the *senescallus hospicii domini prioris.*[51] In close association with the cellarer at some religious houses were obedientiaries who were named *bartonarius* and *granetarius* and who, as the terms imply, were concerned with the procurement of cereal crops for the sustenance

Fig. 11.4   Undercroft below the hordarian's hall in the cellarer's range, on the west side of the great cloister. Engraving by John Le Keux, after a drawing by Owen Carter (Milner, *Winchester,* 3rd edn. (1839), ii, facing p. 169)

of the monastic community. There are no references to a granetar and only two to a bartoner at Winchester, one of which suggests a close relationship with the curtarian, to whom he may have been regarded as an assistant; as at Canterbury, he probably supervised the home farm, which for Winchester was at Prior's Barton.[52]

The obedientiaries at Winchester who were known as *custodes espernii* or *custodes depositi,* or simply *depositarii,* have a somewhat uncertain history. The office first appears in 1286, when the prior and convent were required by Bishop Pontoise to appoint an official by this name to take charge of any surplus funds, and to distribute these to the brethren in pittances of food, drink, or small sums of money, treats which had been withdrawn because of a heavy burden of debt.[53] The regular appearance, on the accounts of the major obedientiaries, of small sums paid to the *depositarius* is frequently accompanied by an explanation of the purposes to which they were to be applied. On All Souls' Day, for example, the monks were served *crespe* or cakes; and on other occasions, such as the feasts associated with the singing of the 'Great O' antiphons for Advent, on Christmas Eve, and the anniversaries of former bishops and priors, they enjoyed pittances of wine, spices or other unnamed treats.[54] For this reason the *depositarius* may be regarded as performing the role of the pittancer in other monasteries like Norwich and Ely.

The chamberlain's department was responsible for clothing and bedding for the community, an operation necessitating substantial revenues, which were provided by the manors of West Meon and Ham (Wilts.). Attached to this office was a small group of workers who cut out and stitched the purchased woollen, linen and canvas cloths to make the monastic habits and undergarments, the bedsheets and covers, tablecloths for the frater, and towels for use in the *lavatorium* in the cloister walk and on the periodic shaving and bath days. The Winchester accounts are few and uninformative, but a chapter decision of 1332 introduced the practice of making cash allowances to each monk four times during the year so that he could buy some of the items for himself.[55] The annual payment amounted to 33s. 4d. from this date onwards for the next 150 years, despite Bishop Wykeham's stern injunction of 1387 ordering this practice, and that of pocket money in place of pittances of food and drink, to cease. Indeed, he was obliged to reconsider on both counts and to allow the brethren to continue their 'ancient custom'.[56]

The infirmary was a separate, self-contained establishment within the Close, with its own hall, kitchen and chapel, and some private chambers for elderly, retired members of the community. Contributions of food and wine were sent by some of the other obedientiaries to assist the infirmarian in his catering, but a resident doctor was probably more often the ideal than the reality; the chapter's neglect in this matter resulted in a severe reprimand by Wykeham.[57]

The final group of obedientiaries is distinguished by its preoccupation with those who lived in the world outside the monastic enclosure, that is, with friends and strangers, pilgrims and the poor. The prior and some of the obedientiaries record charitable donations and almsgiving on their accounts; but it was the almoner and the guestmaster, or hostiller, who came into contact with those in need and whose task it was to put into practice the passage in the Rule requiring them to show special attention to poor men and pilgrims, 'because in them is Christ more truly welcomed'.[58] In addition, the almoner was in charge of a hospital, the Sustern Spital, that stood just outside the south gate of St Swithun's. Each of the 15 to 20 needy women who formed the community there received 3½d. per week out of his funds and an extra sum for clothing.[59] He also paid the stipend of the chaplain appointed to minister to their spiritual needs. From his income in 1316/17 almost half went to the hospital and its inmates, and the same was true a century later. At the same time the almoner fed and clothed the young boys who received a rudimentary education in the almonry school, another charitable institution maintained at St Swithun's as at other monasteries. He purchased six robes for them in 1316/17, but since he does not name them in later years their expenses must have been subsumed under a general heading. Bishop Wykeham called upon them to sing every evening in his chantry chapel after his death, and they probably sang regularly in the Lady Chapel.[60] The almoner was also responsible for the annual *mandatum* ceremony, the washing of the feet of 12 poor men on Maundy Thursday;[61] and on the day of a monk's burial he distributed bread to the poor with the request for their prayers for the deceased. Details of the hostiller's routine at St Swithun's are unknown as no accounts survive, but the revenues of the manor of Littleton had been assigned to his office by Henry of Blois, and supplies of grain, stock, poultry and dairy produce were delivered to St Swithun's regularly, as recorded by the manorial reeve on his account.[62] It was the receiver and prior who bore the heavy cost of the entertainment of visiting royal and government officials and ecclesiastical dignitaries, while the hostiller gave his attention to the others, providing food, lodging and other needs as required. The so-called Pilgrims' Hall in the Close (Fig. 11.5) was probably the site of the hostiller's quarters and of the *hospitium* or guesthouse, and not the conjectural location along the west range of the cloister.[63] The offices and dwellings of both the almoner and hostiller were usually situated near the main entrance gate, where they and their assistants were on hand to greet new arrivals without undue disturbance to the *horarium* of the community.

Fig. 11.5   Reconstruction of the Pilgrims' Hall (*c*.1308), thought to be the priory guest-house. The smaller hall to the right probably provided accommodation for the hostiller. *John Crook*

Monastic Training and Scholarship

Young men who sought admission to the monastic community at St Swithun's would have had to prove that they were literate and had received at least elementary instruction in grammar and, preferably, also in musical chant. Further instruction would follow during their first, probationary year, and would continue after their profession at the end of this trial period.[64] The juniors, as they were called before their ordination, are frequently described as *juvenes in scola* on the accounts of obedientiaries who made annual gifts of small sums to each of them for the purchase of their knives at St Giles' Fair.[65] There were, on average, about four juniors at any one time during the last two centuries before the Dissolution, but there are only two 15th-century references to their scholastic programme, one in the early part of the 15th century, which names a priest employed to give them singing lessons, and the other in 1493, which is the appointment of a grammar master.[66] The 16th-century priory registers name a university graduate who not only taught dialectic in the monastery in 1510 but also dispensed medical advice to the sick; clerics are also found teaching grammar in 1528 and 1538, and in the latter year the appointment specified the instruction of the juniors and of the almonry and chapel boys.[67]

Ordination followed, after several years of instruction not only in the scholastic arts but also in the Benedictine Rule and the customs and observances of the house. The precentor had the responsibility of presenting the monk candidates to the bishop to confer the order of subdeacon on those who were at least 18 years old, and deacon's and priest's orders on those who had attained the minimum ages of 19 and 24 respectively.[68] It was usually at this stage that a few of the most intellectually promising monks were sent to study at the university of Oxford in accordance with a decision of the English Black Monks at their General Chapter Meeting in 1277.[69] Prior to this date all the monks had been educated at the claustral school, usually under the direction of monk lectors. Details of the foundation of Gloucester Hall, at Oxford, which was constructed in the 1290s to accommodate the student monks, were copied into the Winchester cartulary;[70] but the earliest known St Swithun's monk to attend Oxford was Philip de Lustehalle, who was there with one or more companions in 1307. By 1312, and very likely before then, one of his fellow students was Nicholas de Heytesbury, who went on to obtain a doctorate in theology by 1323.[71] Brother Nicholas was the first of 14 monk students who are known to have taken degrees, out of a total of about thirty-two identified as having spent some time at Oxford. The pursuit of higher learning at the university was regarded by the Benedictines as the practical measure best designed to enable them to increase their proficiency in the arts of teaching and preaching, and thus to acquire the necessary skills to match the Friars in the instruction of the faithful and the refutation of heretical opinions.[72] A short period of absence from the cloister was deemed sufficient for this purpose and seems to have been the norm, particularly when houses like St Swithun's were at times financially hard pressed. The Winchester monks were, in fact, reprimanded by the Black Monk Chapter on two occasions for their failure to support any scholars at Oxford; and two 14th-century bishops ordered the chapter to select and send two or three suitable monks without delay.[73] However, in later years—that is, from *c.*1352 to 1532—the evidence suggests that the prior and convent were more regular in maintaining their quota of monk students, as two-thirds of the surviving obedientiary accounts for this period record the payment of student pensions; moreover, all but four of the named students fit into these years.[74]

On their return from Oxford the monk students resumed their place within the chapter and, along with the rest of the brethren, they were assigned to the various departments and offices in accordance with the needs of the community. One of the spheres of work, to which only a passing reference has so far been given, lay within the precentor's domain in his capacity as master of the scriptorium and librarian. After the remarkable achievements of the Winchester School which emanated from the 12th-century scriptorium, the records regrettably fall silent;[75] but there can be little doubt that book production continued and that some monks were regularly occupied in writing and copying manuscripts and in book-binding and repair, probably with the assistance of professional scribes as at Norwich and Ely. Several minor historical works of the later Middle Ages are attributed to Winchester monks. Richard of Devizes, for example, wrote a short chronicle of the early exploits of Richard I in the 1190s, and he may also have been part-author of the *Winchester Annals*;[76] Thomas Rudborne's *Historia Major ... Ecclesiæ Wintoniensis* was written in the mid-15th century, and the 15th-century *Liber Historialis et Antiquitatum Domus S. Swithuni* was copied by the monk John of Exeter in 1531.[77] The monastic library would also have been in constant use by those who were studiously inclined as well as by those who were preparing lectures and sermons; and for these purposes the book cupboards would have been well stocked with basic reference works and biblical commentaries as well as works of theology, history, saints' lives and so on. Unfortunately no medieval catalogue survives, and only about sixty volumes have been identified, of which fewer than ten remain in their original home in the cathedral.[78] A few of the Winchester manuscripts contain inscriptions which provide information about monk users and borrowers. John Drayton's name, for example, is in a copy of the *Legenda Aurea* by James de Voragine, which has been dated to the late 13th or early 14th century, and was thus probably produced during Drayton's own lifetime. In the 16th century John Avyngton, B.Th., bought for his use two printed volumes of the works of Duns Scotus which are dated A.D. 1506 and were therefore probably procured while he was at Oxford.[79] The scriptoria and libraries of other cathedral priories like Ely, Norwich and Worcester are better documented than Winchester, and it is therefore necessary to turn to them for details which would help to fill in many of the *lacunæ* in the records of St Swithun's.[80]

Manorial Administration

No account of St Swithun's Priory can disregard the manorial relationship on which the monks were dependent for their material well-being. A full-length study of the administration of the priory estates has yet to be written, although records of several manors like Crondall and Manydown have been printed and a few specialised articles have appeared.[81] A vast quantity of source material awaits the researcher, including a collection of over one thousand five hundred account and court rolls extending over almost three centuries (1261 to 1540), most of which is preserved in the cathedral library. A study of this kind would encompass a wide range of topics and draw on records from some thirty manors; and it would reveal the changes in policy and organisation of the estates as well as furnish details of farming methods, food supplies to the priory, sales of manorial produce, and accounting methods and procedure. It would also need to examine the large body of personnel involved in these functions, from the supervisory officials to the tenants and casual workers. Since much of this is of more interest and relevance to the medieval economic historian or the specialist whose concern is the rural population and rural husbandry, the following paragraphs will be restricted to a survey of the last-named only, that is of the large labour force of men and women who were in many ways as dependent on the monks for their living as the monks were on them for essential supplies and services.

The general policy among the English Black Monks prior to 1200 had been to take little active part in the exploitation of their lands; it appeared to them preferable to avoid both the 'risks of fluctuating income and the responsibilities of direct supervision',[82] and so their estates were farmed out for an annual rent payable in cash or kind. For a number of reasons, changing economic conditions among them, during the 13th century and for most of the 14th and, in some cases, even longer, the St Swithun's monks like their brethren elsewhere became directly involved with the organisation and supervision of their properties. Around 1400 a new trend becomes evident—or, rather, the recurrence of an earlier trend in response to another shift in the economic and social scene—which resulted in the return to leasing, first of the demesne lands and later of entire manors under specified terms and fixed annual payments. It is with these years, namely the late 14th and early 15th centuries, before the manors were finally let out to farm that we will now be concerned, for it was a time when priory officials and manorial staff came into frequent contact, and records are abundant.[83]

There were indeed numerous occasions when the monastic landlords or their representatives made personal contact with their tenants, manorial servants and workers. The prior himself with his personal staff made fairly regular visits to some of the manors, such as Chilbolton and Silkstead, and at times stayed long enough to cause considerable expense entered on the manorial account in both cash and kind. The manors were also used as convenient stopping places for journeying monks and priory officials *en route* to and from London, Oxford and other points while engaged on negotiations on behalf of the house or pursuing university studies. Crondall, for example, was on the route to London, and Hurstbourne to Oxford.[84] Obedientiaries like the almoner and anniversarian and their stewards are often found visiting the manors in their charge to hold courts, receive money payments, and give directions concerning crops and animals; but it was the receiver himself who, usually with a monk companion, did many of the manorial rounds in order to negotiate sales of wool, and later to collect receipts from these sales and from rents and other dues.[85] In this he was adhering to Bishop Wykeham's stern injunction requiring supervisory visits by two monks twice a year; but Wykeham also found it necessary to warn against the danger of personal involvement in commercial transactions during the course of duty.[86] It may be observed that even the most heavenly minded can scarcely emerge unscathed in the conduct of worldly affairs.

The person in charge on most of the St Swithun's manors was, by *c.*1330, either a sergeant/bailiff or a reeve. The former were selected by the prior and his council on the basis of intelligence and ability, and seem to have formed a corps of trusted and reliable officials who could be transferred from one manor to another as need arose. The latter, on the other hand, were resident farm managers, normally of servile status, and were either appointed by the prior or elected by their fellows at the local court. They sometimes performed additional services such as collecting rents, which they might deliver in person to the receiver at Winchester, where they were obliged to appear each Michaelmas at the time of the annual audit. The degree of mobility between these two positions dispels any presupposition that status and custom posed impenetrable barriers, for some reeves became sergeants and sergeants sometimes became reeves; while reeves in some cases became the farmers who are found leasing demesnes in the 15th century. Under the reeve's supervision was a small group of servants (*famuli curiæ*) who performed essential services within the manorial household (i.e., the court) and on the demesne farm. At Wonston, for example, around 1400 there was a staff of six which consisted of two shepherds, an oxherd, two carters (who transported grain to Winchester) and a dairymaid. The prior sometimes ordered for them six 'duddes', or sets of clothing, to reward and encourage their faithful performance. On larger manors like Enford and Crondall the *famuli* also included ploughmen, cowherds, a granger, a hayward and others; and these additions could bring the manorial payroll to fifteen or more. Supporting this nucleus of more or less full-time workers was the much larger group of customary tenants, who served the lord intermittently in return for their rent-free holdings. These *operarii* filled other essential functions as blacksmiths, woodwards, swan keepers and shearers, in addition to their duties at the time of harvesting, when occasional labourers were also hired. It should be remembered that the distinctions between these groups were clearly drawn only by the manorial accountant when recording the payments to different categories of workers and are therefore unreliable evidence for the historian. The ever lengthening lists of works sold in these years, as the *operarii* commuted more and more of their services for cash payments, are an additional warning of the danger in attempting to impose an artificial order on a manorial population that was never static.

Direct administrative links between the priory and the manor were maintained by the frequent supervisory circuits of a centrally located group of clerical and lay officials appointed by the prior and his council. At the head was the steward (*senescallus domini*), who at Winchester seems always to have been a layman, though monk stewards occur at other houses like Canterbury and Ely. He was usually a prominent local man; between 1380 and 1415, for example, there were three who had served as county sheriffs and two of these, Robert atte More and Edward Coudray, were summoned to parliament.[87] The evidence suggests that some of the manorial supervisors formed a more or less permanent nucleus who served St Swithun's for many years, while others were employed for short periods and often for specified duties only. John Greenfield belonged to the former group, as regular payments of his fee appear on many of the accounts of both Hampshire and Wiltshire manors for much of the first half of the 15th century. There are also a number of priory grants to him in these years, and in 1427 he was provided with a corrody for life; this consisted of a daily food allowance and a room in the monastery situated by the monastic drainage stream called the Lockburn and next to the room occupied by the steward.[88] A few like John Mounter are described as *clericus domini* and the purpose of their visits, as entered on the manorial accounts, was expressed in all-inclusive phrases like 'for negotiations', 'for supervision', as well as more precise ones such as 'for inspection of the stock', 'for [oversight of] the shearing', 'for cider-making', to 'arrange leases' or to 'seek a runaway serf'. One clerk occurs at Wonston as having been sent to make up the account, which must have been a regular necessity.

There are only a few fleeting references in this period at Winchester to the prior's council, which, with the auditorial committee of senior monks, operated as the ultimate source of authority in matters relating to the manorial properties, the former functioning in both a juridical and administrative capacity and the latter acting as the financial executive. For these purposes the council included the prior's steward and several of the more senior among the permanent officials like Greenfield, the Mounters,[89] and Thomas Wellys, the bailiff of Barton.[90] There were a number of occasions, however, when other councillors were brought in to give advice on ecclesiastical and political affairs, of local and national concern, in which St Swithun's was involved. Three of these advisers in the early 15th century were John Forest, archdeacon of Surrey and Master of St Cross, Richard Wyot, and Richard Petworth the English humanist; all three were prominent members of Bishop Beaufort's household and were, at the same time, recipients of retaining fees or pensions from the prior and convent.[91]

The Monastic Community and its Neighbours

It is the historian's aim to reconstruct as accurate and complete an account as possible of his particular segment of the past. For St Swithun's in the later Middle Ages this task is beset with difficulty and, as a result, the monks' involvement with and attitude to their neighbours and fellow Christians in the local community and beyond can only be sketched in broad outline. But, first, how do the individual monks' family connections fit into the picture? There were at least fifteen monks from Basing (now part of Basingstoke), six, including Bishop Woodlock, whose native village was Marwell, six whose name shows a Salisbury origin, and five whose families lived in the parish or manor of Enford.[92] It seems clear that most of the community were closely connected to the Hampshire and Wiltshire areas in or near which many of the priory estates were located. There were also at least fifteen whose name indicates a Winchester background, one of these being John le Devenish de Winton, who was a monk in the 1330s and 1340s, when his namesake was mayor of the city.[93] Attention has recently been drawn to evidence of the remains of a Devenish chantry at the altar of the Holy Cross on the north side of the cathedral.[94] By contrast, Ralph Mascal, who held the combined office of curtarian and cellarer in the 1420s, came of unfree parentage; his father was the farmer of the priory manor of Stockton, who was manumitted in 1417, several years after his son's profession and ordination to the priesthood, and he spent his retiring years in the monastery as a corrodian.[95] A further example of this interweaving of relationships is found in Thomas atte Brygge of Basing, brother of Ralph de Basing, who was hordarian between 1379 and 1400 after obtaining a degree at Oxford. Thomas supervised the stock at the priory manor of Woolstone in 1380 and later years, and with his wife was admitted to the monastic confraternity.[96]

In the city of Winchester, among religious houses St Swithun's was the chief, although in size it was probably not greater than Hyde Abbey, the other local Benedictine monastery. There were also four houses of friars—Augustinian, Carmelite, Dominican and Franciscan—which fluctuated in numbers as the occupants were constantly on the move. Although there were some fifty churches in Winchester, it seems that until the 16th century most citizens were buried in the cemetery on the north and west sides of the cathedral.[97] The cathedral priory also held property in the city and soke, including the manor or liberty of Godbegot on the north side of the High Street, and in the 14th century the monks were paying rent for several stalls at St Giles' Fair.[98] Richard Turnaunt, mayor of the city in 1426/7, leased from St Swithun's a fulling mill and adjoining watercourse at nearby Easton;[99] and another mayor, John Gylmyn, was, with his wife and daughter, given a corrody of a daily supply of food from the convent kitchen.[100] The prior and convent had certain obligations to the mayor and citizens, one of which was the burden of repair of Kingsgate and Southgate, first mentioned in 1266, and probably of the city wall in between.[101] Letters of confraternity, as already noted, were the outward expression of a relation of mutual respect and friendship between monks and laity, sometimes resulting from an exchange of gifts or services, spiritual on the part of the former and temporal of the latter. Thomas Beaufort, brother of Bishop Henry Beaufort, was the recipient of one of these letters in February 1416 at the time when Prior Thomas Neville was languishing in the Tower of London, if he had not already died. Despite the prior's 'voluntary resignation' it is likely that his arrest the previous August, at the time of the discovery of the Southampton Plot, was instigated by the bishop on the grounds of alleged complicity with the perpetrators. There had assuredly been no warmth of feeling between the bishop and the unfortunate prior, who was an Oxford graduate, and whose election to the see in 1404 had been thrust aside by the provision of Beaufort.[102] To secure one powerful Beaufort, then earl of Dorset and admiral of the fleet, as a potential ally in case of need was probably regarded by the chapter as a diplomatic move at a vulnerable moment.

Relations with Bishop, and after 1426, Cardinal Beaufort during his lengthy episcopate were, it may be inferred, distant and not without continued strain, as shown by Prior Aulton's almost grovelling petition for the return of the organist and choirmaster who had been seconded to the episcopal chapel at Wolvesey.[103] More amicable relations obtained with later bishops, although they were rarely more intimate, partly on account of the bishops' frequent and prolonged absences when performing their episcopal functions or engaged in the royal service; this situation, however, must have been viewed as some measure of compensation for the chapter's exclusion from any say in the choice of the diocesan. The bishops for their part appointed monks from time to time to a number of posts within the diocese. One of these was that of confessor or penitentiary, for which university monks like Thomas Neville and Robert Westgate were often chosen;[104] another was the responsibility for the spiritualities of the see in the bishop's absence, for which vicars-general were appointed. At Winchester, however, Prior John Merlawe seems to have been the last to have been given this charge, a further indication that Bishop Edington's successors were not on close terms with St Swithun's.[105] Monks also served on various episcopal commissions; William Wroughton D.Th., for example, was Waynflete's commissary appointed to undertake a visitation of Chertsey Abbey.[106] Little informative detail of the proceedings of episcopal and archiepiscopal visitations of the priory in the 15th and early 16th centuries has been preserved, and the few remaining injunctions that might have shed light on the internal state of the house adhere closely to common form. The record of monastic visitations is better documented, although these too may have been for the most part formalities. They were arranged at each of the triennial chapter meetings of the English Benedictines, which were usually held in Northampton and to which each of the Black Monk houses sent delegates. Thomas Neville served as one of the joint presidents, as did his two successors in the priorate, Thomas Shirebourne and William Aulton,[107] and the Winchester chapter regularly participated by sending visitors when requested and by being, in their turn, visited.[108] During his presidency in 1445 Aulton licensed his own subprior, Robert Puryton B.Th., to go on pilgrimage to the shrine of St James at Compostela. In this undertaking Puryton also served as the envoy of Henry VI by offering a gift at the shrine on the king's behalf, and by returning with letters of thanks and of confraternity for the king and queen from the dean and chapter of St James.[109]

Few of the obligations imposed by the royal command on St Swithun's, as on other religious houses, were as agreeable. The monks were called upon to perform a number of onerous duties, one being the supervision of the collection of tenths and subsidies within the archdeaconry of Winchester or the whole diocese; the royal mandates were normally issued through the bishop, and the collectors were required to present a detailed account at the exchequer within a fixed period of time.[110] Whenever members of the royal family were travelling in the region of Winchester, or of the priory manors situated at a distance from the monastery, the purveyors and other members of the royal household descended like predators and scoured the vicinity, eating and appropriating supplies from all the estates within reach, at the expense of many a reeve and sergeant as their accounts record.[111] The king also demanded corrodies for retiring royal officials and servants, and the prior and convent, like other religious communities, constantly reiterated their claim to exemption from this imposition.[112] The prior and chapter were regularly summoned through the bishop to parliament and to the clerical convocation, which were usually held concurrently. On one occasion Prior Neville was one of a number of prelates invited by Richard II to attend a council in order to advise him on the state of the Church during the Schism.[113] William Clement was among the monks sent by the chapter to parliament and convocation as proxy during the 1460s, and the prior attended in person in 1472, accompanied by Brother John Hampton.[114] Parliament met in Winchester on two occasions during the late 14th century at a time of increasing anticlericalism, and the hostility of the London merchants to government policies necessitated the choice of another location. Representatives from the priory would have participated in the deliberations, and in addition the monastery would have been required to accommodate and entertain some of the delegates. One of the latter, in June 1371, was John Wycliffe, who was about to set out on the later stages of his controversial career.[115]

The cathedral itself witnessed a number of royal ceremonies, including the marriage of Henry IV and Joan of Navarre in 1403 and the baptism of Prince Arthur in 1486. These occasions also necessitated heavy expenditures for St Swithun's, which enjoyed no exemption from such duties on religious grounds. The burden of hospitality which was thus thrust upon medieval monasteries by kings and magnates diminished the resources which might have been allocated to the poor and needy. This is one of the many reasons that prevent any estimate of the extent of monastic almsgiving. Another is the fact that gifts were often bestowed in kind and only sometimes entered on the dorse of obedientiary and manorial accounts. In addition, it is impossible to interpret and classify the long lists of 'donations' (*dona et exennia*) recorded by the accountants, for these included small amounts paid to poor clerks, friars, scholars and others, as well as larger sums to lawyers, noble guests and royal officials.[116] Again, it would be unfair to exclude from consideration the frequent distributions of bread and ale among the poor on the day of a monk's funeral and on the yearly *obits* or anniversaries of deceased monks and benefactors; nor should the provisions made to care for the monks' elderly parents and employees be forgotten. Almsgiving and other charitable acts had their source in the spirit and practice of mutual charity among the brethren which the Rule repeatedly stressed. Thus, it would be fairer to conclude that Benedictine charity was selective and discerning than to dismiss it as a mere token gesture.

Signs of Renewal in an Age of Change and Uncertainty

During the late 1520s monks, secular clergy and educated laity went about their accustomed tasks as before, but many must have been aware of an undercurrent of change and increasing uncertainty. Conflicting ideas and views were being circulated and discussed against a background of political tension brought on by the anticlerical attitudes expressed in Parliament and by the king's determination to obtain a divorce. Among these controversial topics were the validity of Protestant beliefs newly arrived from Germany, the application of humanist scholarship to scriptural exegesis, and the publication of several editions of the Bible in English translation.[117] At the same time there was a movement for reform within the Church among some of the Henrician bishops, including Richard Fox of Winchester, who retired from government office and court circles in 1516 in order to devote himself to the care of his flock. His registers show his special concern for the religious men and women of the diocese, whose laxity in discipline he deplored.

It has often been remarked that visitation records from this period reveal the truth of Fox's judgement and the repeated failure to be wholly and unceasingly committed to the monastic ideal. None of this should occasion surprise among those who acknowledge that it has its roots in man's fallen nature, which is still in the throes of being redeemed.[118] Cardinal Wolsey also displayed his zeal in attempting a reform among the religious by summoning the Benedictines to meet him at Westminster in February 1520 to discuss the statutes he had prepared for their consideration. Prior Silkstede sent five of his senior monks, three of whom were Oxford graduates, to this conference, where once again human nature prevailed, as shown by the refusal to admit that any divine inspiration might be hidden in this outside interference in monastic affairs which were quite capable of regulation from within.[119]

In fact, there are some signs of renewal from within at this time. At Norwich, Ely and Worcester there was a slight but noticeable increase in monastic vocations in the early 16th century, and the same may be true at Winchester, although the surviving statistics are insufficient to permit any certainty.[120] In 1495-6 there appear to have been only about thirty-five monks, in 1532-3 numbers had risen to about forty-five, and on the final surrender list in November 1539 there are 33 names.[121] Of these 35, four are described as priests and students at Oxford, an increase in university attendance which has also been noticed among Glastonbury and Coventry monks in the 1530s.[122] While a rise in the number of monastic professions is in itself a persuasive argument for the presence of renewal, there is also some slight evidence of a different kind that seems to reflect a change in attitude towards university studies. At Winchcombe, Abbot Kidderminster presided over a programme of monastic study and scholarship within the cloister which was intended to obviate the need for university centred training; this was a return to an earlier tradition, and almost certainly arose in response to the concern to purify monastic life.[123]

After the first round of monastic visitations, undertaken by the king's commissioners in 1535 and 1536, at which, in the case of Winchester, Thomas Cromwell was present in person, the major houses were forcibly persuaded to co-operate with government policies. At both Worcester and Winchester the priors were subjected to accusations against their character and competence and induced to resign. In March 1536 a protesting Henry Broke was replaced by William Basing, who was certainly not the freely elected choice of the chapter but one of those who had been named in a petition to the king and had found favour with Cromwell.[124] He was one of the many who formed the new breed of churchmen, who supported Tudor policy and prospered in the new ecclesiastical establishment; not surprisingly he was appointed dean of the new foundation in 1541 (Fig. 11.6).

Although there is no lack of evidence for the Dissolution period, the known facts leave much to be explained. The monasteries were abolished by an act of state; their total and immediate compliance, with only a few exceptions, still requires further research and reflection. There is no doubt that there had been a gradual breaking down of community life; individual monks were continuing to live under the same roof and share the same

Fig. 11.6   Henry VIII hands Letters Patent to Dean Kingsmill (formerly Prior Basing), granting estates to the new Dean and Chapter of Winchester Cathedral. Detail from the initial letter of the Letters Patent, dated 1 May 1541. *Dean and Chapter of Winchester/John Crook*

table—although even this observation requires some qualification—but they were no longer sharing daily in the *koinonia* which is fundamental to the monastic life. The gradual accumulation over five centuries of customs and privileges had overlaid the living core of tradition, concealing it from view; radical pruning was required for survival and fresh growth. The perennial problem of finding 'suitable and constructive employment'[125] within the monastery for a diverse range of abilities, and for temperaments which were often restless and sometimes incompatible, required understanding, discernment and patience in guiding and training young aspirants not only in the life of prayer but also in mutual forebearance and support. At the same time the community's relationship with its neighbours in the changing world outside the monastery gate required periodic adjustment so as to preserve and strengthen the vital bond of Christian charity in whatever form it was needed. When the final day came the only visible resistance, with the single exception of the London Charterhouse, was at individual level. Of those who refused to conform, a few of the most prominent lost their lives, and a few went abroad to continue their monastic vocation elsewhere. Among the latter, at least one was a monk of St Swithun's.[126]

Notes

1. Born in Winchester, Ethelwold became a monk at Glastonbury, where St Dunstan was abbot; he was consecrated bishop in 963. For the arrival of monks from Abingdon and for details of his monastic foundation there, see M. Lapidge and M. Winterbottom (eds.), *Wulfstan of Winchester: the Life of St Æthelwold* (Oxford, 1991), pp. xiii-xxxix.
2. See above, p. 21.
3. D. Knowles (ed.), *The Monastic Constitutions of Lanfranc* (London, 1951).
4. T. Symons (ed.), *Regularis Concordia: the Monastic Agreement of the Monks and Nuns of the English Nation* (London, 1953).
5. Walkelin is said to have 'always had monks around him, and whenever he celebrated mass in his chapel at Winchester he chose monks to celebrate with him as his deacon and subdeacon': *Winchester Annals,* p. 39.
6. There are a few continental examples, e.g. Monreale, Sicily; also Downpatrick in Ireland.
7. In this article all references to the Rule are to J. McCann (ed.), *The Rule of Saint Benedict* (London, 1960).
8. I follow Dr. M. J. Franklin's dating here in 'The Bishops of Winchester and the Monastic Revolution', *Anglo-Norman Studies* 12 (1989), p. 47.
9. Goodman, *Chartulary,* item 1.
10. *Winchester Annals,* p. 49. Giffard died in 1129. The march or procession is described as though it were an early example of widdershins (*ibid.,* p. 46).
11. *Ibid.,* p. 43.
12. D. Knowles, C. N. L. Brooke and V. C. M. London (eds.), *Heads of Religious Houses, England and Wales, I, 940-1216* (Cambridge, 1972), *passim.*
13. Cluny was the mother house of a reformed branch of the Benedictines; the earliest English Cluniac priory was established at Lewes in 1077.
14. See pp. 69-79, 80-96.
15. Goodman, *Chartulary,* items 3-7, 10-12, 26, 33.
16. *Ibid.,* item 7, dated to 1171 (M. J. Franklin, *pers. comm.*).
17. Westminster Abbey was probably unique among the large monastic foundations in being constantly affected by the king's proximity and by his frequent use of the chapter house for meetings of the Commons during the 14th century; but it was richly rewarded by royal donations and bequests.
18. The bull is summarised in Goodman, *Chartulary,* item 45.
19. Postulation is the term used to denote the choice of an ecclesiastic who was already a bishop.
20. D. E. Greenway (ed.), *John Le Neve, Fasti Ecclesiæ Anglicanæ 1066-1300, II (Monastic Cathedrals)* (London, 1971), pp. 86-7, and *Winchester Annals,* p. 89.
21. H. R. Luard (ed.), *Matthæi Parisiensis ... Chronica Maiora,* RS 57, 7 vols. (1872-83), v, pp. 179-83.

22. In such cases the pope disallowed both candidates and substituted his own nominee.

23. C. Deedes (ed.), *Registrum Johannis de Pontissara, Episcopi Wintoniensis, A.D. 1282-1304*, Canterbury and York Society (1915-24), p. 647. John of Pontoise was an Englishman, who obtained a doctorate in civil law at Bologna and may have studied at Oxford: A. B. Emden, *Biographical Register of the University of Oxford to A.D. 1500*, 3 vols. (Oxford, 1957-59).

24. *Pontoise's Register*, pp. xxi and 240.

25. *Ibid.*, pp. 425-37. By comparison with some other cathedral priories St Swithun's achieved a greater degree of autonomy in the election of the prior and appointment of obedientiaries. At Worcester the bishop always retained the right to choose the prior from a list of seven nominees elected by the chapter; he also controlled the appointment of the sacrist. At Canterbury the archbishop appointed to several of the obedientiary offices by selecting in each case one of three names presented to him, while at Ely the bishop had complete freedom to appoint to four of the obediences.

26. G. W. Kitchin (ed.), *Compotus Rolls of the Obedientiaries of St. Swithun's Priory*, HRSoc (1892). There are over one thousand account rolls for Norwich and about five hundred for Worcester but only about one hundred and fifteen for Winchester, of which a few, though preserved in the cathedral library, are not in Kitchin's volume; a few others are preserved elsewhere.

27. The earliest surviving manorial accounts are dated in the 1260s and these, too, are not all to be found at Winchester. The accounts of the episcopal lands begin as early as 1208.

28. D. Knowles, *The Monastic Order in England, 940-1216*, 2nd edn. (Cambridge, 1963), p. 432. For Wulfstan the precentor, see Lapidge and Winterbottom, *Wulfstan*, pp. xvi-xvii; for his *De tonorum harmonia* (i.e. *Breviloquium super musicam*) and other writings, see *idem.*, pp. xvi-xvii.

29. These statistics have been compiled from both published and manuscript sources during the course of my research.

30. Although I have adopted Kitchin's four main groupings as an introduction to this section, the many differences in detail are the result of my current research.

31. Two examples of this pressure are found in J. Greatrex (ed.), *The Register of the Common Seal of the Priory of St Swithun, Winchester, 1345-1497*, Hampshire Record Series, 2 (Winchester, 1978), item 76, which is the papal provision of Henry Beaufort in 1404; and item 314, in which Henry VI orders the chapter to elect William Waynflete in 1447.

32. Winchester was the first cathedral priory to obtain this set of privileges for its priors, although the prior of Canterbury had been granted the use of the mitre in 1221.

33. Goodman, *Chartulary*, item 190 (Bishop John Stratford, 1332/3).

34. See J. Crook, 'Winchester Cathedral Deanery', *HFC Proc.* 43 (1987), p. 144; and Dom A. Watkin, 'Fragment of a Thirteenth-Century Receiver's Roll from Winchester Cathedral Priory', *EHR* 61 (1946), pp. 102, 104, 100.

35. Kitchin, *Compotus Rolls*, pp. 234-9: receiver's account for 1334/5. Unfortunately no accounts of the prior have survived at Winchester, unlike Worcester and Canterbury; but it is possible that there were none.

36. *Ibid.*, p. 39.

37. J. Greatrex, 'The Administration of Winchester Cathedral Priory in the Time of Cardinal Beaufort', unpubl. Ph.D. thesis, University of Ottawa, 1973, pp. 243-4. See also *eadem*, 'Manorial Lord and Manorial Tenant in the Fourteenth Century: St Swithun's Cathedral Priory and the Sprot Family of Woolstone', *WCR* 58 (1989), pp. 8-14, and above, pp. 153-6.

38. *Pontoise's Register*, p. 642; the third prior was also assigned these duties.

39. Kitchin, *Compotus Rolls*, pp. 86, 414, 418.

40. For the most prestigious product of the Winchester scriptorium, the Winchester Bible, see above, pp. 80-96.

41. In addition to the two accounts transcribed in Kitchin, *Compotus Rolls*, pp. 209-23, three further fragments in the cathedral library have recently come to light.

42. The one remaining sacrist's account (dated 1536/7) has been transcribed and translated in full in G. W. Kitchin and F. T. Madge (eds.), *Documents relating to the Foundation of the Chapter of Winchester, A.D. 1541-1547*, HRSoc (1889), pp. 19-31. The one reference to the keepers of the relics is to be found in a newly discovered document in the Spanish national archive at Simancas (MS E.593): P. Bogan, 'Dom Thomas Figg and the Foot of St Philip', *WCR* 61 (1992), pp. 22-6. It is probably safe to assume that the subsacrists and relic keepers took the place of the

obedientiaries known as *feretrarii* and *tumbarii* at other monasteries.

43. Y. L. Kusaba, 'The Function, Date and Stylistic Sources of the Treasury of Henry of Blois in the South Transept of Winchester Cathedral', *WCR* 57 (1988), p. 42. For John Crook, however, the sacristy was located in what is now the Morley Library: 'King Edgar's Reliquary of St Swithun', *Anglo-Saxon England* 21 (1992), pp. 177-202.

44. See below, pp. 178-82.

45. Bromle presided at the Martinmas court at Stockton manor, Wilts., in this year (BL, Add. Roll 24349). The only surviving account for this office is dated 1529/30; it is not in Kitchin's edition, and has recently disappeared. Both Worcester and Ely have 14th- and 15th-century accounts for this office.

46. Some of the anniversarian's accounts are headed 'Anniversarian and Warden (*Custos*) of the Manor of Bishopstone'; Kitchin, *Compotus Rolls,* pp. 202, 205. It should be noted that there are two 16th-century accounts which are not included by Kitchin, and in addition there are ten accounts in Worcester Cathedral Library, Class C, Nos. 1, 2, 531-7.

47. The earliest account, unfortunately incomplete, is dated 1280/1 and has been transcribed and edited by Dom Aelred Watkin (see note 34, above). Both 'receiver' and 'treasurer' are used in the accounts, possibly interchangeably; but perhaps, when two were in office simultaneously, the latter may have been assistant to the former.

48. Kitchin, *Compotus Rolls,* pp. 257-303; in the one year (1334/5) when accounts of both hordarian and receiver are available, the former paid out in weekly amounts and for various provisions over £200, while the latter also paid the monk kitcheners over £250 (*ibid.,* 271, 229). The reduced amount paid by the hordarian may be explained by the fact that there were probably over sixty monks before the Black Death (1349/50) and perhaps not more than forty later in the century.

49. *Ibid.,* pp. 306-62.

50. G. W. Kitchin (ed.), *A Consuetudinary of the Fourteenth Century for the Refectory of the House of S. Swithun in Winchester,* HRSoc (1886), pp. 18-19. There is also an incomplete earlier consuetudinary of the almoner, which begins *'Hec sunt consuetudines elemosin[ari]e ecclesie Sancti Petri et Sancti Swithuni, Winth[onie]'* but includes other offices as well; it probably dates from the first half of the 13th century and is now BL, Add. MS 29436, fos. 72v-81.

51. To the two accounts of the curtarian and cellarer transcribed by Kitchin (*Compotus Rolls,* pp. 380-89) must be added three more which have since been returned to the cathedral library. On two occasions in the 14th and 15th centuries there are references to a monk in charge of spices, *speciarius* (BL, Harley 329, fo. 24v and Greatrex, *Common Seal,* item 316); he too would probably have been associated with the cellarer, and the office, like those of hordarian and curtarian, seems to be unique to Winchester.

52. If the bartoner rendered accounts at St Swithun's, these may have been not in cash but in kind. It would have been his task to arrange for the purchase, transport and storage of grain, some of which would have been brought to the new granary built by the receiver within the precincts in 1334/5 (Kitchin, *Compotus Rolls,* p. 230). Goodman's (and Kitchin's) suggestion that the bartoner was in charge of the manor of Barton (Goodman, *Chartulary,* pp. l-li; Kitchin, *Compotus Rolls,* p. 232, note 3) seems reasonable, but it cannot be confirmed. For an account of some aspects of Prior's Barton, see F. R. Goodman, 'The Home Farm of S. Swithun's 1248-1344', *WCR* 8 (1939), pp. 10-13.

53. Goodman, *Chartulary,* p. l and item 111.

54. Kitchin, *Compotus Rolls,* pp. 401, 406, 421, 294, 297; see also Worcester Cathedral Muniments C.531 and 543. The *depositarius* seems also to have been associated with the subprior in overseeing the money deposited in and borrowed from the Edington chest (see above, p. 147).

55. Goodman, *Chartulary,* item 180. Since one of the 'pay days' was the feast of St Giles, the monks were able to take advantage of the fair for some of their purchases. Other cathedral priories were much later in introducing cash allowances for clothing.

56. J. Greatrex, 'A Fourteenth-Century Injunction Book from Winchester', *Bulletin of the Institute of Historical Research* 50 (1977), pp. 242-6. The monks' successful resistance was no doubt related to the fact that the bishop was concerned to have their co-operation in his reconstruction programme for the nave.

57. BL, Harley 328, fo. 5v.

58. McCann, *Rule,* chap. 53.
59. There is a long series of almoner's accounts in Kitchin, *Compotus Rolls,* pp. 389-466; his main source of income was provided by the manor of Hinton Ampner (i.e., Hinton of the Almoner).
60. See below, pp. 247-56.
61. The 12 poor men were fed in the refectory afterwards.
62. Henry of Blois' charter is in Goodman, *Chartulary,* item 3; the Littleton accounts are in WCL.
63. See T. D. Atkinson, 'Winchester Cathedral Close', *HFC Proc.* 15 (1941-43), facing p. 21. See also J. Crook, 'The Pilgrims' Hall, Winchester; Hammerbeams, Base Crucks and Aisle-Derivative Roof Structures', *Archaeologia* 109 (1991), pp. 129-59.
64. This description is based on evidence drawn from Norwich, Canterbury and Worcester as details are lacking at Winchester.
65. As, for example, in Kitchin, *Compotus Rolls,* pp. 287, 294 (hordarian); p. 213 (*custos operum*); pp. 412, 421 (almoner). The knife was an essential piece of equipment for the monk, as well as for other men in this period. It was listed in the Rule among the basic necessities which were to be issued by the abbot (McCann, *Rule,* chap. 55).
66. Greatrex, *Common Seal,* items 236 and 510. In the latter the grammar master was required to teach selected brethren, which presumably included the juniors, and one of his perquisites for good performance was an extra allowance of sugar.
67. LB II, fos. 46v, 123v; LB III, fo. 83v.
68. No lay brothers or *conversi* occur at Winchester after 1300, and few are known before that date. The precentor and monk ordinands sometimes stopped at one of the priory manors on their way to and from an ordination, thus necessitating an entry on the expense account there, for which information we are thankful; see, for example, in WCL, the Whitchurch manorial account for 1336/7 and the Crondall account for 1398/9.
69. W. A. Pantin, *Documents Illustrating the Activities of the General and Provincial Chapters of the English Black Monks, 1215-1540,* 3 vols., Camden Society, 3rd ser., 45 (i), 47 (ii), 54 (iii) (1931-7), i, p. 75. A few monks were sent up before they had received priest's orders.
70. Goodman, *Chartulary,* items 61-66.
71. Heytesbury, under Heghestbury, has been noted by Emden, *Oxford,* who, however, did not know of the entry on the Hurstbourne manorial account for 1312 (MS, WCL); it records that Heytesbury was at Oxford in that year, and indeed he would have had to continue his studies there for eight to ten years in order to have obtained a doctor's degree.
72. Pantin, *Black Monks,* ii, p. 75.
73. Pantin, *Black Monks,* ii, p. 2 and iii, p. 149 record the lack of Winchester monk scholars. The bishops were John Stratford in 1326 (HRO, A1/5, fo. 174) and Adam Orleton in 1338 (HRO, A 1/6, fo. 67).
74. It must be admitted that in this period the accounts cover only 58 years, but it is reasonable to assume, from the 66 per cent survival rate in these years, that there would have been many similar entries on many of the lost rolls.
75. The silence of the records is, of course, in large part due to the loss of the precentor's accounts.
76. See above, notes 5, 10 and 20, and p. 11, note 20.
77. Rudborne's *Historia Major* was printed by Henry Wharton in *Anglia Sacra sive Collectio Historiarum,* 2 vols. (London, 1691), i, pp. 179-286; the *Liber Historialis* is at present being transcribed and edited by John Crook. For an excellent commentary on all of these texts, see A. Gransden, *Historical Writing in England, I, c. 550 to c. 1307* (London, 1974), pp. 247-524; and, *eadem, Historical Writing in England, II, c.1307 to the Sixteenth Century* (London, 1982), pp. 393-8, 493-4.
78. There can be no doubt that St Swithun's library, like those of the other cathedral priories, contained an impressive collection of volumes, nor that they were in regular use, *pace* Dean Kitchin's disquisition on the monks' reluctant approach to reading and study (*Compotus Rolls,* pp. 88-9). In fact, his remarks drew a swift response from one of his contemporaries. Three months after the publication of his volume a column appeared in the Roman Catholic weekly *The Tablet,* 29 October 1892, entitled 'Only one Book a Year'; it sharply criticized him for his 'fanciful description of monastic life' and for the 'blunders and mis-statements with which his papers abound'. These harsh words would not be forthcoming in today's more ecumenical climate, in which Kitchin's mistakes and inadequacies are freely acknowledged, and his contribution to historical scholarship in making primary sources available in print continues to be widely appreciated.

79. The *Legenda Aurea* is now in the Cambridge University Library (Gg.2.18), as also are the volumes of Duns Scotus (Sel. 3.28-29).
80. Some of these details have been provided in J. Greatrex, 'What Can be Said about the Attitude to Learning in the Later Middle Ages?', *Journal of Ecclesiastical History,* forthcoming. As to the location of the library at St Swithun's, there is no evidence to support the traditional view that it was above the east end of the Slype between the south transept and the chapter house, i.e. the present Morley Library; see Crook, 'King Edgar's Reliquary', pp. 177-202.
81. In the Hampshire Record Society series, for example, there are F. J. Baigent (ed.), *A Collection of Records and Documents Relating to the Hundred and Manor of Crondal in the County of Southampton* (1891), and G. W. Kitchin (ed.), *The Manor of Manydown, Hampshire* (1895). J. G. Drew has produced typescript volumes of account and court rolls, in translation, of Chilbolton (2 vols., 1945), Houghton (1943), Michelmersh (1943) and Silkstead (1947), which are deposited in WCL; he also wrote an article on 'The Manorial Accounts of St. Swithun's Priory, Winchester', *EHR* 62 (1947), pp. 20-41, in which he was chiefly concerned with accounting methods and auditing.
82. D. M. Knowles, *The Religious Orders in England,* 3 vols. (Cambridge, 1948-59), i, p. 35.
83. Most of this section is based on my own unpublished research in my Ph.D. thesis (see above, note 37).
84. To cite but two of many examples of travelling monks, Robert Puryton stopped at Crondall on his way to Convocation in 1426 and 1428 (WCL, accounts for those years), and William Rudbourne and Thomas Shirebourne stopped at Hurstbourne in 1391 on their way to Oxford (Hurstbourne account).
85. In the year 1432/3 entries on the accounts of seven manors show that Peter Cranbourne, receiver, was actively engaged in touring the estates.
86. Wykeham's injunctions: BL, Harley 328, fos. 6v-8.
87. More was probably steward from 1394 to 1406, as he appears on a number of manorial account rolls during these years; he was high sheriff in 1393 according to PRO, *Lists and Indexes No. 9, List of Sheriffs for England and Wales* (1898), p. 55, and his summons to Parliament in 1397/8 is noted in PRO, *Parliaments of England, Return of Members of Parliament 1213-1702,* Pt. I (1878), p. 256.
88. Greenfield's leases are in 'Cathedral Records', MS, WCL, iii, fos. 34, 38, and 39; his corrody, which included the grant of *unam cameram situatam iuxta rivilum vocatum Lorteborne,* is calendared in Greatrex, *Common Seal,* item 133.
89. There were two John Mounters, senior and junior, who together served the priory in the years 1377-1422; for their presence on the council, see the Stockton court roll for 1385 (BL, Add. Roll 24342). William Haiward was one who worked on the Wonston account in 1448 and who was employed for only about three years, as his last appearance was at Crondall in 1451.
90. Wellys was also given a corrody for life with lodging assigned in an upstairs room next to the hay barn and a stable for his use underneath (Greatrex, *Common Seal,* item 232).
91. Forest was Beaufort's vicar-general in 1418 (Greatrex, *Common Seal,* item 107 and note 3); Wyot was Beaufort's chief steward (*ibid.,* item 153). Petworth, papal and public notary, was described by the bishop as *scribus noster* (*ibid.,* items 149, 128 and 220 respectively).
92. The surnames of most of the monks designate their place of origin.
93. Goodman, *Chartulary,* item 149. This monk was elected bishop by his brethren in 1345, but the election was set aside by the provision of Edington.
94. Goodman, *Chartulary,* item 265, and B. Carpenter Turner, 'A Forgotten Chantry in the Cathedral', *WCR* 60 (1991), pp. 16-17.
95. Greatrex, *Common Seal,* items 178 and 188.
96. *Ibid.,* item 30.
97. *Winchester Studies 2,* i, pp. 106-8. See also Dom S. F. Hockey (ed.), *The Register of William Edington, Bishop of Winchester 1346-1366,* Hampshire Record Series, 8 (Winchester, 1987), ii, item 201, where a monk was assaulted while performing a burial.
98. See A. W. Goodman, *The Manor of Godbegot* (Winchester, undated, *c.*1923). The rents for the stalls are on the pipe rolls of the bishopric in HRO.
99. Greatrex, *Common Seal,* item 212.
100. Gylmyn, also known as Loke, was mayor in 1429/30 (Greatrex, *Common Seal,* item 177).
101. Goodman, *Chartulary,* item 316 and also W. H. B. Bird (ed.), *The Black Book of Winchester* (Winchester, 1925), pp. 114-15, in which this agreement was copied in the 15th century.

102. The letter is in Greatrex, *Common Seal,* item 173, and Beaufort's letter of thanks follows in item 174; the resignation is *ibid.,* item 158. See also in this connection G. L. Harriss, *Cardinal Beaufort, a Study of Lancastrian Ascendancy and Decline* (Oxford, 1988), p. 81.

103. Greatrex, *Common Seal,* item 236.

104. For Neville, see T. F. Kirby (ed.), *Wykeham's Register,* 2 vols., HRSoc (1896-9), ii, p. 458; for Westgate, see Waynflete's Register, HRO, A 1/13, fo. 41*.

105. Dom S. F. Hockey (ed.), *The Register of William Edington, Bishop of Winchester 1346-1366,* 2 vols. Hampshire Record Series, pp. 7-8 (Winchester, 1986-7), i, item 1227, dated 1360.

106. Wroughton's career is summarised in Emden, *Oxford.*

107. Shirebourne shared the presidency with the abbot of Hyde from 1411-14. The proceedings of the Black Monk Chapters have been transcribed and edited by W. A. Pantin *(Black Monks).* For Shirebourne, see vol. iii, p. 162; for Aulton, *ibid.,* p. 110.

108. In 1426, for example, the prior was appointed to visit the Benedictine monasteries in the diocese of Winchester, while the abbot of Abingdon was to visit St Swithun's: Pantin, *Black Monks,* ii, p. 169.

109. Greatrex, *Common Seal,* item 290.

110. As, for example, in 1371 in Wykeham's Register, HRO, A1/11, fo. 44 (this item is not in the printed edition).

111. The account rolls of Wootton, Whitchurch, and Chilbolton have numerous entries listing these expenses; some of the king's knights and soldiers actually stayed at the manor of Mapledurham for ten weeks in 1417.

112. This demand was based on the royal right as founder and patron. When Henry VI tried to settle one of his retainers in the priory the monks refused, with the reminder that they had obtained exemption from Edward II (PRO, Chancery Miscellanea, C.47/17).

113. This was in January 1399 at Oxford; see under 'Neville' in Emden, *Oxford.*

114. Clement had a degree in canon law (see Emden, *Oxford*); for his attendance at parliament and convocation, see Waynflete's Register, HRO, A 1/13, fos. 78*, 94*v and A 1/14, fo. 142v. For Hampton and the prior at convocation, see *ibid.,* A 1/14, fo. 150v.

115. For further information on the crises of this period, see May McKisack, *The Fourteenth Century, 1307-1399* (Oxford, 1962), chapters xiii-xvi.

116. See, for example, the receiver's account for 1334/5 in Kitchin, *Compotus Rolls,* pp. 238-40, and also some of the items on the hordarian's accounts under 'foreign expenses', *ibid.,* pp. 263, 277, 282, 292.

117. William Tyndale's translation, completed in Worms, reached England in 1526 and that of Miles Coverdale ten years later.

118. As St Paul vividly describes the human condition in Romans 8:22-3.

119. Pantin, *Black Monks,* iii, pp. 117-24.

120. J. Greatrex, 'Some Statistics of Religious Motivation', *Studies in Church History* 15 (1978), pp. 179-86.

121. The hordarian's accounts provide the first two figures, and the third comes from the surrender deed, PRO, E315/494.

122. For Glastonbury, see R. W. Dunning, 'Revival at Glastonbury 1530-39', *Studies in Church History* 14 (1977), pp. 213-22; for Coventry, see P. Heath (ed.), *Bishop Geoffrey Blythe's Visitations,* Staffordshire Record Society, 4th ser., 7 (1973), p. 86.

123. Knowles, *Religious Orders,* iii, pp. 91-3, and W. A. Pantin, 'Abbot Kidderminster and Monastic Studies', *Downside Review* 47 (1929), pp. 200, 206.

124. J. Gairdner (ed.), *Letters and Papers, Foreign and Domestic, Henry VIII,* 10 (1887), items 480, 485, 511 are all concerned with the appointment of Basyng, who offered £500 to Cromwell for a favourable decision.

125. I owe this succinct phrase to Professor A. G. Dickens, *The English Reformation* (London, 1964), p. 54.

126. Thomas Figg, who had entered St Swithun's in 1527/8 at the age of 18; he fled across the Channel at some unknown date and ended his days as a monk of St Andrew's Abbey, Bruges; see note 42, above.

THE MEDIEVAL TILE PAVEMENTS OF WINCHESTER CATHEDRAL

Christopher Norton

Few visitors to our medieval cathedrals, presented as they are with such a wealth of artistic and historical treasures, pause to consider the floor on which they tread, unless it be to examine the brasses and grave slabs which happily survive in such large numbers in this country. And yet in the Middle Ages most of our great cathedral and abbey churches would have contained extensive pavements of brightly-coloured, glazed tiles. Though overlooked by religious reformers, zealots and vandals, they have suffered a no less thorough destruction over the course of the centuries from the constant passage of feet. Consequently, the few pavements which have survived are for the most part to be found in obscure corners, in libraries and muniment rooms, and in other places where they have escaped the wear and tear of daily use. The survival of substantial remains of the 13th-century tile pavement of the retrochoir of Winchester Cathedral is therefore all the more remarkable. Worn and disturbed though it may be, it is nonetheless a monument of international significance. Like stained glass windows, glazed tiles were a characteristic creation of the medieval period, without any precedent in antiquity. And although they were manufactured over much of north-west Europe, there are probably more pavements surviving in this country than in the rest of Europe put together. Certainly, no cathedral in Europe better enables the visitor to appreciate a floor of medieval tiles in their original context than Winchester. Humble and unassuming though they are, these neglected works of art merit a place in any discussion of the splendid treasures preserved at the cathedral.

The retrochoir pavement is not contemporary with the building, but belongs to the later 13th century.[1] Nor was it the first tiled floor in the cathedral. Scattered around the building, in the more disturbed areas of the retrochoir, sporadically through the nave and transepts, as well as loose in store, are numerous other tiles of different dates, some of which belong to the middle decades of the century. Glazed tiles are rare in England before this date, and there is no evidence of any earlier decorated pavements in the cathedral, with the possible exception of a few extremely worn tiles with patterns in relief reset in the south retrochoir aisle (Fig. 12.1, Nos. 1-2). These have generally been assigned to the 13th century, but they are quite unlike any other Hampshire tiles of the period. Broadly comparable relief tiles were used at a number of sites around the country from the late 12th century, while one of the designs may be compared to some relief tiles from the chapter house of St Albans Abbey, dated *c*.1151-66. The Winchester examples could also be early: is it indeed conceivable that they were originally laid in connection with the alterations to the shrine area in the apse of the Romanesque cathedral under Henry of Blois in the 1150s? Bishop Henry at any rate is precisely the kind of patron who would have both known about this new and expensive form of decoration, and been willing to pay for it.[2]

Fig. 12.1   Nos. 1-2: relief tiles, 12th or 13th century (after Knapp, 1956). No. 3: inlaid tile and plain hexagons (Group 1), 1240s. Scale 1:4. *Christopher Norton*

The earliest properly dated tiles belong to the mid-13th century. To the early 1240s can be ascribed a single small square tile identical to fragments from Winchester Castle; they were probably all made south of Winchester at Marwell, an episcopal manor at that time in the hands of the king because of a vacancy in the see. The small rosette design was probably laid in conjunction with hexagonal tiles, of which fragments are known from the castle (Group 1: Fig. 12.1, No. 3). The castle has also produced a second set dating from the early 1250s, identical to other examples in the cathedral. They include a panel of lions and griffins within circles, reset outside the entrance to the Lady Chapel (Group 2: Fig. 12.2). They are said to have been found *in situ* under the early 16th-century stalls in the chapel. These are all inlaid tiles, a technique which had been developed in northern France around 1230 and was widely adopted thereafter; the 1240s group are among the earliest examples in this country.[3] The red body of the tile was stamped with a wooden stamp bearing the pattern in relief, thus leaving an impression in the surface, which was filled with a plastic white clay. After glazing and firing, the finished product presented a white pattern on a red ground—though as a result of the particular clay used and variations in the firing conditions within the kiln, many of the Winchester tiles turned out to have a grey rather than red body. Their inlay is exceptionally deep—up to 5 mm.—and thus unusually durable, and this largely explains the survival of so many tiles at the cathedral.

The techniques and the designs pioneered in the 1240s and 1250s were widely copied in Hampshire, Wiltshire, Dorset and beyond for the rest of the 13th century and into the early fourteenth. Collectively, they constitute what is known as the 'Wessex School' of tiles.

Very similar in design to the lions and griffins of the early 1250s is a small area of *in situ* tiling recently rediscovered in the virgers' office (formerly the choristers' vestry) in the western aisle of the south transept, which was probably originally used as the cathedral treasury (Group 4).[4] However, in order to get some idea of the overall lay-out of the pavements, we need to turn to the retrochoir. The tiles here (Group 4: Figs. 12.3-12.6) were laid *c*.1260-80, by which time the more important parts of the cathedral, including the presbytery and the Lady Chapel, had presumably already been paved. This must have been one of the largest commissions ever undertaken, covering as it did not only the whole of the retrochoir, but also the north presbytery aisle (where the much disturbed remains of the original floor survived until 1969) and presumably the south presbytery aisle (now paved with Purbeck marble slabs perhaps dating from the time of Bishop Fox's work in the early 16th century). From the surviving remains and from earlier records of lost areas, the overall design can be discerned (Fig. 12.5, top). The pavement was divided into rectangular panels running east-west in the centre of the retrochoir, and north-south in the aisles, with a similar arrangement in the north presbytery aisle. Within each panel the tiles could be laid in sets of nine, or four, or singly, divided by thin plain borders, or else in an uninterrupted mass of decorated tiles (Figs. 12.3 and 12.4). Seventeen different patterns were used (Figs. 12.5 and 12.6, Nos. 4-20), though doubtless many of the other designs now scattered around the disturbed areas of the retrochoir also came from this pavement. The patterns are

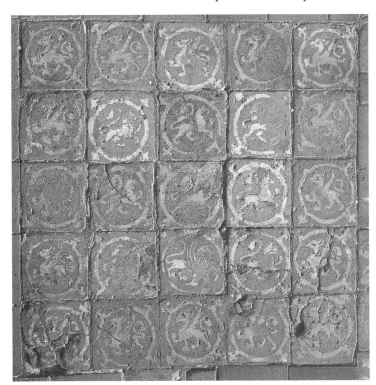

Fig. 12.2 A patch of relaid lions and griffins (Group 2), 1250s, outside the Lady Chapel. *John Crook*

bold and simple, plain even, but they remain legible when laid *en masse* and viewed at a distance. By contrast, the details of many of the more complex, sometimes fussy designs which were more popular later on are lost when set in the floor. Unfortunately the loss of the glaze and the disturbed and dirty condition of the pavement gives it a dull, matt appearance; the rich lustre imparted by the glaze can now be imagined from the excellent replica floor made by Professor Baker for the north presbytery aisle in about 1969. Sadly, the disappearance of the glaze from parts of this floor after less than twenty-five years is a sharp reminder of the wear being inflicted on the medieval originals.

Both the overall lay-out and the individual designs of the retrochoir tiles were copied from the earlier floors of the 1240s and 1250s, as we know them from better preserved examples at other sites; in their turn they were the inspiration for some later groups of Wessex tiles represented at the cathedral (Groups 8-10), including the fragmentary remains of a pavement associated with the refurbishing of the altars in the eastern aisle of the north transept in the early 14th century. Thus between *c*.1240 and *c*.1325 the whole of the eastern arm of the cathedral, including no doubt the choir, was paved by a succession of different tilers all working in very much the same idiom. This consistency of design (or conservatism) is a particular feature of the Wessex tiles—in other areas styles changed

Fig. 12.3   Part of the original retrochoir floor of *c*.1260-80. *John Crook*

much more rapidly—and it must have given an unusual homogeneity to the floors of the cathedral. The only exception were two sets of special tiles which survive in very fragmentary condition at Winchester but which are identical to some much better examples from Chertsey Abbey, near Windsor.[5] They are generally considered the finest medieval tiles in Europe, and were probably associated, directly or indirectly, with royal patronage. They are also some of the very few with figurative scenes and religious figures on them, the latter in particular being generally avoided on the floor, for obvious reasons. The first set, dated to c.1250 and possibly associated with a putative re-ordering of the shrine of St Swithun, includes three splendid roundels (Group 3), each composed of

Fig. 12.4   Detail of part of the original retrochoir floor of c.1260-80. *John Crook*

four pieces (Fig. 12.7, Nos. 26-7). They show combat scenes, one with a mounted knight in armour, another with a trial by combat, the third with a man (perhaps Samson or Richard Cœur de Lion) grappling with a lion with his bare hands.[6] The detail of the pictures is extraordinary, bearing in mind that they are not painted, but made with white clay inlaid into a red body. The second set (Group 5), datable to the 1290s or shortly thereafter, depicts an archbishop standing under an architectural canopy with his hand raised in blessing (Fig. 12.7, No. 28). Their original position within the cathedral is not known.

The later history of the cathedral's pavements is very different. The Wessex school died out, and local production was never more than sporadic thereafter; imports from other areas or even from across the Channel become quite common. Tiling within the cathedral was henceforth episodic. Furthermore, though interesting in themselves as loose fragments, the later tiles have not left us with any significant areas of *in situ* paving. Partly this is a matter of chance; partly it reflects the fact that most of the later products are technically inferior. The designs were now usually made with a liquid white slip poured into an impression on the surface of the tile not more than 1 mm. deep, often much less. Consequently, they were not very durable. Such for instance are some small slip-decorated tiles of the mid-14th century (Group 15) from the tileries at Penn in Buckinghamshire (Fig. 12.6, No. 21). Penn tiles were produced in enormous quantities and have an unusually wide distribution over much of southern England. Their rather cluttered designs contrast markedly with the earlier Wessex products.

Rather better in quality of both design and manufacture are the tiles of Wykeham's chantry chapel, completed before his death in 1404. The pavement is largely intact, though extremely worn, somewhat surprisingly in view of its protected position. There are four designs, including a rose-window motif (Group 16: Fig. 12.6, Nos. 22-25). The other three all show breaks in the wooden stamps used to make the patterns. The identical designs,

Fig. 12.5 *Above:* plan of the retrochoir floor, showing original lay-out. *Below:* Nos. 4-12, nine designs from the original floor (Group 4), *c.*1260-80. Scale 1:4 *Christopher Norton*

Fig. 12.6   Nos. 13-20: eight designs from the original retrochoir floor, (Group 4) *c.*1260-80. No. 21: Penn tile (Group 15), mid-14th century. Nos. 22-5: Otterbourne tiles in the original floor of Wykeham's chantry chapel (Group 16), *c.*1400. Scale 1:4.   *Christopher Norton*

26.

27.

Fig. 12.7.
Nos. 26-7: two roundels from Chertsey Abbey, identical to worn fragments found in the cathedral
(Group 3), *c*.1250. Scale 2:9.

No. 28: tile panel from Chertsey Abbey, identical to fragments found in the cathedral (Group 5), 1290s. Scale 1:4. *Trustees of the British Museum*

28.

Fig. 12.8   Nos. 29-31: Newbury tiles (Group 19), *c.*1410. No. 32: 'Have Mynde' tile (Group 20), mid-15th century. No. 33: Richard Fox tile (Group 24), *c.*1520. Scale 1:4. *Christopher Norton*

but, interestingly enough, with the cracks in the stamps considerably less developed, are preserved at Wykeham's nearby scholastic foundation, Winchester College, where the accounts reveal that they were made by William Tylere of Otterbourne (just south of the city) in 1395-96.[7] William does not seem to have stayed in business very long, however; at any rate in 1411-12 the college purchased tiles from Newbury, and examples of the Newbury group also appear at the cathedral, notably in protected corners of the nave and south transept (Group 19: Fig. 12.8, Nos. 29-31). They were perhaps associated with the completion of the nave after Wykeham's death, but there is nothing to suggest that the nave was tiled throughout, to match the east end: it was surely too vast an area to contemplate.

One reason for the disappearance of local workshops was the flooding of the market from the late 14th century right through until the early 16th with plain glazed tiles, green and yellow, imported from Flanders and the Netherlands. They were utilitarian products of no artistic merit; numerous examples can be seen scattered around the cathedral. Bishop Fox's work on the presbytery aisles *c.*1525 also resulted in the laying of some plain tiles, this time in a distinctive white clay with vivid green or pale yellow glazes. They were probably imported from Normandy, from the lower Seine valley. Patterned tiles, on the other hand, were seldom imported from abroad, and the latest examples in the cathedral are all local products, perhaps specially commissioned in connection with some of Winchester's famous series of episcopal chantry chapels. Some large tiles bearing the inscription 'Have Mynde' (Group 20: Fig. 12.8, No. 32) may have been connected with Waynflete's chapel in the retrochoir, while a single fragment preserved in the Victoria and Albert

Museum bears what appear to be part of the letters **R F** for Richard Fox (Group 24: Fig. 12.8, No. 33); the same initials can be seen carved on his chantry chapel on the south side of the feretory.[8] Finally, some unusually large tiles decorated with foliate designs (Group 25) may be connected with the construction of Bishop Gardiner's chantry chapel. This was the last of the structural additions to the cathedral in the medieval tradition, though its decorative details—if not the tiles—are distinctly Renaissance in character. Gardiner's chapel therefore provides a fitting conclusion to three remarkable centuries of tiling which witness to the continuing concern of the cathedral authorities for the embellishment of their great church, from the vault to the floor.

Notes

1. The main publications on the cathedral tiles are: A. B. Emden, 'The Medieval Tile Pavement in the Retrochoir', *WCR* 17 (1948), pp. 6-12; G. E. C. Knapp, 'The Medieval Tiles of Winchester Cathedral', *WCR* 25 (1956), pp. 16-24; and E. C. Norton, 'The Medieval Tile Pavements of Winchester Cathedral', *BAA Winchester*, pp. 78-93, with full discussion and references to all earlier publications. In the following notes I cite only new references to the cathedral tiles. The Group numbers used here are the same as in my previous article. The drawings used to illustrate this chapter are taken from Winchester tiles, though in some cases, where there are no good examples surviving in the cathedral, I have used identical designs from other sites. The drawings of the Chertsey-type tiles, however, are taken from the British Museum catalogue (see note 5, below), by kind permission of the Trustees of the British Museum.

2. Group 6. For new evidence on the dating of the early relief tiles, see M. Biddle and B. Kjølbye-Biddle, 'England's Premier Abbey: the Medieval Chapter House of St Albans Abbey and its Excavation in 1978', *Expedition* 22 (1980), pp. 17-32; G. Zarnecki, J. Holt and T. Holland (eds.), *English Romanesque Art 1066-1200,* Exhibition Catalogue, Hayward Gallery (London, 1984), p. 392; E. C. Norton, 'Early Cistercian Tile Pavements', in E. C. Norton and W. D. Park (eds.), *Cistercian Art and Architecture in the British Isles* (Cambridge, 1986), pp. 228-55, at pp. 240-4. For mid-12th century work around the apse, see J. Crook, 'Excavating the Holy Hole', *WCR* 58 (1989), pp. 34-42, and above, pp. 59-61. For some glimpses of 12th-century stone and mortar floors in the eastern arm, see *ibid.,* p. 35 and E. S. Eames, 'An Investigation of the Tile Pavement in the North Aisle of the Presbytery, Winchester Cathedral, in 1969', *BAA Winchester,* pp. 73-7.

3. E. C. Norton, 'The Origins of Two-Colour Tiles in France and in England', in D. Deroeux (ed.), *Terres Cuites Architecturales au Moyen Age,* Mémoires de la Commission Départementale d'Histoire et d'Archéologie du Pas-de-Calais, 22.2 (Arras, 1986), pp. 256-93, including discussion of the Winchester tiles.

4. J. Crook, 'The Choristers' Vestry', *WCR* 60 (1991), pp. 44-9. They belong to Group 4, like the retrochoir pavement.

5. Groups 3 and 5. For Chertsey, see E. S. Eames, *Catalogue of Medieval Lead-Glazed Earthenware Tiles in the Department of Medieval and Later Antiquities, British Museum* (London, 1980), pp. 141-71.

6. Note that the extremely worn design 3.4 illustrated in Norton, 'Medieval Pavements', fig. 1, can now be identified as the bottom left-hand quarter of the trial by combat roundel. For the latest ideas on the shrine, see J. Crook, 'The Typology of Early Medieval Shrines—a Previously Misidentified "Tomb-Shrine" Panel from Winchester Cathedral', *Antiq. J.* 70 (1990), pp. 49-64, and above, pp. 57-68.

7. For the college, see E. C. Norton, 'The Medieval Paving Tiles of Winchester College', *HFC Proc.* 31 (1974), pp. 23-42.

8. Now dated 1513-18; see A. Smith, 'The Chantry Chapel of Bishop Fox', *WCR* 57 (1988), pp. 27-32, and P. Lindley, 'The Sculptural Programme of Bishop Fox's Chantry Chapel', *ibid.,* pp. 32-37.

THE DEVELOPMENT OF THE EAST END OF WINCHESTER CATHEDRAL FROM THE 13TH TO THE 16TH CENTURY

Peter Draper and Richard K. Morris

Introduction
Peter Draper

The building history of the east end of Winchester Cathedral provides a fascinating illustration of changing priorities in the liturgical life of the cathedral from the late 11th century to the eve of the Reformation. The successive building campaigns pose several complex archaeological problems but are best understood in relation to the display of the numerous relics housed in the cathedral, particularly those of St Swithun, and to the changing emphasis on the high altar, which remained in almost exactly the same position throughout.[1]

Fig. 13.1   General view of the retrochoir, facing north-west. *Kit Galbraith*

The first major building work to be undertaken following the completion of the Norman church was probably initiated by Bishop Godfrey de Lucy shortly before his death in 1204, and completed by his successor, Peter des Roches (1205-38).[2] The new work, commonly referred to as the retrochoir,[3] extended the church to the east and took the form of a three-bay aisled hall giving access to a two-bay Lady Chapel flanked by rectangular chapels terminating the aisles. Reference to the plans (Figs. 3.1 and 13.2) shows that this arrangement followed very closely the lay-out of the original east end of Walkelin's church, even to maintaining the same size for the respective chapels.[4] As the high altar remained within the Norman apse and there was no change to the space allotted to the liturgical choir, what was gained was a spacious three-bay aisled hall. The motivation for building this eastern extension is undocumented and can only be surmised. The typological association of the architectural form, a hall-like structure at the east end of the church, lies with outer crypts, which were usually built to improve access to shrines.[5] Such an association would also be consistent with the degree of architectural elaboration evident at Winchester, particularly the extensive use of Purbeck marble. There is, however, no unequivocal evidence that the shrine of St Swithun was placed in the retrochoir before the 15th century,[6] and it may be pertinent to note that this space was almost exactly the same size as the liturgical choir and could therefore have accommodated the entire community for the daily Mass of the Virgin.[7] It would also have provided space for a considerable number of pilgrims to congregate when visiting the shrines.[8]

There is, as we shall see, clear archaeological evidence that the retrochoir was originally intended to extend one bay further west to link with the piers on the chord of the Norman apse. However, this bay, which housed the area now known as the feretory, behind the high altar, was not in fact rebuilt until the next period of building, which began in the early 14th century. This campaign included, in addition to the rebuilding of the presbytery, the construction of splendid new choir-stalls and the piecemeal remodelling of the eastern chapels of the transepts. It would be reasonable to expect that the presbytery aisles would have been remodelled at the same time as the presbytery, but this work was not undertaken until the early 16th century, probably because Bishop Edington turned his attention to the west end of the church. His start on the remodelling of the nave was continued by William of Wykeham and work was not resumed on the east end until the latter part of the 15th century with the construction of the Great Screen, which gave greatly enhanced importance to the high altar. The new reredos completely obscured the traditional display of relics in the feretory behind the high altar, and it may be significant that it is at this time that we have the first clear evidence of the shrine of St Swithun being placed in the centre of the retrochoir.[9] It was immediately adjacent to this site that the magnificent chantry chapel of Cardinal Beaufort (d.1447) was built in the place of honour on the south side of the shrine.[10] His successor, Bishop Waynflete (d.1486), then placed his equally impressive chantry on the north side (Fig. 13.1).

The next building work was undertaken by the two succeeding bishops, Peter Courtenay (d.1492), who reconstructed the east bay of the Lady Chapel, and Thomas Langton (d.1501), who remodelled the adjacent south chapel as his chantry chapel. Bishop Fox (d.1528) was responsible for the final phase of work: the remodelling of the upper parts of the presbytery, including the wooden vault, and the belated reconstruction of the presbytery aisles. He chose to be buried in the most prestigious position remaining, the south side of the feretory, which then housed the capitular altar. With the building of the chantry chapel of Bishop Gardiner (1531-51, 1553-55) on the north side of the feretory the east end of the church reached very much the state seen today.

In the light of John Crook's conclusions on the probable position of Swithun's shrine during the 13th century, the precise function (or functions) of the retrochoir remains uncertain. The design of the 13th-century feretory platform implies that at that date the display of the shrines above and behind the high altar was firmly turned westwards towards the monastic community, though the shrines would presumably have been partially visible through the apse arcade to visiting pilgrims gathered in the retrochoir, and the Holy Hole would have provided a means of getting closer to the relics housed on the platform itself. The construction of the screen in the early 14th century shut out the pilgrim even more effectively from the feretory though some of the relics remained visible, prominently displayed in caskets on massive beams around the presbytery. The erection of the spectacular reredos known as the Great Screen placed the focus of the religious community very firmly on the high altar and would have necessitated some reorganisation of the shrines, as these would now have been completely enclosed between the 14th-century screen and the new reredos. It may have been only at this point that the retrochoir took on its role as a feretory to house the shrine of Swithun.

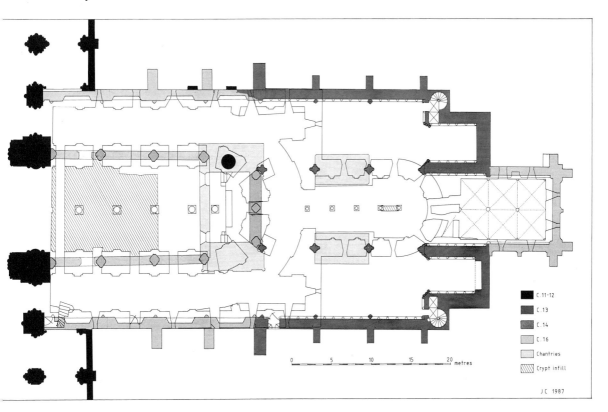

Fig. 13.2 Winchester Cathedral, plan of east arm, showing present structure superimposed on outline of Romanesque crypt. *John Crook*

The Architectural Work of the 13th Century
Peter Draper

Apart from the rebuilding of the east bay of the Lady Chapel in the 15th century, the remodelling of the south chapel by Bishop Langton and the insertion of the magnificent Waynflete and Beaufort chantry chapels, the 13th-century work survives in a fairly complete state,[11] though it does pose several challenging archaeological problems.[12]

In a number of respects the new work was governed by the 11th-century building. The outer walls continue the line of the Norman aisle walls, and the new arcade piers are placed directly over the walls of the former axial chapel, which serve as secure foundations (Fig. 13.2). As a result, the aisles of the retrochoir are nearly as wide as the central vessel, giving the effect of a hall church. The western piers of the arcade were, however, built over the vault of the ambulatory of the Norman crypt, just east of the apse, and so had to be provided with additional supports in the crypt.

The regularity and continuity of the external plinth shows that the new work was laid out in one campaign, and the consistency of the main architectural elements suggests that it was largely carried out to a single design, although there were certainly minor changes to details and at least one substantial break in the sequence of construction. In his magisterial study Willis was the first to observe that the eastern responds of the arcade are not bonded into the walls of the Lady Chapel.[13] He noticed that the bases of these responds have a straight joint with the Lady Chapel wall but that the first shaft rings are continuous with those of the adjacent chapels; from this level the work was going on as one build. From this observation he rightly surmised that the walls had been laid out around the Norman church and brought to a certain height before the Norman axial chapel and ambulatory were demolished in order to provide the foundations for the new arcade.

Work on the retrochoir arcade certainly proceeded from east to west, as is clearly evident from the changes to the design of the piers. The eastern piers follow the east responds in having eight detached Purbeck shafts, the cardinal axes being marked by shafts of substantially larger size. This arrangement is followed in the lower half of the western piers, but above the shaft rings the four subsidiary shafts are coursed with the core of the pier, and this is also true of the west 'responds'. Close examination reveals that the latter were once free-standing piers and that these piers are intentionally asymmetrical. The west face of the pier is angled to follow the line of the present 14th-century arch in order to support an arcade, which was intended to spring from the Norman piers on the chord of the apse.[14] This would have given the retrochoir four bays and would have included within it the shrine area behind the high altar, creating through this canted bay a funnelled effect from the Norman presbytery to the new east end, analogous to the arrangement at Canterbury. This does, however, pose the question as to how the retrochoir was to be related to the three-storey Norman presbytery. It may have been intended that the east bay of the presbytery should have a two-storey elevation with the new clerestory windows at the same level as the Norman clerestory, but with the taller arcade, necessitated by the wider span of this arch, occupying most of the combined height of the arcade and gallery openings of the Norman elevation.[15] But was the retrochoir to continue at the same height? There is no archaeological evidence to support such a hypothesis and the slenderness of the piers in the retrochoir would make it seem unlikely. It may be noted that the buttresses opposite the western 'respond-piers' are much larger and would seem intended to support a high eastern gable, even if the piers beneath do not seem adequate to support a substantial wall.

The central vault of the retrochoir was built slightly higher than the vaults of the aisles but there is no clerestory. There is, however, clear evidence of a change of plan in the construction of this vault, particularly apparent in the confusion of shafts and supports for the vault at the entrance to the Lady Chapel (Fig. 13.3).[16] This is best explained as the result of a decision during construction to raise the height of this vault and to substitute much heavier chamfered ribs for the finer, more elaborate ribs found in the aisles and the Guardian Angels Chapel.[17] This change may be connected with the decision not to rebuild the east bay of the presbytery, which meant that the retrochoir had to be joined to the Norman apse.

Stylistically, the retrochoir is an interesting monument in the emergence of a distinctively English version of Gothic. It has close parallels in the degree of architectural elaboration with the new work under construction at Lincoln, particularly in the use of slender piers and wide arcades,

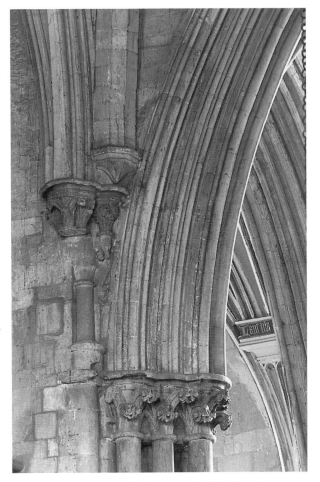

Fig. 13.3   Confusion of shafts on south side of arch at entrance to Lady Chapel. *Peter Draper*

though Winchester lacks the famous idiosyncrasies of the Lincoln design.[18] One of the most striking features of the Winchester retrochoir is the lavish use of Purbeck marble for the bases, shafts and capitals of the arcade piers, for the free-standing shafts in the jambs of the entrances to the chapels and for the small arcade which runs around the outer wall (Fig. 13.4). The pierced foiled motifs in the spandrels of this arcade also have Purbeck marble as a background,[19] and constitute another characteristic elaboration which is used to even more striking effect in the Lady Chapel.

The possible extent of the painted decoration which may once have adorned this part of the church is hard to assess. The north-east chapel, known as the Guardian Angels Chapel, has well preserved decoration,[20] and it is likely that comparable paintings were formerly in all the eastern chapels and perhaps on the central vault as well. Shortly after its completion the retrochoir was also provided with one of the earliest tiled pavements in this country, much of which survives in remarkable condition.[21] Also to be noted in connection with this 13th-century work are fragments of what once must have been a

Fig. 13.4 Wall arcade in north-east corner of retrochoir, facing east. *Peter Draper*

Fig. 13.5 Retrochoir: western respond of north arcade, showing junction with 14th-century presbytery. *Peter Draper*

Purbeck marble screen of considerable quality. The reconstruction of these fragments has been attempted but the precise original location and function of this screen cannot be established with certainty.[22] It is possible that it may have been associated with the feretory platform, which was certainly remodelled during the first half of the 13th century.

The Architectural Work of the 14th Century
Peter Draper and Richard Morris

After *c*.1230 there was no building work of any consequence in this part of the church until the extensive activity in the early 14th century. New choir-stalls were commissioned in 1308;[23] the refurbishment of individual eastern chapels in the transepts was undertaken between *c*.1300 and *c*.1330;[24] the entrances to the crypt were reorganised, perhaps around 1320;[25] but the main campaign, the reconstruction of the presbytery, was probably begun *c*.1310, starting with the rebuilding of the eastern bay. While the amount of work undertaken at this time was quite extensive it seems to have been a series of largely uncoordinated campaigns rather than a coherent building programme.

There are no surviving documents relating to this part of the building so the dating and the sequence of construction can only be established by the analysis of the architectural details and their relation to a wider context. There is, however, a record of a document in a medieval index to documents now missing from the cathedral cartulary in which the mason 'T. of W.' undertook to work on the presbytery at the joint cost of the bishop and the priory.[26] The archival work of John Harvey combined with the meticulous analysis of the moulding profiles have demonstrated sufficiently close links between the Winchester presbytery and the documented work of Thomas of Witney at Exeter to establish beyond doubt the identity of the mason.[27] Thomas is recorded as owning property in Winchester before 1311 and it is probable that this can be related to his involvement with the work at the cathedral. This date in Thomas's career accords well with the likely date for the architectural details on stylistic grounds. The mouldings of the north-east arcade and the east arcade and screen of the presbytery at Winchester show very close correspondences with Witney's work at Exeter, especially the bishop's throne and the pulpitum (designed by 1317) but such as to indicate that the work at Winchester came first. Thomas of Witney took over as master mason at Exeter in 1316 but his documented visit there in 1313 could have provided the opportunity to study the most recent work there at first hand. The design of the two-storey elevation of the Exeter presbytery goes back to the 1290s and the subsequent addition of the balustrade to the choir elevation is datable on documentary evidence to c.1300-10. The marked similarities evident in the design of the two-storey elevation in the two buildings, including the moulding profiles of the pierced balustrade and the clerestory window, and the use at Winchester of two of the three variant designs for the clerestory passage openings found at Exeter, raise further interesting questions about the possible inter-relationship between the work on the two buildings in the early 14th century, given that it would be a little surprising for wealthy Winchester to copy the design of a provincial cathedral.

The archaeological evidence indicates that the eastern bay of the presbytery was built to its full height before work proceeded further west, so the campaign may have been confined initially to the completion of the 13th-century intention to rebuild only the east bay and not the entire Norman presbytery.[28] Work began with the demolition of the Norman apse and the construction of the north-east pier and the arch which finally linked the western pier of the retrochoir with the presbytery (Fig. 13.5). As this arch, and the wall it supports, is much thicker than the 13th-century pier, the eastern screen wall and surmounting arcade had to be built at the same time to support the marked overhang on the inside face.[29] At that stage the 13th- and 14th-century piers would have been separate (Fig. 13.6),[30] as the awkward infilling of re-used Norman masonry was inserted at a later date, possibly when the east gable wall was rebuilt by Bishop Fox.[31] The south-east arch (Fig. 13.7) poses a problem because it is quite unlike the north-east arch and the junction with the 13th-century pier is also arranged quite differently (Fig. 13.8). Alternative explanations have been suggested to account for this anomaly: either that the original arrangement was similar to that on the north but that at some time after construction it showed signs of failure so that the pier was reconstructed and the arch rebuilt to the present design, or that a new team took over during construction and modified the design.

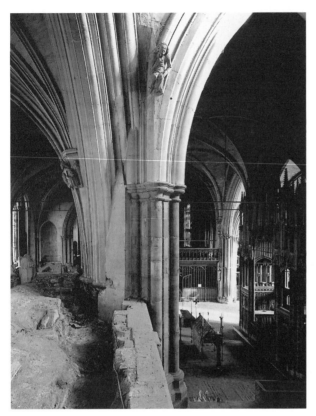

Fig. 13.6 Junction of north-east arch of presbytery and north arch of the arcade supporting the presbytery gable, with infill masonry. *John Crook*

There are strong reasons for thinking that the second is the correct explanation. A vital piece of evidence shows that the south-east pier is original and not subsequently rebuilt. Inside the small chamber behind the altar of the Fox chantry there survives on the south face of the pier a tabernacle clearly of the same date as those on the east side of the screen, though simpler in form. Beneath this complete tabernacle survive the hacked-off remains of the continuation of the cavetto and the projecting cornice mouldings which surmount the eastern screen wall and below that the mutilated remains of another tabernacle. These two tabernacles were designed to mask' the otherwise blank face of this substantial pier. This evidence, which has not hitherto been used in this connection, taken together with the neatness of the junction effected between the south-east bay and the eastern screen, and the absence of any sign of disturbance in the spandrels above the arch, shows that the present pier was part of the original scheme and thus must represent a conscious revision of the arrangement on the north side, possibly to take account of the apparent instability of this part of the building.[32] From this it follows, if we take into account the evidence of the clerestory above this arch (discussed below), that there is good reason to accept as original the mouldings of this arch, too, even though they appear to be later in date than those of the north-east arch.[33]

Analysis of the mouldings of the south-east arch shows that they bear no relationship to those of the north-east and east arcades, nor to work elsewhere which can be reliably assigned to Thomas of Witney. The dramatic change of style (Fig. 13.9a-b) testifies almost certainly to a change of master mason, though the simpler, shallower mouldings may also have been selected to facilitate the awkward assembly of the south-east arch in a confined space and with a redesigned pier system at its east springing.[34] The moulding consists of large waves and shallow hollow chamfers in alternation, each with a delicate roll moulding or bowtell in the centre (Fig. 13.9b), an unusual combination in the Decorated period and thus helpful in narrowing down the field of possible attributions. In the early 14th century the closest parallel is provided by window arches in the transept of of St Thomas's, Winchelsea (complete perhaps by *c.*1312), and related arch profiles are to be found in contemporary Kentish works such as the gatehouse of St Augustine's,

Canterbury. Otherwise the nearest parallels appear in the second quarter of the century, in a series of works in the West Country which have been linked by Harvey with Master William Joy: Wells Cathedral (where he was master mason by 1329), Ottery St Mary (1337 onwards), and St Mary Redcliffe, Bristol.[35] The combinations of miniature waves, hollows and bowtells in the undated south porch of St Mary Redcliffe approximate most closely to the overall design spirit of the Winchester arch, but the reinforcing arches added around the crossing area at Wells after 1338 include bowtells in hollows and a wave moulding identical in size to those at Winchester.

From the evidence of the profiles one can understand why Willis and subsequent authorities judged the south-east arch to be considerably later in date than the others in the presbytery east bay. However, the archaeological re-assessment of the fabric presented here leaves little doubt that the arch is earlier than has been thought, and was probably executed very shortly after Thomas of Witney's departure for Exeter in 1316. At this date the connection with Winchelsea could imply that the new designer was a

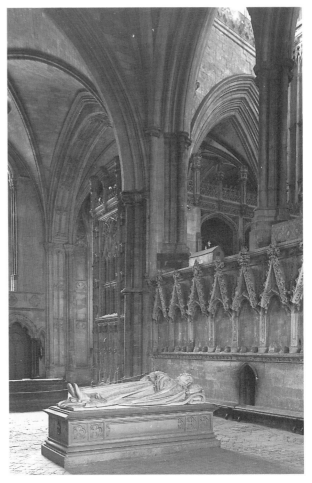

Fig. 13.7   South-east arch from south-east, viewed over feretory screen. *Peter Draper*

Kentish mason rather than William Joy, whose firmly dated works are later. But the case for an attribution to Joy is strengthened by the appearance in the clerestory window directly above the arch of a distinctive deep chamfered profile identical in its geometry to the mullions of Joy's presbytery clerestory at Wells Cathedral. In the south-east window at Winchester this profile survives only in the stubs on the sill, and although it may have been the intention to carve these into a more elaborate mullion shape (the present window tracery and mullions are later, as explained below) the specific geometrical link with Wells remains valid. Moreover, the broader roll and chamfer mullion design introduced by Witney in the north-east clerestory window clearly pre-dates the deep chamfered profile: the former cannot be cut out of the latter because their geometry is quite different. In summary, the south-east arch and some details in the clerestory above are most appropriately assigned to William Joy, and constitute his earliest known work, in a style evidently influenced by the Kentish/Court school of masons.

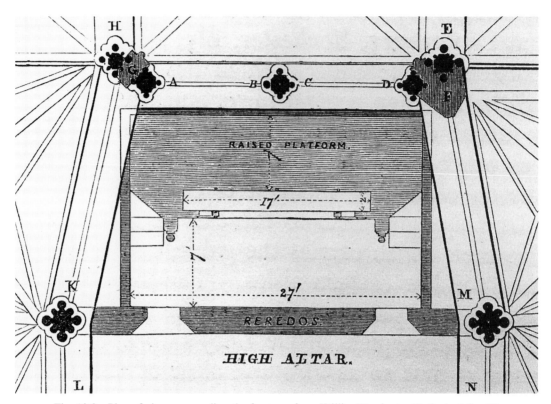

Fig. 13.8   Plan of piers surrounding the feretory, from Willis, *Winchester Cathedral,* fig. 19

The design of the remaining bays of the presbytery was taken largely from the south-east bay.[36] The piers, bases and capitals of the presbytery arcades are all fairly conventional productions of the Purbeck marblers, and thus provide little help with date or attribution. Only the surviving west respond base of the north arcade (its southern equivalent is mutilated), with the bell base mouldings cut in freestone, is suggestive of a date in the second quarter of the 14th century.[37] It can be related to a group of early bell base designs found at Wells Cathedral and other churches where William Joy worked, and the specific detail of the double bell effect is repeated in the nave south arcade of St Mary Redcliffe.

Much more rewarding for the purpose of attribution is the profile of the arcade arches, which is a modification of the south-east arch, as previous authorities have observed. However, the drawings published by Willis fail to bring out clearly the major difference,[38] namely that in the south-east arch what was actually a continuous wave moulding (with bowtell) has been transformed into a double ogee moulding (interrupted by a bowtell) in the main arcade arch (Fig. 13.9c). Another interesting aspect of the latter is that the double ogee is asymmetrical in the dimensions of the two parts. A similar combination of these unusual features occurs at Salisbury Cathedral, in the strainer arches of the east transept and in various flying buttresses added about 1330 to correct movement in the new crossing tower.[39] These additions can be dated by their close association with the tomb of Bishop Mortival (d.1329) and, significantly, some of the other mouldings they employ connect them to the style of William Joy at Exeter Cathedral (west porches),

Fig. 13.9   Moulding profiles,
Winchester Cathedral
presbytery arcades.
(a) East bay, north-east arch;
(b) East bay, south-east arch;
(c) Main arch type, bays 2-4
(drawn on the south arcade,
bay 4). *Richard Morris*

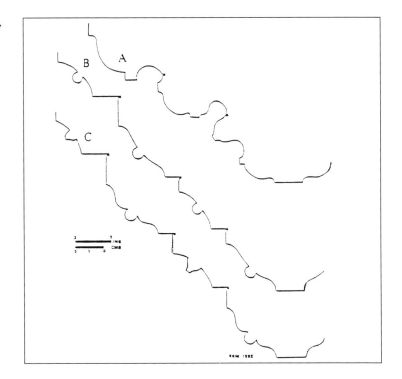

St Mary Redcliffe, and Wells. Indeed, combinations of ogees and bowtells of comparable
scale to those at Winchester are also found in Wells in work of Joy's period in the choir and
in the arcade arches around the crossing.

Thus the evidence suggests that William Joy designed the presbytery arcades, rework-
ing his earlier mouldings for the south-east arch into a profile more typical of his later work.
He is also likely, therefore, to have supervised the rebuilding of the presbytery as a whole to
completion as a shell with a wooden roof,[40] even though there is very little in the clerestory
level which can be specifically linked with him. The deep chamfered profile from Wells
continued to be employed at sill level for a while, but otherwise the mouldings of the window
frames and rere-arches are closely based on those established by Witney. As to the date when
the presbytery was rebuilt, the mouldings in themselves cannot produce a definitive answer,
but some clues may be gleaned from a reconstruction of William Joy's career, for which the
mouldings have provided vital information. Documentary evidence suggests that Joy would
have been preoccupied with the Wells presbytery shortly after 1326, probably with the Wells
crossing arches after 1338, and was busy at Exeter by 1345-46. On these assumptions among
others, the most likely periods for the Winchester work would be either in the early 1320s,
shortly after his appearance in the east presbytery bay, or in the early to mid 1330s.[41]
Stylistically, the presumption is slightly in favour of the latter, but one cannot be certain.
Either date would be appreciably earlier than the mid 14th-century date favoured by Willis,
who associated the design of the clerestory windows with the work of Bishop Edington at the
west end of the nave.

It might be thought that a protracted building campaign would not have been tolerated
by the monastic community in this important part of the church, and it would seem equally

unlikely that work would begin on the west end of the church unless the presbytery was fully operational. However, apart from the evidence of the mouldings there are other indications that the presbytery campaign was indeed protracted. Careful examination of the stonework in the clerestory reveals evidence of careless setting out (so that the alignment of the clerestory wall had to be corrected during construction), of poor workmanship, and a number of minor changes, all of which indicate that the sequence of building was not altogether orderly. It is also curious that the aisles were not remodelled when the presbytery arcade was built. Willis assumed that the Norman aisles survived intact until the early 16th century, suggesting that there must have been some arrangement similar to that to be found at St Albans, where the Norman aisles survive up against the 13th-century elevation of the choir. This hypothesis, however, cannot be sustained. The presbytery piers must have been built complete, and their

Fig. 13.10   External and internal elevations of the presbytery, showing window tracery (Britton, *Winchester Cathedral,* pl. XXVIII)

placement in relation to the alignment of the Norman piers, with the changed size of the bay divisions, makes it impossible for the Norman aisle vaults to have remained. The Norman outer aisle walls were, however, retained and a temporary wooden roof must have been erected over the aisles when attention was diverted to the nave.[42]

Finally, there is one architectural feature of the presbytery which is not compatible with a date as early as the 1330s: the tracery of the clerestory windows (Fig. 13.10). The east window was certainly remodelled by Bishop Fox and, as we have seen, the tracery of the north and south windows of the east bay is not original and has been changed to bring it into conformity with the other clerestory windows. But when were these built? Neither the moulding profiles of the window jambs and the mullions nor the pattern of the tracery provides a definitive answer. Certain elements in the geometry of the mouldings are current from the 1330s but not the precise configuration found in these windows, which is unlikely to be earlier than c.1380. By that date it occurs in buildings associated with the patronage of William of Wykeham. If the windows had been completed in the 1330s it would mean that the jambs of the windows have been either recut or replaced. It is hard to accept that this would have happened within fifty years.[43]

Any date for the presbytery clerestory after the mid-14th century raises the question of its relation to the work of Edington and Wykeham in the nave. In fact, these windows are not at all similar to any of those in the nave, nor are they like the presbytery aisle windows built by Bishop Fox: they seem to belong to a completely separate campaign. In general terms the design of the tracery can be seen to be of a type which became fashionable in the late 14th century with works like New College, Oxford, but as it remained popular through the 15th century it cannot be used to provide a secure date. The most obvious possible explanations are: that the presbytery campaign was indeed very protracted, perhaps interrupted by the Black Death, and was only finally completed around 1380; or that the presbytery was completed in the 1330s and that the clerestory was subsequently remodelled in the later 15th century when the Great Screen was built;[44] or that the clerestory was remodelled by Bishop Fox when the east window was replaced and the present wooden vault inserted. At the present stage of research it is not possible to come to a definitive conclusion and this tricky question will have to remain open.

The final stages in the remodelling of the east end of the church were undertaken by Bishop Fox. He certainly rebuilt the east gable, adding the octagonal turrets, and the appearance of his heraldry on the wooden vault leaves little doubt that he was responsible for this. He rebuilt and vaulted the presbytery aisles, taking full advantage of the light flooding through the enlarged aisle windows by constructing the open-work tracery screen on the north and south sides of the presbytery.[45] On top of this screen were displayed the relics of Winchester's illustrious monarchs and bishops, enclosed in newly-made wooden caskets. There is evidence that Fox's work was to have been even more ambitious. Embedded in the masonry between the presbytery aisle and east aisle of the transept was constructed the complete tracery of yet another aisle window. This implies that it was intended to demolish the eastern aisle of the transept, possibly as part of a grand scheme to remodel the transepts as well. Had this been carried through, the new work in the presbytery would have been linked directly with Wykeham's work in the nave, and Winchester would have acquired a much more consistently Perpendicular character. The chance survival of much of the Norman work may destroy the consistency of the effect but it does leave us with a much more interesting building.

Notes

1. The evidence concerning the shrine of St Swithun through the Middle Ages is discussed fully in this volume by John Crook; see above, pp. 57-68.

2. This assumption rests on the reference in *Winchester Annals,* 78, under the year 1202, to the institution of a confraternity to support the fabric but it is not certain that this was specifically for the retrochoir nor, if it was, that it marked the start of work.

3. Strictly, *retrochorus* referred to an area west of the choir, not east of the high altar, but the current use of the term indicating the area behind the high altar is now established. See P. Draper, 'The Retrochoir of Winchester Cathedral', *Architectural History* 21 (1978), p. 15, note 3.

4. John Crook has pointed out that the archaeological evidence surviving in the crypt suggests that a 12th-century eastern extension to the axial chapel preceded the construction of the retrochoir. He will discuss this more fully in a forthcoming publication. Over the 13th-century lateral chapels are the vestiges of unfinished structures which seem to have been intended as towers, perhaps to reflect a similar feature over the aisle chapels in Walkelin's church: R. Gem, 'The Romanesque Cathedral of Winchester: Patron and Design in the Eleventh Century', *BAA Winchester,* p. 8 and note 33.

5. The associations of this form with outer crypts are discussed more fully in M. F. Hearn, 'The Rectangular Ambulatory in English Medieval Architecture', *Journal of the Society of Architectural Historians* 30 (1971), pp. 187-208 and in Draper, 'Retrochoir', 1978.

6. See pp. 63-6, above.

7. For the Anglo-Saxon background to this practice see A. Klukas, 'The Continuity of Anglo-Saxon Liturgical Tradition in Post-Conquest England as Evident in the Architecture of Winchester, Ely and Canterbury Cathedrals', *Les Mutations Socio-Culturelles au Tournant des XIe-XIIe Siècles,* Proceedings of the Colloques Internationaux du Centre National de la Recherche Scientifique (Paris, 1984), pp. 111-23; for contemporary practice see P. Draper, 'Seeing that it was Done in all the Noble Churches in England', in E. Fernie and P. Crossley (eds.), *Medieval Architecture and its Intellectual Context,* Studies in Honour of Peter Kidson (London, 1990), pp. 137-42.

8. For a fuller discussion of the importance of pilgrimage and the cult of relics see J. Sumption, *Pilgrimage: an Image of Medieval Religion* (London, 1975) and for the architectural consequences see C. N. L. Brooke, *Medieval Church and Society* (London, 1971). The need for such a space in the 13th century may be connected with increasing difficulties in using the crypt due to flooding, though we do not know the intended function(s) of the Norman crypt nor how it was used. It may be noted that de Lucy's crypt for the Lady Chapel does not seem to have been connected to the Norman crypt as it might have been had that crypt still been in active use. See J. Crook, 'The Romanesque East Arm and Crypt of Winchester Cathedral', *JBAA* 142 (1989), pp. 5-20, for a full discussion of the history of the crypt. The reference in the mid-12th century to the removal of relics from a *locus indecens* need not refer to the crypt, as *indecens* does not carry any topographical implication.

9. It may be significant, however, that St Swithun's name is not included in the *tituli* on the east face of the 14th-century screen, perhaps implying that his shrine was not with the others. In that case the only possible alternative location for his shrine would be the centre of the retrochoir.

10. See above, p. 64. St Albans provides a close parallel for such an arrangement of 15th-century chantries flanking a shrine.

11. Subsidence, especially on the south side, has been a long-standing problem and is probably the cause of the modifications to the roof of the retrochoir. It is possible that the original aisle roofs were of shallow pitch but there is some evidence on the south side that this was at one time roofed with transverse gables in order to reduce the outward pressure on the aisle wall.

12. For successive discussions of these problems see Willis, *Winchester Cathedral*; C. R. Peers and H. Brakspear in *VCH Hants,* v, pp. 51-6; N. Pevsner, 'A Note on the East End of Winchester Cathedral', *Arch. J.* 116 (1959), pp. 133-5; Draper, 'Retrochoir' 1978; F. Woodman, 'The Retrochoir of Winchester Cathedral: a New Interpretation', *JBAA* 136 (1983), pp. 87-97; P. Draper, 'The Retrochoir of Winchester Cathedral: Evidence and Interpretation', *JBAA* 139 (1986), pp. 68-74; Crook 'East Arm'.

13. Willis, *Winchester Cathedral, p.* 41.

14. The evidence is clearer on the north side. Francis Woodman ('New Interpretation') was the first to observe this and to see its implications, but some aspects of that article are incorrect or misleading; see Draper, 'Retrochoir' 1986. To build the new western piers of the presbytery a portion of

the Norman piers on the chord of the apse would have had to be cut away.

15. Unlike the 14th-century elevation, where much greater emphasis was placed on the clerestory windows. A two-storey elevation on the lines proposed would provide sufficient distance between the apex of the arcade and the clerestory sill to allow for the lean-to roof of the aisles. Woodman's suggestion of a three-storey elevation does not seem compatible with the archaeological evidence.

16. For a fuller discussion of this problem see Draper, 'Retrochoir', 1978.

17. This central vault is certainly 13th-century and not later, as Woodman suggested, as is clearly shown by the character of the foliage on the bosses.

18. The way that the vault responds stand proud of the wall captures something of the skeletal effect of Lincoln and this is enhanced by the wall passage in front of the windows. Often described as a 'Rémois' or 'Champenois' passage, as its origins seem to lie in the region of Reims, this feature occurs in other buildings of the period, e.g. Tynemouth. It is not known if it had a specific function.

19. The hole visible in the centre of each foiled motif indicates the loss of an attached feature, probably some foliate feature in metal.

20. The paintings are discussed above by David Park and Peter Welford (pp. 129-30).

21. The tile pavements are discussed above by Christopher Norton (pp. 169-71).

22. See P. Tudor-Craig and L. Keen, 'A Recently Discovered Purbeck Marble Screen of the Thirteenth Century and the Shrine of St Swithun', *BAA Winchester,* pp. 63-72; and, more recently, J. Crook, 'The Thirteenth-Century Shrine and Screen of St Swithun at Winchester', *JBAA* 138 (1985), pp. 125-31; see also above, p. 104.

23. The stalls are discussed fully below by Charles Tracy (pp. 193-206).

24. See G. Russell, 'Decorated Tracery in Winchester Cathedral', *BAA Winchester,* pp. 94-100 and E. C. Norton, 'The Medieval Tile Pavements of Winchester Cathedral', *BAA Winchester,* pp. 78-93. On the evidence of the moulding profiles and the design of the window tracery, the remodelling of the Silkstede Chapel (Russell's 'South 2' window) may be Witney's earliest work at Winchester. It is possible that the updating of the transept chapels may have been in preparation for the antici- pated rebuilding of the presbytery.

25. Crook, 'East Arm', pp. 11-15.

26. Goodman, *Chartulary,* p. 242.

27. J. Harvey, *English Mediæval Architects: a Biographical Dictionary down to 1550,* revised edn. (Gloucester, 1984), p. 339; and R. Morris, 'Thomas of Witney at Exeter, Winchester and Wells', *Medieval Art and Architecture at Exeter Cathedral,* British Archaeological Association Conference Transactions for 1985 (London, 1991), pp. 57-84.

28. The archaeological evidence can be seen at clerestory level where there is an obvious rough break in the masonry and a clear change of intended alignment on both north and south sides at the junction between this bay and the adjacent bay to the west. This 'break' is confirmed by the nature of the mouldings and the foliage of the capitals of the rere-arches of the eastern bay, which, particularly on the north side, are quite distinct from those of the bays to the west.

29. The thickness of this wall clearly implies the intention to have a clerestory passage. Woodman ('New Interpretation') suggested that the east wall was inserted 10 to 15 years later but he failed to notice the degree of overhang. R. Morris ('Thomas of Witney', p. 69) has demonstrated that the affiliations of the unusual sunk chamfers employed on the eastern piers are with buildings associated with royal patronage, the dates of which would support the earlier dating. There he tentatively raised the possibility that the tabernacles on the screen may have been added *c.*1320, but he now agrees that the niches are integral with the screen and must be dated closer to 1310.

30. It is possible that in order to increase stability the piers may have been bound together at this time by the bands of iron which are clearly visible around the 13th-century capitals.

31. The infilling certainly post-dates the iron bands which are buried within it, and a late medieval date is indicated by the style of the corbel figures added at the base of the re-used half-shafts.The dimension of the half-shafts does not match any of the existing shafts in the church and it is not known where they came from.

32. The south side has always shown the most instability. The obvious misalignment between the arch mouldings and the south-western pier of the retrochoir supporting them shows that adjustments were made during construction of the 13th-century work.

33. Willis was the first to suggest that the south-east arch might have been rebuilt and Woodman

('New Interpretation') proposed, unconvincingly, a date as late as the 15th century.

34. Close examination of the mouldings at the springing of the arch on the west side shows that the arch was begun on an alignment similar to that of the north-east arch and that it was skewed to its present alignment during construction.

35. Harvey, *Mediæval Architects,* pp. 164-65; *idem, The Perpendicular Style* (London, 1978), p. 82.

36. Including the height of the clerestory sill in relation to the apex of the arcade arch. The north-east arcade arch is wider and therefore higher, and its apex cuts into the sill.

37. For bell bases see R. K. Morris, 'The Development of Later Gothic Mouldings in England', *Architectural History* 22 (1979), pp. 1-48, at pp. 28-29.

38. Willis, *Winchester Cathedral,* fig. 36, G and H.

39. Richard Morris, in a paper to be published in in *Medieval Art and Architecture at Salisbury,* British Archaeological Association Conference Transactions for 1991.

40. A stone vault does not seem to have been envisaged in the original design. The present wooden vault was inserted by Bishop Fox in the early 16th century (for the date, see the observations in this volume of Phillip Lindley and Martin Biddle, at pp. 115-18 and 298, note 41 respectively), and presumably replaced an earlier wooden structure. Wooden vaults simulating stone were not uncommon.

41. These dates would accord better with the style of the foliage of the capitals of the clerestory rere-arches than the date of *c.*1350 first proposed by Willis. See Russell, 'Decorated Tracery', p. 94.

42. It may be significant that the presbytery campaign does not seem to have been associated with the direct patronage of a bishop unlike the high quality work of Edington and Wykeham in the nave.

43. Would the tracery of the north and south windows of the east bay have been replaced so early? The jambs in this eastern bay were not altered when the tracery was replaced.

44. John Crook's findings on the translation of St Swithun's relics in 1476 now provide confirmatory evidence for the date of the screen; see above, pp. 63-4.

45. This may replace an earlier screen, as the present bench beneath Fox's work appears to be 14th-century. For the presbytery screens, see Martin Biddle's analysis, below, pp. 268-74.

THE 14TH-CENTURY CHOIR-STALLS

Charles Tracy

The early 14th-century choir-stalls at Winchester Cathedral (Fig. 14.1) are not only the finest set of choir furniture in Europe of their date but, with their échelons of decorative gabled canopies and the, now lost, series of sculpted Old and New Testament panels above the seats, they are unique.[1] Within the constraints of a short essay, an attempt will be made to provide a stylistic context for the architectural and sculptural components of the furniture, so as to reflect the monument's true importance in the history of English 14th-century art.

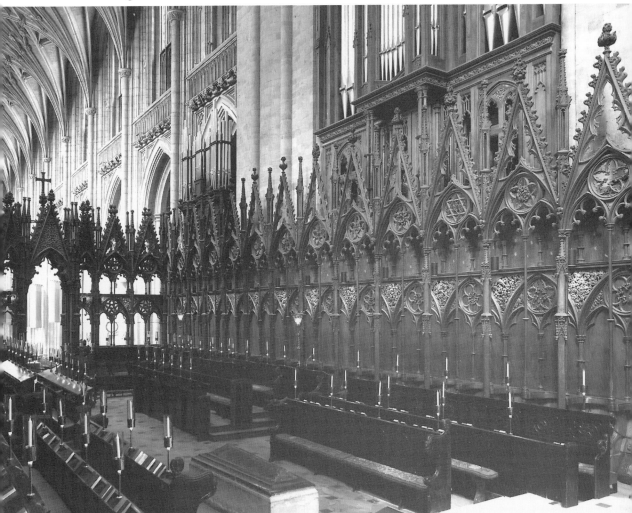

Fig. 14.1 Winchester Cathedral. View of NW corner of stalls. *John Crook*

Fig. 14.2   Winchester Cathedral. North return substalls. *Charles Tracy*
Fig. 14.3   Winchester Cathedral. East end of south lateral stalls. *Charles Tracy*

The designer was almost certainly William Lyngwode, a master carpenter from Norfolk. His family must have come from Lingwood, some five miles from Blofield in Norfolk, where William held a tenancy of land. The patron was Bishop Henry Woodlock. He was from a local gentry family with an older kinsman also at the monastery who was elected subprior in 1295, the year that Henry himself was elected prior. Ten years later he was appointed bishop, the only prior of the cathedral church to be promoted to the post. If a comparison with Bishop Stapledon (1308-26) at the secular cathedral of Exeter is allowed, we can say that a bishop who was formerly intimately associated with his episcopal church is more than usually likely to intervene personally on the level of patronage. Evidence of Woodlock's connection with the choir-stalls at Winchester is to be found in the letter which he wrote in the summer of 1308 to John Salmon, bishop of Norwich, asking him to excuse William Lyngwode from attendance at the manor courts until he had finished in the choir 'a piece of work belonging to his craft of carpentry which he had already begun'.[2]

The early 14th-century choir straddles the two western bays of the crossing, the same position as its Romanesque predecessor.[3] There were probably 66 back stalls, corresponding with the known number of monks at that time.[4] The monastic cathedrals like Winchester tended to have more back stalls than the secular establishments, although they did not always have substalls. Early 14th-century Canterbury, for instance, had eighty back stalls, while 13th-century Rochester has sixty. Unfortunately, our conception of the original choir-stalls at Winchester is impoverished by the almost total loss of the substalls, which, apart from the survival of some fifteen stall ends, are reduced to a rump of six seats at the west end (Fig. 14.2).

It has to be said that the seating at Winchester, although giving an impression of solidity and massiveness, is not a success. The seats are rather too low and shallow, and

Fig. 14.4   Winchester Cathedral. North side of prior's seat. The elbow of this seat has been cut back to accommodate the later buttressing. *Charles Tracy*

the seat elbows are too low for comfort. It is a pity that more of the talent that went into the embellishment of the stalls' superstructure could not have been employed on the basic task of providing seats that were comfortable to sit in. Moreover, the canopy-work, however architecturally and sculpturally impressive, betrays a similar inexperience in furniture-making.

The Winchester choir-stalls represent an attempt to translate the design of *rayonnant* stone furniture into the medium of wood.[5] In order to construct an échelon of towering gables, Lyngwode departed from the established arrangement, as seen in the 13th-century Westminster Abbey choir-stalls, of one gable to each bay.[6] By using a system of doubled arches (Fig. 14.3) he was able to display gables on a sufficiently monumental scale to vie with the productions of the stonemason. He also gained extra height so that sculpted panels could be inserted where they could be easily seen above the cornice of the stall backing.[7]

Fig. 14.5   Winchester
Cathedral. Engraving of the
return stalls (Britton,
Winchester Cathedral, pl. XIV)

But he did not want his system of alternation to be over-stressed in the treatment of the stall uprights, which were to vary between a single column and a quatrefoil cluster of extremely thin columns. In the event, the weight of this impressive superstructure proved too heavy for the seat capping below. Soon after the stalls were completed, special measures had to be taken to shore up the edifice by means of the buttresses which we see today (Fig. 14.4). These emphasise the double-bay arrangement by accentuating the major supports of the system. Subsequent important alterations to the return stalls should be noted. Originally the return back stalls were treated similarly to the main ones, with solid panelling behind (Fig. 14.5). This was removed by Sir George Gilbert Scott in 1874. Unobtrusive pinnacles on either side of the gable over the choir entrance have been replaced by clusters of large pinnacles designed by Scott. The gable itself would originally have been carried by four clustered columns of the kind which supported the main uprights. The seats for the prior and subprior on either side were treated as if they had been a major bay with their own (solid) gables above.

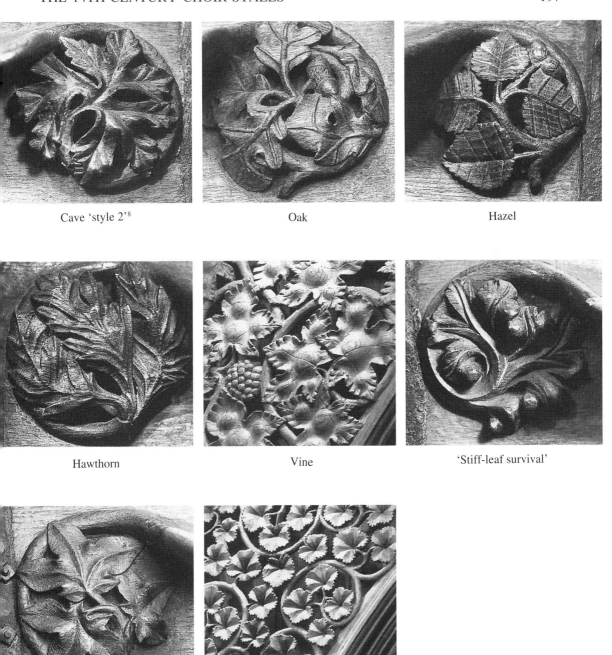

Cave 'style 2'[8]   Oak   Hazel

Hawthorn   Vine   'Stiff-leaf survival'

Ivy or possibly sycamore   Geranium

Fig. 14.6 Winchester Cathedral choir-stalls. Leaf forms. *Charles Tracy/ John Crook*

Fig. 14.7a Spandrel of seat backing. Falconer. *John Crook*

Fig. 14.7b Spandrel of seat backing. Lion. *John Crook*

Fig. 14.8 Cley Church, Norfolk. Clerestory on south side of nave. *Charles Tracy*

As is usually the case, the two most important stalls were given special decorative treatment. The subprior's stall to the north of the entrance-way, curiously, is the more dignified of the two (Fig. 14.5). It is larger. Its sides would have been open like the prior's stall, if John Britton's engraving is to be relied upon. Both stalls have a larger boss than usual in the centre of the vaulting above, but the subprior's is the bigger of the two. Wilfrid Carpenter Turner suggested that it might have been used temporarily as the bishop's throne, noting that the misericord displays a mitred head. We have no evidence that a bishop's throne was intended elsewhere as part of the early 14th-century furnishings, and it is quite possible that Woodlock planned to use the return stall on the north side for his official throne.[9] As a former prior he might have wanted to sit in the body of the choir-stalls without, as was the normal practice in these circumstances, usurping the position of the prior.

The canopy-work at Winchester has lost almost all traces of its medieval colouring and gilding. As is to be expected for a monument of this period, an early 18th-century description of the stalls characterises them as 'adorned with spire-work gilded'.[10] A water-colour drawing of the stalls by James Cave in 1801 (Fig. 21.1) shows that the cusps and bosses were then gilded. This painting also discloses the panelling above the stall cornice at the back painted blue with gold stars superimposed. Simon Jervis suggested that this decoration may date to the Restoration, possibly following earlier colouring executed as a background to the carvings which were probably placed at this level.[11]

The repertory of sculptured leaf forms on the stalls—including geranium, vine, oak, a late survival of stiff-leaf, hawthorn, hazel, and ivy—is generously wide for a single monument of this period (Fig. 14.6). The treatment of the foliage still recalls the naturalism

Fig. 14.9 St Ethelbert Gate, Norwich, west side. (J. Britton, *History and Antiquities of the See and Cathedral Church of Norwich* (London, 1816), pl. XXIV)

of Southwell more strongly than the conventionalism of the full-blown English Decorated style. The human and animal carving is equally vivid in its naturalism (Fig. 14.7a-b).

The Winchester furniture's East Anglian stylistic origins are confirmed in a number of respects. Much of the foliage can be recognised in the pages of the Ormesby Psalter, of about 1310,[12] such as the ivy, oak and vine. The ubiquitous cinquefoiled circle at Winchester can, as it happens, be instanced in the clerestory at Cley Church, Norfolk (Fig. 14.8), although the characteristic foliage terminations of Winchester are missing. The foils of the oculi at Winchester are normally pointed and subcusped, but they can be semi-circular and subcusped, as at Cley, or uncusped. The use of subcusping on both monuments, a 13th-century *rayonnant* motif, is a significant parallel. The sculpture on the St Ethelbert Gate at Norwich (Fig. 14.9), although later than the Winchester furniture and now completely restored, points to a common artistic tradition.[13] The way that the motifs are disposed in the spandrels resembles the formula used on the Winchester stalls. Also the carving itself at Norwich reminds us of the spandrel carving at Winchester. At the cathedral in Norwich the foliage carving on the bosses in the east cloister walk is close in type to that in the Winchester choir-stalls. In the carnary chapel at Norwich the hood-mould label head-stops are like those on the Winchester choir-stalls.[14] Much of the stone sculpture in the gatehouse of Bishop Salmon's hall at Norwich is closely reminiscent of the wood-carving at Winchester.[15] Also in the medium of stone, outside Norwich, closely comparable parallels with the heads and figures at Winchester can be found. At Snettisham Church the corbel heads look very like those at Winchester, and there are similar small figures in a crouching position, emerging from the wall at the junction of the hood-moulds of the arches (Figs. 14.10 and 14.11). At Cley there is a Winchester-type head, again used as a label-stop. Most of the label-stops at Cley are figures in long flowing robes, pressed back against the wall in unnaturally contorted positions, very like the stance of the 'Green Man' on the Winchester stalls (Figs. 14.12 and 14.13).

Fig. 14.10 (*above*) Snettisham, Norfolk. Label-stop of nave arcading. *Charles Tracy*

Fig. 14.11 (*above right*) Winchester Cathedral. Label-stop of choir-stalls. *John Crook*

Fig. 14.12 (*right*) Cley Church, Norfolk. Label-stop of north nave aisle arcade. *Charles Tracy*

The proximity of the style of the stone corbel figure at Winchester itself, on the south side of the west face of the east presbytery arcade (Fig. 14.14), to the 'Green Man' on the stalls suggests that Norfolk stone sculptors as well as wood-carvers may have been employed. Both figures are in the same crouched position with one shoulder pushed forward awkwardly. The hair-style and tunic with buttoned sleeves are identical. The facial types are similar, and they both have long stick-like fingers.

The articulation of the choir-stalls is in many ways more finely drawn than any comparable monuments in stone. Even allowing for the difference of medium, it is possible to say that this is not the spirit of the 'metropolitan' style productions in London, such as the Edmund Crouchback tomb at Westminster Abbey. Neither the design, particularly if we accept that there were no pinnacles in Lyngwode's work,[16] nor the sculptural detail of these monuments is comparable. Nor will we find any connections on the shrine, of about 1302-08, or the sedilia, of before 1308, at St Albans Abbey. In the last-named cases the principle of movement in depth is found as well as the liberal use of the ogee arch, both motifs practically absent at Winchester. The difficulties encountered in finding a model for these stalls are a mark of their originality. The sculptural vocabulary is essentially *rayonnant*, well exemplified by the gabled motifs on the lower stage of the Waltham Cross, of 1291-92.[17] But Lyngwode dispenses with the buttresses and pinnacles, the solid spandrels and the cornice of his English models for the front plane of his stalls, reminding us in many

Fig. 14.13 Winchester Cathedral. 'Green Man' in spandrel of seat backing. *Charles Tracy*

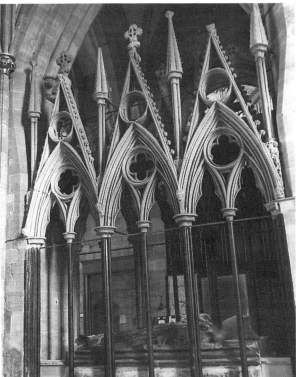

Fig. 14.14   Winchester Cathedral. Stone corbel figure on SE end of west side of presbytery east arcade. *John Crook*

Fig. 14.15 Hereford Cathedral. Tomb of Bishop Aquablanca. *Charles Tracy*

ways of the Aquablanca tomb, of about 1268, at Hereford Cathedral (Fig. 14.15), and the intermediate bays on the south portal at Notre-Dame, Paris, of about 1257-67 (Fig. 14.16). The design of the Winchester stalls, self-evidently experimental, is remarkable for its stylistic integrity, adapting the language of *rayonnant* stone architecture for use in wooden furniture, and transforming it in terms of the original and spirited vocabulary of East Anglian decorative motifs. But it must be said that the residual impression is of a monument designed by someone who was not familiar with the very latest stylistic tendencies being worked out in London. Lyngwode appears to have been not completely up-to-date and to have relied upon the classic statements of *rayonnant* architecture of some fifty years earlier.

On the question of whether there were originally pinnacles, it must be remembered that in the London-type examples they were ultimately attached to a back wall. Exceptions to this were the Aveline (*c*.1292) and Crouchback (d.1296) tombs at Westminster Abbey, where the pinnacles were supported on stout buttresses. As already noted, Lyngwode's uprights were too slight to take the weight of the elaborate free-standing superstructure. He must have realised that the deployment of pinnacles would have been inadvisable. Those that were added in about 1315, after Lyngwode's departure, do not look out of place on the lateral stalls but self-evidently can never have been intended above the return stalls

Fig. 14.16   Paris, Notre-Dame Cathedral. South transept portal. *James Austin*

between the gables of the prior and subprior's seats, and the adjacent bays (Fig. 14.5). The arcading on the west side of the upper storey of the St Ethelbert Gate at Norwich (Fig. 14.9) can, I believe, be legitimately adduced in support of the argument for the lack of pinnacles on the Winchester choir-stalls in the first place.

     Judging from the abundance of carving on the remaining stalls[18] and from the estimated extent of the original furniture, a large team of carpenters must have been involved. The consistency of style throughout the first phase of the work suggests that Lyngwode brought most of the craftsmen with him from Norfolk. But the unequivocally experimental nature of the design of the stalls is based on the principals of stonemasonry translated, unsuitably, into wood. Doubtless, carpenters of varying degrees of talent were involved, although the standard of the carving is consistently high. It seems that one craftsman found employment afterwards making choir-stalls for the parish church of Headbourne Worthy just outside Winchester. He must have had a rather unimportant function in the cathedral because his construction and workmanship are crude. He certainly cannot have been someone who Lyngwode would have considered worth importing from Norfolk. Lyngwode's career before he came to Winchester and after his departure is quite unknown. If he worked on any more wooden furniture we have no evidence of it. But if the hypothesis is correct that he was primarily a stone-carver by training, he may well have been responsible for the design and execution of several of the later works in Norfolk, already adduced for the sake of comparison, in particular, the St Ethelbert Gate, the carnary chapel and the gatehouse of Bishop Salmon's hall at Norwich. It is probable, however, that one of his principal assistants was later employed on the choir-stalls at Wells Cathedral. We are ignorant, also, about the carpenters who were used to renovate the stalls but it is likely that they came from London.

Notes

1. Modern studies of the choir-stalls have been of a specialist nature. In 1927 Canon Goodman published the letter from Bishop Woodlock to Bishop Salmon, referred to below, in its original Latin and in English translation: A. W. Goodman, 'The Choir Stalls, Winchester Cathedral', *Arch. J.* 84 (1927), pp. 25-6. In the same publication, T. D. Atkinson, then cathedral architect, contributed a short article on the furniture (*ibid.*, pp. 127-8). The decorative sculpture on the choir-stalls is discussed by C. J. P. Cave, 'Carvings on the Spandrels of the Quire Stalls', *WCR* 1943, pp. 4-5. For other contributions to the subject, see Alan Rannie, 'Decorated Architecture in the Cathedral', *WCR* 35 (1966), pp. 14-23; Edward T. Joy, *Woodwork in Winchester Cathedral* (Winchester, 1964); and S. Jervis, *Woodwork of Winchester Cathedral* (Winchester, 1976). A useful comment on the restoration work to the choir-stalls effected after the Civil War was supplied by Barbara Carpenter Turner: 'The Return of the Church; Cathedral and Close, 1660-62', *WCR* 29 (1960), p. 22. During the restoration of the choir-stalls in the late 1960s, the then cathedral architect published a series of articles in the local press: W. J. Carpenter Turner, 'Winchester Choir-Stalls', *Hampshire Chronicle*, 14, 21 and 28 January 1967. In 1976 his successor, Corinne Wilson (now Mrs. Bennett) contributed an important note on the construction of the choir-stalls: C. G. Wilson, 'The Medieval Quire', *WCR* 45 (1976), pp. 16-18. The fullest account of the furniture can be found in Charles Tracy, *English Gothic Choir-Stalls, 1200-1400* (Woodbridge, 1987), pp. 16-24.
2. Goodman, 'Choir Stalls'. A year later a second letter was sent asking for a similar concession.
3. See above, p. 22 .
4. In the year 1325 we have the names of all the monks in a list given in Bishop John of Pontoise's register: Goodman, *Chartulary,* p. li. There are only 62 back stalls extant. The lateral stalls were truncated when the medieval pulpitum was replaced in 1637 by the Inigo Jones structure. A foliate boss from the removed section was acquired in 1897 by the Victoria and Albert Museum (Acc. No. 236-1897). For a discussion of the changes made in the 17th century, see Charles Tracy, 'A Boss from the Winchester Cathedral Choir-Stalls at the Victoria and Albert Museum', *HFC Proc.* 44 (1988), pp. 87-93.
5. *Rayonnant* was primarily a French architectural style, which succeeded the High Gothic from the middle of the 13th century. Structure became formalised, and from that moment decoration became the first priority. The prime characteristics were tracery and, finally, cut mouldings. There was much less emphasis upon the logic of structure, members merging into their supports. The best example for our purposes is at Notre-Dame, Paris (Fig. 14.16), where the style was introduced by Pierre de Montreuil and his associates in the 1250s. Here in stone can be found the heavy acute crocketed gables, cusped oculi, triangles, and decorative panels of the Winchester choir-stalls.
6. See the reconstruction of the abbey choir-stalls in W. R. Lethaby, *Westminster Abbey and the King's Craftsmen* (London, 1906), p. 272, and the early 18th-century painting by an anonymous artist in the Westminster Abbey museum. The Westminster Abbey choir-stalls were removed by order of the Dean and Chapter at the end of the 18th century.
7. For a discussion of these panels, their iconography and placing, see Tracy, 'A Boss', pp. 90-1.
8. C. J. P. Cave, 'Carvings in the Spandrels of the Quire Stalls', *WCR* 12 (1943), pp. 4-5.
9. But see below, p. 299, note 59, for evidence that the episcopal throne was located in its present position, on the south side of the presbytery, by 1525.
10. Lord Clarendon and S. Gale, *The History and Antiquities of the Cathedral Church of Winchester* (London, 1715), p. 26.
11. Jervis, *Woodwork*, p. 19.
12. Oxford, Bodleian Library, Douce 366: esp. fos. 71v and 147v. Both pages are given by Nigel Morgan to the second pair of artists working on the manuscript from about 1310-20: P. Lasko and N. J. Morgan (eds.), *Medieval Art in East Anglia 1300-1520* (Norwich, 1973), pp. 18-19.

13. Dated by Alan Borg and others to 1316-17 in *Medieval Sculpture from Norwich Cathedral* (Norwich, 1980), pp. 30-35. The west side of the gate is illustrated in J. Britton, *The History and Antiquities of the See and Cathedral Church of Norwich* (London, 1816), pl. XXIV.
14. The basement of the Carnary Chapel at Norwich, founded by Bishop Salmon in 1316, incorporates octofoiled subcusped oculi.
15. Bishop Salmon obtained a licence to buy the land for his new hall in 1318.
16. See below.
17. *Vetusta Monumenta, III,* Society of Antiquaries (London, 1796), pl. XVI.
18. Carpenter Turner counted over 500 images of kings, queens, bishops, monks and priors, together with ordinary men and women: W. J. Carpenter Turner, 'Winchester Choir-Stalls', *Hampshire Chronicle,* 21 Jan 1967, p. 6.

THE VENERABLE CHAPEL ARMOIRE

Simon Jervis

In Memoriam Horst Appuhn

On the south side of the Venerable Chapel stands an oak armoire (Figs. 15.1 and 15.2), which has attracted little attention since it was extracted from the fittings of the neighbouring Silkstede Chapel, repaired, and placed in its present position in 1965.[1] It may have been put in the Silkstede Chapel in 1816, when the chapel was fitted with cupboards made from old panelling 'for the reception of the surplices of the singing men and choristers', but it might have been there already, as the cathedral architect, Wilfrid Carpenter Turner, suggested in 1965.[2] It now contains a miscellany of old books.

The armoire is 2.01 m. (79 ins.) high in total (Fig. 15.3). It has four corner posts, connected at top and bottom by tenoned and pegged horizontal rails to form a box frame. The corner posts project some 100 mm. (4 ins.) at the bottom to form feet, and some 50 mm. (2 ins.) at the top to form corner finials. The frame at the back is rebated at the sides, top, and bottom, to house five vertical boards of riven tapered section, set clinker-fashion with an overlap of about 20 mm. (0.75 ins.) and nailed to the rebate at top and bottom, and to the supports of the upper and lower shelves (see below). The top and bottom of the armoire are similarly constructed, with two horizontal boards of riven tapered section, set clinker-fashion lengthwise, and engaging in grooves in the front and side rails. Both top and bottom boards are supported by two through-jointed cross-members, whose ends are easily visible on the outside of the top and bottom rails at front and back. The bottom boards are set some 55 mm. (2.25 ins.) below the top of the lower front rail, which thus constitutes a substantial sill.

On the sides of the armoire, whose total depth measures 655 mm. (25.75 ins.), the frame is carved to form simple roll mouldings on the outer and inner edges. The outer mouldings on the posts are returned at right-angles to meet the outer mouldings of the cross-rails, but also extend upwards on the outer edge of the corner finials and downwards for about 25 mm. (1 in.) to match the treatment of the front (see below). Between the mouldings, the side, top and bottom rails have been chamfered to each side, while their centres have been left flat; the arrises so formed have been gently rounded, so that the profile presented is pulvinated, but slightly angular. The feet are chamfered below the cross-moulding and inside the continued outer moulding, but continue vertically below this level. The sides of the finials are tapered from the corresponding extended outer mouldings at the top down to the level of the upper side of the top rail, in a gentle concave curve.

The side frames are filled in each case by two vertical planks, butted in the centre, and engaging in grooves in the frame at the sides, top and bottom. The planks are uneven,

Fig. 15.1 Winchester Cathedral, armoire in the Venerable Chapel, c.1325-50. Front view. *John Crook*

Fig. 15.2 Winchester Cathedral, armoire in the Venerable Chapel, c.1325-50. Oblique view. *John Crook*

the visible widths of those on the left being about 170 mm. (6.75 ins.) at the front and 210 mm. (8.25 ins.) at the back, and those on the right about 200 mm. (8 ins.) at the front and 190 mm. (7.5 ins.) at the back. At approximately one-third and two-thirds levels are rows of three large, shallow domed iron nail-heads, about 22 mm. (0.8 in.) in diameter. These levels correspond to those of the internal shelves.

On the front of the armoire, whose total width is about 1.365 m. (53.75 ins.), the frame is chamfered from inside to outside at the sides and top to leave a moulding on its outer edges; the moulding is square at the top and rounded at the sides. The tops of the posts are not chamfered above the level of the lower edge of the square moulding on the top rail, and rise as vertical, rectangular finials. The feet are also vertical below the lower rail; the mouldings stop at this point, and the chamfer, stopped at a right-angle, dies towards the inner sides of the posts.

The frame is rebated at the sides and at top and bottom to receive lateral planks, 210 mm. (8.25 ins.) wide on the left and 215 mm. (8.5 ins.) wide on the right. At top and bottom, and at the level of the upper shelf (see below) these planks sport rows of three shallow domed iron nail-heads, similar to those on the sides. Between the lateral planks are hung two sets of doors, the lower 1.22 m. (48 ins.) high, the upper 410 mm. (16 ins.) high. Each door consists of two vertical planks butted together, of widths varying, in no particular pattern, from about 185-210 mm. (7.25-8.25 ins.). The horizontal gap between the two sets of doors is filled by rebated cross-pieces, fixed to the doors; thus the original four doors now open as two.

Five sets of applied iron strap hinges extend from the side posts to the opening of the doors (Fig. 15.1). On the lower doors one set of hinges is set centrally, and two others occur at roughly identical intervals of 500 mm. (19.75 ins.) above and below the central set. The top hinges on the upper doors are 500 mm. (19.75 ins.) above the upper hinges on the lower doors. Only the spacing of the lower hinges of the upper doors does not seem to fit obviously into this regular series of intervals; they are about 265 mm. (10.4 ins.) below the upper set. Each strap hinge follows the same design, and is positioned similarly. The finials are formed as simple, bifurcated scrolls, issuing from a rounded terminal, embellished with two small angular projections at the points where the terminal swells from the strap. Three nails, one in each scroll, and one in the centre of the terminal, affix each finial. In the centre of the lateral planks the straps are embellished with further rounded sections, with small angular projections at each of the four joins with the straps; these rounded sections are nailed, and there is another nail through the strap towards the inner side of each lateral plank, immediately before the hinge proper. On the doors there is another nail through the strap next to each hinge, then another, then a third nail through a rounded section similar to that already described. The strap is then held by a ninth nail before the three which fix the bifurcated inner finial. Each strap hinge is thus held by 12 nails in all.

On the inner planks of each door, between the strap hinges of the upper doors and between the top and centre strap hinges of the lower doors, are pear-shaped loop handles with hexafoil back plates, with small angular projections between each foil. Below and to the left of the handle on the lower right door is a rectangular iron keyhole escutcheon with concave corners and triple notches top and bottom. It is fixed by four nails.

The interior of the armoire (Fig. 15.2) was divided by two shelves. These were secured by supports at back, sides and front. These supports, of rectangular section, chamfered at top and bottom on their visible edges, are tenoned into the corner posts, grooved to receive the shelves, and incorporate housings for lateral supports, similar to those supporting the top and bottom of the armoire. The clinker-set planks of the armoire's back are channelled to receive the shelf supports. The nails with shallow domed heads already noted on the sides, and at the level of the upper shelf on the lateral planks at the front, engage in the shelf supports, as do further nails through the back and through the outer sections of the central strap hinges of the lower doors.

The rebated cross-pieces now joining the two sets of doors are of a similar section to the remaining shelf supports, although on the inside of the right front lateral plank is an unchamfered fragment. The evidence is not definitive, but is seems probable that these elements, although cut and refinished, may be the original front support of the upper shelf, which also divided the upper doors from the lower.

Although there are numerous repairs and infills, the armoire seems, externally at least, to be in more or less its original form. The only later additions appear to be the rectangular keyhole escutcheon, which is probably late 19th-century, and the four handles and their escutcheons. Although the latter are congruous with the strap hinges, and do not seem modern, they appear sharper in treatment, different in colour, and of thinner metal. It is possible that they are late Gothic replacements. The position of the original handles may be marked by circular ghosts set more or less symmetrically outside and slightly above the present handles on the upper doors, and in approximately corresponding positions below the central strap hinges on the lower doors.

The front of the armoire also bears ten circles or parts of circles heavily scored with a compass. Their arrangement follows no very obvious pattern, although they appear to have been executed when the planks forming the front of the armoire were in roughly their present positions (some extend over the joins between two planks) but before the strap hinges were put on (some extend behind the strap hinges). It is difficult to account for these circles; given the carefully integrated design of the whole armoire, the lack of any evidence for a different hinge system, and the apparent homogeneity of the oak, it seems very unlikely that the hinges were not part of the original conception.[3] A geometric arrangement of intersecting circles and a group of four concentric circles are also visible on the front, lightly incised with a compass on the left lateral plank, between the central and upper strap hinges of the lower doors, and on the neighbouring part of the left door.

The armoire appears to have been thoroughly cleaned, perhaps before its thorough repair by Mr. J. L. Viney in 1965,[4] but there are what appear to be traces of paint and/ or gesso preparatory for paint, in the incised circles, on the domed nail-heads and elsewhere. Green is widespread, but red or pink also seem to be present, and it is possible that the nail-heads and the hinges were gilded.

The purpose of this lengthy but by no means exhaustive description (no mention has been made of the elaborate system of scribing lines, nor of the numerous pegs which were an essential part in the armoire's construction) is to demonstrate that what may now appear a subfusc, even unprepossessing survival was a highly calculated and complex structure which in its original condition—especially if, as seems likely, it was painted—must have seemed refined and impressive.

The interior of the armoire shows some signs of later vicissitudes. The insides of the doors are painted buff, there is a later strut across the back, some hat-pegs have been inserted, and there are various inscriptions, the latest dated 1964, while one of the earlier reads, 'Xmas

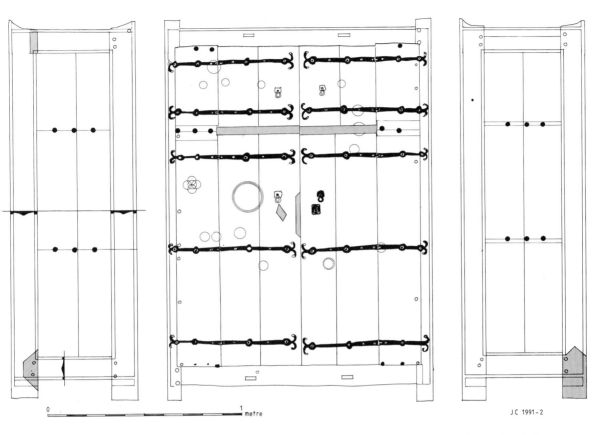

Fig. 15.3   Winchester Cathedral, armoire in the Venerable Chapel, *c.*1325-50. Scale drawing. Solid black: ironwork; small circles: wooden pegs; shaded: replacement timber. *John Crook*

1887 New Altar Cloth'.[5] This raises the question of function. The armoire—and here it should be explained that this term is here used in preference to the modern English 'cupboard', because the medieval 'cupboard' was an entirely different furniture type,[6] on which plate was displayed—was a flexible and ancient form. Two-doored pedimented armoires containing books are depicted in mosaic in the mausoleum of Galla Placidia, in Ravenna, of about A.D. 440,[7] and in the Northumbrian Codex Amiatinus of about A.D. 700,[8] the former with two shelves, the latter with four. Later uses include archives, gold, silver and jewellery, clothes, armour, vestments, food, drink and eating utensils. The Winchester armoire was presumably for ecclesiastical utensils, ornaments, or vestments.[9]

The earliest surviving free-standing armoire is a magnificent Romanesque specimen, with two round-arched doors and countersunk strap hinges, and arcading on its sides, at the church of Saint-Etienne in Aubazine (Corrèze), which is convincingly dated to about 1176.[10] The next is a smaller but massively constructed armoire, with concealed countersunk hinges, the whole painted and gilt inside and out, in the cathedral museum at Halberstadt, probably made in about 1230-40.[11] At Bayeux Cathedral is another free-standing armoire (Fig. 15.4) which, although mutilated and rearranged, still has 14 doors in two registers, within a narrow rectilinear framework, with surface-mounted strap hinges and all-over painted decoration; it probably dates from about 1240.[12] Later painted specimens include the early 14th-century example at Noyon, tragically destroyed in 1918,[13] and a late 14th-century armoire from Perpignan.[14]

The pedimented armoires noted at Ravenna and in the Codex Amiatinus had distant descendants in a large series of gabled armoires with fixed lateral planks flanking single narrow doors, often divided horizontally; there was sometimes also a small extra door in the gable. The type crops up in Sweden, Austria and Germany.[15] A variation on this theme is at Kloster Medingen in Lower Saxony, one of a group of five convents for noble ladies, originally founded in the late 12th and early 13th centuries (comprising Medingen, Ebstorf, Lüne, Wienhausen and Isenhagen), which possess a remarkable accumulation of about two hundred pieces of medieval furniture.[16] The Medingen armoire, constructed of massive nailed planks bound with iron, about the same height as that at Winchester but some 355 mm. (14 ins.) wider, has lateral planks and double doors with strap hinges, but no gable; its conformation is thus broadly similar to that of the Winchester armoire. The late Horst Appuhn (1924-90) suggested a date in the second half of the 13th century for the Medingen armoire; he also noted that it was originally painted with scrolled ornament.[17]

Although the Winchester armoire bears similarities to that at Medingen, its construction, with a framework, is quite distinct and much more refined. The sides of the Winchester armoire are particularly remarkable in that they seem to represent a very early version of panelled construction. Fully evolved panels would not normally have been of this

Fig. 15.4   Bayeux Cathedral, armoire, *c.*1240. From a photograph in the Fitzwilliam Museum, Cambridge, entitled 'Le Chartrier in the Sacristy, Bayeux', and inscribed 'ENE [ELIE?].JEAN'. *Fitzwilliam Museum*

length, nor would they have been formed of two butted planks, nor would they have been nailed to internal shelf supports so that these play a stiffening role similar to that of internal ledges on doors. The mouldings which decorate the framework of the Winchester armoire's sides and run round the top and sides of its front, are carved, with no use of the moulding plane. It has been observed that the Winchester choir-stalls, of about 1308, although in part turned, did not employ the plane.[18]

The few English free-standing armoires with doors include one in the exchequer at Winchester College, probably of 1413,[19] another in the muniment room of Westminster Abbey,[20] and a third at York Minster, closely related to fitted cupboards in the Zouche Chapel, which must have been made between 1361 and 1394; the latter have been dendrochronologically dated to about 1380 to 1400.[21] William Bell Scott illustrated two 'Almeries' in his *Antiquarian Gleanings in the North of England* of about 1850: one, with foliate iron decoration, in Wetheral Church but said to come from another church, and since disappeared; the other, in St Catherine's Chapel at Carlisle Cathedral, with painted decoration including the initials **TG** for Prior Thomas Gondebour (1484-1507).[22] A further substantial armoire is in King's College Chapel in Cambridge.[23] None of this small group is very close to the Winchester armoire, although, interestingly, the handles on the York armoire are in positions roughly corresponding to the circular ghosts of the putative original handles noted on the Winchester example.

The comparisons so far adduced tend to suggest a date for the Winchester armoire in the late 13th or early 14th century. Nearby in the south transept of Winchester Cathedral is a curved bench, with roll mouldings on its frontally visible edges, which bears traces of green paint, with red below. This has been dated to the late 13th century, and may provide a context for the armoire.[24] The iron strap hinges of the armoire may also be evidence for dating. Their bifurcated ends may be compared with those on four chests: one at Kloster Ebstorf,[25] which has been dendrochronologically dated to about 1177 or later; a chest at Merton College, Oxford,[26] dated to 1280-1300; a chest at St Peter's, Cound,[27] dated to 1340-80; and the Richard of Bury chest in the Burrell Collection, of about 1340.[28] Even closer is a chest in Laneham Church (Notts.), of the type called in German a *Frontstollentruhe,* on which bifurcated scrolls issue from a rounded terminal. The Laneham chest is decorated on its front with chip-carved roundels and on its feet with blank Gothic arcading, suggesting a late 13th-century date.[29] The strap hinges on the Winchester armoire, with their repeated circular widenings, embellished with angular projections where they meet the straight sections of strap, are more elaborate than any of these examples. This may be a feature endemic to strap hinges—the much earlier countersunk hinges on the furniture at Aubazine of about 1176 incorporates comparable widenings[30]—but it may also suggest a later date, particularly as the angular projections seem cut with the chisel.[31] On balance it seems most probable that the armoire was produced in the second quarter of the 14th century.

The Winchester armoire is the most sophisticated surviving piece of its type in England. It seems to stand on the cusp between the massive planked furniture of the early Gothic period, and the carved, moulded and panelled furniture of the late Gothic. Not as spectacular as the armoires at Halberstadt, Bayeux and Noyon, the latter now destroyed, the Winchester armoire must nevertheless, if it was indeed originally painted, have been an extremely showy product. Even in its present subdued condition and inconspicuous position its refinement and quality are readily discerned. It deserves to be better known.

Notes

1. 'Cupboard in the Cathedral', *Country Life,* 9 December 1965.
2. S. Jervis, *Woodwork of Winchester Cathedral* (Winchester, 1976), pp. 10 and 38; *Country Life,* 'Cupboard'.
3. A possible but unlikely explanation is that the circles may have played some part in the original painted scheme. The hinges on the armoire at Bayeux (see note 12, below) took relatively little account of its painted scheme.
4. See note 1, above.
5. This refers to the so-called 'Transfiguration Frontal', which was received the week before Christmas: *Hampshire Chronicle,* 24 December 1887; see also M. Wileman, 'The Altar Frontal for the Feast of the Transfiguration', *WCR* 56 (1987), pp. 10-11.
6. See Penelope Eames, 'Furniture in England, France and the Netherlands from the Twelfth to the Fifteenth Century', *Furniture History* 13 (1977), p. 1.
7. Illustrated in F. Windisch-Graetz, *Möbel Europas von der Romanik bis zu Spätgotik* (Munich, 1982), p. 156.
8. Florence, Bibliotheca Laurenziana, illustrated in H. Hayward (ed.), *World Furniture* (London, 1965), facing p. 32.
9. Eames, 'Furniture', pp. 4-9, with quotes from 1212 to 1482.
10. *Ibid.,* pp. 21-25, pls. 10-11.
11. H. Kreisel, *Die Kunst des Deutschen Möbels, I, Von den Anfängen bis zum Hochbarock,* 2nd edn. (Munich, 1974), p. 27 and pl. 27; Windisch-Graetz, *Möbel,* pl. 3.
12. Eames, 'Furniture', pp. 25-7.
13. M. Polonovski and G. Perrault, 'Le trésor de la Cathédrale de Noyon retrouvé', *L'Estampille,* November 1987, pp. 44-7. This article also describes (pp. 36-9) a further 13th-century armoire at Noyon, of massive iron-bound construction.
14. M. Carmé Farré Sanpera, *El Museo de Arte de Cataluña* (Barcelona, 1983), p. 115.
15. Windisch-Graetz, *Möbel,* figs. 89-91, 101; Kreisel, *Kunst des Möbels, I,* figs. 29-34.
16. Kreisel, *Kunst des Möbels,* fig. 25; Horst Appuhn, 'Mittel-alterliche Truhen in Kloster Ebstorf', *Jahrbuch des Museums für Kunst und Gewerbe Hamburg* 3 (1984), p. 49.
17. Kreisel, *Kunst des Möbels, I,* pp. 20, 295.
18. C. Tracy, *English Gothic Choir-Stalls, 1200-1400* (Woodbridge, 1987), pp. 68-9.
19. Eames, 'Furniture', pp. 27-30.
20. *Ibid.,* pp. 30-33.
21. J. B. Morrell, *Woodwork in York* (York, 1949), pp. 121, 125 (see also Eames, 'Furniture', pp. 15-17 and Jane Geddes, review of Eames in *JBAA* 131 (1978), pp. 123-4).
22. W. B. Scott, *Antiquarian Gleanings in the North of England* (London, *c.*1850), pl. 32; see also J. C. Cox and A. Harvey, *English Church Furniture* (London, 1908), pp. 310-11.
23. Eames, 'Furniture', pp. 52-4.
24. Jervis, *Woodwork,* p. 12; *Country Life,* 'Cupboard'.
25. Appuhn, 'Truhen' (see note 16, above), p. 51.
26. Eames, 'Furniture', p. 155.
27. *Ibid.,* p. 156.
28. C. Tracy and J. Geddes, entry for Bury with further ironwork comparisons, in J. Alexander and P. Binski (eds.), *Age of Chivalry: Art in Plantagenet England 1200-1400,* Catalogue, Royal Academy Exhibition (London, 1987), p. 477.
29. E. Mercer, *Furniture 700-1700* (London, 1969), fig. 28.
30. Eames, 'Furniture', figs. 2a-b, 3, 10, 11a-b.
31. J. Geddes, 'Decorative Wrought Iron', *Age of Chivalry,* p. 175.

THE PERPENDICULAR REMODELLING OF THE NAVE: PROBLEMS AND INTERPRETATION

John Crook and Yoshio Kusaba

The account published in 1846 by Robert Willis, 'father of British cathedral archaeology',[1] of the remodelling of the Romanesque nave of Winchester Cathedral is arguably the most accomplished chapter of his enduring architectural history of the church.[2] He traced the progress of the extended building campaign initiated by Bishop William of Edington (1345-66) and taken up by his successor, William of Wykeham (1367-1404). By means of masterly descriptions, supplemented by fine analytical drawings, he convincingly demonstrated how the main elevations of the Romanesque nave were refashioned *in situ* under the direction of Wykeham's architect, William Wynford, into the soaring Perpendicular profiles admired by visitors today.[3]

Willis did not address some questions in the detail demanded by modern scholars, particularly regarding the west end of the cathedral (Figs. 16.1 and 16.2) and the relationship between the works that he attributed to Edington and Wykeham.[4] These limitations are partly the result of Willis's method of exploration and the circumstances under which the paper was composed. He concentrated particularly on stylistic features, such as mouldings, but all his comparisons were from Winchester Cathedral alone; the current state of knowledge did not permit him to relate the mouldings to those occurring in other contemporary buildings, as would be done today. He mentioned only briefly the equally important evidence provided by construction techniques, such as coursing and jointing; some of this evidence is to be seen in concealed parts of the building, such as the roof spaces. No doubt his failure to discuss such matters in detail is partly explained by the fact that his paper was composed as an introduction to an analytical tour of the cathedral; it would have been impractical to take his audience into the inaccessible recesses. Willis tended, also, to emphasise Wykeham's work at the expense of that which he attributed to Edington; this may reflect the much greater volume of extant documentary material relating to the operations of the later bishop.[5] In this paper we re-examine the evidence and attempt to refine Willis's findings. We add new observations to those of Willis, identifying some of the problems which invite further research.[6]

The Romanesque West Front

The Romanesque west front is the subject of a forthcoming study by Philip McAleer,[7] and it is not our intention to discuss it in detail here. Suffice it to say that the limited available evidence seems to indicate a structure comprising twin towers flanking a narthex at ground level with a gallery above. All of these elements are extant or evidenced in contemporary churches in Normandy.[8] One interesting question is why the Romanesque west front was demolished at all. Was it structurally unsound?[9] This seems unlikely: the Romanesque

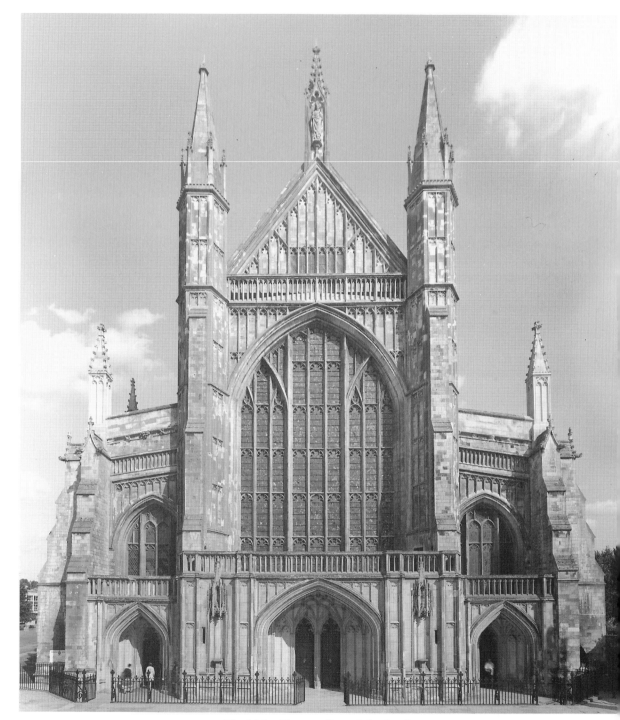

Fig. 16.1   The west front. *John Crook*

foundations towards the western end of the cathedral are more firmly established than those further east, as was convincingly demonstrated when the cathedral was underpinned in 1905-12,[10] and the surviving foundations are immensely thick,[11] unlikely to have been affected by the subsidence so evident, for example, in the south wall of the 13th-century retrochoir.[12] Another suggestion, for which there is however no evidence, is that the Romanesque west front was removed because it had never been completed.[13] The mostly likely explanation remains that the Romanesque west front was taken down because it was considered stylistically outmoded. At several other cathedrals, however, the Romanesque west fronts survived or were merely remodelled.[14]

The plan of the Romanesque west front is known to us from the short section of flint and mortar core now forming part of the wall between the churchyard and No. 11, The Close, and from the wide footings whose core protrudes in places through the gravel in the cathedral forecourt; these footings have been excavated on at least four occasions.[15] The evidence visible within the roof spaces and stair turrets of the west end of the cathe-

Fig. 16.2   Internal elevation, section and plan of the west front, dated 1816, by Edward Blore (Britton, *Winchester Cathedral*, pl. V)

dral is less well known. In the roof spaces above the nave aisles there are indications of the junction between the main elevations of the nave and the east wall of each flanking tower. This evidence has been partially obliterated by the rough piercing of passages from the stair turrets, but fragmentary remains of three or four courses of the alternately-bonded eastern walls of the towers survive in the north roof space, confirming the Romanesque plan determined by excavation.

The 14th-Century Remodelling of the West Front

Willis proposed a simple two-phase division for the remodelling works: he was of the opinion that most of the west front was built before Edington's death, and that the work was completed under Wykeham's patronage at the end of the century. In fact, the west front shows several constructional anomalies which suggest that this was an over-simplification. Willis was undoubtedly correct in attributing the greater part of the nave remodelling, including the aisle and nave vaults, to the campaign initiated by Wykeham in the 1390s; the remodelling of the west front and the westernmost aisle bays seems, however, to have involved more than one phase of building. The most significant point to have emerged from our examination is that the triple porch block appears to have been constructed against the eastern walls of the Romanesque west front: these walls remained standing in this phase. Only when the porch block had been completed was the rest of the Romanesque western structure eventually taken down in preparation for the completion of the west front more or less as we see it today.

Phase 1: The Triple Porch Block

The first identifiable phase of new building consists of a triple porch block,[16] built in Caen stone.[17] It comprises three widely-spaced, deep, splayed porches, under four-centred arches, leading to doorways opening into the nave and aisles; the central porch (Fig. 16.3) is wider,

Fig. 16.3   The central porch. *John Crook*

taller and deeper than the flanking ones, which are set back by 1.22 m. The splays of the lateral porches are unequal, to allow their doorways to be centrally placed with respect to the nave aisles.[18] The top of the porch block is marked by a cornice, surmounted by a balustrade.

Apart from a drawing of an arch-moulding section,[19] Willis scarcely discussed the stylistic features of the triple porch block.[20] The design of the interior of each porch is characterised by a busy linearity and a fastidious repetition of features such as the clusters of tiny hexagonal bases carrying all the vertical shafts. A similar concern for stylistic logic is displayed in the way in which the outermost order of the porch arches runs behind the moulded course at the top of the plinth, reappearing below it. The wide splays of the porches are decorated with blind panels under narrow cinquefoil tracery with foliate cusps; there are two bays of panelling each side of the deeper, central porch, and one in the side porches. The close-set intricacy of the lierne vaulting adds to the impression of linear complexity. The spandrels above the porches are decorated with blind vertical panels, with trefoil tracery and foliate cusps.

On the western face of the triple porch, between the central and lateral porches, the severity of what are essentially solid blocks of masonry buttressing the main nave elevations and containing the stairs is relieved by canopied niches for statuary flanked by shallow salients, part-hexagonal on plan, decorated with narrow traceried panels with trefoil heads. The tracery and vaulting of the niches echo the busy design of the porches. Projecting from the angles of the salients are small plain pilaster buttresses running from ground level to the cornice.

Phase 2: Interior and Upper Parts of the West Front

The construction of the triple porch was followed by further work that Willis attributed to Edington, comprising most of the remainder of the west front. Several reasons may be advanced for assigning this work to a later phase than the triple porch. Evident disjunctions in the coursing between the outer and inner walls are visible in the reveals of the three doorways, especially the central one. It appears that the masonry of the internal walls at the west end of the nave was toothed into that of the back of the triple porch. The most plausible explanation is that this procedure was necessary because the triple porch had first been built against the eastern walls of the Romanesque west front, which had survived the initial demolition.[21] The masonry of the porch block was roughly toothed into the core of the east walls of the Romanesque towers until these walls were ready to be taken down; later the Phase 2 masonry was toothed back into the earlier work.

Another feature supports this conjecture. At the westernmost end of each aisle wall are bands of blind, traceried panelling, 870 mm. wide (Fig. 16.4). Close examination shows that these bands, which are now truncated by sculpted corbels supporting the aisle vault, formerly continued upwards, following the curve of the arches of the windows at the ends of the aisles; it seems that they were intended to run right around the windows. The following argument explains the necessity for this treatment. The west end of the westernmost Romanesque bays of the nave aisles had been defined by the inner face of the eastern wall of the Romanesque western towers. These massive walls (perhaps 2.00 m. thick after the removal of the facing masonry from the west side) were, however, replaced by much thinner 14th-century ones (1.10 m.), whose position was pre-determined by the fact that they were constructed against the east side of the porch block, which had already been built

Fig. 16.4   Panelled band at west end of north aisle wall, with later inserted corbel. *John Crook*

in Phase 1. So the east face of these new walls was approximately 900 mm. west of that of their Romanesque predecessors. To avoid having a westernmost bay that was this much longer than the others, and to avoid difficulties when vaulting, the gap was bridged by the panelled bands. If the Romanesque west front had been entirely demolished before its 14th-century successor was erected, the inner face of the new west wall would have been aligned to the west end of the westernmost bay, and there would have been no need for this compromise.

There is some evidence that a similar panelled band was also intended to frame the great west window. When the aisles and main vessel were eventually vaulted by Wykeham a different design was introduced, with transverse arches standing well forward from the window plane in a rather clumsy way (Fig. 16.4, top).

A study of the mouldings of the inner face of the west front compared with those of the triple porch also reveals dissimilarities which may not be explained merely by their different architectural context. The tracery of the panels is more robust, and the bases—now restricted to the major mullions—though still hexagonal, do not display the complexity observed in the porch block.[22] The simplification of style may indicate that we are dealing with a new phase of building, possibly after a pause of some years.[23] It is possible, furthermore, that the triple porch was intended to support a structure very different in design from the west front that was actually built in the second phase.

West Windows, Stair Turrets and West Gable

Internally, the elevation of the central vessel consists of two tiers of cinquefoil headed panels, above which are four tiers of similar window lights in the great west window, followed by the tracery lights at the head of the window (Fig. 16.2). The mullions that run up through the entire elevation from the ground to the window-head appear to be all of one constructional phase. These major and minor mullions are arranged in a rhythm of A-B-B-A; a simpler A-B-A pattern is employed in the lateral windows, and the central, minor mullions stop at window sill level. The mullions of the great west window and the lateral windows have almost identical profiles, the only difference being that the minor mullions of the lateral windows are slightly narrower.[24]

Externally, the great west window is framed within deep jambs comprising two wide casement mouldings,[25] which Willis identified as a feature of the building works carried out under Edington's patronage. The inner moulding runs right around the arch, while the outer one on each side stops against a string-course on the diagonal face of each stair turret. Willis could not accept that this formed part of the original design, and suggested (implausibly in our view) that the string-courses marked the upper limit of Edington's work.[26] Above this window and the flanking ones at the ends of the aisles, the spandrels are decorated with blind panelling terminating in trefoil heads with cusps decorated with foliate knobs.

Flanking the great west window are hexagonal stair turrets, rising to the full height of the elevation and terminating in pinnacles approximately at the same height as the pinnacle over the western gable. Most of the faces of the turrets are decorated with narrow, paired panels with trefoil heads, similar to those of the panelled bands at the west end of the aisles. However, the western face of each turret is plain, and a plain buttress with three off-sets is built against it. The masonry at the base of these buttresses logically continues that of the porch block, and is properly coursed with the stair turrets, as is all the original masonry where it has survived,[27] indicating that these buttresses were designed from the outset in Phase 2, rather than being an afterthought.

Willis 'was inclined to think' that the gable above the west window belonged to Wykeham's post-1394 campaign.[28] Stylistically, however, the gable shares many features with the remainder of the west front. The major mullions of the rectangular six-light window in the gable are identical in external profile and dimensions to the major mullions of the windows at the end of the aisles.[29] Major and minor mullions follow the same (A-B-B-A) rhythm as that of the great west window below. These mullions are carried up through the head of the window, meeting the projecting moulded coping of the gable. Flanking the window are similar vertical elements (again with an A-B-B-A rhythm), exactly aligned with those above the extrados of the west window. They all form a system of panelling terminating in cusped cinquefoils. All these stylistic features suggest that the gable was constructed in the same phase as the rest of the west front above the porch.[30]

The Remodelling of the Aisles

Two bays of the north aisle and one of the south were remodelled in this phase, including windows identical to those at the ends of the aisles. Although stylistically no significant change is visible between the west wall and the aisle walls, further localised coursing disturbances may be detected. On the south side, there is a notable change in internal coursing just east of the band of panelling. However, the external masonry of the aisles is consistently coursed with the clasping buttresses at the south-west corner of the nave, which form part of Phase 2. If, as seems possible, the remodelling was essentially a refacing of the Romanesque core, work might have progressed at different rates internally and externally. Another possible factor determining these anomalies was the insertion of a doorway in the first bay, presumably leading into the southernmost part of the burial ground.[31]

On the north side, where two bays were remodelled, a break in the external coursing occurs in the angle between the north-facing clasping buttress and the aisle wall, up to a level corresponding to the string course; above this level the courses run together.[32]

Fig. 16.5   North elevation of the west end of the nave, showing Phase 2 and Phase 3 aisle windows and Phase 3 clerestory. *John Crook*

Internally no such anomalies are discernible, but the walls here are partly obscured by the subsequent insertion of the consistory court (now the cathedral treasury).[33]

The fact that two bays were remodelled on the north side compared with one on the south may reflect the fact that immediately north of the two westernmost bays of the nave stood a chapel dedicated to St Swithun, a focus of pilgrimage activity situated over the saint's original grave. This was rebuilt in smaller form at the time of the mid 14th-century alterations, and a new doorway was created leading to it.[34] This doorway, like the one on the south, mentioned above, shows the moulding characteristics attributed to Edington's mason by Willis, notably the wide hollow chamfer.[35]

Intended Height of the Aisles

Willis drew attention to the fact that the aisle walls of the work that he attributed to Edington were lower than the final height of those produced by Wykeham's post-1394 campaign. This is clear externally, where a set-off in the masonry just above the apex of the westernmost aisle windows represents the head of the main wall, upon which a parapet would have been set (Fig. 16.5).[36] The profile of the aisle roof is reflected in the line of the cornice at the head of the blind panelling above the lateral windows (Fig. 16.6).

There is also evidence within the roof spaces for the raising of the aisle parapet. The most important evidential features are the short lengths of sloping weathering courses on the eastern face of the walls at the west ends of the roof spaces, at a level corresponding to the cornice mentioned in the previous paragraph (Fig. 16.7).[37] These give the precise position of the intended lead roof over the Phase 2 aisles.[38] Clearly very little space was envisaged between the top of the vault and the roof. Vestiges of an intended opening from the stair turrets on to the aisle roofs survive on the south side (Fig. 16.8). On this side, the weathering course is returned for a short distance along the back of the gallery wall.

Inside the building, the blank spandrels above the windows at the west end also suggest that Wykeham's final aisle vault was set at a somewhat higher level than originally intended in Phase 2. The springing of the proposed vaulting is unlikely to have been markedly different from the level eventually adopted by Wykeham, however. There is no evidence that any such vaulting was commenced in Phase 2.

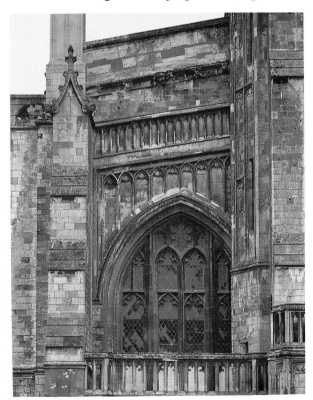

Fig. 16.6   Phase 2 window at the west end of the north aisle.
John Crook

Fig. 16.7   West wall of
north aisle roof space,
showing fragment of
weathering course associated
with the proposed Phase 2
aisle roof. *John Crook*

Fig. 16.8   North-west corner of south aisle
roof space, showing remains of door on to
proposed Phase 2 roof. *John Crook*

A discontinuity in the masonry of the responds in the Phase 2 bays at the level of the springing of the later vault is not necessarily significant; such a break is found at the springing of all of Wykeham's aisle vaults, and two or three courses of the Phase 2 vaulting respond shafts appear to have been replaced when Wynford's octagonal capitals were inserted (Fig. 16.4).[39] Likewise, the sculpted corbels supporting the transverse arches at the west ends of the aisles also date from the late 14th century,[40] and were inserted above the truncated panelled bands.

No vaulting actually took place in Phase 2, therefore, nor is it clear whether the aisles were re-roofed at this stage. If the alterations to the aisle walls consisted essentially of a re-casing, it might have been possible to leave the aisle roofs provisionally *in situ.*[41]

Despite these difficulties in interpretation, there can be little doubt that the aisles were to be revaulted as part of Phase 2, and this implies in turn an intention also to remodel the main elevations of the nave. The plan must have been to suppress the main arcade, and produce a two-storey elevation. The level of the proposed clerestory windows is suggested by the lowered pitch of the aisle roof. The most likely treatment is presumably that found in the presbytery, dating from earlier in the century.[42]

Phase 3: The Remodelling of the Main Elevation of the Nave

There is no evidence that the remodelling of the nave piers, analysed so penetratingly by Robert Willis, was started in Phase 2, and if this was the intention we have no evidence for the form the piers and the elevations above them might have taken. The most economical interpretation is that the main elevations remained unaltered at this stage; if a lower roof was actually built over the westernmost aisle bays, the gallery openings must have been blocked. There is no evidence that the clerestory was remodelled in Phase 2, and the entire clerestory undoubtedly forms part of Phase 3 (Fig. 16.5).

Work began with the main elevation on the south side, working from west to east, then continued on the north side, working in the same direction.[43] As Willis showed, some Romanesque masonry of the piers was left *in situ* and was actually cut into new profiles.[44] However, this method of working was neither as consistent nor as extensive as Willis implied. Working eastwards along the south side we find that in those piers that received this treatment the Romanesque shaft on the nave side and its associated dosseret survive; on the aisle side the respond shafts of the main order usually survive, while the masonry on the diagonal faces of the piers is usually replaced and only occasionally is recut Romanesque stone. Obviously new facing masonry had to be added at the level where the springing of the main arcade had been cut away, so the recut Romanesque masonry is limited to a band between the top of the Perpendicular bases and the level of the bottom of the former Romanesque main arcade capitals. In other words, the re-use of existing facing masonry was limited; and it was eventually found far simpler to strip off the Romanesque masonry in its entirety and re-case the piers.

In the main vessel of the nave, the junction between Phases 2 and 3 occurs within the main arcade responds at the west end, which are illustrated by Willis.[45] On the main vessel side, Wykeham's recut Romanesque masonry abuts that of Phase 2 with a straight joint. On the aisle side of the responds, the panelled band was replaced by shafts supporting Wykeham's aisle vaulting.

As already noted, this aisle vaulting was set at a higher level than originally envisaged in Phase 2. This involved alterations to the west wall, above the terminal windows of the aisles. The masonry here was cut back above the vault as far as was necessary, nearly to the line of the outer wall, where it continues in the form of the north-south clasping buttresses (Fig. 16.7), and the greater part of the west wall above the aisle vaulting was rebuilt. Internally, Romanesque masonry was re-used in this wall.

The treatment of the walls above the blind balustrades over the terminal aisle windows is visually the least satisfactory part of the west front, and it is hardly surprising that it has often been supposed that 'Wykeham's' post-1394 work began at the level of these balustrades. Set on each balustrade are a few courses of plain masonry, then a cornice with grotesque heads and square fleurons; this cornice returns along the entire length of the nave, at the foot of the parapet. In fact the balustrades themselves should probably be assigned to Phase 3. They abut the tracery panels of the hexagonal stair turrets in a clumsy way, suggesting that they are secondary. Furthermore, the masonry of the balustrades appears to be integral with the rebuilt sections of the walls above the aisle vaults and must therefore belong to the same phase. As Willis observed, the cusps of the trefoils of the balustrading have no terminal foliage, which may also imply a post-1394 date. The open balustrade above the triple porch, though now a modern rebuild, may originally have been of the same date; it is similar to the internal balustrades below the clerestory windows of the main nave elevation, built in that period.

Examination of the timber high roof shows that it was completely reconstructed in the early 15th century;[46] its pitch was altered, as may be seen by the weathering courses against the west face of the tower. The upper parts of the walls were also raised slightly, and the walls themselves were thickened out, partly covering the surviving Romanesque wall-shafts and dosserets above the extrados of the Perpendicular high vault.

Willis's account of the actual remodelling of the main nave elevations appears still to be broadly valid, and is perhaps the most satisfactory part of his 1845 paper. In his view the heraldry of the nave vault indicates that it was not completed until the episcopate of Cardinal Beaufort.[47] Wykeham's coat-of-arms appears in every bay of the nave vault, but this may merely indicate his role of benefactor. The extended building campaign produced one of the most admired features of Winchester Cathedral.

Documentary Evidence and the Problem of Dating

So far in this paper we have deliberately avoided assigning absolute dates to the various phases. There can be little doubt, on stylistic grounds, that Phase 1, the triple porch, should be assigned to the period of Edington's episcopate. The good documentary evidence for Wykeham's post-1394 campaign provides a secure date for the remodelling of the greatest part of the nave, including all the vaults of the nave and aisles. Between these two limits has to be placed our Phase 2, traditionally attributed to Edington: we propose an alternative interpretation.

Edington's Will

Edington's will, partly quoted by Willis,[48] makes clear that by 1366 he had begun work 'upon the nave'. Willis believed that this work comprised most of the west front, together with two aisle bays on the north side and one on the south. However, we have divided Willis's single building campaign of 'Edington' into two clearly separated phases; and further documentary evidence discussed in the following sections implies that the will alluded merely to the unfinished state of the west end of the nave, with the half-demolished east walls of the Romanesque western structure still standing, and the new triple porch built against them.

The Building Works of 1371

Important evidence for building works at Winchester Cathedral in 1371 occurs in Wykeham's episcopal register. On 7 April he admonished persons unknown who, 'fearing neither God nor men, stole from that place [the graveyard of Winchester cathedral] ashlar blocks and unhewn stone, lime, cement and scaffolding poles belonging to the new work of our church (*'novi operis ecclesiæ nostræ predictæ'*), which had been prepared at great cost for the execution of its construction works'.[49]

In his *Life of Wykeham* George Moberly suggested that this accumulation of building materials marked 'the inception of the great design of the transformation of the whole of the nave into the Perpendicular style of architecture'.[50] The terminology certainly broadly supports this idea; for when work did actually begin, in 1394,[51] a careful distinction was made between the 'old works' and the new campaign, the *nova opera*. We now propose that the works apparently beginning or in progress in 1371 may have comprised our Phase 2, i.e. the work between the triple porch and Wykeham's well-documented building campaign of 1394 onwards. The reference to the theft of building materials seems to imply that the cathedral churchyard, north of the cathedral itself, was being used as an active building site rather than a place where materials were being stock-piled for building works that never took place.[52]

Moberly suggested that Wykeham's work on the nave was interrupted 'after three or four years' because of lack of co-operation from two successive priors, Hugh Basing and Robert Rudborne. Only with the appointment of the more complaisant Thomas Neville could the works continue. But apart from his political difficulties at that time, the bishop was also busily engaged in the construction of New College, Oxford (1380-86) and Winchester College (1387-94), as well as repairs to other episcopal buildings.[53]

The Visitation Injunctions of 1393

Nevertheless, arrangements for the resumption of building work were made before the death of Prior Rudborne in 1395. Wykeham's visitation injunctions of 23 August 1393 are a key document, as yet unpublished. The bishop drew attention to the ruinous state of the church, and ordered Prior Robert Rudborne to pay £700 sterling in seven annual instalments to the 'Clerk of the New Works', Brother John Wayte, towards repairs. The subprior and convent were likewise to pay 700 marks in seven annual instalments.[54] Meanwhile similar financial arrangements were made regarding the 'Clerk of the Old Works'. Old and new building work were kept apart for accounting purposes. The visitation injunctions of 1393 mark the start of the main phase of Wykeham's construction programme at the cathedral.

Wykeham's Will

Wykeham's will of July 1403 is an invaluable source-document for the later stages of the work and provides the sequence of operations.[55] By then the aisles were partly completed. Though the text implies that work had not yet started on the central nave vessel, the fact that Wykeham's chantry chapel was apparently complete suggests that the remodelling of the nave elevations had in fact reached at least the fifth bay from the west on the south side. He ordained that 'the body or middle of the church, between the south and north aisles, from the entrance to the choir to the west end should be refashioned in its walls, windows and vaulting following the form and manner of the new work of the aisles, now begun'.

Conclusions

It seems to us that the works of 1371 were more substantial than previous authorities have proposed, and we suggest as a working hypothesis that the works of 1371 comprised our Phase 2, namely the main work of the west front and the westernmost bay(s) of the aisles. Our hypothesis does not, of course, disqualify the traditional view that Wykeham's main work on the nave was held up either because of a disagreement with the prior and convent or because he was occupied elsewhere in work on New College, then Winchester College.

The study of moulding types, facilitated by the present scaffolding of the west front, may help to answer these questions, which are presented as working ideas which may help elucidate the problems of this complex period in the constructional history of Winchester Cathedral.

Notes

1. The felicitous phrase of T. Tatton-Brown, *Great Cathedrals of Britain* (London, 1989), p. 9. See also R. Mark, 'Robert Willis, Viollet-le-Duc, and the Structural Approach to Gothic Architecture', *Architectura* 7.2 (1977), pp. 52-64.
2. Willis, *Winchester Cathedral,* pp. 54-75: chap. IV, 'On the Nave'.
3. This aspect of Willis's work was not entirely new, however: the process by which the nave had been remodelled had already been alluded to by Garbett in his letter of 1817 published in Britton, *Winchester Cathedral,* p. 59.
4. The problems are summarised by John Harvey, *The Perpendicular Style* (London, 1978), p. 84: '... [the west front] is an enigmatic work. Just how much was designed at the start, and when that start was, is a problem compounded by the question of what was under construction for Edington's successor Wykeham in 1371, and how much of the front itself was designed by Wynford in or after 1394.'
5. Willis's text reveals, too, some aesthetic prejudice in favour of Wykeham's post-1394 work: he describes, for example, the windows of the west front and the westernmost bays as 'most cavernous and gloomy' (Willis, *Winchester Cathedral,* p. 59), and his attitude may have affected the balance of his analysis.
6. The scaffolding now erected for the repair of the west front will undoubtedly facilitate research, allowing a detailed study of the structure to be made.
7. *HFC Proc.,* forthcoming.
8. See above, pp. 24-6 and p. 35, note 19.
9. As Peers and Brakspear believed (*VCH Hants,* v, p. 58): 'The whole west front of the Romanesque church must have been very ruinous at the time ...'.
10. I. T. Henderson and J. Crook, *The Winchester Diver* (Winchester, 1984), pp. 20-3.
11. The footings of the north-western presumed tower, excavated by Martin Biddle and Birthe Kjølbye-Biddle in the mid-1960s, were over 4 m. thick. The surviving upstanding length of core at the south-west corner is 2.80 m. thick, implying walls at least 3.15 m. (10 ft. 4 ins.) thick.
12. Towards the east end of the nave, however, there is evidence for the poor condition of the south aisle wall: a fragment of a Romanesque respond shaft survives opposite the third pier from the crossing (it was presumably covered by a screen associated with the rood screen which stood in this bay); it inclines considerably from the vertical.
13. For the problem of the completion date of the west end of the nave, see above, p. 32. Evidence in the roof spaces (see below) shows that the tower walls had reached at least the level of the crown of the gallery arcade.
14. At Canterbury, where Lanfranc's nave was remodelled like Winchester's in the 14th century, the south-west tower was remodelled in the first half of the 15th century by Archbishop Chichele; the Romanesque north-west tower survived until its demolition in 1831.

15. The Romanesque west front was excavated by Owen Carter *c*.1845, as reported by Willis, *Winchester Cathedral*, p. 65 (see also *Hampshire Chronicle*, 10 January 1846: 'The ancient foundations at the west end of the Cathedral have lately been re-opened and examined ... by Mr Owen Carter'); by John Colson in 1862: *Hampshire Chronicle*, 22 March 1862; by Martin Biddle and Birthe Kjølbye-Biddle in 1966 (M. Biddle, 'Excavations at Winchester, 1966: Fifth Interim Report', *Antiq. J.* 47 (1967), pp. 267-8 and pls. LIIb and LIX); and by the office of the Winchester City Archaeologist in June/July 1990 (K. E. Qualmann, unpublished report, 'Archaeological Evaluation of Areas to the North and West of No. 11, The Close, Winchester', dated 10 September 1990).

16. For William Garbett, writing in 1817, the porch block was also of a different phase from the rest of the west front; he proposed, however, that it was constructed subsequently and attributed it to Cardinal Beaufort: Britton, *Winchester Cathedral*, p. 66.

17. See above, p. 43 for a discussion of the stone types of the west front. As well as the other types of stone enumerated by Tim Tatton-Brown, there is also considerable use of artificial 'plastic stone'. A full survey of the stones used in the west front is being carried out as part of the current repair programme.

18. This feature is not shown in Blore's plan (our Fig. 16.2).

19. Willis, *Winchester Cathedral*, p. 76, moulding 'I'.

20. Richard Morris (*pers. comm.*) hopes to undertake a study of the stylistic features of the porch. He provisionally detects a link between the porch moulding profiles and bases and those in the south transept at Gloucester, which might point to John Sponlee; but the profiles also appear to be connected with work in the style of the Wells lodge in the north transept at Milton Abbas (Dorset), and the best parallel for the vaulting of the Winchester porch appears to be the Lady Chapel at Wells, indicating the Thomas of Witney/William Joy partnership (see above, pp. 184-7).

21. It seems likely that what survived were the eastern walls of the two flanking towers, and the terminal wall of the nave, which probably comprised a wide arch between a western gallery and the nave itself. Leaving as much of the Romanesque work for as long as possible seems a more likely procedure than taking everything down and leaving the entire nave and aisles open to the elements, and producing, as it were, a cross-sectional view of the cathedral.

22. The moulding of the major mullions of the west wall of the nave is similar to those of the central mullions of the chantry chapel of Bishop Edington (d.1366).

23. J. H. Harvey, *The Perpendicular Style* (London, 1978), p. 85, also suggests that a pause in construction may have occurred, which he attributes to the Black Death of 1347-48.

24. Externally, the mullions are step-chamfered, and the angles (120 degrees) are again based on the hexagonal form. The major mullions differ from the minor ones by the addition of a part-hexagonal nosing. Internally, the mullion profiles are characterised by hollow chamfers and rolls mouldings. In the great west window the major mullions are 560 mm. wide and the minor mullions exactly half that width (280 mm.); the major mullions of the lateral windows are 560 mm. wide and the minor ones 240 mm. wide.

25. That is to say, elliptical hollow mouldings.

26. Willis, *Winchester Cathedral*, p. 64 and fig. 29, which illustrates the mouldings.

27. The considerable amount of post-medieval refacing of the buttresses in Portland stone is less satisfactorily integrated with the turrets.

28. Willis, *Winchester Cathedral*, p. 63.

29. Internally, these mullions have a step-chamfer profile.

30. Unfortunately the clumsy integration of the timber roof with the internal masonry of the gable cannot be taken as evidence to corroborate this deduction; Wykeham's post-1394 roof at the western end of the nave was rebuilt after a fire in 1698: J. Munby and J. Fletcher, 'Carpentry in the Cathedral and Close at Winchester', *BAA Winchester*, p. 105.

31. The burial ground is now shown to have extended well south of its present boundary. The City Archaeologist's investigations have established that the Carnary Chapel of 'St Mary's *in cœmiterio*' clearly did stand well *within* the cemetery rather than on the south side as the present walls imply (see note 15, above). Burials are found in the present garden of No. 11, The Close, well south of the present south wall of the churchyard.

32. It should, however, be noted that both the north-west and the south-west clasping buttresses appear to have been refaced in post-medieval times, in Portland stone. Anomalies in the coursing may

therefore have been removed or introduced.

33. The Romanesque plinth is visible at the foot of the wall in the second bay from the west, on the north side.

34. The chapel in existence when the Romanesque west front was demolished probably dated from the 13th century (M. Biddle, 'Excavations at Winchester, 1966: Fifth Interim Report', *Antiq. J.* 47 (1967), pp. 267-8; *idem,* 'Excavations at Winchester, 1967: Sixth Interim Report', *Antiq. J.* 48 (1968), pp. 278-80), and abutted the east side of the north-west tower. Its north and west walls were rebuilt further south and east respectively in the mid-14th century, giving a chapel less than half the size of the previous one.

35. The mouldings of Edington's south door were revealed in the summer of 1950, when post-medieval infill was removed: W. Carpenter Turner, 'Curle's Passage', *WCR* 20 (1951), p. 11.

36. Cf. Willis, *Winchester Cathedral,* p. 60, fig. 24.

37. Only short lengths survive; much of the wall at the west end of the aisle roof spaces was rebuilt when Wynford's vault was inserted (see below).

38. The weathering courses were noticed by Garbett in the early 19th century (Britton, *Winchester Cathedral,* p. 64), who realised that they marked the intended level of the aisle roof in this phase.

39. In the respond between the two Edington bays on the north side there is a clear change in the jointing pattern two courses below the Wykeham capital, and the stone is of a different colour.

40. See above, p. 110.

41. A weathering crease cut into the south (external) side of the main elevation below the present roof in the westernmost bay of the south aisle (visible in Fig. 16.8) suggests that a temporary roof was erected here, possibly between our Phases 2 and 3; however, the crease also cuts through the infill of the Romanesque gallery arches, which is Wykeham's work. There is, furthermore, no such crease over the north aisle.

42. See above, pp. 182-9 and Fig. 13.10.

43. See our comments on Wykeham's will, below.

44. Willis, *Winchester Cathedral,* pp. 68-70.

45. Willis, *Winchester Cathedral,* p. 62, fig. 26, showing the respond of the south arcade.

46. Munby and Fletcher, 'Carpentry', pp. 101-5.

47. Willis, *Winchester Cathedral,* p. 59.

48. Willis, *Winchester Cathedral,* p. 54, note 's'.

49. T. F. Kirby (ed.), *Wykeham's Register,* 2 vols. HRSoc (1896-9), ii, p. 127. At the same time (*ibid.,* pp. 127-8) an appeal was made for workmen and means of transport to bring stone from quarries in the Isle of Wight to the cathedral, so that repair works could be carried out.

50. G. H. Moberly, *Life of William of Wykeham,* 2nd edn. (Winchester and London, 1893), p. 271. Moberly believed, however, that the west front had been completed, together with modifications to the aisle walls of the westernmost bay(s) (i.e. our Phase 2), between Wykeham's appointment and 1371; this is implausible.

51. A Winchester College document, quoted by R. Lowth, *The Life of William of Wykeham, Bishop of Winchester,* 3rd edn. (Oxford, 1777), p. 195, note 9 states that work began in November 1394: '*Novam fabricam [Ecclesiæ Wynton.] incepit die Mercurii prox. post festum omnium Sanctorum anno regni Regis Richardi II. xviii*'.

52. Moberly believed (pp. 101-2, 272) that the works of 1371 included the remodelling of the eight piers on the south side of the nave where the Romanesque masonry was partly recut, rather than refaced. This is implausible; there is no stylistic progression between the profiles or the bases of the 'recut' as opposed to 're-cased' piers.

53. Work on these other buildings is specifically mentioned in Wykeham's appeal for stone from quarries in the Isle of Wight: *Wykeham's Register,* i, pp. 127-8.

54. BL, Harley 328, fo. 16.

55. For the text of the will, see Lowth, *Life of Wykeham,* Appendix, pp. xxxii-vvvvi. Part of the will is quoted in translation by Willis, *Winchester Cathedral,* pp. 57-8.

THE LADY CHAPEL STALLS

Charles Tracy

The Winchester Cathedral Lady Chapel is the only pre-Reformation example to survive with a complete set of oak stalls (Fig. 17.1). Stone stalls were more usually provided, as in the original, 13th-century design of the Winchester Lady Chapel. In fact, evidence has only ever been adduced in a couple of instances for the use of wooden stalls in Lady

Fig. 17.1   View of Lady Chapel stalls from east, *c.*1865. *Winchester City Museums*

231

Chapels elsewhere.[1] Winchester's furniture has tended to be overlooked by modern writers on the cathedral.[2] Nowhere is this more starkly and inexplicably exemplified than in the *Buildings of England* volume for Hampshire, which, under 'furnishings' in the Lady Chapel, omits any mention of the very component upon which the proper liturgical functioning of the space depended.[3] At least one previous cathedral architect seems to have felt that the furniture had been somewhat neglected in modern times by the Dean and Chapter.[4] Perhaps the comparative gloom of the western bay of the Lady Chapel, often making the woodwork difficult to see, has played a part.[5] But for whatever reason, this superb specimen of early Tudor joinery and decorative wood-carving has tended to be passed over.

Across the entrance to the Lady Chapel is a plain but handsome late Gothic oak screen of Perpendicular design (Fig. 17.2). Six tall six-light pierced tracery arches, with an answering dado below, are set on either side of a wider three-tiered opening for the double-doored entrance-way. This structure is topped by a substantial veranda-type loft, with coved ceiling and repeated two-light arcading each side. The screen must have formed part of an earlier set of Lady Chapel furniture, which was either never completed or later

Fig. 17.2   View of western screen of Lady Chapel from west. *John Crook*

discarded when the existing stalls were put in. It has been noted that the double doors of the screen have been adapted to open outwards instead of inwards.[6] It was suggested that this alteration was made to facilitate access to the return stalls of the later furniture. It is probable that the coving under the loft is coeval with the original screen, rather than added when the stalls were put in. The housings for a beam, cut through the parapet of the wall passage on the north side of the chapel (at the top of the stairs discovered by Wilfrid Carpenter Turner) coincides with the eastern extension of the extant screen loft.[7] If the present stalls are to be associated with Prior Silkstede (1498-1524), which seems most probable, the screen cannot have been erected later than 1498, the date of the death of his precursor, Hunton,[8] and is probably somewhat earlier.

The existing stalls represent a reclothing of the 13th-century Lady Chapel. Above them to north and south survives the original treatment of the walls—six open arches in pairs under three blank trefoil heads. Higher still is a pierced quatrefoil between two trefoils, originally lighted through three arched openings in the outer thickness of the

Fig. 17.3   View of internal stair on north side of Lady Chapel, from top. *John Crook*

wall. Arcading with Purbeck marble shafts ran round the chapel at ground level, as it does in the retrochoir aisles to this day.

An important change to the chapel, carried out during the last quarter of the 15th century, was the insertion of a stone stair on the north side in the thickness of the wall (Fig. 17.3). This was discovered by Carpenter Turner in 1969. Although its original purpose is unrecorded, the stair must have had a liturgical function in providing access during services to the western screen, an approach from the north and south stair turrets being relatively inconvenient.[9] The entrance has a finely moulded stone doorcase of 15th-century type, and the date of *c*.1475 which has been assigned to these alterations must be about right.[10] The stair must have been inserted in association with the new entrance screen, which, therefore, can also be assigned the same date, as suggested by Carpenter Turner.[11] Subsequently, structural problems affected the floor of the gallery above, resulting in the need for a strengthening wall to be built directly opposite the entrance at the base of the stair (Fig. 17.3, left). This is of rough-and-ready workmanship and is composed of re-used 13th-century masonry and a few bricks.[12] It made access difficult, and necessitated the removal of the wooden entrance door. Quite reasonably, Carpenter Turner surmised that the strengthening wall was inserted at the same time as the remodelling of the east bay of the Lady Chapel, *c*.1500. However, he also dated the erection of the wooden stalls to the

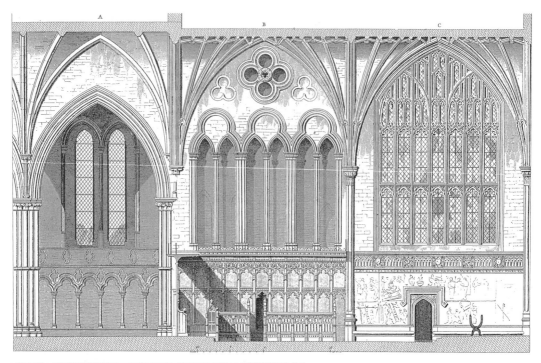

Fig. 17.4   Engraving of Edward Blore's drawing of north side of Lady Chapel and retrochoir (Britton, *Winchester Cathedral,* pl. XX)

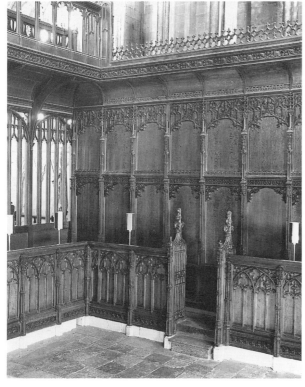

Fig. 17.5   View of north side of Lady Chapel stalls. *John Crook*

Fig. 17.6   Original 'preaching' figure on desk end, north side of Lady Chapel. *Charles Tracy*
Fig. 17.7   Desk front buttress of Lady Chapel stalls. *John Crook*

same time, which is probably about fifteen years too early. Judging from the considerable wear in the centre of the treads now exposed, the passage in its new and very much less convenient form must have been in use for a long time. Moreover, the timber sill at the bottom of the framing, where the stairway penetrates the later stalls, is significantly worn on each side.[13]

The 13th-century stone arcading at ground level was almost completely removed to accommodate the new stalls.[14] Interestingly, the drawing of the north side by Edward Blore in 1817 shows that access to the earlier staircase doorway was incorporated in the new furniture, through one of the panels behind the seats in the sixth bay from the west (Fig. 17.4).[15] Indeed, the break in the seating is still there today, with the original bench ends on either side of the opening. A parallel for a doorway behind a set of stalls can be found on the south side of the roughly contemporary furniture at the chapel at The Vyne, near Basingstoke.

At Winchester, although Carpenter Turner noticed that the framing in the stall backs opposite the stair entrance has been rebated for a door, '... one was never fitted nor could have been without fouling the stone opening behind'.[16] Perhaps, if the furniture had been made elsewhere for assembly on site, the possible requirement for a door in this position

Fig. 17.8 Back panelling of Lady Chapel stalls, detail. *Charles Tracy*

Fig. 17.9 Desk tracery infilling of Lady Chapel stalls. *Charles Tracy*

Fig. 17.10   Door of Fox
chantry chapel. Detail.
John Crook

might have been allowed for just in case it was needed. It is hard to reconcile the refinement of the Winchester stalls with the notion of an open panel being left in the stall backs
giving directly on to a dark entrance through which there was only inconvenient access to
a stair beyond. At least, there is some evidence that the gap between the stalls and the back
wall was lined with panelling.[17] This would have improved the appearance of the arrangement.

A photograph of the Lady Chapel from the east, of *c*.1865, records the condition of
the stalls before the most recent restoration work was undertaken (Fig. 17.1).[18] It can be
seen that the stair entrance had been blocked up by that date. Indeed, from Carpenter
Turner's investigations we know that access was sealed off, above and below, in 1821.[19]
In the period 1817-27, when there was a considerable amount of work going on in the
major spaces of the cathedral, we learn that 'in several years choral services without organ
were held daily in the Lady Chapel'.[20] In order to increase the congregational capacity, the
13th-century wall passages were pressed into service, necessitating the boarding-over of
the staircase on the north side.

The stalls are of the 'single screen' type. They have bench seating, without misericords,
a tendency which began to appear throughout England at about this time. On the north side
the benching is broken into by two original bench ends between which was the entrance
to the staircase. The traceried elevation behind and above the seats consists of two tiers of
arcading, divided by uprights, surmounted by a coved canopy with vine-trail frieze and
cresting.[21] There are 11 seats each side with desks in front, and a further three bays on the
returns. The desks are carried on ventilated stone plinths with elaborate buttressing and
tracery to their fronts (Fig. 17.5). The desk ends are of traditional form with trefoil-shaped
carved poppy heads. On their leading edges they incorporate traceried polygonal buttresses,
similar to those at the divisions of the desk fronts. The buttresses on the desk ends
accommodated lively half-length figures of Tudor ecclesiastics as if standing in pulpits,
preaching (Fig. 17.6). The shorter desk front buttresses resemble architectural tourelles
with capped and finialed roofs (Fig. 17.7).

In spite of the high restoration content, it is evident that in this furniture an exceptional standard of both joinery and decorative carving was achieved. This can be

recognised in the imaginative handling of the decoration, from the treatment of the friezes and crenellation (Fig. 17.8) to the filling of tracery cells (Fig. 17.9) and the details of the buttressing. The carving itself is of an extraordinary delicacy, miraculously supple and plastic for the medium. As Simon Jervis has pointed out, this work is stylistically close to the Fox chantry chapel door, probably datable to *c*.1520 (Fig. 17.10). A local craftsman, Mr. James Thomas Laverty, trading under the name of 'Thomas and Co.', appears to have been responsible for the thorough but sensitive restoration of the furniture in the 1890s.[22]

The disjunction of the desks and stall backs in the Blore drawing, and still today, has been noticed by previous writers.[23] It is certainly curious that before 1821, when the staircase was accessible, the lateral stall entrance-way on the north side appears not to have

Fig. 17.11   Unrestored desk end poppy head on north side of Lady Chapel stalls, from west.
Charles Tracy

lined up with it. It is clear that the desks of the north and south sides must have been moved at some time between their erection and 1817. The unusually wide gap between the return seats and desking, visible even in the Blore drawing, must be authentic as the alignment of the desks depends upon the siting of the two wooden columns supporting the coving of the western screen. The unnecessary and unauthentic gap of just under a seat's width at the east ends suggests that there may have been a rearrangement of the desking at some time in this area. Indeed, it is almost certain that desks and stall bays would have lined up originally throughout. There would have been three bays of desking west of the lateral stall entrance-ways, instead of the existing two and one third, and five further bays east of them. The stall entrance-way on the north side would have aligned with the staircase door.

Apart from repairing and making good, Thomas and Co. were busy in 'restoring' the lost decorative carving, such as the cornice cresting, already mentioned, and a considerable part of the cornice vine-trail frieze. A major preoccupation must have been the restoration of the poppy heads, the 'preaching' figures on the stall end buttresses and the tracery on the western desk ends.[24] All the missing parts were replaced, with more or less authentic results, on the basis of what remained, usually a thigh, shoe, animal foot, hand or paw. The shoes, at least, look convincingly contemporary. Taken together with the treatment of the carving, well represented by the only completely unmutilated desk end to the east of the central entrance-way on the north side (Fig. 17.11) and, selectively on the superstructure, it is possible to build up a composite picture of the carver's style. This is characterised by an admirable fluency, and certain 'trademarks' such as the pricked and decorated backgrounds to the main motifs.[25] An essential element of the luxuriance and imaginativeness of the carving

Figs. 17.12 a & b   Tracery at top of Lady Chapel stall backs; and St George's Chapel, Windsor. Panelling behind stalls. Detail. *Charles Tracy*

style is the wide range of foliage and floral motifs, and the attention to detail throughout.

The eastern desk end on the north side is shown in the 19th-century photograph to be without tracery (Fig. 17.1). This has since been rectified, although the later decoration is merely applied. All the other authentic desk ends have tracery carved in the traditional way in the solid, except for the eastern desk end on the south side, which must have been embellished sometime before the date of the photograph. Given the lavish treatment afforded all the others, it is not easy to understand why the easternmost desk ends were originally plain. Of the 'preaching' figures on the desk end buttresses, only the hatted and cloaked cleric on the easternmost north lateral stall centre desk end is preserved intact (Fig. 17.6). The others have at least lost their heads and many are completely modern replacements.

It was certainly during the priorate of Hunton that the 15th-century easternmost bay of the Lady Chapel was begun. It is generally accepted that, whereas Hunton was responsible for most of the building works, his successor, Prior Silkstede was in charge of the furniture and decoration. Hunton's rebus can be seen on the inside and outside of the eastern bay, and inside in the spandrels of the door on the north side, formerly leading to a vestry. On the bosses in the western bay the arms of Henry VII, and Bishops Courtenay (1487-92) and Langton (1493-1501) can be seen. According to Milner, in both parts of the chapel the names and rebuses of Priors Hunton and Silkstede were painted on the interstices of the vaulting.[26] There is a proprietorial inscription under Silkstede's portrait over the piscina.[27] Jervis also noted the close relationship between the carved wood grape cornice on the stalls, and the stone vine frieze above the wall paintings in the east bay.[28]

In the stalls themselves, the horse on the north-east side of the north-eastern central poppy head could be a reference to Silkstede. On the south side of the desk end south of the main entrance-way the arms of the diocese are displayed. This, perhaps, suggests that it was intended that the bishop should sit in the seat of honour in this position, with the prior on the north side, as often happened in choir-stalls where there was no bishop's throne.[29]

The screenwork in the south transept of the cathedral, which bears Silkstede's initials, presents a striking stylistic contrast to the Lady Chapel stalls. This appears to be slightly later, and recalls another local monument, the English Renaissance style choir-stalls at Christchurch Priory of 1520-25.[30] The Lady Chapel stalls, on the other hand, are still purely Gothic in treatment, recalling a classic *rayonnant* prototype such as the late 13th-century choir-stalls at Poitiers,[31] or the more restrained element of the English Decorated architectural style emanating from London, such as the wall arcading inside St Stephen's Chapel, Westminster. Later examples of the same type in wood are at the Fitzalan Chapel, Arundel of *c*.1385, St Laurence, Ludlow, *c*.1415-25, or even the choir-stalls at Tong Church (Salop.), *c*.1480. The simplicity and conservatism of the Lady Chapel stalls recalls in a general sense the aesthetic of the classically Perpendicular Wykeham chantry chapel in the cathedral itself, completed by 1403.[32] The screenwork in the south transept cannot have been made more than ten years later than the Lady Chapel stalls. This underlines the extreme conservatism of the last-named monument for its date.

Fig. 17.13   The Vyne, Basingstoke. View of south side of chapel stalls. Detail. *Charles Tracy*

Fig. 17.14 Langton Chapel. West screen from the drawing by E. Blore (Britton, *Winchester Cathedral*, pl. XVII, detail)

A progressive feature in these stalls is, of course, the eschewal of the traditional misericords. Yet they recall in many ways the features of the typical 15th-century stereotype. In particular, the desking, ventilated stone plinths, seat standards, buttressing, and the choice of decorative foliage types are typical for their date. What we most emphatically do not find is any late Gothic influence from abroad or any hint of the impending classical revolution. The decorative sculpture barely represents any advance over that on the stalls of St George's Chapel, Windsor of 1478-83.[33] The tracery and decoration at the top of the stall backs at Winchester is very similar indeed to that on the panels behind the stalls at Windsor (Figs. 17.12a and 17.12b). The vine-trail friezes in both buildings are very close. The desk ends at Windsor have similar buttresses with 'preaching' figures. The tracery and decoration on the desk fronts is a simplified version of the same at Windsor. The tourelles on the desk front buttresses at Winchester are scaled-down versions of those on the western lateral screens at Windsor. There is no question of the two sets of furniture being carved by some of the same craftsmen. But the Winchester artists must have known the Windsor work.

Two other sets of stalls should be passed briefly in review, before a reasonable approximation of the date of manufacture of the Lady Chapel furniture can be effected. The chapel stalls at The Vyne are very similar in design to those in the Winchester Lady Chapel, with the double tier of tracery on the stall backs, coved ceiling with crested

Fig. 17.15   Langton Chapel. South side stall backs and canopy-work. *Charles Tracy*

architrave, and benches for seats fronted by comparable desks (Fig. 17.13). The style of the decorative carving is similar, but the execution was by a different workshop. Stylistically, these stalls look as if they must have been made at about the same time. The presence on the battlements of the chapel of the Sandys arms encircled by the Garter strongly suggests that the Vyne chapel could not have been started before 1518. The window glazing was probably finished by 1524.[34] The similarity of the Vyne furniture to that at Winchester could be explained by the friendship of Bishop Fox (1501-28) with William Sandys.[35]

The canopied stalls in the Bishop Langton chantry chapel (Fig. 17.14) were described by Blore in 1817 as 'one of the most elaborate and exquisitely delicate specimens of oak carving in the kingdom' (Fig. 17.15).[36] Unfortunately, in 1818 the woodwork was badly mutilated, the original 14-bay screen with double doors in the centre being moved a few feet eastwards. To fit into the narrower available space the screen was cut down to ten bays. At the same time the coved canopy-work on top of the screen was removed and placed above the altar at the east end of the chapel. The dating of the Langton Chapel stalls is rather a puzzle. Although they should have been made well before the Lady Chapel furniture, since the bishop died in 1501, stylistically they seem more advanced in date.

Again, there are connections with the St George's Chapel stalls, in general terms in the canopy-work, but more specifically in the treatment of the lettered frieze (Fig. 17.16a and 17.16b). But there are some hints also of the style of the Henry VII Chapel stalls at Westminster Abbey, of *c.*1512, in such details as the twisted columns, decorative sculpture, 'twig-cusping', and the human figures on the uprights, although the two monuments are hardly directly comparable.[37] Perhaps there is a hint here of that late-Gothic continental influence, completely lacking in the Lady Chapel. This suggests that the Langton Chapel woodwork cannot have been completed much before the end of the first decade of the 16th century.

Figs. 17.16a & b   Langton Chapel and St George's Chapel, Windsor. Lettered frieze on stalls. Detail. *John Crook and Charles Tracy*

It is understandable that the Lady Chapel stalls have, in the past, been dated to around 1500. Their style is rooted in the English Gothic tradition and their design is strictly conventional. However, Prior Silkstede's responsibility for the embellishment and decoration of the eastern bay of the Lady Chapel, let alone his patronage of the furniture, adds up to an ambitious artistic programme. Given the workload of the new prior, it is difficult to envisage the stalls being erected much before c.1515. It is some reassurance that also on comparable projects, in the cathedral on the Bishop Fox chantry chapel and, elsewhere, on the stalls at the Vyne chapel, the carving and architectural design was for the most part as traditionalist as at the Lady Chapel.[38]

Acknowledgements

I am indebted to John Crook for his practical assistance and useful suggestions, particularly on the archaeological problems associated with the staircase, and for supplying some of the photographs. My thanks to the National Trust for permission to photograph and examine the Vyne chapel stalls. I have benefited from the thorough study of the monument made by Simon Jervis in 1976. He was kind enough to read a draft of this paper, and supplied a number of pertinent comments.

Notes

1. At Westminster Abbey, see P. Tudor-Craig, 'The Embellishments and Furnishing of the Medieval Church', in C. Wilson and others, *Westminster Abbey* (London, 1986), p. 139; and at Norwich, see A. B. Whittingham, 'The Stalls of Norwich Cathedral', *Annual Report of the Friends of Norwich Cathedral* (1948), facing p. 25.
2. An honourable exception is the succinct analysis in Simon Jervis's *Woodwork of Winchester Cathedral* (Winchester, 1976), pp. 34-5.
3. N. Pevsner and D. Lloyd, *The Buildings of England: Hampshire and the Isle of Wight* (Harmondsworth, 1985), p. 675.
4. 'If the Lady Chapel stalls are ever cleaned and restored as they should be...': W. Carpenter Turner, 'Discoveries in the Lady Chapel', *WCR* 39 (1970), p. 35.
5. A complete set of new desk lights has recently been fitted.
6. Carpenter Turner, 'Lady Chapel', p. 35.
7. For a discussion of these stairs, see below. The alternative adduced by Carpenter Turner ('Lady Chapel', p. 35), that the beam housing had been for the existing screen, which would have been sited some 3 ft. further east than at present, seems somewhat far-fetched.
8. Howard and Crossley's reported dating of c.1524 and Vallance's of c.1500-25 are, surely, too late: A. Vallance, *Greater English Church Screens* (London, 1947), p. 53.
9. For the liturgical function of the Lady Chapel, see pp. 247-54.
10. Carpenter Turner, 'Lady Chapel', p. 35. John Crook has pointed out that there is no evidence for any form of door fastening. There are hinge bolts but no wear. The only evidence that the door was ever hung is the round indentation on the ceiling at the east end of the passage.
11. *Ibid.*, p. 35.
12. John Crook has observed that some of the masonry is also of 11th- and 12th-century origin. The 13th-century material is whitewashed and is marked in red ochre as pseudo-ashlar blocks. The bricks are very thin, typically 175 x 40 mm.
13. John Crook has pointed out that, whereas there is some wear on the Lady Chapel or south side, there is much more on the stairs side, where a new piece has been inlaid to compensate.
14. Carpenter Turner ('Lady Chapel', p. 33) explained that: 'When the stalls were fitted the pillars, caps and arcading were removed but the quatrefoils above them were left in position with all projecting mouldings hacked off. To support the stonework formerly carried by the pillars a rough stone wall was built in place of the shafts.'
15. Britton, *Winchester Cathedral,* pl. XX.

16. Seen from the back the framing has been clearly interrupted to form a rectangular opening.
17. John Crook has noted nails in timber posts and nail holes in the masonry.
18. Winchester City Museums, PWCM 3421 (W. Savage Collection). I am grateful to John Crook for bringing the existence of this important 19th-century record of the Lady Chapel to my attention.
19. Written in chalk by the workmen on the back of the panel which blocks the entrance is 'the floor laid over 1821—2 year of George 4 reign'. See Carpenter Turner, 'Lady Chapel', p. 32.
20. Quoted in Carpenter Turner, 'Lady Chapel', p. 33.
21. The modern cresting has replaced that shown in Blore's drawing. See Britton, *Winchester Cathedral*, pl. XXI.
22. CA, 27 February 1894 and 27 November 1894. The firm 'Thomas and Co.' comprised James Thomas Laverty (*alias* Mr. Thomas) and the architect G. H. Kitchin, who together restored the Old Chesil Rectory in Chesil Street in 1892 and then took it over as a business premises: cf. *Hampshire Chronicle*, 4 September 1992; 5 May 1978. Simon Jervis (*pers. comm.*) suggests that the firm was not called 'Kitchin and Laverty' because at that time a commercial partnership between an architect and a craftsman would have been professionally outlawed.
23. Carpenter Turner, 'Lady Chapel', p. 32, and Jervis, *Woodwork*, p. 35.
24. A detailed catalogue of the restorations by Thomas and Co. on the desk ends in the Lady Chapel is as follows:

South-east desk end
Buttress and 'preaching' bishop new. Applied tracery probably modern but inserted before 1865. Tracery on the back in the solid. Both poppy head figures restored from the waist up. (The adjoining stall end also preserves a similar remnant of a human figure with wide shoe/slipper tied at the ankle. The comparability of these details, with their handling is useful evidence that most of the stall ends are authentic.)

North-east desk end
Shown as plain in 1865. New applied tracery inserted. Both the figures of monkeys are mainly new. Only feet, hands and thighs remain from original. Buttress renewed above cornice level, including 'preaching' bishop figure.

South-east centre desk end
Tracery in the solid both sides. New figures inserted into old poppy head. 'Preaching' buttress figure of ecclesiastic reading a book old but with new head.

South-west centre desk end
Tracery in the solid both sides. New figures inserted into old poppy head. 'Preaching' buttress figure modern.

North-east centre desk end
Tracery in the solid both sides. Original poppy head, with two hares on the west side and a squirrel and horse (?rebus for [Silk]steed) on the east intact. Gowned, cloaked and capped 'preaching' figure original. Is this a portrait?

North-west centre desk end
Tracery in the solid both sides. Old poppy head original with carving of addorsed griffins on the north. Replacement on the south. Reading cleric on poppy head old with new head.

South-west return desk end
Tracery in the solid both sides. Although the poppy head with foliage is original, the addorsed griffins are entirely new. Buttress 'preaching' figure renewed.

North-west return desk end
Tracery in the solid both sides. Modern figures skilfully applied to old poppy head. Buttress 'preaching' figure renewed.

25. Notice, for instance, the pricked and mosaic background decoration to the hares (Fig. 17.11) and the horse (?) on the wholly authentic north-west centre desk end.
26. Milner, *Winchester,* ii, 63. For the interpretation of the rebuses, see below, pp. 257-8.
27. In translation: 'Silkstede also caused these polished stones, (O Mary) to be ornamented at his expense': *ibid.,* p. 64, note 1.
28. Jervis, *Woodwork,* pp. 34-5.
29. The bishop may have sat, unconventionally, on the north side of the entrance-way of the main choir-stalls, when these were first built (see above, p. 199), but there is some evidence that by the early 16th century the bishop's throne was in the more usual position (see below, p. 299, note 59).
30. A date of *c.*1515 has been suggested for this furniture: K. F. Wiltshire, *Christchurch Priory: the Choir Stalls and Misericords* (Christchurch, undated). Simon Jervis has surmised that the south transept woodwork may be the remnants of a projected scheme for a new Lady Chapel screen (Jervis, *Woodwork,* p. 35); but see below pp. 262-3 for Martin Biddle's interpretation.
31. For the following examples, see C. Tracy, *English Gothic Choir-Stalls, 1200-1400* (Woodbridge, 1987), pls. 66, 94 and 187; and *idem, English Gothic Choir-Stalls, 1400-1540* (Woodbridge, 1990), pls. 26 and 144.
32. The tracery in the desk fronts at Winchester are of a typical early Perpendicular type, such as John Sponlee's work in the Dean's Cloister at Windsor of 1353-56. See J. Harvey, *The Perpendicular Style* (London, 1978), pl. 17.
33. For a full discussion of this furniture, see Tracy, *Choir-Stalls, 1400-1540,* pp. 47-58, and, in particular, pls. 94, 162, 170 and 189.
34. See H. G. Wayment, 'The stained glass of the chapel of The Vyne and the chapel of the Holy Ghost, Basingstoke', *Archaeologia* 107 (1982), 148-49.
35. Lord Sandys, together with Bishop Fox, obtained from the king a charter in 1524 for the establishment of the Fraternity of the Holy Ghost in Basingstoke. See Chaloner W. Chute, *A History of The Vyne in Hampshire* (Winchester and London, 1888), p. 39.
36. *Gentleman's Magazine* 87 (1817), p. 225. See the description of the monument in Jervis, *Woodwork,* pp. 36-37.
37. For a full discussion of the Henry VII Chapel, Westminster Abbey furniture, see Tracy, *Choir-Stalls, 1400-1540,* pp. 47-58, and, in particular, pls. 161, 175-6 and 179.
38. The figured frieze on the stalls at The Vyne is only half-hearted in its classicism.

THE LADY CHAPEL AND ITS MUSICIANS, *c.*1210-1559

Roger Bowers

Except in the broadest terms, little is now known of the manner in which, by the end of the Middle Ages, even the greater English Benedictine monasteries were undertaking the central function for which they existed, namely the perpetual worship of God in the monastery church. Few late service books of ritual text and plainsong chant have survived, and barely a handful of consuetudinaries. That the maintenance of the *Opus Dei* continued to exercise its historic priority is evident. Moreover, the greater monasteries were energetic in keeping up with, and even inaugurating, developments in the practice of liturgy, especially in respect of the worship of the Virgin Mary. During the 15th century, this latter devotion was manifest particularly in the creation, maintenance and development of small groups of trained singers, boys and (eventually) men, who constituted specialist choirs established to lend particular distinction to the services of worship of the Blessed Virgin. By the time of the Dissolution, some fifty such Lady Chapel choirs are now known to have existed at the more prominent of the Benedictine and Augustinian houses; none is at all well documented, but by good fortune both the origins and the last years of that at Winchester can be traced with greater clarity than has yet proved possible elsewhere.

When, early in the 13th century, the bishop and the cathedral community undertook the substantial enlargement of the east end of Walkelin's original Norman church to its present dimensions, their principal objective was the provision of an eastern chapel dedicated specifically to the conduct of the worship of the Virgin Mary, and in particular to the daily celebration of Lady Mass—the votive mass of the Virgin—observed as a festive mass with full ceremonial and chant. No examples of any of the principal service books of either ritual text or plainsong chant employed at the cathedral at this period are known to be extant. However, the handful of missals and consuetudinaries that survive from other Benedictine houses do convey a reasonably clear overall vision of the content and style of daily Lady Mass,[1] and it is evident that in no significant respect did the nature of its plainsong or ritual differ from that of High Mass of the day. Decent and seemly observance therefore predicated the presence of at least a small chorus of competent singers from among the monks in addition to the celebrant and his assisting deacon and subdeacon; probably the required daily attendance was of some six or eight, as elsewhere.[2] Others, of course, were likely to wish to be present and attend without actually participating; for them, as well as for the singers, were provided the stonework stalls incorporated into the north and south walls of the Lady Chapel, remains of whose arcaded canopies can still be seen behind the later wooden stalls.[3]

By *c.*1225 William of Trumpington, abbot of St Albans, could observe, when inaugurating a daily sung Lady Mass in his own church, that 'in all the noble churches of

247

England a mass of the Blessed Mary is solemnly observed with plainsong daily';[4] in every probability this was, and remained, the case at Winchester also, even though for some two hundred years following its likely inception virtually no documentary notice of this entirely unexceptional and routine observance appears to have survived. However, in 1402 there was made to its manner of performance a major alteration and expansion which elevated its celebration to a much enhanced level of prominence in the life of the monastery. Towards the last years of the 14th century there occurred quite generally in England a fashion—albeit short-lived—for greatly enlarging the number of singing-boys appointed for the choirs of newly-founded collegiate churches, and in particular for employing the resources of boys' voices in the plainsong chant of the daily Lady Mass.[5] The most prominent of the Benedictine monasteries were as subject to this fashion as any other churches, and happened to be in a particularly good position to make an immediate and positive response. At Winchester, as in all other monastic churches, it had been a long time since young boys with unbroken voices had served in the monks' choir in any capacity; the practice of child oblation had been discontinued since about the middle of the 12th century, and by not later than early in the 13th the Benedictine order was applying regulations preventing its monasteries from admitting as novices youths of any age earlier than the late 'teens.[6] However, a pool of young boys was being maintained elsewhere in the priory, as scholars of its almonry grammar school, where a small group of boys nominated by individual monks were given the usual education of the day in reading, writing, and Latin grammar and literature by a secular schoolmaster appointed for the purpose.[7] Numerous such schools are known to have been inaugurated from c.1290, and especially in the early 14th century; among their principal purposes was the provision of boys sufficiently well educated to serve the monks at their private masses. For Winchester, documentation is unfortunately lacking; however, an apparent reference to boys of an almonry school occurs at neighbouring Hyde Abbey as early as c.1325,[8] and it seems reasonable to suggest that the inauguration of an almonry school at the cathedral priory may have been undertaken at much the same period.[9]

Given the ready availability of a team of educated boys already trained to attend the altar, therefore, all that was needed at the beginning of the 15th century to respond to current fashion and turn a group of those blessed with good singing voices into a boys' choir for Lady Mass was the appointment of a qualified musician to instruct and coach them in the necessary skills. Commonly in monasteries of the period, the occupant of this new office was given the title of 'cantor'. The first monastery known to have implemented this departure was Westminster Abbey, some time in the 1390s or a little before; Winchester Cathedral may well have been the second. This innovation was facilitated by the receipt of a substantial endowment conferred on the monastery by John and Alice Talmache, consisting of lands in the manor of Up Somborne (Hants.), of which the priory apparently took seisin in 1400-1.[10] The immediate wishes of the Talmaches were that for the welfare and good estate of their souls a special collect in their names should be recited daily in the course of the celebration of the Lady Mass, and also that an annual commemorative *obit* (the services of Mattins and Mass for the Dead) should be observed in the choir of the cathedral by the monastic body, this *obit* to be specially distinguished by the participation of a (professional) cantor.[11] When, however, in September 1402 the prior and convent were ready to implement these conditions, it was perceived that the generosity of the Talmaches would stretch further than just this; it was found that not merely their *obit*,

Fig. 18.1   View of the Lady Chapel *c.*1900. *Winchester City Museums*

but also the daily Lady Mass at which they were henceforth to be remembered, could be enhanced by the presence of a professional musician and singer, and by a team of boys under his direction.

Consequently, on 29 September 1402 John Tyes, formerly of Westminster Abbey,[12] was appointed as cantor for a term of 20 years, with a two-fold obligation. Firstly, he was to attend every day at Lady Mass celebrated in the Lady Chapel, participating in the singing of its music and also playing the Lady Chapel organ; and secondly, he was to teach up to four boys of the priory in chant whenever assigned to him for the purpose. The monks also proposed to employ his expertise to enhance the music of the services in the principal monastic choir. He was to participate there whenever the liturgy was to be adorned with performances of settings of music in polyphony (*cantus organicus*), and indeed, on all festival days of sufficient rank to warrant the celebration of High Mass by the prior or his substitute.[13] That the four singing-boys whom Tyes was to teach were drawn from the boys of the almonry school (as in all other known Lady Chapel choirs) is strongly suggested by the terms of an extra duty laid upon them two years later. On 16 August 1404 the prior and convent concluded an agreement with the bishop, William of Wykeham, to have masses said for his soul in perpetuity in his chantry chapel in the nave of the cathedral; further, arrangements were made for the boys of the almonry to gather each evening at Wykeham's chantry chapel to sing in honour of the Virgin Mary a Marian votive antiphon (either *Salve regina* or *Ave regina cœlorum*), followed by the psalm *De Profundis* and prayers for the repose of Wykeham's soul.[14] This double duty—of singing daily both at Lady Mass and an evening Marian votive antiphon—became the standard obligation of Lady Chapel singing-boys in all monasteries which maintained them.

Tyes was appointed to be an all-round church musician. His contribution to the monks' choir was to join with the handful of enthusiasts who undertook to enhance the choir service at festive times of the year with performances of the relatively elaborate polyphony of this period, in the form (mostly) of settings of the ordinary and of extra-liturgical motets at High Mass.[15] As organ player, his duties extended only to the Lady Mass. Some primitive and rather raucous brute of an organ had been built for the Anglo-Saxon cathedral as early as the days of Ethelwold and Ælfheah;[16] references to its early 12th- and 14th-century successors may also be found,[17] but at the present period the player of this organ in the body of the church was evidently one of the monks. However, towards the end of the 14th century there had arisen at the greater monasteries the practice of locating a second, smaller, instrument in the Lady Chapel for use at Lady Mass.[18] It was an organ of this type that Tyes was now to play as part of his attendance at Lady Mass, though the nature of the contribution of the instrument to the conduct of the service at this period is wholly obscure.

From 1402 onwards, therefore, the daily Lady Mass was observed by a celebrant and two other monks acting as deacon and subdeacon, attended by a further group of monks to serve as a choir augmented now by the four singing-boys, all directed by John Tyes as professional cantor. Tyes remained in office certainly until around 1418 or 1419, and was still active in the city in 1423.[19] He is remembered as a composer; his two surviving works, both for the ordinary of Mass, are preserved in a manuscript of Lady Mass music probably compiled *c*.1419 and so appear certain to have been written for his Winchester Cathedral singers. One is an elaborately isorhythmic setting of the Gloria, for three voices (Fig. 18.2); the other, mostly in sonorous note-against-note counterpoint, is a four-voice setting of the Sanctus.[20] These pieces, for men's voices (alto and tenor), require no mean level of musical expertise in performance, and create a clear impression that the singers of polyphony among the Winchester monks under Tyes' direction were more than decently competent at their hobby.

In general, the Lady Chapel boys' choirs of the monastic houses proved successful and durable throughout the 15th century, and it is probable that the choir at St Swithun's survived and throve likewise, though lack of documentation leaves such a likelihood impossible to substantiate. The names of two of what appear to be Tyes' successors as lay musicians of the priory are known, though not so much in the capacity of masters of the Lady Chapel choir as of players of the organ in the monks' choir and instructors of the young monks in chant. Robert Bygbroke appears already to have been in office by 1429, but his talents were sufficiently great to attract the predatory attentions of a more

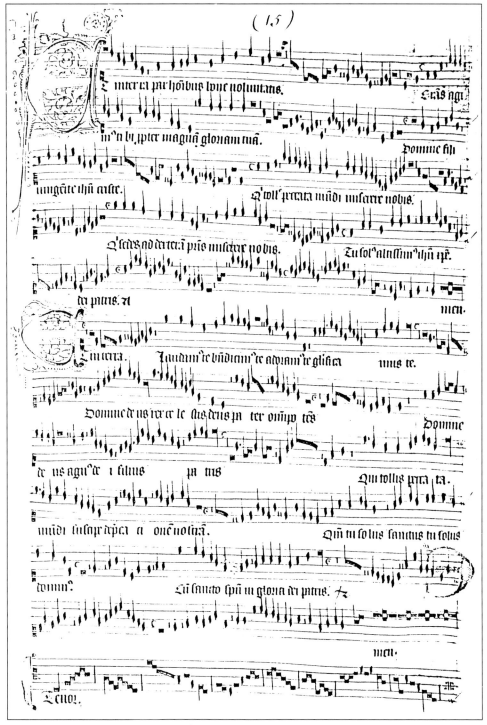

Fig. 18.2　John Tyes, *Gloria in Excelsis,* now BL, Add. MS 57950, fo.15 .

powerful employer. In July 1435 or 1436 his services were requisitioned by the bishop, Cardinal Beaufort; the prior lamented that in his absence 'the chorus of singers is mutilated gravely, the melody of the organ is silent',[21] but there is no reason to imagine that Beaufort relented. Bygbroke was perhaps succeeded by Robert Derby, who in November 1444, described as a clerk of the prior of St Swithun's, was rewarded for playing the organ in the chapel of Winchester College on the occasion of a visit by King Henry VI.[22] However, Beaufort died in 1447, and Bygbroke appears then to have returned to his previous employment; two years previously he had taken up the lease on a home in the city, and in 1453 the prior conferred on him membership of the confraternity of the priory in terms that suggest that he had returned to service there, which the prior expressly hoped would continue thenceforth.[23] It is most unlikely that the priory would at this time have employed a lay organist for the monks' choir separate from and in addition to the master of the Lady Chapel choir, and the likelihood is that Bygbroke and Derby did indeed manage the music of the Lady Chapel in addition to making their contribution to the music of the principal monastic choir.

In respect of the period prior to the last 20 years of the 15th century, the scope and character of the music of the Lady Mass, and of the evening Marian antiphon at Wykeham's chantry, should not be misconceived. The voices of singing-boys were not yet used in the execution of composed and written polyphony; their accomplishments for Lady Mass and the Marian antiphon extended only to the performance of plainsong, though a skilled teacher could coach them in the techniques of improvising descant to plainsong where appropriate. Moreover, the polyphony of men's voices which the cantor directed in the Lady Chapel and the monks' choir required only the forces standard for this period, namely a small ensemble of three or four voices (alto and tenor) singing one to a part. However, from about the 1460s, the composers who were working in the household chapels of royalty and the upper aristocracy and at the secular cathedral and collegiate churches began to develop a new style of church music, which employed for the first time the full chorus of singers, including the voices of the boys, and cultivated a highly demanding and technically virtuosic style. These composers engaged the full range of vocal timbres from treble to bass, and indeed created thereby what has been considered ever since to be the quintessential sound of English cathedral music, sung by a chorus combining the voices of boys and men.[24]

In monastic institutions, Lady Chapel boys could not be admitted to services in the monks' choir, so the adoption of these developments was limited to the Lady Chapel services and to other votive services sung out of the monks' choir. Even so, the reception of music in this very demanding and coloratura 'Eton Choirbook' style could not be undertaken without an enlargement in the number of singing-boys, and also—eventually— the employment of professional singing-men with whom to supplement the enthusiasts among the monks. At Winchester, it appears that this modernisation of the choral force was begun in 1482 with the appointment of Edmund Pynbrygge as cantor. Many of his duties were the same as those that had been expected of John Tyes 80 years earlier; they extended to his attendance at daily Lady Mass, and also at a newly-instituted Mass of Jesus celebrated each Friday at an altar in the nave of the church, plus attendance in the monks' choir to sing and play the organ at High Mass and both Vespers on all feast-days and Sundays. However, the crucial development related to the singing-boys; these were now doubled in number to eight, and it was expressly required of the cantor that he teach to them the skills of singing composed polyphony from written notation as well as in plain-song chant.[25]

It seems clear from the terms of Pynbrygge's contract that it was the priory's expectation from now on that the Lady Mass under his direction would be distinguished on most days, and perhaps every day, by the incorporation of composed polyphonic music sung by the cantor, boys and monks who constituted the Lady Chapel choir. The contents of early 16th-century manuscripts show that particularly amenable to this manner of execution were the movements of the Ordinary, with the Kyrie, Alleluia and Sequence; unfortunately, no sources of Winchester provenance are known to survive. Moreover, at much the same time as the appointment of Pynbrygge, the priory began the refurbishment—and ultimately the partial rebuilding—of the Lady Chapel itself as a fit milieu for the offering of the mass. The western screen and loft were installed, from which (facing east) the Epistle and Gospel could be chanted as at High Mass, and presently the chapel furnishings were completed with the provision of the present set of choir-stalls.[26]

The Lady Mass now possessed in all respects the potential and resources to become the most individually distinguished of all celebrations of divine service observed in the cathedral, and between 1510 and 1529 the choir was raised to full professional standing by the appointment of a team of skilled singing-men to perform with the boys. The group numbered four, presumably so chosen as to permit each to take one of the four lower voices (alto, two tenors and bass) in the standard five-part music of the day. In March 1510 Pynbrygge's duties were divided; he retained his role as specialist organ-player and singing-man, while a second musician, Thomas Goodman, was appointed to be cantor and teacher of the singing-boys, whose number was now raised to ten.[27] By 1529 at the latest (and probably some years before) the team of four singing-men appears to have been fully in place. Four *coadiutores* (assistants) at Lady Mass were recorded in that year, almost certainly to be identified with the group of four 'singingmen' recorded in 1539,[28] though doubtless, competent enthusiasts among the monks were still welcome to augment the lower voices and fill out the sound. The four men in office in 1529 appear to have been Thomas Goodman (cantor and master of the boys), Henry Perrat (organist, succeeding Pynbrygge),[29] John Netter (alias Baker) and Henry Stempe.[30] Perrat died in the autumn of 1534,[31] and was eventually succeeded as organist by Stempe, the vacancy thus arising being filled by Henry Jaye (or Joye);[32] and, as cantor, Thomas Goodman was succeeded by Matthew Fuller on 5 February 1538. Fuller's duties were the same as those of Goodman before him, except for a slight expansion of his duties of helping the monks' choir on festivals;[33] meanwhile, Stempe's contract of 1537 recorded that by then the professional choir was required to sing a Jesus antiphon weekly on Fridays in addition to singing the Jesus Mass.[34] Of the actual repertory of the choir, unfortunately, nothing is known; however, there is no reason to imagine that it was any less ambitious or competent than its counterparts at the cathedral priories of Worcester and Canterbury, which normally sang in four and five parts, and sometimes six, and maintained a substantial repertory principally of music for the Lady Mass and the Marian antiphon.[35] And Matthew Fuller (cantor), Henry Stempe (organist), John Netter and Henry Jaye were the men who, with eight boys, composed the professional lay choir on the day that all was overtaken by the Dissolution, 14 November 1539.[36]

The policy of Henry VIII's government was to minimise the degree of disturbance arising from the suppression. Not only were suitable ex-monks to be engaged as canons and minor canons of the New Foundation; express order was also given that the services of all existing singing-men and boys should be retained to form the nucleus of the professional choir of seculars which was now to take the place of the monks in observing the full round of liturgy in the high choir of the cathedral.[37] It had already been decided that Winchester should be equipped with a choral force matching those of Durham and Canterbury as the largest of the New Foundation choirs, with 12 minor canons, a gospeller and an epistoler, 12 lay vicars, a master of the choristers and organist, and ten choristers; and the recruiting necessary to expand the existing choir to these dimensions was complete at least by the autumn of 1541.[38] Fuller, Stempe, Netter and Jaye (and also Thomas Goodman) were all appointed to be lay vicars; to teach the chorister boys 'in playne songe, prycke song and descante' (that is, in plainsong and polyphony). Richard Winslade was recruited in January 1540 from his previous employment at the parish church of St Mary at Hill, London, to be master of the choristers and organist.[39]

The Benedictine liturgical use of the cathedral priory was discarded at the Dissolution, and order was given that the new choir should observe divine service according to the secular (that is, non-monastic) use of Salisbury.[40] Although the body of text, ceremony and chant comprising Salisbury Use differed much in detail, it departed not at all in principle from the historic practice of the former monastery; to the sometime monks who comprised 11 of the 12 minor canons, little would seem to have changed, though for the former singing-boys and men of the Lady Chapel their new employment as members of a full-time choir must have come as rather an abrupt shock. It was ordained expressly that the New Foundation choirs 'shall kepe in the church dayly service with our ladys mass';[41] the Lady Chapel now had to share with the principal choir the focus of music-making of professional standard in the cathedral, but its established prominence as the site of a mass distinguished by the daily performance of elaborate music was in no way compromised. Even at Rochester Cathedral, one of the least favoured and smallest of the New Foundation choirs, it was expected that the Lady Mass would be enhanced daily with the polyphonic music of both choir and organ,[42] and the same could hardly be less true of the Lady Mass at Winchester, endowed with choral resources nearly twice those of Rochester.

However, the Lady Chapel continued to enjoy use for this, its original and historic purpose, only until 1559—with an interruption, moreover, between 1549 and 1553. It was axiomatic of the new vernacular liturgy stipulated for the English church by the Protestant politicians of the government of Edward VI in 1549, discarded in 1553 at the accession of Mary Tudor but re-applied in 1559 by Elizabeth I and her politicians, that it repudiated utterly all reverence for the sacrifice of the Mass, and all address to the Virgin Mary as intercessor. Lady Mass was heard no more in the cathedral after June 1559; the Lady Chapel was silenced, and the music of the cathedral generally was launched upon the long, bleak night of Elizabethan belittlement, austerity and impoverishment.

Notes
  1. See especially J. B. L. Tolhurst and the Lady Abbess of Stanbrook (eds.), *The Ordinal and Customary of the Abbey of St. Mary, York,* Henry Bradshaw Society, 73, 75, 84 (1934-50), pp. 56-8; J. W. Legg (ed.), *Missale ad Usum Ecclesie Westmonasteriensis,* Henry Bradshaw Society, 1, 5, 12 (1891-7), cols. 1119-29.
  2. H. T. Riley (ed.), *Gesta Abbatum Monasterii Sancti Albani,* 2 vols., RS 28 (1867), i, pp. 284-5 (St Albans: *c.*1225); R. Graham (ed.), *The Register of Archbishop Winchelsey,* Canterbury and York Society, 51-2 (1952-6), p. 820 (Christ Church, Canterbury, 1290s). For some further examples, see

F. Ll. Harrison, *Music in Medieval Britain,* 2nd edn. (London, 1963), pp. 77-9.

3. See above, pp. 231-46.
4. *Gesta Abbatum Monasterii Sancti Albani,* i, pp. 284-5.
5. R. Bowers, 'Choral Institutions within the English Church: their Constitution and Development, 1340-1500', unpubl. Ph.D. dissertation, University of East Anglia, 1975, pp. 4051-3, 4068-100.
6. D. Knowles, *The Monastic Order in England, 940-1216,* 2nd edn. (Cambridge, 1963), pp. 421-2; *idem, The Religious Orders in England,* 3 vols. (Cambridge, 1948-59), ii, pp. 230-3 (esp. p. 230, note 6).
7. There is some account of monastery almonry schools in general in N. Orme, *English Schools in the Middle Ages* (London, 1973), pp. 243-5.
8. J. C. Cox, 'The New Minster or the Abbey of Hyde', in *VCH Hants,* ii, pp. 118-19.
9. The earliest certain reference to the existence of an almonry school occurs in 1404: LB I, fo. 18v (calendared in J. Greatrex (ed.), *The Register of the Common Seal of the Priory of St Swithun, Winchester, 1345-1497,* Hampshire Record Series, 2 (Winchester, 1978), item 63).
10. Charters: Edward III 50, 52, 62-6, 73; M. Perry, 'King's Somborne Hundred', *VCH Hants,* iv, p. 474; *Calendar of Close Rolls 1364-8,* pp. 484, 485; *Calendar of Patent Rolls 1381-5,* p. 530; WCL, accounts of hordarian, 1400-1 onwards: G. W. Kitchin (ed.), *Compotus Rolls of the Obedientiaries of St. Swithun's Priory,* HRSoc (1892), pp. 283, 285, 290.
11. Cartulary of William Basyng, hordarian, MS, WCL, fo. 7v.
12. Westminster Abbey Muniments, Book I (*Liber Niger*), fo. 86v.
13. LB I, fo. 15v (Greatrex, *Common Seal,* item 53); this calendar is not quite accurate in respect of the interpretation of the term *cantus organicus.*
14. LB I, fo. 18v (Greatrex, *Common Seal,* item 63).
15. For the use of polyphony in the cathedral in Anglo-Saxon times, see A. Holschneider, *Die Organa von Winchester* (Hildesheim, 1968); M. Berry, 'What the Saxon Monks Sang', in B. Yorke (ed.), *Bishop Æthelwold: his Career and Influence* (Woodbridge, 1988), pp. 149-60.
16. J. W. McKinnon, 'The Tenth-Century Organ at Winchester', *Organ Yearbook* 5 (1974), pp. 4-19.
17. Goodman, *Chartulary,* items 3, 10, 260; Kitchin, *Compotus Rolls,* pp. 402, 404.
18. For some examples, see R. Bowers, 'The Performing Ensemble for English Church Polyphony, *c.*1320-*c.*1390', in S. Boorman (ed.), *Studies in the Performance of Late Mediæval Music* (Cambridge, 1983), p. 182 and note 51.
19. W. H. B. Bird (ed.), *The Black Book of Winchester* (Winchester, 1925), p. 50; *Winchester Studies 2,* ii, pp. 786, 1373.
20. M. Bent and A. Hughes (eds.), *The Old Hall Manuscript,* 2 vols., Corpus Mensurabilis Musicae, 46 (Rome, 1969-73), i, pp. 32-5, 369-72.
21. LB I, fos. 49v, 54r (Greatrex, *Common Seal,* items 211 and 236).
22. H. Chitty, 'The Basins Given by Henry VI to Winchester College', *Notes and Queries,* 12th ser., 1 (1916), p. 442.
23. *Winchester Studies 2,* ii, pp. 999, 1011, 1181; LB I, fo. 80v (Greatrex, *Common Seal,* item 330).
24. R. Bowers, 'The Performing Pitch of English Fifteenth-Century Church Polyphony', *Early Music* 8 (1980), pp. 21-8; *idem,* 'The Vocal Scoring, Choral Balance and Performing Pitch of Latin Church Polyphony in England, *c.*1500-1558', *Journal of the Royal Musical Association* 112 (1987), pp. 38-76.
25. The requirement that he play the organ in the monks' choir was not expressly included in his 1482 indenture, but was spelled out when his contract was renewed in 1510: LB I, fo. 106v (Greatrex, *Common Seal,* item 402); LB II, fo. 44v.
26. See above, pp. 231-46.
27. LB II, fos. 44r, 44v.
28. Compotus Rolls, MSS, WCL, Box 66, roll SS.23 (account of warden of Lady Chapel, 1529-30); PRO, E315/494, p. 2.
29. Compotus Roll, MS, WCL (no reference), account of anniversarian, 1530-31.
30. Both were singing-men in 1539 (PRO E315/494, p. 2), and both had been resident in Winchester since at least the 1520s: *Winchester Studies 2,* pp. 1304-5, 1357.
31. HRO, B Wills 1534-1536, No. 34.
32. PRO, E315/494, p. 2.

33. LB III, fo. 73r.
34. LB III, fos. 35r (in English) and 69v (in Latin).
35. J. W. Legg and W. St. J. Hope (eds.), *The Inventories of Christ Church, Canterbury* (London, 1902), p. 164; BL, Harley 604, fo. 118r. At Winchester, in deference to the terms of Wykeham's will (see above, p. 250), it appears that the daily Marian antiphon continued to be sung by the boys' voices alone, rather than by the full polyphonic chorus, as elsewhere.
36. PRO, E315/494, p. 2.
37. PRO, E36/116, pp. 19-20. Ultimately, though five of the 12 inaugural canons were ex-religious, only three were former monks of Winchester.
38. H. Cole (ed.), *King Henry the Eighth's Scheme of Bishopricks* (London, 1838), p. 36; TA 1541-2, fos. 2r-8r, 11v.
39. H. Littlehales (ed.), *The Medieval Records of a London City Church: St Mary at Hill, 1420-1559,* Early English Text Society, 1st ser., 128 (1905), pp. 380, 384; LB IV, fo. 15r; B. Matthews, 'Winslade of Winchester', *Musical Times* 119 (1978), p. 711.
40. PRO, E36/116, p. 19; WCL, TA 1541-2, fos. 10v-11r.
41. PRO, E36/116, pp. 19-20.
42. W. H. Frere (ed.), *The Use of Sarum,* 2 vols. (Cambridge, 1898-1901), ii, p. 235.

EARLY RENAISSANCE AT WINCHESTER

Martin Biddle

Classical decorative motifs and architectural forms appear on some nine different structures erected in Winchester Cathedral in the first sixty years of the 16th century. No other building preserves so many works illustrating the successive aspects of the Early Renaissance style in England. No other building illustrates so clearly the course that style might subsequently have taken, nor, when it failed, the length of the pause which ensued before a more fully realised classical idiom became firmly established in the 1630s.

The purpose of this paper is to provide a description of the Early Renaissance work in the cathedral, and to give sufficient annotation to place each example as far as possible in its chronological and stylistic context, and to explain its genesis.

1. Langton's Chantry Chapel

The Lady Chapel was reconstructed and refurbished with sculpture, wall paintings and new woodwork in the time of Priors Thomas Hunton (1470-98) and Thomas Silkstede (1498-1524),[1] and was probably completed before the appointment of Bishop Fox in 1501, whose arms, pelican badge, and motto (*Est Deo Gracia*) do not appear. No Renaissance detail can be seen in any surviving part of these works.[2]

During these same years the chapel to the south was converted to a chantry for his own use by Bishop Thomas Langton (1493-1501), revaulted, and provided with a wooden screen and canopied stalls, 'one of the most elaborate and exquisitely delicate specimens of oak carving in the kingdom'.[3] The existing 14th-century reredos was retained, but repainted and regilded, and the crockets and pinnacles of its canopies were cut off and replaced by a cornice decorated in an Early Renaissance manner (Fig. 19.1).[4]

The new cornice, which ran across the full width of the chapel and was returned for a short distance along the north and south walls, displays a series of confronted and addorsed cockatrices (i.e. basilisks, mythical beasts with the head, body and claws of a cock combined with the wings and tail of a 'serpent'), their tails bound together to a floret, their claws and beaks holding an upright barrel (tun). Above the heads of each pair a semicircular pediment carries the bishop's initials, **T L**, in crudely serifed Roman letters, framed by volutes, slashed and crocketed, which come together at the top in a flower-like device. The cornice was taken down in 1818 and is now displayed in the Triforium Gallery.[5]

The date of this cornice is a delicate matter, for on any count it represents the earliest appearance of Renaissance motifs in the cathedral. The initials can refer only to Bishop Langton, but the cockatrices and tuns present some difficulty.[6] The rebus of a cockatrice on a tun appears many times in the vault of Langton's Chapel, but so does another rebus which can only mean 'Long-tun': a capital T above a horizontal tun with a lower case L (a 'long L') passing vertically through both.[7] Langton's initials occur individually on many

257

Fig. 19.1   Langton's chantry chapel, cornice, 1501-?10. *John Crook*

of the bosses, but no other initials are present to identify the cockatrice rebus, although the latter is as prominent as the 'Long-tun'. The cockatrice rebus has usually been taken to indicate Prior Hunton, a 'hen on a tun'. This cannot be correct: Hunton's rebus, which appears in the Lady Chapel, e.g. in the spandrels of the north door leading to the now demolished sacristy, is an H (elsewhere in the chapel 'Hun') piercing a horizontal tun.[8] The problem reappears on the cornice, for it is difficult to believe that the bishop's initials would appear so intimately related to another's rebus.

The medieval Latin name for Winchester was *Wintonia,* adjective *Wintoniensis,* frequently abbreviated to *Winton',* and passing into English as 'Winton'. Langton, and perhaps his predecessors, used as a rebus for Winton a vine issuing from a tun, a 'vine-ton'. Here lies the clue to the cockatrice on a tun, and the text is Proverbs, 23:31-2:[9]

> Do not look at wine (*vinum*) when it is red,   31
> when it sparkles in the cup
> and goes down smoothly.
> At the last it bites like a serpent (*coluber*),   32
> and stings like a cockatrice (*regulus*).[10]

Thus a cockatrice on an tun indicates a 'wine-tun', and appears as such many times on the bosses of the vault of Langton's chapel. On the cornice (Fig. 19.1) the message is clear and manifold: the bishop's initials above the rebus for his diocese, which in turn echoes the rebus for his surname; and the wine tun supported by cockatrices, which identify the tun and in their mixed form and their pairs, echo the *coluber* and the *regulus* of the Vulgate, Proverbs, 23:32.[11]

Langton died of the plague on 27 January 1501, five days after his election as archbishop of Canterbury. Since the arms of the see of Canterbury appear on the woodwork and in the vault of the chapel impaling Langton,[12] the works can only have been finished after his death, presumably by his executors. Langton may have founded the chantry in his lifetime,[13] but may not have completed or even begun the construction of his chapel. The work cannot have been long delayed, and should have been complete well before the end of the decade.

The difficulty is that this cornice would then appear to offer the earliest appearance of Renaissance elements so far recognised on any English monument. Anthony Blunt saw the problem, but did not explore it, grouping the Langton cornice with the other works of Renaissance character carried out in *le style de Gaillon* during the long episcopate of Richard Fox (1501-28).[14] A finer chronology now seems possible. At the latest, delayed for whatever reason, it seems difficult to place the completion of the Langton chantry chapel after *c*.1510. It would then be followed in 1513-18 by Fox's chantry chapel (No. 2, below), at some date shortly before 1524 by the canopied seats in the south transept (No. 3), and in 1525 and the immediately following years by the group of works which refurbished the presbytery (Nos. 4-6).

This sequence seems broadly reflected in the character of the classical detail. This is coarse and crudely applied to Langton's cornice and Fox's chantry chapel, but relatively delicate and well integrated where it appears on the south transept canopies and more particularly on the presbytery tombs and screens.

The scrolled semicircular pediments or 'flattened shells', the most distinctive element of the Langton cornice, appear in more elaborate form on the East Anglian terracotta tombs of *c*.1525-30 at Oxburgh (Norfolk) and Layer Marney (Essex),[15] and, on a grand scale with the shell-ribs visible, as acroteria on the Layer Marney gatehouse (pre-1527/9),[16] and in the scrolled shell-hood over the entrance to the English palace at Guisnes for the Field of Cloth of Gold (as recorded in a later painting).[17] On a small scale, very similar volutes composed of slashed scrolls provide the arch of the architectural frame to an illumination in the French manuscript book of the pageants for Princess Mary's ceremonial entry into Paris in 1514.[18]

All these must ultimately derive from sources similar to those which gave rise to the scrolled and topped semicircular shell-hoods over some of the windows of Gaillon (*c*.1502-10).[19] In the years before the French war of 1513 knowledge of such Italian details may have come to Winchester in the course of contacts with the diocese of Rouen, whose archbishop at that time was Cardinal Georges d'Amboise (d.1515), the builder of Gaillon.[20]

2. Fox's Chantry Chapel

Bishop Richard Fox (1501-28) had chosen the position of his chantry chapel by the eve of the French war in June 1513. It was described in December 1518 as 'newly built' and three months earlier, on 30 September, the bishop had laid down detailed instructions regarding the duties and qualifications of his two chantry priests.[21] Even so, the bishop's cadaver effigy may not have been installed in its niche in the south side of the chapel until later, for the bill for the 'parclose of yron standing byfour my lordys pyctor' was not issued until 22 March 1522/3.[22]

Fox's chantry chapel was probably designed by William Vertue, the king's master

Fig. 19.2   Fox's chantry chapel, volutes of interior dado, 1513-18. *John Crook*

mason, who was employed by the bishop on the construction of Corpus Christi College, Oxford.[23] A design attributed to Vertue for one bay of the chapel shows a wholly Gothic structure in the latest Court fashion; there is no sign of classical ornament.[24] Yet inside the chapel, the vertical ribs of the blind arcades of the dado on the north, west and south walls are cut off short and supported on classical volutes, ribbed, and decorated with leaves below and to either side (Fig. 19.2).[25] It was to be another ten years until Fox was buried beneath the floor of his chantry chapel on the day of his death, 5 October 1528.[26]

3. The Canopied Seats in the South Transept

Set across the south end and against part of the west wall of the south transept are a series of canopied wooden seats or benches backed for the most part by linenfold panelling but interrupted by the wood-cased Norman column supporting the tribune and by two doors.[27] The coved canopy is surmounted by a cornice composed of framed panels of Early Renaissance ornament and supporting a series of carved finials (Fig. 19.3). The linenfold panelling in the southern section is divided by seven fine pilasters each carved with different Renaissance candelabra patterns (Fig. 19.4). To either side of the two doors there are slender posts, their upper parts decorated with imbricated ornament interrupted by cubical sections bearing

Fig. 19.3   Silkstede's canopied seats against the west wall of the south transept, shortly before 1524, rearranged 1816. *John Crook*

the arms of the see of Winchester and of Thomas Rennell (dean, 1805-40).[28]

The frieze on the western section has medallion heads at each end of a line of six panels (Figs. 19.3, 19.5). The two outer panels contain urns supported by pairs of fantastic bird heads, their bodies composed of slashed and vegetal scrolls (Fig. 19.5). The inner four panels display pairs of griffins supporting alternately the arms of the see and the initials **T S** to either side of a knot.

These initials are those of Thomas Silkstede (prior, 1498-1524) and the character of the detail suggests that the canopies belong to the last years of his life. But in its present arrangement the woodwork as a whole cannot all be attributed to him, for in the frieze panel above the south door are the initials **T R** and the date 1816. These refer, like the arms on the door posts, to Dean Rennell, but the extent of his work is unclear.[29] The present arrangement can be seen in John Coney's view of the south

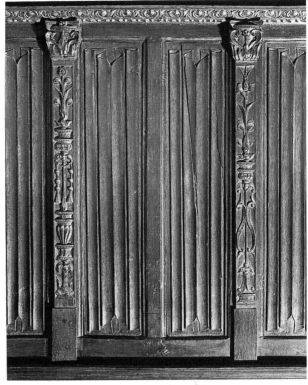

Fig. 19.4   Silkstede's canopied seats across the south end of the south transept, detail of pilasters, shortly before 1524, rearranged 1816. *John Crook*

transept drawn in 1817,[30] but some at least of the woodwork was in this area earlier for in 1760

> the remains of a Canopy, under which the Presses for the Choir vestments are placed, which formerly seems to have been the Covering of Stalls, and still preserves in the Cornice the initial Letters of *Silkestede's* name, often repeated,[31]

were noted 'opposite' Silkstede's chapel, i.e. on the west wall of the transept. Milner confirms this:

> Against the west wall of the transept we see certain ancient presses, bearing upon them the device of Silkstede; the original use of which seems to have been to keep the great habits of the monks or large outside garments, the use of which was frequently dispensed with, but which they were obliged always to appear in on solemn occasions in the choir. These presses are still made use of for containing the surplices of the choristers and singing men. In the south wall, under the clock, is a door ... [32]

By 1818 Charles Ball could note 'the modern entrance to the chapter room' on the west side of the transept

> ornamented with a rich wainscotting of oak, carved in various devices to correspond with the ancient presses which are ranged along the *south* [my italics] wall of the transept. These presses are carved in scrolls and terminate in canopies, bearing on the cornice the initial and

Fig. 19.5   Silkstede's canopied seats against the west wall of the south transept, detail of cornice, shortly before 1524, rearranged 1816. *John Crook*

device of Prior Silkstede, by whom they were probably erected for the purpose of containing the rich vestments worn on all solemn occasions by the monks of the cathedral.[33]

These accounts suggest that before 1816 the canopies were ranged along the west wall of the transept and were then used as presses, perhaps in the form of a series of alcoves, in which to store vestments. Sometime before April 1818 the west aisle of the south transept was remodelled to provide a chapter room and treasury.[34] It was presumably as part of this work that the woodwork was rearranged in 1816, the greater part being placed across the end of the transept, with new doorways being formed to open west into the new chapter room and south beneath the tribune. Rennell's work will thus have involved the movement and re-erection of most of the woodwork, the insertion of two doors, the plain panelling around the Norman column of the tribune, and probably the installation of the seats or benches, which are not mentioned earlier, with the addition of the plain panels forming their backs.

But were these canopies originally erected on the west side of the transept? A possibility first suggested by Warton in 1760 is that they belonged originally to Prior Silkstede's chapel in the east aisle of the transept immediately opposite their then (and in part their present) position.[35] This must still seem the most likely explanation, given the prominent display of Silkstede's name **T h o M A s S** (a play on his initials and possibly on the name of Mary and the words *'hominum salvator'*) on the cornice of the screen dividing the chapel from the body of the transept, and the present bare condition of the interior from which, if it was ever completed (which there seems no reason to doubt), the fittings must have been removed.

An alternative suggestion is that the canopies may be survivals of Silkstede's new screen for the Lady Chapel, in view of the evidence there for disruptions in the original scheme.[36] The south transept canopies belong, however, to the end of Silkstede's long term of office, the Lady Chapel screen to the beginning. Woodwork already in use in the south transept in the 18th century, bearing the name of a prior whose own chapel was in that transept, seems more likely to have been there from an early date, particularly since its use as canopied stalls in Silkstede's now empty chapel seems to explain all its various features.

At all events we have in these canopies evidence for the character of Renaissance detail on wood-carving in the cathedral in the years immediately before Silkstede's death in 1524. The arrangement of the frieze panels and their Renaissance patterns are closely matched in the cornices of the terracotta tomb of the first Lord Marney at Layer Marney, and in the cornices of the screen and tomb at Oxburgh, as well as by other terracotta monuments of the 'East Anglian' group (Barsham, Braconash, Norwich and Wymondham).[37] The parallels, notably the urns with fantastic supporters,[38] are sufficiently close to suggest derivation of the decorative patterns from a related or similar set of sources, probably the decorated borders of printed books and manuscripts produced in France in the first two decades of the 16th century.[39]

The arabesques of the pilasters and the design of the capitals with inturned volutes, which are not closely matched in the East Anglian group, must ultimately derive from similar drawn or printed sources. The ready availability of such materials in an easily movable form shows that there need be no question of any specific links to, for example, the makers of the East Anglian terracottas. Indeed, as we are now beginning to learn, terracottas with Franco-Italian motifs were made at different sites, for different patrons, and with rather different details.[40] All the more so with wood-carving, which will usually have been carried out on the site where the work was required, and probably by incumbent craftsmen rather than by specialists brought in for the task. This may perhaps explain why some of the Winchester wood-carvings with Renaissance detail are less accomplished than contemporary work in stone. Silkstede's canopies in the south transept, however competent their friezes, are in general no match for the carving of the presbytery screens of 1525 (Nos. 4 and 5, below); and these in turn surpass the carved panels of 1540/1 in the choir-stalls (No. 7), some of which are no more than journeyman work. The wooden mortuary chests (No. 6) are an exception, as we shall see.

4. The Tombs in the Presbytery Screen

The chronology of Fox's works in the eastern arm of the cathedral now seems to have been as follows:[41]

Presbytery high vault	1503-5
New bosses on high vault	1506
Presbytery aisle vaults	1506-9
Chantry chapel	1513-18
Reordering of the presbytery	1525

This last marks the culmination of Fox's work in the cathedral and involves three distinct elements: the treatment of the tombs he found in position below the arcades to either side of the presbytery (this item); the screens to close in the presbytery (No. 5); and the wooden mortuary chests set upon the screens (No. 6). His work can perhaps best be seen as the completion of a process which had begun 50 years before when the construction of the Great Screen separated the presbytery from the retrochoir and from the shrine of St Swithun, and concentrated the focus of attention upon the high altar. As will be seen, however, responsibility for the presbytery works was not Fox's alone. It is a simplification to regard him as their sole author, for the screens and the friezes upon them show variations of style which can only be explained by the personal preferences of the donors.

When Bishop Fox and his associates set out to enclose the presbytery with new stone screens running between the piers of the 14th-century arcades, they faced the problem of incorporating the tombs already lying beneath the arches to north and south. Numbering the three bays from the crossing eastward, the tombs are as follows (there is space for two burials west and east lengthways beneath each arch):

THE NORTH SCREEN

North Aisle Side		Presbytery Side
	EAST	
Harthacnut (king of England, 1040-42)		None
	Bay N3	
Aymer de Valence (bishop, 1250-60)		None
John of Pontoise (bishop, 1282-1304)		John of Pontoise (reconstituted tomb-chest)
	Bay N2	
None		None
North door of presbytery		North door
	Bay N1	
None		Richard Toclyve (bishop, 1173-88)

WEST

THE SOUTH SCREEN

Presbytery Side		South Aisle Side
	EAST	
None		None
	Bay S3	
None		None
None[42]		Richard, son of William the Conqueror, and Earl Beorn[43]
	Bay S2	
None[44]		Nicholas of Ely (bishop, 1268-80)
South door of presbytery		South door
	Bay S1	
None		None

WEST

Fig. 19.6 John of Pontoise's tomb-plaque on the north side of the north screen of the presbytery (Bay N2 N), the central panel, 1525. *John Crook*

Fig. 19.7 John of Pontoise's tomb-chest against the north screen of the presbytery (Bay N2 S), looking north-east, 1525. *John Crook*

Fig. 19.8   Harthacnut's tomb-plaque on the north side of the
north screen of the presbytery (Bay N3 N), the left and
central panels, 1525. *John Crook*

Fig. 19.9   Aymer de Valence's tomb-plaque on the north
side of the north screen of the presbytery (Bay N3 N), the left
and central panels, 1525. *John Crook*

Fig. 19.10   Richard Toclyve's tomb-plaque on the south side
of the north screen of the presbytery (Bay N1 S), 1525.
John Crook

The tombs appear to have been left in position as far as possible, but they were treated in different ways. Seven burials are involved. The most elaborate treatment was given to Bishop John of Pontoise: a tomb-plaque facing the north aisle (Fig. 19.6) and an 'elegant Early Renaissance tomb-chest'[45] (Fig. 19.7) in the corresponding position on the north side of the presbytery. The tomb-chest incorporated an earlier Purbeck marble slab decorated with a delicate frieze of alternating right and inverted trefoils which may have come from the bishop's original tomb.[46] Three other burials were provided with new tomb-plaques on the north screen: King Harthacnut (Fig. 19.8)[47] and Bishop Aymer de Valence (Fig. 19.9)[48] facing the north aisle, Bishop Toclyve (Richard of Ilchester) facing the presbytery (Fig. 19.10).[49] All four memorials were carved in low-relief with classical motifs and incorporated new inscriptions.

The burials along the line of the south screen were treated differently, emphasising the other contrasts between the two screens (see below, No. 5). All three lie on the south side of the screen in Bay 2 in what may have been their original positions. The burial place of the heart of Bishop Nicholas of Ely lying beneath a low many-cusped Gothic arch was opened in 1887 and found to contain an inscribed lead plate and a lead box in which was what may be a silver-gilt vase.[50] In the same bay immediately to the east Duke Richard and Earl Beorn lie together in a lead coffin also seen in 1887 below a similar low arch and covered by an inscribed late 12th- or 13th-century tomb-slab.[51] Neither of these burials was treated with decoration in the Renaissance manner like those in the north screen, but the right-hand spandrels of the two low arches have Renaissance motifs. Both tombs were identified with new inscriptions in 'Romano-Gothic' capitals on the screen wall above them. Lettering of this type is most unusual; I am grateful to Sally Badham for confirming the broad appropriateness of the description 'Romano-Gothic', and for pointing out that there is a broad similarity to the script on some early 16th-century German monuments from the workshop of Peter Vischer the Elder, albeit with fewer flourishes. A comment on this script form, in particular on the A, will appear shortly in Pamela Tudor-Craig's *Catalogue of the Pictures of the Society of Antiquaries of London.*

The monuments of those whose burials were disturbed by the screens were either incorporated (Duke Richard and Earl Beorn), reconstructed (John of Pontoise), or replaced (Harthacnut, Toclyve, Aymer de Valence, and Nicholas of Ely).[52] Of the latter one at least (the heart tomb of Aymer) and possibly a second (the tomb-slab of Toclyve) still survive elsewhere in the cathedral, but their mortal remains were apparently left in place, for the hearts of both Aymer and Nicholas have both been seen in more recent times.[53]

The inscriptions placed on the new screens to commemorate those whose monuments were altered reflect the differences in the way their tombs were treated: those on the south screen were in Romano-Gothic, and here the new arrangements were Gothic in style; those on the north screen were in Roman capitals, corresponding to the Renaissance treatment given to all four monuments (Figs. 19.6 and 19.8-10).[54] This difference is seen again in some of the lettering used for the mottoes on the screens (see below, No. 5).

The style of the Renaissance tomb fronts is considerably more advanced than that of Silkstede's canopies (No. 3). Here for the first time at Winchester we see ribbons with rippling surfaces used as frames and also to hang the elegant rectangular panels upon which the inscriptions appear in correctly serifed Roman capitals. The candelabra patterns of Pontoise's tomb-chest are close to those of Silkstede's woodwork (cf. Fig. 19.4 and Figs. 19.6-7), but the armorial cartouches with their scrolled ends on the front of John of Pontoise's tomb-chest (Fig. 19.7) are advanced for 1525 and hint at the use of *les cuirs,* the leathery scrolls developed to and perhaps beyond perfection by Rosso in the high Fontainebleau manner of the next decade, and seen in Winchester in the great cartouche of the Mason tomb of 1559 (No. 9; Figs. 19.22-3). 'La finesse de la décoration de ces deux monuments [des évêques Richard Toclyve et John Pointes] permet de supposer qu'ils furent exécutés par des artisans français, venus probablement de Gaillon ou de Rouen'.[55] Anthony Blunt's suggestion may underestimate the ability of English masons to produce such work by the middle of a decade which had opened in 1520 with the English palace at Guisnes for the Field of Cloth of Gold and the Round House at Calais for the entertainment of the Emperor Charles V,[56] and had continued with the decorations carried out for Charles's London entry in 1522.[57]

The leaves on Richard Toclyve's tomb-plaque are distinctively flat, like cardboard or leather cut-outs, without surface modelling (Fig. 19.10). Flat leaves appear again in the foliage around the cartouche of the inscription panel of the tomb-plaque on the north side of John of Pontoise's tomb (Fig. 19.6), but are absent from the face of his tomb-chest, where the leaves are fully modelled (Fig. 19.7). This 'flat style' may be no more than the work of less skilled carvers, but it appears again in some of the Nonsuch slate carvings 15 years later. It is perhaps a trait to be looked for elsewhere.

5. The Presbytery Screens

The screens fill the three bays to either side of the presbytery with four-light windows 'in the purest and most finished style of the Gothic',[58] set in square frames standing on the low dado which contains the tombs just described (No. 4). A Gothic string-course runs across each pair of windows from pier to pier and on top of the string there is an elaborate Renaissance frieze carved on both faces (Figs. 19.12 and 19.13).

Although the two eastern bays (N2 and N3, S2 and S3) are filled with windows, the western bays (N1 and S1) each have a door in the eastern half of the bay giving entry from the aisles to the presbytery. The north screen has a full-length panel of four-light blind tracery to the west, but in the south screen this space is occupied on the presbytery side by the bishop's throne.[59] Both doors occupy the lower two-thirds of the screen: the north door is covered by a battlemented cornice below a shortened four-light window; the ogee canopy over the south door rises through a six-light window of different type. The north door is framed externally to either side by semi-octagonal shafts with battlemented and crocketed pinnacles; the south door by semi-octagonal shafts externally and internally by slender rectangular buttresses with crocketed pinnacles. Since 1849 the screens have been glazed with plain sheets topped by floriated crosses set on metal transoms, and before this they were filled with quarry glazing,[60] but their original treatment is unknown.

THE SOUTH SCREEN

Presbytery Side	EAST	South Aisle Side
	BAY S3	
Edward the Confessor[61]	*EAST*	Dimidiated rose and pomegranate badge of Henry VIII and Katherine of Aragon
Fox as Bishop of Winchester	*CENTRE*	See of Winchester
Pelican badge of Fox[62]	*WEST*	Pelican badge of Fox
	BAY S2	
Initial **R** for Ricard[us]	*EAST*	Initial **W** for Winton[iensis]
Fox as bishop of Winchester	*CENTRE*	Fox as bishop of Durham
Initial **W** for Winton[iensis]	*WEST*	Initial **R** for Ricard[us]
	BAY S1	
St George (England and the Garter)	*EAST*	St George (England and the Garter)
Pelican Badge of Fox	*CENTRE*	Fox as bishop of Bath and Wells
[The bishop's throne][63]	*WEST*	Fox as bishop of Exeter

The hollow roll of the string-course is inscribed on both faces of both screens with mottoes, many times repeated. Overriding the string on each face are shields of arms, three to a bay, 35 in all (since one is missing behind the bishop's throne), the central shield in each bay wreathed, gartered, mitred, or crowned, as appropriate, the mitres and crowns rising up from the string in front of the Renaissance frieze above (cf. Fig. 19.12). This frieze is unfinished: the tops of the motifs rising from the urns sometimes look cut off and a cornice is needed to complete the entablature. As David Park says, the friezes 'have a curious tacked-on appearance. Although the vocabulary is Italianate, the syntax—a frieze without a surmounting cornice—is not'.[64]

The incompleteness of the friezes is not the least problem of the screens. There are significant differences between the two, and their heraldry, mottoes, and initials, never previously fully described, have often been misunderstood.[65] The heraldry is best set out in plan. All the arms, badges, and initials are on shields, except for the initials **W F** appearing twice on the string-course in Bay N3.

THE NORTH SCREEN

EAST

North aisle side		Presbytery Side
	BAY N3	
Frost impaling Hampton	*EAST*	Frost[66]
See of Winchester		Fox as bishop of Winchester
	CENTRE	
[Initials **W F** on string, for William Frost]		[Initials **W F** on string, for William Frost]
Frost	*WEST*	Hampton[67]
	BAY N2	
Initials **H B** with **p** below for Henry Broke, prior	*EAST*	Frost
See of Winchester	*CENTRE*	Edward the Confessor
Frost	*WEST*	Initials **W F** for William Frost
	BAY N1	
Sword severing Malchus' ear (John, 18:10)	*EAST*	Frost
Five wounds of Christ	*CENTRE*	See of Winchester
Pillar of the Flagellation and scourges	*WEST*	Initials **W F** for William Frost

The South Screen

Fox's motto, **EST DEO GRACIA** ('God is Grace' or 'Grace is an attribute of God' rather than 'Thanks are to God', as it is usually translated),[68] is repeated six times cut in the hollow of the Gothic string-course on each face of the screen in Romano-Gothic capitals (Fig. 19.12), with the date **A D 1525** carved in Arabic numerals on both sides of the screen

Fig. 19.11   The north face of the door in the north screen of the presbytery (Bay N1 N), with the initials of Henry Broke (prior, 1524-36) in the spandrels, 1525. *John Crook*

in Bay S1. The south screen is entirely Gothic in form and detail, with the minor exception of the decoration of the spandrels of the two tomb-arches in the south face (see above, p. 266). The door in the south screen is 'flamboyant' Gothic in its crocketed ogee form and detail and appears old-fashioned in its setting.[69] The heraldry on this screen refers to the see of Winchester and to Bishop Fox and his previous bishoprics (e.g. Fig. 19.12), with references to the royal house.

The North Screen

The mottoes **IN DOMINO CONFIDO** (Psalm 11:1, 'I trust in the Lord') and **SIT LAVS DEO** ('Praise be to God') are repeated alternately three times each on each face of the screen in the hollow of the Gothic string-course. Those on the presbytery side are painted (not cut) in Romano-Gothic capitals, with the date **1525** painted in Arabic numerals in Bay N1. The mottoes on the north face are in serifed Roman capitals (with the single exception of one 'round' D in Bay N2 N), and are painted (not cut) in Bay N1 and cut in Bays N2 and N3. The initials **W F** for William Frost appear on a label on the string-course in Bay N3 on both the south and north faces. The door in the north screen is Gothic in form but the north face of the jambs and lintel 'offrent une décoration à la française',[70] with repeating Italianate candelabra and foliage patterns of great delicacy, while the spandrels contain shields with **H** and **B** flanked by further floral and urn-derived forms (Fig. 19.11). The initials identify Prior Henry Broke and occur again on one of the shields on the north side of the screen (Bay N2 N). The decoration of the north door echoes the treatment of the earlier tombs incorporated in the dado of the north screen, which, in contrast to those in the south screen, is entirely Renaissance in character (see above, No. 4). The heraldry of the north screen refers principally to William Frost of Avington (d.1529), steward to Bishop Fox, and his wife Juliana Hampton (d.1526), with additional references to the See of Winchester and Bishop Fox, and to Henry Broke (prior, 1524-36).[71] The three shields in Bay N1 N display the *Arma Christi,* with the principal shield of the five wounds crowned by a papal tiara with infulae. The owners of the mottoes IN DOMINO CONFIDO and SIT LAVS DEO have not been identified, but it seems likely that they are either William Frost and Prior Broke or the Frost and Hampton families.

There are thus substantial differences between the two screens in style as well as in reference. The south screen is the more traditional and the more clearly identified with Fox; and it is on the south side of the presbytery, the side where the bishop's throne stood in Fox's time. The north screen makes more of the new Franco-Italian style of decoration in the dado tombs and in the doorway; it is identified with a different set of persons, notably with Fox's steward, William Frost, and the family of Frost's wife, Juliana Hampton, but also with Henry Broke, the prior.

The screens bear the same date, 1525, and they must be assumed to be contemporary, although one date is painted on and the other incised, and the dates are differently expressed. Moreover, the overall design is identical. The differences between the screens are probably therefore best seen as reflecting the tastes and attitudes of the donors, and may in turn be related to the positions they occupied in choir, and especially to the location of the bishop's throne on the south and the possible position of the prior's stall on the north.[72]

The Renaissance Frieze

The richly ornamented Renaissance frieze which runs along the top of both screens provides another set of problems. Eighty years ago the authors of the *Victoria County History of Hampshire* called attention to 'fine Italian work' of the cornice, 'that on the south being rather richer than the other ...'[73]. The difference is in fact striking, in style, content, and reference (Figs. 19.12 and 19.13), the southern frieze florid and overcrowded where the northern is cool and sparse, the southern providing numerous perches for Fox's pelican and once incorporating his initials (S3 S), the northern anonymous except for a single owl of Frost perching on an urn on the remoter aisle side (N3 N).

The southern frieze contrasts sharply with the screen on which it stands, which is notable for its almost complete lack of Renaissance detail. In the relief and roundness of its forms the southern frieze differs also from the Renaissance decoration of the northern screen and its tombs, which is altogether lighter and shallower (compare, for example, Figs. 19.6 to 19.11 with Fig. 19.12). There are two versions of the southern frieze. In the heavier and more elaborate of the two, on both faces in all bays except S3 S, the decoration consists of confronted and addorsed foliate scrolls bound together by urn-like bands and curving into slashed scrolls with tightly rolled tips. The upper elements—shields, winged cherubs, and Fox's pelicans—perch on top of the centre of each pair of scrolls, while between each pair rises an urn supported by the adjacent scrolls. In the lighter version, which appears only in Bay S3 S, the shields are absent and the scrolls are less fleshy, sometimes little more than shallow loops between each principal element, but nevertheless supporting alternately large urns with 'plants' (perhaps the lower parts of candelabra) and small urns on the flat tops of which perch the pelicans of Fox.

The rhythm of the frieze is quite complex and varies slightly from bay to bay. In the heavy version the sequence in Bay S2 S is:

cherub A / urn / shield 1 / urn / cherub B / urn / shield 2 / urn / cherub C / urn / pelican right / urn / central cherub D / urn / pelican left / urn / etc.

the pattern centring on cherub D, which is partly hidden behind the mitre over Fox's arms rising from the string below (Fig. 19.12). In Bay S3 S the whole effect is lighter:

plant A / urn / small cherub / urn / plant B / urn / plant C / urn / plant D / urn / pelican right / urn / central blank / urn / pelican left / urn / etc.,

the mitre over the arms of the see at the centre of the pattern rising in front of the blank space. The crests rising above the principal arms in the centre of the cornice below sometimes obscure the central element in the frieze, as in Bay S2 S. Sometimes a blank has been left, as in Bay S3 S. In other places the central element has been adjusted (e.g. the slimmed-down cherubs in Bays S1 S and ?S1 N and S2 N) or copied by a cruder hand (Bay S3 N). The lack of a clear relationship between the crests and the frieze shows the awkwardness of the fit between the south screen and the frieze which stands upon it.

The northern frieze is quite different and at the same time more consistent, although there are small variations between the various elements (Fig. 19.13). The pattern consists of tall calyx-like vases containing three elaborate flowers alternating with simpler low vases from which rise five stylised plants. The vases are linked by slashed fronded scrolls bound base to base by horizontal bands. The carving is crisp, precise, and elegant, and the only concession to informality is the owl perched on one of the tall vases in Bay N3 N to hint at the involvement of William Frost. As in the southern frieze, however, so too here there are problems in the relationship of the pattern to the crests rising above the principal coats-of-arms in the string-course below.

In both friezes there is a great deal of variation in the way the patterns end at the adjacent piers. Usually there are blank vertical bands terminating the pattern (e.g. Fig. 19.13), but these can vary greatly in width, and sometimes they are absent, in which case the pattern terminates in the middle of an element (e.g. S3 N). When these oddities in fit

Fig. 19.12 The frieze on the south face of the south screen of the presbytery (Bay S2 S), with Fox's arms as bishop of Durham wreathed and mitred rising from the string-course below, and with a painted monogram on the frieze to the left of the left-hand winged cherub, c.1525-30. *John Crook*

Fig. 19.13 The frieze on the south face of the north screen of the presbytery (Bay N1 S), with William Frost's arms on the string-course below, c.1525-30. *John Crook*

and in the relationship of string-course to frieze pattern are added to the absence of a cornice (see above, p. 269) and the differences in style and reference between the two friezes (and even within the southern frieze), it becomes clear that the monument we have today is not only unfinished but may not be at all as was originally intended. The constant repetition of Fox's pelican badge and the inclusion of his initials show that the southern frieze was certainly being carved during his lifetime, but the work may well have been brought to a halt by his death in October 1528. William Frost died the following summer and was buried not at Winchester but at Netley. With the departure of the two principal donors (for that is what the heraldry suggests they were), Prior Broke may have been anxious simply to bring the work to a reasonable conclusion. It might be permissible to speculate that the southern frieze was originally being prepared for something else, but that with Fox's death it was appropriated to 'complete' the screens, that the northern frieze was provided by the surviving donor to finish the work, and that he in turn died before it could be done. Some such scenario may account for the principal problems, but does not seem to explain why the northern frieze shows the same problems of fit that we see in the southern, whether to the piers or to the screen below. Screens and frieze cannot be much different in date, but they may not originally have had the same destination.

The decoration of the screens is in the Franco-Italian style of the first quarter of the 16th century, *le style de Gaillon,* but there are variations: the cool and delicate low relief of the tomb-plaques (No. 4, Figs. 19.6 to 19.10) and the north door (Fig. 19.11), the elegant but relatively light scroll-work of the northern frieze (Fig. 19.13), and the hot-house tendrils of the southern (Fig. 19.12). Clearly several hands were at work, and there may be chronological differences between the parts. The decoration of some of the tomb-plaques hints at future developments (see above, p. 267),[74] the overwrought southern frieze seems to look back.

We do not know who the carvers were, but on the south side of the southern frieze in Bay S2 there are four monograms painted on the flat ground between the upper elements. They are difficult to read and require further work.[75] They appear to be as follows:

to the left of cherub B	**h' B** (*or* R B)
to the left of cherub C	**I B** (*ligature, ?for* J B)
to the left of cherub F	**R** (*?no ligature apparent*)
to the right of cherub F	**T B** (*ligature*)

It seems possible that these may be the monograms of the carvers working on the southern frieze, and it may be significant that in at least three cases the surname appears to begin with B.[76] The mason Thomas Bertie has often but wrongly been associated with the construction rather than the repair of the presbytery vaults in 1532-33.[77] By 1515-16 a Thomas Bartue, probably the same man, was living in High Street; by 1531-32 our Thomas was bailiff of the Soke, and he went on to become in 1544 captain of Hurst Castle, of which he had been the mason. By 1538 he was clearly a craftsman of some standing, engaged in the works at Titchfield for Thomas Wriothesley, and it was probably through Wriothesley that he came to play a major role in the construction of the coastal defence forts of Hampshire from 1539 onwards. His career before 1538 is obscure. By 1531-32 he was receiving an annual fee of 13s. 4d. as the cathedral mason, and the same year he received 100s.—by far the largest single payment—for his part in the *repair* of the vault over St Swithun's shrine.[78] We have no other certain evidence of his activity as a mason before 1538, but, in view of his role as cathedral mason from at least 1532-33, it seems possible that the monogram **T B** on the southern frieze is his and indicates that in the 1520s he was still a practising mason, whether or not he was also already a designer and administrator. The other monograms may be members of his family: those whose names we know are his father Robert (d.1501), his brother William, and his son (born *c.*1517) Richard, so that R at least ran in the family. Might the single R (if that is what it is) be a sign that the young Richard, later to marry Katherine Brandon, widow of Charles Brandon, Duke of Suffolk, helped his father at the lodge bench when not in school?[79]

6. The Mortuary Chests

At some date in the 16th century, presumably at the end of the episcopate of Richard Fox (1501-28), the bones of the Anglo-Saxon kings, queen, and bishops, which had formerly rested in lead-lined wooden chests on top of the screen wall flanking the Holy Hole, east of the feretory, were moved and placed in chests set on top of the new north and south screens of the presbytery. Originally there may have been ten of these new chests, five on each side, but Parliamentary troops threw out the bones and destroyed several of the chests in December 1642. When the bones were put back in 1661, four of the original chests were replaced and replicas were provided in place of two of the missing chests, but these were left uninscribed until the time of Thomas Gray (precentor, 1683-92). Today there are thus six chests, three on each side, one in each bay, the two western chests (in Bays N1 and S1) being the replacements of 1661.[80]

The four original chests (in Bays N2 and N3, and Bays S2 and S3) have occupied the same positions since they were first recorded in detail in 1715,[81] but Hammond's account shows that they occupied different positions before the Civil War. The present positions are probably those in which the chests were placed in 1661.[82]

We do not know when the chests were made. They are entirely Renaissance in character, the first monuments in the cathedral without any trace of Gothic detail, and they are inscribed in fine Roman capitals, but they bear no date, nor any indication, whether badges, initials, or arms to show at whose expense they were made. They are invariably ascribed to Bishop Fox, perhaps for no other reason than that they stand on screens always attributed to him. Now that the screens can be seen to be the result of the shared patronage of Fox, Frost, and Broke (see above, p. 271), it is no longer possible to be so certain of Fox's responsibility for the chests. Moreover, the screens suggest that Fox's taste was conservative, preferring the Gothic to the new Franco-Italian manner. As the first purely Renaissance artefacts in the cathedral, the chests may not therefore be Fox's. If that is so, they should probably be dated *c.*1525-30 rather than *c.*1525 as has usually been the case.

The four original chests (the two chests provided as replicas in 1661 are in a cruder style) 'are unique documents of the high quality of early Renaissance painted furniture in this country'.[83] Writing from another perspective, and contrasting the chests with the style of the tomb-plaques of Toclyve and Pontoise in the north screen, Blunt thought the chests 'ont l'air d'être des imitations par des maçons [*sic*] anglais qui n'avaient pas encore l'habitude du style italianisant de la Normandie'.[84]

To some extent, critical appreciation is hindered by the repainting of the chests on at least two occasions, in 1662 and in 1824,[85] for this is bound to have blurred the line and detail, even if it has preserved the original colouring.[86] There is a sense therefore in which the chests may be appreciated better through the medium of black-and-white detail photographs, as here, than through colour reproductions.[87]

The chests are rectangular, averaging 1.48 m. long by 0.61 m. wide overall at cornice level, and are covered by lids with vertical sides and a ridged top. Turned finials stand on some of the gable ends and the attributed arms of the Saxon kings are displayed on pairs of shields set centrally on top of the lids. In elevation each chest comprises a side panel set on a low moulded plinth and topped by an elegant entablature consisting of a narrow architrave, a tall frieze, and a strong cornice. On each long face the entablature is supported by turned half-balusters, applied to the broader vertical end pieces, which act as pilasters. The elevations thus provide a proper architectural composition on which to place the gabled lids.

The gable ends of the lids are filled with shell-hoods, each surrounded by a semicircular frame (Fig. 19.16). The lids are otherwise undecorated but their vertical sides carry painted inscriptions in modified Roman capitals identifying the bodies whose remains are contained within.

Architrave and cornice are undecorated, but the tall friezes display a variety of decorative patterns, those on the two southern chests (S2 and S3) consisting of openwork metal (?lead) designs nailed to the wood, while those on the two northern chests are carved into the wood of the frieze (N2 and N3). The friezes, which continue round all four sides of each chest, are different from chest to chest, displaying scrolls of various kinds (S2 and S3), sometimes interspersed with shields (N3), mythical beasts (N2 S), or addorsed cornucopiae (N2 N). The metal openwork designs on S2 and S3 are the simpler, but can be extraordinarily delicate for what is probably cast and trimmed lead (S3). The carving of the friezes on the northern chests is of very high quality, especially the beautiful pattern of flowers and scrolls on N3 S.

The sides of the chests have rectangular inscribed panels between supporters. The panels are ansate, that is, they have tray-like handles at either end. No two pairs of handles are alike, nor any two pairs of supporters, even from side to side of the same chest. The variety of invention is as remarkable as the quality of the carving. The 'human' supporters hold the handles and top corners of the panels; the 'animals' hold the handles:

N3	
North side	Standing cherubs with ribbons
South side	Demi-cherubs rising from scrolls
N2	
North side	Eagles with floral tails
South side	Standing cherubs with shields
S3	
North side	Standing cherubs
South side	Standing cherubs with ribbons (Fig. 19.15)
S2	
North side	Demi-cherubs rising from fronds
South side	Lions with floral tails (Fig. 19.14)

The ends of the chests have short rectangular panels filled with medallions over which shields have been fixed (Fig. 19.16).

Forty years ago, James Lees-Milne suggested that Fox brought these chests from Italy.[88] Lees-Milne is a perceptive critic of the Italian and French Renaissance, but like most of his generation has been reluctant to accept that high quality work was often produced by English craftsmen working in the new idiom. Documentary research and a growing realisation of the importance of the temporary works undertaken for entries and entertainments has done much to correct the balance. To take two examples from the 1540s: the stuccoes of Nonsuch may have been designed by Nicholas Bellin of Modena but they were for the most part made by 'Kendall and his company',[89] while the windows and sculpture of Lacock were the work of John Chapman.[90] Nevertheless, Lees-Milne's suggestion that the Winchester chests came from Italy may not be as far-fetched as it might seem.

Fig. 19.14   Mortuary chest of Eadred (king of Wessex, 946-55), south side (Bay S2, formerly in Bay S3), *c*.1525-30. *John Crook*

Fig. 19.15   Mortuary chest of Edmund (?Edmund Ironside, d. 1016, see note 44), detail of south side (Bay S3, formerly in Bay S2), *c*.1525-30. *John Crook*

Their form, as Simon Jervis has pointed out, is like that of medieval *châsses* containing the relics of saints.[91] More precisely, they are similar to Italian Early Renaissance reliquary chests.[92] But this may be too specific. The Winchester chests are as secular as they are anonymous. Unlike almost every other high medieval work in the cathedral, they give no indication of their donor; and if we omit the inscriptions, which may have been written only when the chests reached their destination, they carry no sign that they were intended to serve any religious or mortuary function. They could as well be domestic as ecclesiastical. Moreover, they appear to have been adapted, for the shields on the ends have been fixed over the medallions, and the lids may not be original: they are plainer, flimsier, and the detail of the

Fig. 19.16   Mortuary chest of Eadred (king of Wessex, 946-55), east end (Bay S2, formerly in Bay S3), *c.*1525-30. *John Crook*

shell-hoods at each end is coarse by comparison with the decoration of the chests themselves.[93]

The mortuary chests deserve a detailed new investigation. The lids may be replacements of 1661, and the shields on the ends may have been added then, but this does not change the chests' strange anonymity. Not even Fox's pelican, so prominent on all his works, is to be seen. It is true that there are a few shields integral with the decoration (e.g. on N3), but like the main panels they need not have been painted when the chests were obtained. For obtained, probably on the London market, I think we can assume they were, and adapted to contain the relics of the Saxon kings. But whether they were imports from Italy, as Lees-Milne suggested, or were products of the finest workshops of the capital, it is difficult to say.

There are two, perhaps conflicting, indications. The metal strip-work forming the friezes of the southern chests (S2 and S3) is certainly an English trick, for lead leaves had long been used in the decoration of ceilings, and lead strap-work, fixed with iron pins like the friezes on the Winchester chests, formed part of the decorations of Nonsuch.[94] But this is not to say that metal fittings like these were not also used abroad. However, the style of the figures and other carved decorations provides a further clue. This is not 'le style italianisant de la Normandie'. It is either Italian or Italian through English eyes and hands, and skilled ones at that. On balance, I suspect these chests are London work, produced in a shop with close access to guidance and inspiration from Italians working in the capital in the 1520s. Such a workshop might be thought to have close connections with the Court, and might seem to suggest that the chests were presented by the king to preserve the relics of his predecessors. But their anonymity is surely against this, for if they had been royal gifts they would certainly have carried the royal arms and badges.

It seems on balance very unlikely that the chests were specially ordered for Winchester. But wherever they were obtained, the carvers were well aware of Italian models: the cherubs on the chest containing the remains of Edmund (Fig. 19.15) may be poor things if compared to those supporting the royal arms on the tomb of Henry VII but they are siblings of those who support the arms of a Rovere cardinal on the altar-rail of the Capella della Rovere in Santa Maria del Popolo in Rome, carved about 1480.[95]

7. The Panels Fronting the Choir-Stalls

In 1539 the priory of St Swithun was dissolved and 'quietly turned into a Dean and Chapter ... much as if the great reform of St. Ethelwold were to be quietly reversed'.[96] The year before the convent had been 'very conformable' to the destruction of St Swithun's shrine.[97] Now they received their reward. By Letters Patent of 28 March 1541, Henry VIII established the new body with William Kingsmill, prior since 1536, as dean and with 12 prebendaries appointed in part from among the brethren.[98]

In celebration of the establishment and dignity of the new cathedral body carved wooden panels were inserted into the fronts of the desks standing before 16 of the choir-stalls. Although forming the backs of the sub-stalls, these panels can only be seen as referring to the canopied stalls behind, the easternmost eight on each side. The subjects are as follows, numbered from west to east:[99]

East

N8	Cherub rising from fronds between two confronted dolphin scrolls (cf. N6) (Fig. 19.17a)	S8	Fleur de lys between tendril scrolls
N7	Medallion ?helmeted head looking up right (outwards), within a slashed roundel between floral scrolls (Fig. 19.17b)	S7	Medallion head wearing a cap and looking right (inwards), within a wreath, between floral scrolls
N6	Label bearing the date **1540**, suspended by ribbons from a knot between two confronted dolphin scrolls (Fig. 19.17c)	S6	Portcullis between its own scrolled chains, beneath a hooped crown
N5	Arms of Stephen Gardiner (bishop, 1531-51, 1553-55), mitred and gartered, between **S W** for Stephanus Winton[100]	S5	Arms of the New Foundation, supported by *putti* (Fig. 19.17d)
N4	Arms of Henry VIII (1509-47), crowned and gartered, with lion and dragon supporters, beneath the initials **H R**, for Henricus Rex[101]	S4	Arms of William Kingsmill (dean, 1541-49), beneath an ecclesiastical cap, between the initials **W K**[102]
N3	Tudor Rose supported by floral scrolls, beneath a hooped crown	S3	Tudor Rose supported by rose scrolls, beneath a hooped crown
N2	Medallion head with curly hair, looking left (outwards), within a wreath between floral scrolls (Fig. 19.17e)	S2	Medallion head with curly hair, looking left (inwards), within a wreath between floral scrolls
N1	Elaborate grotesque with central downward-hanging plant and outward-looking masks, between candelabra (Fig. 19.17f)	S1	Candelabrum urn between supporting floral scrolls

West

The date 1540 on Panel N6 anticipated the issue of the Letters Patent establishing the capitular body on 28 March 1541—but in theory only by three days, for the year changed on 25 March. In practice the Patent must have been in draft for some months and its issue

(a) Fronded cherub (N8)

(b) ?Helmeted medallion head (N7)

(c) Date label, **1540** (N6)

(d) Arms of the New Foundation, granted June 1541 (S5)

(e) Curly medallion head (N2)

(f) Grotesque (N1)

Fig. 19.17   Choir-stalls, desk fronts. *John Crook*

a foregone conclusion, perhaps somewhat delayed.[103] The arms of the new body on Panel S5 likewise anticipated (supposing the panels are all the same date) the grant of arms on 1 June 1541,[104] but again the issue will have been agreed and the design finalised long before the date of the actual grant.

It is less easy to account for the embellishment of 16 stalls with the new panels. The capitular body consisted of a dean and 12 canons, the vice-dean, receiver, and treasurer being chosen from among their number.[105] For whom then were the other three stalls? Although it is not possible to be certain, the most likely candidates for the remaining stalls are the precentor, the sacrist, and possibly the seneschal (i.e the chapter clerk), the first two chosen from among the minor canons.[106]

The arrangement of the panels 'reads' within each row and from side to side of the choir. The four central panels have the arms of king and bishop on the north (N4 and N5) and dean and the New Foundation on the south (S4 and S5). These are flanked by the royal badges, to the west roses (N3 and S3) and to the east a portcullis and—an exception—-the date 1540 (S6 and N6). These eight panels have clear symbolic meanings. They are flanked in their turn to either side by four panels of apparently purely decorative content, first by pairs of medallion heads (N2 and S2, N7 and S7) and then by grotesque and floral patterns (N1 and S1, N8 and S8). But the medallion heads are so arranged that the northern pair looks outward and the southern pair inward, as if guarding the central devices of secular and ecclesiastical authority.[107] The panels bearing the arms of bishop and dean do not, of course, indicate the location of their stalls, any more than does that of the king. The whole arrangement is a decorative and tutelary celebration of the New Foundation and its royal supporter, not a collection of stall plates.

Pevsner thought the Renaissance motifs on these panels 'rather uninspired'.[108] In reality they are a mixture in which at least two carvers seem to have been involved. The *putti* supporting the arms of the New Foundation (Fig. 19.17d) are even flabbier than the cherubs on the mortuary chests (Fig. 19.15), their outlines insipid. But the dolphin scrolls flanking the label bearing the date (Fig. 19.17c) and those supporting the extraordinary four-winged fronded cherub on Panel N8 are taut and menacing beasts, even if the cherub is epicene and more knowing than he should be (Fig. 19.17a). The medallion heads are good, their encircling wreaths well carved and their supporting floral scrolls sparse and elegant (Figs. 19.17b and 19.17e).[109] The coats-of-arms and badges are standard stuff, but the strength of the series lies throughout in the floral zoomorphic scrolls, some of which are exemplary (e.g. Fig. 19.17f).

The carving of the panels is rather old-fashioned for 1540, looking back to Franco-Italian models of the 1520s and unaffected by the new mannerist style already becoming established in the royal works of the London region in the later 1530s. It was to be another fifteen years or more before the influence of Fontainebleau was to be felt in the cathedral.

8. Gardiner's Chantry Chapel

Stephen Gardiner (bishop, 1531-51, 1553-55) died at Whitehall on 12 November 1555 and was buried temporarily at Southwark. In February 1556 his body was removed to Winchester and on the 28th was buried in a makeshift brick structure standing above ground north of the high altar 'tyll soche tyme as a chapell sholde be made for hym, as was apoynted by his executors'.[110] In his will made on 8 November the year before Gardiner had left money for his burial, together with £400 'for the erection of a chantry that I may be prayed for', and

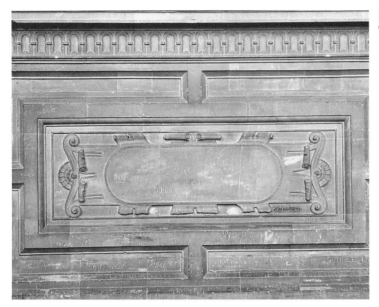

Fig. 19.18   Gardiner's chantry chapel, cartouche on north side, 1556-58. *John Crook*

£300 for a tomb.[111] Since Edward VI's act of 1547 dissolving chantries had not been repealed by Mary, the establishment of a chantry would have been technically illegal. Only the form of Gardiner's tomb, identical in all essentials to Fox's chapel of 40 years before, shows that Gardiner's executors had in mind the eventual establishment of a chantry (Fig. 5.2).

John White, who sang the Requiem Mass and was Gardiner's successor in the see (1556-59), was one of the executors. In December 1558 White gave the sermon at Mary's funeral, and was at once placed under house arrest. Freed in January, he opposed the Supremacy Bill in March, was committed to the Tower, and in June deprived of his bishopric. Although soon released, he died in January 1560 and was buried in the cathedral in an unmarked grave. White's short reign, the strong Protestant views of his successor, Robert Horne (1561-79),[112] and the form of Gardiner's chapel, with its obvious structural reference to the eventual establishment of a chantry, suggest that the chapel was built in the years 1556-58. The date 1568 scratched in the recessed field between the frame and outer border of one of the cartouches on the north face provides a *terminus ante quem* (Fig. 19.18).

Gardiner's chantry chapel, Gothic and Renaissance, has always disturbed the critics: 'an absurd medley of the Gothic and Ionic, both indifferent in their kinds' (Milner);[113] 'a compound mixture of bad Italian and bad English' (Britton);[114] 'a singular mixture of Gothic and Ionic ... executed with considerable beauty' (Ball);[115] 'far from homogeneous ... Gothic in parts, Early Renaissance in parts, and as early as anywhere in England High Renaissance in a few parts' (Pevsner);[116] work of 'untainted and vigorous classicism that it would not be an absurd mistake to post-date by over a hundred years' (Girouard).[117] Like Fox's, Gardiner's chapel consists of a stone cage standing on a high substructure containing the burial chamber. The cage is of three bays, divided internally into a two-bay chapel and an eastern sacristy. The structure is Gothic, the tracery of the four-light openings comparable to the presbytery screens of thirty years before, the stone vaults of both compartments still entirely late medieval. It is the decorative detail, here playing a very prominent role, which is almost entirely Renaissance in character.

Fig. 19.19   Gardiner's chantry chapel, frieze and pedimental sculptures, east end, 1556-58. *John Crook*

The surface of the substructure is treated on both faces with long scrollwork panels, 'very subdued in the details',[118] set within rectangular frames attached to the outer borders by short axial ties (Fig. 19.18). Between the two cartouches on the north face an oblong recess contains the *transi* figure of the bishop's decayed body, another echo of Fox's chantry chapel on the other side of the presbytery.

Above the cartouches and the recess a fluted frieze runs between the buttresses and beneath the sills of the windows (Fig. 19.18). From this level upwards the buttresses become fluted pilasters which make the transformation from the octagonal medieval shafts of the substructure to the classical entablature above. This entablature carries a triglyph frieze, the metopes decorated alternately with *bucrania* (ox-heads) and *paterae* (dishes), very correctly done, but quite independent of the verticals of the Gothic openings below (Fig. 19.19). Above the entablature there is a band of bead-and-reel below a frieze of flutes, and over this an elaborate scrolled cresting, rather like a low balustrade. The scrollwork supports lion and grotesque masks and is flanked by rectangular bases carved with circle-in-square ciphers. Upon these bases Gardiner's griffins rise like acroteria (some are now missing),[119] while his arms as bishop of Winchester, mitred and gartered, stand at the centre of the east and north faces, flanked on the latter by the arms of the see of Winchester.[120]

The chapel is entered at its north-west corner by a flight of steps from the north aisle. Inside, the space is dominated by an Ionic reredos filling the east wall (Fig. 19.20). The upper and lower parts of this two-storey composition are out of kilter, the altar off-set southwards to allow for the sacristy door. The plain ashlar panel above the altar is framed by a double guilloche rising from demi-roses at the base, returning beneath acanthus fronds at the angles, and centred on a cartouche containing the bishop's initials **S G**. The frame was presumably intended to take a panel painting, either never provided or long removed. The door north of the altar leading to the sacristy, and the sacristy itself, are entirely Gothic

Fig. 19.20   Gardiner's chantry chapel, reredos, 1556-58. *John Crook*

in character, like the vaults above both compartments, except that the chapel vault springs from corbels carried by winged cherubs of entirely Renaissance inspiration.[121]

Another winged cherub, set on a scrollwork label, hovers centrally on the frieze of the entablature/stylobate carrying the upper half of the reredos. The middle of this entablature is carried by massive decorated consoles, but its ends are curiously unsupported. Pairs of winged cherubs, in profile and face to face, creatures of astonishing skill and beauty, decorate the frieze.

The upper half of this composition is divided into three round-headed niches of equal size, the outer pair shallow with flat backs, the central niche apsidal, covered with a shell head and flanked by fluted Ionic columns supporting a full entablature. The underside of the architrave has a scrolled pattern in which the bishop's initials appear a second time. The frieze is decorated with a more elaborate version of the wave pattern which also appears on Thomas Mason's tomb (Fig. 19.24). The cornice is complete where the composition breaks forward above the columns, but stops awkwardly to either side, as do all the elements of the upper half of the reredos where they meet the curve of the vault and the ribs of its square cusped panels. Good as the Renaissance work is in itself, it is almost wholly unintegrated with the rest of the chapel.

There is no figure in the central niche. The southern contains the figure of *Synagoga*, blindfold, displaying the Tablets of the Law; in the northern stands *Ecclesia*, open-eyed, holding the Cup of Sacrifice in her left hand, with the New Testament under her arm and a cross, banner, or spear, now missing, in her right.

The chapel may be unfinished: the principal figure is absent; there is no memorial inscription; there was until recently no altar; and the painting behind the altar—the reredos proper—is missing. The brevity of White's tenure of the see and his replacement by the severely Protestant Horne might be the explanation, but the missing elements could as well have been removed as offensive, whether by Horne or later.[122]

More significant is the dissonance between the Gothic and the Renaissance features. This is starkly obvious where the horizontals of the classical composition seem to disappear behind the vault—as if the latter had been built up against it as an afterthought (Fig. 19.20), but the same lack of coherence appears on the exterior where the triglyph frieze is unrelated to (instead of controlling) the verticals, and the cresting sits roughly on top of the entablature (Fig. 19.19). Only the cartouches of the substructure seem to run logically with their surrounds. Pevsner saw this substructure as 'entirely English mid C16',[123] a fair description of the coherence of its Gothic and Renaissance elements and not inconsistent with Blunt's judgement of the cartouches: 'panneaux de cuir purement bellifontain'.[124]

The upper works are not homogeneous, and can only be the work of two groups: one team which built the walls and vaults, including the cartouches and the 'irreproachably orthodox' triglyph frieze,[125] and another which provided the east wall of the chapel. The second perhaps also provided the cresting, for the latter is anything but 'subdued in the details', Pevsner's description of the cartouches which applies equally well to the triglyph frieze.[126] But if there were two teams, as the lack of structural coherence suggests, they shared the same classical repertoire, as the details show.

The two-tier reredos forming the east wall of the chapel is one of the most intriguing compositions of the first English Renaissance. Lees-Milne found it 'very bewildering, for the classical trimmings down to each detail pay strict regard to the rules of the orders used, and are besides exceedingly finely carved'.[127] There ought to be no surprise at the scholarship or the quality. The tomb of Sir Robert Dormer at Wing displays both as early as 1552,[128] and the stuccoes made at Nonsuch in the years from *c*.1540 to 1546, although very fragmentary, show an understanding of the human form and of the figure beneath drapery unsurpassed in England for another century.[129] The order used in the Winchester reredos seems to be identical to John Shute's Ionic, the notes for which were in this country well before Gardiner's death.[130] To my eye, *Ecclesia* offers another link to Shute: the positions of her arms are dictated by her attributes—cup, book, and ?cross—but the leftward curve of her figure, the pose of her legs, high waist, and the set of her shoulders and head, can all be seen in the caryatid figure on Shute's Ionic plate. Margaret Whinney thought these figures 'puzzling and somewhat provincial ... French rather than English', while Pevsner regarded them as 'full Cinquecento'.[131]

Iconographically *Synagoga* and *Ecclesia* remain puzzling: often set to either side of a portal, their presence here might suggest the gate to Heaven, but the absence of the central figure makes all interpretation dangerous. The suggestion sometimes made that they were chosen because they were neutral, neither saints nor the Holy Family, seems to me anachronistic: executors who could contemplate the establishment of a chantry chapel in these years are not likely to have been ready to compromise on imagery. As for their

Fig. 19.21   Thomas Mason's tomb-chest, looking north-east, 1559, reconstructed *c*.1818. *John Crook*

appearance, the figures of Faith, Hope, and Charity at Nonsuch, had they survived, would perhaps have provided the mixture of style and religious content that we are seeing here.

There are distinct references to Nonsuch: the frame behind the altar recalls the setting of the Nonsuch stuccoes surrounded by frames of slate carved with guilloches and gilded. At Nonsuch such frames were the controlling element in the decoration, and can be traced directly back via Fontainebleau to Giulio Romano's work at Mantua.[132] The winged cherub above the altar panel has an even closer parallel at Nonsuch, for there such cherubs with outspread wings were set directly above plain stucco fields bordered with bead-and-reel, which seem to have been designed like the blind panel at Winchester to take paintings.[133]

The wave ornament on the frieze of the entablature links the Gardiner scheme to a series of other contemporary monuments, most immediately to the slightly simpler version on the Mason tomb in the cathedral (Fig. 19.24; see below, No. 9), but more exactly to the floriated waves on the frieze of the chimneypiece of c.1554 at Broughton Castle, Oxfordshire.[134] This wave design also appears on the contemporary tomb of Sir James Worsley (d.1557) and his wife in Godshill church, Isle of Wight, and later in a group of chimneypieces in and around Longleat.[135]

The wave ornament is only one of several details linking the Gardiner chantry chapel to the Mason tomb. The guilloche frame of the panel behind the altar is very close to the guilloche frames of the inscription tablets on the tomb (Fig. 19.21), and Anthony Blunt noted the tiny detail of the fans seen on both monuments, where each section of the fan is cut at the circumference by a tiny rounded nick (cf. Figs. 19.18 and 19.21).[136] There seems little doubt that the chantry chapel and the tomb, the one of 1556-58 the other of 1559, were carved by the same masons.

Then there is the question of the two-tiered arrangement. The anonymous reviewer of James Lees-Milne's *Tudor Renaissance* in the *Times Literary Supplement* for 22 February 1952 drew attention to the reredos and canopy dated 1539 over the altar of the chapel of Francis I's château at Villers-Cotterêts (Aisne).[137] This is on a much larger scale, an ornate triumphal arch with a lower register of three niches set between four Corinthian columns on pedestals, and an attic with a large shell-headed niche surmounted by a dominant entablature as at Winchester. The original ceiling was barrel-vaulted, again as at Winchester, but although Villers-Cotterêts is certainly a parallel, I very much doubt whether there is any direct relationship. The Winchester reredos derives, I suspect, from a tradition of shell-headed niches long established at Winchester,[138] combined with a penchant for two-tiered compositions originally derived from the design of chimneypieces. For a better understanding of this we must turn finally at Winchester to the almost contemporary tomb of Thomas Mason (d.1559).

9. Thomas Mason's Tomb

Thomas Mason, the only son of Sir John Mason, died at the age of 18 on 23 July 1559 and was buried in the cathedral of which his father had been lay dean from 1549 to 1554.[139] His tomb stood against the north wall of the retrochoir where its position is shown on the plan drawn by E. W. (William) Garbett published by Britton on 1 January 1818.[140] Very shortly after this the tomb was dismantled, probably in the course of the campaign of restoration undertaken by Prebendary Nott and William Garbett. They may have wished to clear the Early English arcading of the north wall of what they saw as unnecessary clutter,

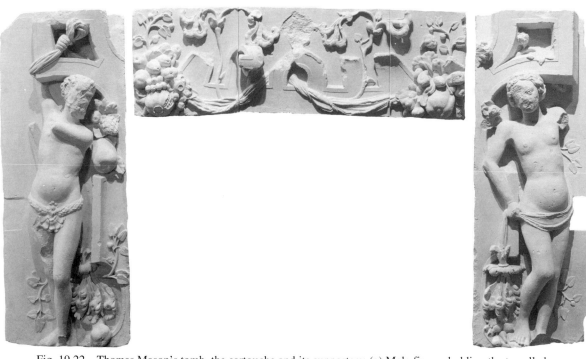

Fig. 19.22   Thomas Mason's tomb, the cartouche and its supporters: (a) Male figure, holding the tasselled end of a swathe of drapery; (b) the top of the cartouche, with drapery, fruit and flowers; (c) Female figure, holding the other end of the swathe of drapery with its tassel; 1559, dismantled *c*.1818. *John Crook*

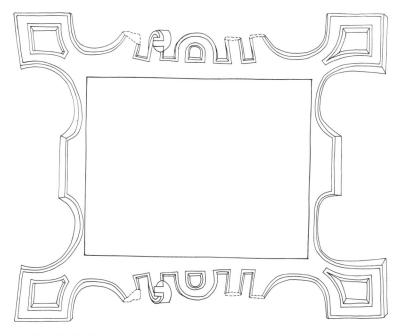

Fig. 19. 23 Thomas Mason's tomb, the cartouche of 1559 reconstructed.
Martin Biddle

but if so they did not extend their efforts to the removal of Sir John Clobury's equally intrusive monument against the south wall.[141] Or they may have felt that the Mason tomb was in some way offensive, perhaps because of the nude figures. Whatever the reason, they took the tomb down, replacing it with a tomb-chest made up from a few of the pieces (Fig. 19.21).[142] Some of the remainder they set aside for safe-keeping, but (as will appear) a good deal more, if ever kept, has since been lost.

The original form of the tomb has never been established. Garbett's plan suggests that the size and position of the base remain unchanged, but no traces can now be seen on the wall above to indicate its original height. The tomb seems never to appear in early drawings and engravings and, of all the historians of the church, only Ball provides a description. Leaving the [Guardian Angels] chapel, he wrote,

> we observe, against the north wall of the church, a handsome monument of free-stone, consisting of a rich pediment, supported by pillars of the Corinthian order, over an oval tablet decorated with figures and foliage. Upon the top of this design, which is of considerable height, are coloured shields of arms; and the tablet bears the following inscription, in capital letters ...[143]

With the help of this description some sense can be made of the surviving fragments. These are now widely distributed in the cathedral.

Incorporated in the present tomb-chest
1. Two inscribed panels framed by double guilloche. The panels are individual flat slabs, the west panel 500 mm. high by 636 mm. wide, the east panel 495 mm. by 625 mm. The frames, each consisting of several stones which extend into the surrounding masonry, are 680 mm. by 810 mm. and 677 mm. by 793 mm. respectively.
2. Two coloured coats-of-arms in scrolled cartouches, on separate blocks, the upper 355 mm. high by 348 mm. wide, the lower 325 mm. high by 349 mm. wide. Although now set one above the other, the lower block sliced off at the top to fit, the foreward curve at the bottom of both stones suggests they were originally set side by side.
3. Two panels, one at each end, of large double guilloche emerging from behind a long, two-level, rippled 'leaf', over which is set a half fan, the west panel 675 mm. high by 262-274 mm. wide, the east panel 676 mm. high by 255-266 mm. wide. Both panels are set in plain raised borders, in some cases cut on the same blocks as the panels, the west border overall 890 mm. by 539 mm., the east border overall 890 mm. by 545 mm.
4. Two apsidal niches, one at each end, fluted and covered with shell hoods, the west niche 570 mm. high by 155 mm. wide, the east niche 603 mm. high by 150 mm. wide. Both niches are set in plain borders, in some cases cut on the same blocks as the niches, the west border 723 mm. by 270 mm., the east border 750 mm. by 260 mm.

In the Triforium Gallery (Fig. 19.22a-c)[144]
5. Panel with a male 'caryatid' supporter, nude except for a floral belt and a fan-like apron, with a swag of drapery and part of a cartouche, height 872 mm., width 340 mm. (Acc. No. 278).
6. Decorative panel with swag of drapery, flowers, fruit, and the top of a cartouche, length 860 mm., height 280 mm. (Acc. No. 279).
7. Panel with a female 'caryatid' supporter, nude, with a swag of drapery and part of a cartouche, height 870 mm., width 333 mm. (Acc. No. 277).

Over the vault of the Guardian Angels Chapel
8. Pair of fluted column shafts, 1020 mm. between bed faces, diameter at top 121 mm., at base 128

mm. Entasis. Twenty-two flutes, the lower 390 mm. of the fluting cabled, i.e. filled with solid cylindrical pieces. Drilled centrally top and bottom to take dowels from capital and base (Acc. Nos. 1150-1).

9. Base for one of these columns, height 80 mm. between bed faces. The upper torus is imbricated, the lower has a three-strand pelleted guilloche. Drilled centrally (Acc. No. 1152).

10. Pair of fluted engaged colonette shafts, 765 mm. between bed faces. Diameter at top 92 mm., at base 120 mm. Entasis. Eleven (i.e. 22) flutes. The fluting not cabled. Not drilled. One of the colonettes is cut on two blocks (Acc. Nos. 1153, 1154-5).

11. Base for one of these colonettes, height 100 mm. between bed faces. The mouldings are plain. Not drilled (Acc. No. 1156).

In the tribune of the north transept

12. Pair of architrave blocks, 87 mm. high, for an entablature returning over two sets of coupled columns, each projection 508 mm. wide and *c*.177 mm deep. Three astragals with bead-and-reel below a *cyma reversa* with waterleaf. The soffit of both blocks decorated with a recessed rectangular rosette panel between dowel holes, 325 mm. apart, to take the dowels from the capitals (Acc. Nos. 260, 264-5).

13. Six or more fragments making up a complete frieze, 183 mm. high, decorated with wave ornament centred upon a grotesque mask (Fig. 19.24; Acc. Nos. 159-63, 238).

14. An engaged Ionic capital. Not drilled. Possibly not associated (Acc. No. 221).

The principal element appears to be a great cartouche supported by male and female figures who hold a swag of drapery which loops around them and up over the cartouche, and ends on both sides in an enormous tassel (5-7: Fig. 19.22; the cartouche is reconstructed in Fig. 19.23).[145] This must be Ball's 'oval tablet decorated with figures and foliage ... [which] bears the ... inscription.' The space available inside the cartouche is however only just sufficient to take one panel of the inscription (1: overall width of one panel including guilloche 810 mm., height 680 mm.). We must therefore assume that while the first panel (now the west one) was placed here, the second was set in the lower part of the monument, centrally on the face of the tomb-chest.

This provides a possible clue to the location of the two guilloche panels (3) and the fluted niches (4) now all set on the ends of the tomb-chest, for the second inscription panel would not have been sufficient alone to fill the face of the lower part of the monument. If the panel was flanked by the niches and the ends of the chest were decorated with the guilloches, a satisfactory arrangement might emerge. It is also one which involves the least movement of the pieces, for those originally in the lower part of the monument are still there, joined by the first panel of the inscription brought down from above. The engaged columns and base (10 and 11) may also have been on the face of the tomb-chest, as we shall see.

Ball's 'rich pediment, supported by pillars of the Corinthian order' over the cartouche is represented today by the pair of tall fluted, partly cabled, shafts and base (8 and 9), by

Fig. 19.24   Thomas Mason's tomb, the frieze from the canopy, 1559. *John Crook*

Fig. 19.25 Sir John Mason's tomb in Old St Paul's, London, engraved by Wenceslaus Hollar, 1658 (W. Dugdale, *The History of St Paul's Cathedral* (London, 1658), p. 94)

the pair of architrave blocks (12), and by the fragments making up the whole of the frieze (13). When the frieze is correctly assembled it reveals a central bay 1199 mm. long, flanked by rectangular projections 508 mm. wide returned 177 mm. in front of the central panel. The frieze can be reassembled on top of the architrave where the faces of the projections fit exactly to the mason's lines inscribed on the upper surface of the architrave blocks. The architrave over the central bay is missing, as is the whole of the cornice.

'Upon the top of this design, which is of considerable height, are coloured shields of arms.' The loss of the cornice of the main entablature means that we have no direct evidence for the arrangement of the upper part of the monument. The engaged columns and base (10 and 11), if they belong to this tomb, and there seems no reason to suppose they do not, may suggest an attic flanked by engaged columns and crowned by a second entablature, nothing of which seems to survive. An Ionic capital (14) might belong to this order but it has not so far been possible to work out how it fits. The two coloured coats-of-arms in scrolled cartouches (2), now somewhat cut down, would have been set within the attic.

An alternative and perhaps better solution might be to see the engaged columns and base (10 and 11) as elements on the front of the tomb-chest rather than as part of an attic. This would place a shorter order (10 and 11) below a taller (8 and 9), and possibly an Ionic below a Corinthian. But just such a shorter engaged ?Tuscan order below a taller free-standing Corinthian is found on the much later monument of Bishop Thornborough in Worcester Cathedral, erected in 1627, and cannot be excluded. If this were the arrangement of the Mason tomb, the shields of arms would have been set in some less architectural framework over the main order.

By either solution we arrive at a two-storey monument of superimposed orders, Corinthian and possibly Ionic. The design of the 'podium', that is to say the tomb-chest, situated below the main order and below the great cartouche and its supporting figures, remains uncertain, for the bases of the Corinthian columns must have been set upon it, perhaps supported by the smaller engaged order. A further difficulty is provided by Ball's use of the word 'pediment'. Did he mean a triangular structure over the cornice of the main entablature, perhaps containing the coats-of-arms, or was he using the word loosely when he meant the entablature itself? No pieces of a triangular pediment have yet been recognised, but it is clear that much is missing and it is not safe to argue from their absence.

Sir John Mason, Thomas Mason's father, died in 1566. He had intended to be buried in his son's tomb at Winchester, as the inscription states, but in the event was buried in Old St Paul's. His tomb there, dated 1566, seems to provide a guide to the general arrangement of the Winchester tomb, for the main features suggested by the surviving fragments and by Charles Ball's brief description all appear (Fig. 19.25).[146] The setting of Sir John's arms in a scrolled cartouche at the centre of a curious 'fencework' pediment above the main entablature, and the arrangement of the face of the tomb-chest, with pedestals below the columns and the incorporation of decorated panels, may help to explain the more obscure elements in the design of the Winchester tomb.

The design of Thomas Mason's tomb is linked to Bishop Gardiner's chantry chapel by a series of shared features, as we have seen.[147] The two-tier composition, the use of the guilloche frames, the wave ornament on the frieze, and the detail of the rounded nicks at the outer edge of each section of the fans, all suggest that the same team worked on both monuments. The links to Nonsuch seen in the chantry chapel are reinforced by the Mason tomb, for nothing is perhaps more characteristic of the stuccoes of Nonsuch than the bunches and garlands of fruit and flowers here displayed around the cartouche.[148] Leathery scrolls and cartouches were another prominent feature of the Nonsuch stucco, together with the semicircle-on-square motif which appears on top of the Winchester cartouche. The Nonsuch stucco is too fragmentary to recover the design of whole cartouches, and by the 1550s their invention had become so varied, as the Dormer tomb at Wing amply displays, that the search for a specific parallel for the Winchester cartouche is perhaps pointless: the elements could be recombined in almost endless ways. There are nevertheless strong similarities to the cartouches in the gallery of Francis I at Fontainebleau, notably in the appearance of the semi-circle motif on the axis of the frame, and in the employment of large-scale scrollwork in the round.

In one particular the Mason tomb shows clearly the passage of time from the first introduction of the Fontainebleau style into England. The surfaces of the human figures, still mannerist in their posture, are becoming vaguer, and the torsos show that an under-

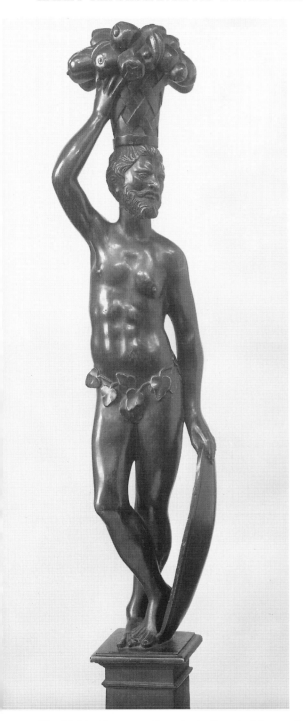

Fig. 19.26   Bronze andirons in the Fontainebleau style, *c.*1540-50. Otis Norcross Fund. *Courtesy, Museum of Fine Arts, Boston*

standing of the underlying musculature is beginning to fade. These figures are already not as accomplished as those on the reredos of Gardiner's chantry chapel.

Margaret Whinney suggested that as a structure of superimposed orders with a sculptured back panel the Mason tomb to some extent resembled the tomb of Louis de Brézé, the husband of Diane de Poitiers, in Rouen cathedral, probably in part at least by Jean Goujon and dating to *c*.1540.[149] To the similarities she noted may be added the use of framed square panels of inscription and even the pose of the figures, for the right-hand caryatid of the right-hand pair on the Brézé tomb, although draped, is close to that of the Winchester female figure.

I doubt, again, however, that these similarities indicate any direct derivation from either Rouen or Fontainebleau. They are as likely to have arisen from a general acquaintance with the work done at Fontainebleau and elsewhere in northern France in the 1530s and 1540s. The lineage of the supporting figures illustrates this relationship in a particularly apposite way. These figures have usually been identified, with some hesitation, as Adam and Eve, but since Adam wears his apron and Eve conceals her nakedness with the drapery swag they must be after the Fall (Genesis 3:7), a curious and inappropriate image on the tomb of a youth. In fact they are closely related to the male and female figures of about the same size, each nude except for a garland of flowers, which decorate a pair of bronze andirons of *c*.1530 in the Fontainebleau style now in the Museum of Fine Arts, Boston (Fig. 19.26).[150] The andiron figures each support with one raised arm a wicker basket of fruit, a frequent Fontainebleau trait, and their pose is derived from a famous pair of giant marble caryatid figures of Pan now in the Capitoline Museum in Rome.[151] In 1540-50 the Pan figures were cast in bronze by Primaticcio and Vignola for the Salle de Bal at Fontainebleau and 'inspired generations of new admirers north of the Alps'.[152] So far then from representing Adam and Eve, the Winchester figures are the typical anonymous male and female caryatid-like supporters of many a Fontainebleau work, their ultimate inspiration not Genesis but Pan. They illustrate not only the close association of this phase of the English Early Renaissance with Fontainebleau, but the influence of Primaticcio in particular.

More prosaically perhaps, the use of a two-tier composition for both the Mason tomb and in Gardiner's chantry chapel is as likely to have been influenced by the design of chimneypieces. The provision of elaborate overmantles necessarily involved the use of a two-storeyed design, and this is exactly what we see in early examples. Moreover when Nicholas Bellin of Modena first came to England he was at once engaged in the construction of chimneypieces at Whitehall: 'all antique of suche stuff as the said Modon makith Your Majesties chemenyes' was the English ambassador's description of the stuccoes at Fontainebleau in 1540.[153]

Although the only artist working in England known to have had direct experience of Fontainebleau, Nicholas Bellin of Modena, left France in 1537, it is quite clear that either by the receipt of drawings and engravings, or by the arrival of new recruits from France, or both, artists in England obtained some knowledge of developments taking place across the Channel.[154] The Winchester monuments of the late 1550s suggest, however, that this knowledge was no longer quite up-to-date. While technical understanding of the orders encouraged by the publication of books such as Serlio's *Orders* in 1540 and the circulation and later publication of Shute's *Chief Groundes* was good, the quality of the figure sculpture was already beginning to fall back.

Conclusions

The first isolated hints of the new classical forms appear very early in the cathedral, in the Langton chantry chapel of *c.*1501-?10 and in Fox's chantry chapel of 1513-18 (Nos. 1 and 2). But it is only in the 1520s that there can be any question of the presence of a group of carvers reasonably well acquainted with the franco-italian style of northern France and Normandy. Between about 1524 and 1530 these men created a small series of monuments (Nos. 3, 4, and 5), among which the tombs, door, and frieze of the northern presbytery screen are of some distinction. The friezes of the screens show the work of at least two hands or teams, one more refined, the other knowledgeable but over-enthusiastic in the application of the new forms. This latter team, whose principal work is the south screen frieze, may be associated with Thomas Bertie, an Englishman.[155] The other team, which was responsible for the tombs, door, and frieze of the north screen, certainly included someone much better informed and skilled, but whether he was French or English we do not know: by 1525, in my view, there is no need to invoke a foreign hand in decoration of this by now standard and widespread kind.

These works were certainly undertaken in Winchester. But the mortuary chests (No. 6), the crowning achievement in both senses of this early phase, were probably purchased ready-made from outside, perhaps on the London market, possibly direct from Italy. Could they, one wonders, be *cassoni* of a simpler kind than normally find their way into museums? The replacement of lids originally flat by the ridged form more proper to their adaptive use may provide a clue, to be explored when the chests are next taken down.

These works of the 1520s are entirely decorative. Only the modest pilasters of Silkstede's canopied seats give any hint of the architectural forms to come. The 1530s have nothing to show, and in this troubled decade perhaps nothing was done.[156]

The New Foundation of 1541 was marked with old forms. The panels fronting the choir-stalls look back not forwards (No. 7). They may have been carved in Winchester, but could as well have been carved by any reasonably competent carver working for one of the newly rich, for Thomas Wriothesley, for example, later to be earl of Southampton, or William Paulet, Lord St. John, who in 1540 was responsible for building the coastal fortifications of Hampshire and was in touch with all the best artisans in the south, for they are light enough to have been carried to the cathedral to be installed in celebration of the New Foundation.

From the next 16 years nothing survives and little may have been done. The second phase, covering at most the four years 1556-59, sees the sudden and short-lived introduction to the cathedral of the High Renaissance in the mannerist guise of Fontainebleau. Here again the question of what was actually done in Winchester has to be faced. The extraordinary misfit between the structure of Gardiner's chantry chapel (No. 8) and its reredos suggests the work of two teams. It may also suggest that the reredos was carved elsewhere. The stone used is a fine-grained oolite, possibly Caen, relatively light in weight, and the individual blocks are not large: the figures of *Synagoga* and *Ecclesia*, for example, are both carved on two pieces. So too with the Mason tomb (No. 9), the weight of the individual blocks of which can easily be tested. The links between these two monuments are so close that they must be the production of the same workshop, but there is no reason to suppose that this was in Winchester rather than in London or elsewhere, for the transport of the carved blocks would have caused no problem. It is most unlikely, of course, that the basic structure of the Gardiner chantry was carved anywhere other than Winchester. The classical elements in its decoration could have been achieved by the provision of drawings and profiles by the designer, their better integration into the structure a tribute to the skill of the local masons working for the most part in well-tried traditional forms.

Anthony Blunt noted that the style of these two monuments was 'quelque peu démodé, concluding that the carvers must have been in England for some years. Were they, he asked, members of Nicholas Bellin's workshop or part of Chapman's team which had worked for Sharington until his death in 1553?[157] We can see now even more clearly that the stylistic evidence points to a team well versed in the Fontainebleau manner. Nicholas Bellin's may not have been the only team with this experience by the later 1550s, for those who had worked with him or to his designs at Nonsuch, or on Henry VIII's tomb in the 'tomb-house' at Westminster,[158] will by now have been making their own way and have been able to undertake commissions of this kind. Such teams may have travelled the country, but it is at least as likely that they worked from London, as Modena did, and as did the Southwark marbellers of the next generation, for it was in the capital that reputations and contacts were to be made, and commissions obtained.

After 1559 there is no significant work in the Renaissance style in the cathedral for over seventy years. In the 1630s the tomb of Richard Weston, Lord Portland (d.1634), 'the most progressive and one of the finest monuments of its time in England',[159] and Inigo Jones's rood screen of 1634-38, both with their bronze figures by Le Sueur, place the cathedral once again in the forefront of English artistic endeavour.[160]

Notes

1. Lindley, this volume, p. 114; Park and Welford, this volume, pp. 132-4; S. Jervis, *Woodwork of Winchester Cathedral* (Winchester, 1976), pp. 34-5.
2. But see above, p. 246 note 30, for the suggestion (in my view, unlikely) that the Silkstede panelling now in the south transept was originally intended for the Lady Chapel.
3. Jervis, *Woodwork,* pp. 36-7, quoting from *Gentleman's Magazine* 87 (1817), p. 225.
4. Park and Welford, this volume, pp. 134-5.
5. J. Hardacre, *Winchester Cathedral: Triforium Gallery,* Catalogue (Winchester, 1989), item 73.
6. As John Hardacre noted, *Catalogue,* item 73.
7. The vertical element has in the past been wrongly identified as the (medieval) musical notation for 'long'. It is in fact a lower case Black Letter L with the split top which appears elsewhere early in the sixteenth century, e.g. in the inscriptions painted in 1516 on the Round Table: see Sally Badham in M. Biddle, *King Arthur's Round Table* (London, 1993), chap. 8.
8. [Thomas Warton], *A Description of the City, College, and Cathedral of Winchester* (London, [1760]), p. 95, adds to the confusion by claiming that the 'Roof is painted with a Hen on a Tun, being a Rebus on *Henton,* the place of his Nativity, and partly on his Name'. Langton was born at Appleby in Westmoreland, as was his nephew Robert Langton, and both were benefactors of the town and its institutions: S. H. Cassan, *The Lives of the Bishops of Winchester,* i (London, 1827), pp. 317-18. For the authorship, date, and editions of the anonymous *Description of Winchester,* and its anonymous derivative, *The History and Antiquities of Winchester,* 2 vols. (Winchester, 1773), see J. M. G. Blakiston, 'Thomas Warton's *Description of Winchester* and its Derivatives', *HFC Proc* 35 (1979), pp. 227-38.
9. As first suggested in R. J. King (ed.), *Handbook to the Cathedrals of England, Southern Division,* i (London, 1861), p. 23.
10. Both the Authorised and Revised Standard Versions translate as 'adder', but the Vulgate *regulus* is the cognate of basilisk, hence cockatrice.
11. The same device appears below Langton's initials on two shields, one on the north, the other on the

south side of the nave of Sherborne Abbey, Dorset, as Brenda Kipling points out to me. Sherborne was in the diocese of Salisbury, of which Langton was bishop 1485-93, but the shields need not imply that Langton used the cockatrice rebus before he became bishop of Winchester in the latter year, for the reconstruction of the nave of Sherborne, the work of Abbot Peter Rampisham, or Ramsam (1475-1504), continued for many years, and the bosses include a number of arms having no immediately direct connection with the abbey, although we may suspect they all commemorate donors. They include Henry VII and Elizabeth of York, Archbishops Bourchier and Morton of Canterbury (1454-86 and 1496-1500), and what Pevsner describes as 'a bishop of Exeter who ruled in 1509-19', who must be Hugh Oldham (*recte* 1505-19): John Newman and Nikolaus Pevsner, *The Buildings of England: Dorset* (Harmondsworth, 1972), p. 374. Langton may first have given a contribution as bishop of Salisbury, but was commemorated as bishop of the senior see.

12. J. Vaughan, *Winchester Cathedral: its Monuments and Memorials* (London, 1919), p. 58.
13. Some bishops built their chantry chapels in their lifetime, as did Fox; others, like Gardiner, left this task to their executors (see below, pp. 281-2). For Langton's foundation of his chantry chapel, see John Leland, *Collectanea,* ed. T. Hearne, 2nd edn. (London, 1774), p. 116.
14. A. Blunt, 'L'influence française sur l'architecture et la sculpture decorative en Angleterre pendant la première moitié du XVIe siècle', *Revue de l'Art* 4 (1969), pp. 17-29, at p. 21.
15. A. P. Baggs, 'Sixteenth-century Terracotta Tombs in East Anglia', *Arch. J.* 125 (1968), pp. 295-301; Margaret Whinney, rev. by J. Physick, *Sculpture in Britain 1530-1830,* 2nd edn. (Harmondsworth, 1988), pp. 34-6, illus. 5, who uses (p. 34) the terms 'flattened shells', 'flattened shell-hoods'. In the debate over the date of these tombs, it is important to remember that, insofar as the terracottas were made from the same moulds, the date of the decoration is the date of the making of the moulds, i.e. no later than the date of the earliest tomb. This seems to be *c.*1525.
16. Whinney, *Sculpture in Britain,* p. 35, note 14.
17. S. Anglo, 'The Hampton Court Painting of the Field of Cloth of Gold Considered as an Historical Document', *Antiq. J.* 46 (1966), pp. 287-307, at pp. 289-96, pls. 50-1.
18. BL, Cotton. Vespasian B.ii, fo. 6, illustrated in colour in D. Starkey (ed.), *Henry VIII. A European Court in England* (London, 1991), p. 49 (item III.8). The MS was edited by C.R. Baskerville, *Pierre Gringore's Pageants for the Entry of Mary Tudor into Paris* (Chicago, 1934); it probably came to England with Mary in 1515, and was later in the possession of Nicholas Poyntz of Acton Court (*ibid.,* p. xxx).
19. A. Blunt, *Art and Architecture in France 1500-1700,* 4th edn. (Harmondsworth, 1982), pp. 23-5.
20. Blunt, 'Influence française', p. 17.
21. A. Smith, 'The Chantry Chapel of Bishop Fox', *WCR* 57 (1988), pp. 27-32, at pp. 27, 30.
22. *Ibid.,* p. 29; the bill is dated 22 March 1522, i.e. 1523.
23. *Ibid.,* p. 30; Phillip Lindley, 'The Sculptural Programme of Bishop Fox's Chantry Chapel', *WCR* 57 (1988), pp. 33-7, at p. 33.
24. Reproduced in Smith, 'Chantry Chapel', pl. 3.
25. First noted in *VCH Hants,* v, p. 56, but missed by subsequent observers including Sir Nikolaus Pevsner (*Hampshire and the Isle of Wight* (Harmondsworth, 1967), p. 679), until rediscovered by Phillip Lindley, 'Sculptural Programme', p. 33, note 1; see also Lindley, this volume, p. 122, note 86.
26. Note by F. T. M[adge] in W. W. Capes, *The Bishops of Winchester, II, Walkelin to Gardiner* (Winchester and London, 1907), pp. 77-8.
27. The description which follows is adapted from Jervis, *Woodwork,* p. 9.
28. Rennell's arms were [sable] a cross moline [or]; I am grateful to Brenda Kipling for this identification.
29. Simon Jervis took the view that Rennell 'vigorously extended and restored Silkstede's surviving work' (*Woodwork,* p. 9), but much of the carved work appears to be of 16th-century date.
30. Reproduced in F. Bussby, *Winchester Cathedral 1079-1979* (Southampton, 1979), p. xiv.
31. [Warton], *Description of Winchester,* p. 98.
32. Milner, *Winchester,* 2nd edn. (Winchester, 1809), ii, p. 31.
33. C. Ball, *An Historical Account of Winchester, with Descriptive Walks* (Winchester, 1818), p. 101.
34. *Hampshire Chronicle,* 13 April 1818: the Chapter Room 'lately restored'.
35. [Warton], *Description of Winchester,* p. 98.
36. Jervis, *Woodwork,* p. 35.
37. Baggs, 'Terracotta Tombs', pls. XXIX-XXXVI; Whinney, *Sculpture in Britain,* illus. p. 5.

38. For example, Baggs, 'Terracotta Tombs', pls. XXIX, XXXVIB (1st Lord Marney, Layer Marney), XXXIA (Braconash); Whinney, *Sculpture in Britain,* illus. 5 (1st Lord Marney).

39. Whinney, *Sculpture in Britain,* p. 36, note 18, quoting J. Lieure, *La Gravure dans le Livre et l'Ornement* (Paris and Brussels, 1927), pls. iii, iv, and ix-xi; cf. Blunt, *Art and Architecture,* p. 16.

40. M. Howard, 'Laughton Place: the Tudor House and its Terracottas', *Sussex Archaeological Collections* 129 (1991), pp. 133-52, at pp. 142-52, for a recent review of work in progress.

41. The evidence is as follows: the high vault is datable after 1503 by its heraldry (Lindley, 'Sculptural Programme', p. 33 and note 4); the change in the bosses of the high vault, giving special prominence to Henry Prince of Wales by the larger size of his shield, albeit in the correct heraldic position relative to his father, Henry VII, should probably be associated with the Prince's visit to Winchester in January 1506 (Biddle, *Round Table,* chap. 11); the Prince of Wales' feathers appear repeatedly in the heraldry of the aisle vaults, which must therefore be earlier than 1509; the date of Fox's chantry chapel is discussed above, No. 2, p. 259; the presbytery screens are dated 1525, see below, No. 5, pp. 270-1. On Fox's intention, never achieved, to vault the three aisles of the retrochoir and the transepts, see pp. 117 and 189.

42. This position is now occupied by the modern tomb-chest of Peter Courtenay (bishop, 1487-92). Courtenay was originally buried in the Guardian Angels Chapel, reburied in the Lady Chapel crypt, and moved to this newly constructed monument in 1896: Vaughan, *Winchester Cathedral,* pp. 39-40; G. H. Blore, *The Monuments of Winchester Cathedral,* 2nd edn. (Winchester, 1983), p. 16. The lid of his lead coffin is now set in the top of the modern tomb-chest.

43. Son of the Danish Earl Ulf, nephew by marriage of Earl Godwin of Wessex, and thus cousin of both Swein and Harold (later Harold II, d.1066). Beorn was murdered by Swein in the West Country in 1049 and buried there, but his body was almost immediately exhumed and brought to Winchester, where he was buried in Old Minster 'with King Cnut, his other uncle': Charles Plummer (ed.), *Two of the Saxon Chronicles Parallel,* 2 vols. (Oxford, 1892, 1899), i, pp. 168-71; ii, pp. 229-31. See further below, note 51.

44. In 1818 the late 12th- or 13th-century memorial slab inscribed +HIC:IACET:EDMUNDUS: REX:EÞELDREDI:REGIS:FILIUS, now lying at the foot of the north side of the screen in this position, was 'till lately' in the floor of Gardiner's chantry chapel (Ball, *Historical Account,* pp. 115-116; cf. Milner, *Winchester,* 2nd edn. (Winchester, 1809), ii, p. 58. The slab was presumably moved to its present position between the date of Milner's second edition in 1809 (or his first edition of 1799, if he had failed to revise this part of his text) and 1818, on the mistaken assumption that the Edmund commemorated on this stone and the Edmund recorded on the mortuary chest on top of Fox's screen at this point were one and the same. On the confusion and conflation of the two memorials, see Vaughan, *Winchester Cathedral,* pp. 22-3. The two figures involved may be an infant son of King Alfred, and Edmund Ironside (d.1016), son of Æthelred the Unready, but the confusion appears to have been at least as old as the 14th century and may have been compounded by the inscription placed by Fox on the mortuary chest above. On this, see now further, J. Crook, 'The Bones of King Cnut', in Alexander Rumble (ed.), *The Reign of Cnut* (Leicester University Press, forthcoming).

45. Pevsner and Lloyd, *Hampshire,* p. 679, where the owner of the tomb is not identified.

46. Vaughan, *Winchester Cathedral,* pp. 38-9.

47. *Ibid.,* pp. 81-2.

48. *Ibid.,* pp. 34-7; Lindley, this volume, pp. 101-2.

49. Vaughan, *Winchester Cathedral,* pp. 31-2, supported F. J. Baigent's view that Bishop Richard's original effigy was the one usually identified as that of Peter des Roches (bishop, 1205-38) in the north aisle of the retrochoir. Phillip Lindley (see above, p. 102) supports the traditional view.

50. Vaughan, *Winchester Cathedral,* pp. 37-8; Lindley, this volume, pp. 102-4.

51. Vaughan, *Winchester Cathedral,* pp. 82-3, records that the inscription on the lead coffin seen below the recess in 1887 was read by F. J. Baigent and dated by him to the 12th century. Misled perhaps by Fox's inscription, *'Intus est corpus Richardi Wilhelmi Conquestoris filii et Beorniæ Ducis',* and following earlier writers, Vaughan took this to mean that Richard was duke of Beorn, 'that is, of Bernay in Normandy' (p. 82). But the inscription on the lead coffin, RICARDVS FILIVS WILLLELMI SENIORIS REGIS ET BEORN DVX, shows that the pre-Conquest Earl Beorn (for whom see above, note 43) is almost certainly intended. Baigent's beautiful pencil drawing of the open tomb

showing the lead coffin in position, and his meticulous drawing of the inscription are both published in W. T. Warren, *Illustrated Guide to Winchester* (London and Winchester, 1907), pp. 64-5.

52. In Bay S2 N, behind Nicholas of Ely's tomb, but set in the screen wall above the inserted inscribed grave slab of Edmund (see above, note 44), there is a plain vertical slab of polished Purbeck marble, the south face of which forms the rear wall of Nicholas's tomb-recess. It is perhaps part of his original tomb. A corresponding vertical slab (a fine-grained limestone, not Purbeck) forms the rear face of Duke Richard's tomb-recess, but its north face is hidden behind the late 19th-century tomb-chest of Peter Courtenay (see above, note 42).

53. Vaughan, *Winchester Cathedral,* pp. 35-8.

54. There was originally a painted inscription in Roman capitals on the south face of John of Pontoise's tomb-chest (Fig. 19.7). This is now virtually obliterated.

55. Blunt, 'Influence française', p. 22.

56. Anglo, 'Hampton Court Painting', pls. 50-1.

57. Biddle, *Round Table,* chap. 12, and the further references there given.

58. Milner, *Winchester,* 1st edn. (Winchester, 1798-9), ii, p. 45.

59. The Gothic string-course and the Renaissance frieze both stop at the point where the east side of the canopy of the present throne erected in 1826 (Jervis, *Woodwork,* pp. 25-6) rises past them. This can just be made out from the ground, but has been confirmed by inspection from the scaffolding which recently (August 1992) filled the choir. The date 1525 is carved on the string-course imme-diately next to the throne, well to the east of where it would have been if the string had continued to its full length (cf. the date in Bay N1 S). This shows that the stopping of the string at this point is an original feature and implies that an earlier throne occupied this position in 1525. The whole of the north face of the screen in this bay (S1) is set forward by comparison with the screen in Bays S2 and S3, and the string-course (and hence the Renaissance frieze upon it) is set higher. In addition, the north face of the screen to the west of the door is built of small ashlars, somewhat rough by comparison with Fox's large and finely cut ashlars in the rest of the screen. It thus seems clear that the door and the north face of the screen between it and the bishop's throne belong to an earlier arrangement. Phillip Lindley points out to me (letter dated 8 September 1992) that the south door is probably Waynflete's work and notes detailed comparisons with the stonework of the Great Screen, on which he has a paper in preparation for the *Burlington Magazine.*

60. *Hampshire Chronicle,* 27 October 1849, a reference kindly supplied by Brenda Kipling. The spandrels of the transoms carry the initials **P N**, **W N**, and **J N**, presumably with reference to the donors. Might these be members of the family of Dr. G. F. Nott (canon, 1810-41), who with the architect William Garbett directed the restoration of the cathedral in the early 19th century? The *Hampshire Chronicle* records only that the new glazing was the gift of 'some liberal gentleman who has not given his name', and since Dr. Nott was a bachelor, and his sister was Charlotte Georgina, the problem is at present unsolved.

61. The attributed arms of the Confessor, that is, with five martlets and not four, which would have denoted the Saxon kings in general.

62. Fox, who was probably not from an armigerous family, seems to have chosen the pelican as his badge for its religious symbolism and then adopted it as his arms.

63. See above, note 59.

64. See above, p. 138, note 62.

65. The motto IN DOMINO CONFIDO does not (*pace* Milner and *VCH Hants,* v, p. 56) refer to Henry Cardinal Beaufort, whose motto was *A honor et lyesse* (G. L. Harriss, *Cardinal Beaufort* (Oxford, 1988), p. 370 and note 80). The misidentification of the arms of William Frost as those of Fox's friend, Hugh Oldham (bishop of Exeter, 1505-19), in *VCH Hants,* v, p. 56, is even more deceptive, for it might be taken to imply that Fox, Oldham, and Frost were joint donors of the screens, as they had earlier been founder and benefactors together of Corpus Christi College, Oxford. The arms of Frost were first correctly identified in 1889-90 in E. C. Batten (ed.), *The Register of Bishop Fox* (privately printed, 1889), p. 116, and in G. W. Kitchin and F. T. Madge (eds.), *Documents Relating to the Foundation of the Chapter of Winchester A.D. 1541-1547,* HRSoc (1889), p. 53, probably as a result of the researches of A. C. Radcliffe, the rector of Stoke Charity, where the Hampton tombs are preserved in the church. Radcliffe identified the Frost and Hampton arms on the presbytery screen, and his help was acknowledged by Thomas Fowler, the President of Corpus, in *The History*

of Corpus Christi College, Oxford Historical Society, 25 (Oxford, 1893), pp. 32-4. The same conclusions were reached and fully explained with useful drawings of the heraldry on the north screen by N. C. H. Nisbett, 'Notes on Some Armorial Bearings on the Presbytery Screens, Winchester Cathedral', *HFC Proc,* 5.ii (1905), pp. 179-83, and were followed by A. J. Smith, 'The Life and Building Activity of Richard Fox, *c.*1448-1528', unpubl. Ph.D. thesis, University of London, 1988, pp. 279-85, as Dr. Phillip Lindley kindly points out to me. It should be noted that the Frost arms on the Hampton tomb in Stoke Charity church do not today display a quatrefoil on the chevron, a consistent feature of the arms on the Winchester screen. In 1890, writing to President Fowler of Corpus, Radcliffe noted 'In the Chantry Chapel here there is a very dilapidated copy of the [Frost] arms, on which the azure quatrefoil appears distinctly, & the chevron appears to be sable, but I can't be certain.' Clearly, Radcliffe's careful statement can be accepted, although nothing can be seen a century later. I am most grateful to Mrs. Christine Butler, archivist of Corpus, for her help in providing me with the correspondence between President Fowler and Mr. Radcliffe, and for allowing me to see material relating to William Frost, who was second only to Bishop Oldham as a benefactor of the college.

66. The arms are incorrectly painted; they should be: argent on a chevron sable between three owls gules a quatrefoil azure.

67. Argent on a chevron gules between three cinquefoils azure as many bezants.

68. I am grateful to David West, Emeritus Professor at Newcastle University, and Mr. Guy Clarke of Winchester for their comments on the meaning of this motto.

69. See above, note 59.

70. Blunt, 'Influence française', p. 22.

71. For Frost and the Hamptons, see Fowler, *History of Corpus,* pp. 32-4; B. W. Greenfield, 'Old Stoke Charity', *HFC Proc* 3.i (1894), pp. 1-27; *VCH Hants,* iii, pp. 447-8, 451; *VCH Hants,* iv, p. 151. Juliana died 18 June 1526 and was buried at Netley Abbey, where her husband in his will of 6 July 1529, preserved at Corpus Christi College, Oxford (CCC, *Rejectanea Hants.,* p. 29), directed he should also be buried. There may have been some family association between Henry Broke, William Frost of Avington, and Walter Froste, *custos operum* in 1532-33, for the pension granted to Walter in 1540 refers to him as Walter Froste *alias* Broke (J. Gairdner and R. H. Brodie (eds.), *Calendar of Letters and Papers Foreign and Domestic, Henry VIII,* xvi (London, 1898), p. 719); for Walter, see G. W. Kitchin (ed.), *Compotus Rolls of the Obedientiaries of St. Swithun's Priory,* HRSoc (1892), pp. 106-7, 215, 479.

72. See above, pp. 199 and 240. For the position of the bishop's throne in Fox's time, see above, note 59.

73. *VCH Hants,* v, p. 56.

74. I am not convinced that delicacy of execution or the up-to-the moment character of the detail need imply the presence of French craftsmen. I return to this question below (pp. 276, 294-5).

75. John Crook was the first to notice one of these monograms which appears in his photograph reproduced as Fig. 19.12. I am grateful to him for drawing it to my attention.

76. For a comparable case of a 16th-century French mason setting his name inconspicuously on the face of his work, see the scratched inscription *Pairar Besl ... masson* on a slate border from Nonsuch: Martin Biddle, 'Nicholas Bellin of Modena: an Italian Artificer at the Courts of Francis I and Henry VIII', *JBAA* 29 (1966), pp. 106-21, at p. 114.

77. J. Harvey, *English Mediæval Architects: a Biographical Dictionary down to 1550,* rev. edn. (Gloucester, 1984), p. 21 (s.n. Berty); Pevsner and Lloyd, *Hampshire,* p. 674. For the evidence, see below, note 78. For Bertie's career as a citizen of Winchester, see now Derek Keene in *Winchester Studies 2,* ii, p. 1155 (s.n. Bart[e]u). With the caveats given here, his family life and career as a mason can be followed in Harvey, *Mediæval Architects,* pp. 21-2. For his work on the coastal forts, see Martin Biddle in H. M. Colvin (ed.), *The History of the King's Works,* IV, *1485-1660,* ii (London, 1982), pp. 512, 527, 537, 540, 541 note 2, 557.

78. Kitchin (ed.), *Compotus Rolls,* pp. 219, 222

79. Richard was admitted to Corpus Christi College, Oxford, Fox's foundation, in February 1534, aged just over 16 years: Fowler, *History of Corpus,* pp. 86, 384.

80. Vaughan, *Winchester Cathedral,* pp. 15-18; Jervis, *Woodwork,* p. 29. The best published account

of the inscriptions on the chests, including the texts on two of the lost chests, is B. B. Woodward, *A History and Description of Winchester* (Winchester, n.d. but *c*.1860-1), pp. 70-1. For the two surviving inner chests of *c*.1425, see T. D. Atkinson and A. W. Goodman, 'The Mortuary Chests', *WCR* 2 (1933), pp. 11-14; and cf. Jervis, *Woodwork,* pp. 31-2. An important series of notes and watercolours made by F. J. Baigent in 1874 is preserved in the cathedral library: Vaughan, *Winchester Cathedral,* p. 27. There has been much uncertainty about the original number of chests. Lieutenant Hammond saw ten in 1635 (R. N. Quirk, 'A Tour of the Cathedral before the Civil War', *WCR* 22 (1953), pp. 9-15, esp. p. 11, note 10) and his contemporary observation is probably to be preferred to Thomas Gray's note of ?1684 that there had been eight (Vaughan, *Winchester Cathedral,* p. 18). Hammond's ten may, however, have included two or more of the 15th-century chests, as Atkinson and Goodman suggested in discussing Gray's number of eight, concluding that there had been six of Fox's time.

81. Henry, Earl of Clarendon, and Samuel Gale, *The History and Antiquities of the Cathedral Church of Winchester* (London, 1715), i, p. 27, ii, pp. 26-9.

82. Since the publication of Canon Vaughan's *Winchester Cathedral* in 1919, perhaps as a result of the work recorded by Atkinson and Goodman in 1932, or of a more recent intervention, the chests in Bays S2 and S3 have been reversed, so that Edmund is now in Bay S3 and Eadred in Bay S2. This should be corrected at the first opportunity. Atkinson and Goodman recorded that the easternmost chest on the south side (i.e. the chest then in Bay S3) 'is a reconstruction in 1661 of one of the chests damaged by the Commonwealth soldiery in 1642'. Because of the switch, it is not at present possible to be sure whether this refers to Eadred's chest (as seems likely) or to Edmund's.

83. Jervis, *Woodwork,* p. 29.

84. Blunt, 'Influence française', p. 22. Although Blunt's pioneering account of the Winchester monuments contains many factual errors, his comments on style command attention.

85. Barbara Carpenter Turner, '"The Return of the Church"; Cathedral and Close, 1660-1662', *WCR* 29 (1960), pp. 15-23, at p. 22; Atkinson and Goodman, 'Chests', p. 13; Jervis, *Woodwork,* p. 29. The Chapter Act Books record, 23 June 1824, 'that Mr Garbett be instructed to draw specification for ... colouring the mortuary chests ...'.

86. The repainting of the Round Table in Winchester Castle Hall by the Cave family in 1787 transformed the style of the original of 1516, while preserving the scheme and approximate colouring: Stephen Rees-Jones and Pamela Tudor-Craig in Biddle, *Round Table,* chaps. 7 and 9.

87. The only colour reproduction of one of the original chests currently available shows the north side of that of Eadred, at present in Bay S2: John Crook, *Winchester Cathedral,* Pitkin Guide (Andover, 1990), p. 11, and cf. here Fig. 19.14. The only colour postcard available shows the south side of the 1661 replica in Bay N1.

88. James Lees-Milne, *Tudor Renaissance* (London, 1951), p. 33.

89. Biddle, 'Nicholas Bellin', pp. 113-14; for the quality of the stuccoes, see Martin Biddle, 'The Stuccoes of Nonsuch', *Burlington Magazine* 126 (July 1984), pp. 411-16.

90. Lees-Milne, *Tudor Renaissance,* pp. 52-5. The significance of the work of Sharington and Chapman was established by W. G. Clark-Maxwell, 'Sir William Sharington's Work at Lacock, Sudeley, and Dudley', *Arch. J.* 70 (1913), pp. 175-82; and by W. Douglas Simpson, 'Dudley Castle: the Renaissance Buildings', *Arch. J.,* 101 (1944), pp. 119-25. For an important stylistic assessment, see Blunt, 'Influence française', p. 27.

91. Jervis, *Woodwork,* p. 29.

92. Cf. for example the chest containing the relics of St Nicholas at Bari shown in an altarpiece painted by Gentile da Fabiano in 1425, illustrated in C. Wilson, *The Shrines of St William of York* (York, 1977), fig. 1.

93. Shell-hoods first appeared at Winchester, as far as we can tell from the surviving material, in 1526 when they were used by the painter *T G* to decorate the niches behind the grisaille figures of SS. Birinus, Hedda, and Ethelwold on the back of the altar-piece from Winchester now at Knole: Edward Croft-Murray, *Decorative Painting in England 1530-1837* (London, 1962), p. 23, pls. 30-1.

94. M. Biddle, *Nonsuch Palace, II, The Domestic Material* (London, 1994), 'Lead', by G. Egan.

95. Illustrated by Lees-Milne, *Tudor Renaissance,* figs. 19, 41. Lees-Milne (p. 43) suggested that the

Rovere cherubs, 'a favourite Renaissance convention ... found throughout Italy', were the proto-type for the design of Wolsey's arms upon Ann Boleyn's gatehouse at Hampton Court. So they may be, but they are much more closely related to the Winchester cherubs.

96. Kitchin and Madge, *Documents,* pp. 1, 6.

97. *Ibid.,* p. 7.

98. *Ibid.,* pp. 6, 39.

99. Edward T. Joy, *Woodwork in Winchester Cathedral* (Winchester, 1964), p. 19, numbered the panels from east to west. I have numbered them from west to east, i.e. from the centre of the crossing outwards, in conformity with normal practice.

100. Illustrated in Jervis, *Woodwork,* p. 22; and (larger) in Joy, *Woodwork,* fig. 11.

101. Illustrated in Jervis, *Woodwork,* p. 22; and (larger) in Joy, *Woodwork,* fig. 12.

102. Illustrated in Jervis, *Woodwork,* p. 22.

103. The process of suppression and refoundation between 14 November 1539 and 28 March 1541 can be traced in *L & P Henry VIII,* xv (1896), Nos. 139 (i.1), Nos. 321-2, 809; xvi (1898), Nos. 678 (53), 878 (1).

104. Kitchin and Madge, *Documents,* pp. 7-8, 107-9, with a contemporary heraldic description of the arms, p. 109.

105. *Ibid.,* p. 152.

106. *Ibid.,* pp. 155-6, 160.

107. Jervis, *Woodwork,* p. 22, points out that although the present framework containing the panels does not appear to be older than the 1820s, they seem to have been in their present position since the late 18th century, 'and it seems likely that they were placed in the quire from the first'. The logical arrangement of the panels suggests that, even if reframed, their order has been carefully preserved. The only point where confusion might have arisen is with the medallion heads: it is possible that both pairs originally looked in the same direction, either outward or inward. A simple inversion on one side or the other could have brought about the present situation—but equally the present arrangement may have been that originally intended.

108. Pevsner and Lloyd, *Hampshire,* p. 679.

109. The medallion head N7 appears to be helmeted, but may perhaps be a woman wearing a fanciful head-dress: cf. some of the exactly contemporary medallion heads decorating the ceiling of the King's Presence Chamber in the palace within Stirling Castle: J. G. Dunbar, *The Stirling Heads* (Edinburgh, 1975), Nos. 18, 20, 25, 26, 29, and 40.

110. J. A. Muller, *The Letters of Stephen Gardiner* (Cambridge, 1933), pp. 502-19, at p. 517, quoting College of Arms MS. I.II. Burials, fo. 133.

111. J. A. Muller, *Stephen Gardiner and the Tudor Reaction* (London, 1926), p. 290. For Gardiner's career, see now also Glyn Redworth, *In Defence of the Church Catholic. The Life of Stephen Gardiner* (Oxford, 1990).

112. See below, note 122. Horne died 1 June 1579, *not* 1580: J. M. Horn (ed.), *John Le Neve, Fasti Ecclesiæ Anglicanæ,* III, *Canterbury, Rochester and Winchester Dioceses* (London, 1974), p. 80, note 3.

113. Milner, *Winchester,* ii, p. 58.

114. Britton, *Winchester Cathedral,* p. 97.

115. Ball, *Historical Account,* p. 115.

116. Pevsner and Lloyd, *Hampshire,* p. 679.

117. Mark Girouard, *Robert Smythson and the Architecture of the Elizabethan Era* (London, 1966), p. 42.

118. *Ibid.,* pp. 679-80. Pevsner calls the decoration 'strapwork', but most of it is scrolled.

119. A drawing of Gardiner's chantry chapel and the Holy Hole by John Coney dated 1826 shows Gardiner's griffins all in position: Winchester City Museums, Acc. No. 253.

120. Gardiner's arms were argent, on a cross sable between four griffins' heads erased azure, a garden lily: Muller, *Letters of Gardiner,* p. 502.

121. Compared by Margaret Whinney to those on the altar at Écouen: *Sculpture in Britain,* p. 429, note 28.

122. Horne was a man that 'could never abide any ancient monument, acts, or deeds that gave any light of or to godly religion', destroying images, pictures, missals, painted glass, both at Winchester and

Durham and in Oxford colleges: S. H. Cassan, *The Lives of the Bishops of Winchester* (London, n.d. but *c*.1820), pp. 25-31, esp. pp. 28-9.

123. Pevsner and Lloyd, *Hampshire,* p. 679.

124. Blunt, 'Influence française', p. 29.

125. Lees-Milne, *Tudor Renaissance,* p. 34. The frieze is very close to John Shute's Doric: *The First and Chief Groundes of Architecture* (London, 1563; Gregg reprint, n.d. [1964]), pl. opp. fo. vi and text, fo. vii^v. The differences are that the chapel has ox-heads instead of Shute's ox-skulls, and three guttae rather than five. Shute was sent to Italy by the Duke of Northumberland in 1550 and returned before Edward VI's death in 1553, to whom Northumberland showed Shute's 'trikes and deuises as well of sculpture & painting as also of Architecture' (*ibid.,* sig. Aii). Although not published until 1563, these 'trikes and deuises' were available in the years Gardiner's chantry chapel was being built.

126. Pevsner and Lloyd, *Hampshire,* pp. 679-80.

127. Lees-Milne, *Tudor Renaissance,* p. 34.

128. Whinney, *Sculpture in Britain,* pp. 39-40; Blunt, 'Influence française', p. 26.

129. Biddle, 'Stuccoes of Nonsuch', figs. 24, 26-37.

130. Shute, *Chief Groundes,* pl. opp. fo. viii, text, fos. viii^v-x^v. See further above, note 125.

131. Whinney, *Sculpture in Britain,* p. 39; Pevsner and Lloyd, *Hampshire,* p. 680.

132. Biddle, 'Nicholas Bellin', p. 119, pls. X and XIII.

133. Biddle, 'Stuccoes of Nonsuch', fig. 34. This fragment has now been pieced together to show the complete cherub with wings outstretched across the entire width of a blind panel below.

134. M. Biddle, 'A Fontainebleau Chimneypiece at Broughton Castle', in H. Colvin and J. Harris (eds.), *The Country Seat. Studies in the History of the British Country House Presented to Sir John Summerson* (London, 1970), pp. 9-12. Margaret Whinney has drawn attention to counterparts of the wave and double guilloche motifs at the Carnavalet, at Écouen, and at the Louvre (Whinney, *Sculpture in Britain,* p. 429, note 28), and Anthony Blunt has noted their similarity to the work of Jean Goujon (Blunt, 'Influence française', p. 29). This wave pattern, sometimes called the 'running dog' or 'Vitruvian wave, is a typical Greek decorative ornament, seen for example on the Choragic Monument of Lysicrates and on the Tholos at Epidauros. It was used on the Temple of Mars Ultor in the Forum of Augustus in Rome, and by Raphael on the windows of the Pandolfini Palace in Florence, thence passing into the repertoire of the Fontainebleau School and so to England.

135. M. Girouard, 'New Light on Longleat. Allen Maynard: A French Sculptor in England in the 16th Century', *Country Life* 120 (1956), pp. 594-7. Mark Girouard suggests (p. 596) that Maynard might have worked on the architectural setting of the Gardiner reredos, but notes that the statues 'are far beyond' his range.

136. Blunt, 'Influence française', p. 29: 'un motif d'évantail dont chaque section est découpée à la circonférence par un petit élément incurvé.'

137. Referred to by G. H. Blore, 'Stephen Gardiner and his Chantry Chapel', *WCR* 22 (1953), pp. 15-21. For Villers-Cotterêts, see G. Outardel, 'Villers-Cotterets', *Bulletin Monumental* 86 (1927), pp. 407-12; Louis Hautecoeur, *Histoire de L'Architecture Classique en France,* 1.i (1943), pp. 104, 123, 132, note 3, p. 265, Fig. 84; Jean-Pierre Babylon, *Châteaux de France au Siècle de la Renaissance* (Paris, 1989), pp. 213-18, 717.

138. Seen, for example, in *T G*'s altarpiece of 1526: see above, p. 278, and note 93.

139. For Sir John Mason, the Mason family, and their tombs, see Vaughan, *Winchester Cathedral,* pp. 220-5.

140. Britton, *Winchester Cathedral,* pl. I, No. 29, referred to on p. 85 only as 'a large monument to some persons of the Mason family'. Although the plate is dated 1 January 1818, Britton's title page is dated 1817.

141. Britton expressed his contempt for such monuments, *ibid.* pp. 79-81. The *Hampshire Chronicle* recorded the 'improvements' in the east end of the cathedral in its issues of 13 April 1818 and 3 May 1819. Five years later, when the alterations under Dr. Nott's management were drawing to a close, the *Chronicle* noted (22 December 1823) that they would do away with the bad taste which had crept into the cathedral buildings at the Restoration: the cathedral 'would display the finest specimen of architecture of the Middle Ages in the kingdom'.

142. Vaughan, *Winchester Cathedral,* p. 225, refers to F. J. Baigent for information about Nott and Garbett's 'disturbance' of the tomb, noting that 'the canopy was removed, the width of the altar-tomb was reduced, and a new marble slab was placed on top'.

143. Ball, *Historical Account,* p. 127, with the Latin text of the inscription on pp.127-8; for a translation, see Vaughan, *Winchester Cathedral,* p. 222. Ball's work was published in 1818. In his preface dated 1 January 1818—the date of publication of Garbett's plan—Ball explains that the text was begun in the summer of 1815. It thus describes the situation in 1815-17 and suggests that the Mason tomb survived until at least 1818.

144. Hardacre, *Catalogue,* items 77-9.

145. In Fig. 19.23 the upper two-thirds of the cartouche has been traced from a montage of the photographs in Fig. 19.22, and the lower part supplied by reversing the upper part of the tracing. The scrolls to either side of the semi-circle on the upper border are broken off and cannot at present be restored with certainty. The breaks are indicated by dashed lines.

146. Engraved by Wenceslaus Hollar in William Dugdale, *The History of St Paul's Cathedral* (London, 1658), p. 94. See also Vaughan, *Winchester Cathedral,* pp. 222-3.

147. See above, p. 287.

148. Biddle, 'Stuccoes of Nonsuch', figs. 30, 31, and 37, and complete garlands now reconstructed.

149. Whinney, *Sculpture in Britain,* p. 429, note 29. For the tomb, see Blunt, *Art and Architecture,* pp. 123-4. Anthony Blunt saw links with 'l'atelier de Goujon' in both the Mason and Gardiner tombs: 'Influence française', p. 29.

150. Museum of Fine Arts, Boston, Acc. No. 57.8a & b. Fort Worth Art Center/University Art Museum, University of Texas, *The School of Fontainebleau. An Exhibition of Paintings, Drawings, Engravings, Etchings and Sculpture 1530-1619* (Fort Worth, 1965), p. 60, and illustrated on the title page; *Art Quarterly* 20 (1957), pp. 320 (Nos. 1, 3), 323.

151. Phyllis Pray Bober and Ruth Rubinstein, *Renaissance Artists and Antique Sculpture. A Handbook of Sources* (London and Oxford, 1986), pp. 109-11, Nos. 75, 75a, 75b.

152. *Ibid.* p. 110; S. Pressouyre, 'Les Fontes de Primatice à Fontainebleau', *Bulletin Monumental* 127 (1969), pp. 223-39, fig. 17.

153. *State Papers during the Reign of Henry VIII,* I (Record Commission, London, 1830), p. 484. For discussion and further examples, see Biddle, 'Nicholas Bellin', pp. 112-13, pl. XI.

154. A point made to me by Mme Sylvie Béguin, Musée du Louvre: Biddle, 'Stuccoes of Nonsuch', p. 412. Sir John Wallop's famous letter of 1540 to Henry VIII, already quoted in relation to Nicholas Bellin's chimneypieces, shows how royal rivalry led to the flow of such information between the French and English courts: *State Papers during the Reign of Henry VIII,* I (Record Commission, London, 1830), p. 484.

155. Son of Robert Berty, mason, of Bearsted, Kent: see above, note 77. Pevsner, *Hampshire,* p. 674, says he may have been of French origin. Whatever the evidence (? his surname), his life and training seem to have been entirely English.

156. In the gallery of the north transept there are some lengths of 'frieze' decorated in the style of the early phase which must come from some unknown monument of the 1520s or 1530s.

157. Blunt, 'Influence française', p. 29.

158. Biddle, 'Nicholas Bellin', pp. 110-11, 114-15, 117.

159. Pevsner and Lloyd, *Hampshire,* p. 675.

160. I am most grateful to all those who have helped me in the writing of this article, and not least to those who in earlier years have been so generous with their time and help, especially Mr. Howard Colvin and the late Sir John Summerson. I have benefited greatly from discussions with the late Professor André Chastel and Mme Sylvie Béguin on the questions of Fontainebleau and Nonsuch. Dr. Phillip Lindley has been most helpful in discussing the works of Bishop Fox. Mrs. Brenda Kipling has read the whole text, made many helpful suggestions, and added a number of important references. On almost every point regarding the structure of the cathedral I have enjoyed the advice of Mr. John Crook, the most helpful of editors and photographer *sans pareil.*

THE CATHEDRAL CHOIR AND ITS MUSIC, 1660-1800

Andrew Parker

When, in August 1660, the Dean and Chapter repossessed their cathedral they were faced not only with the task of repairing the fabric and rebuilding suitable houses in the Close, but also with that of re-establishing the choir, its music and the organ. In a surprisingly short time, between 8 August, when the Dean and Chapter were reinstalled, and the next statutory chapter meeting that November, the choir had been brought up to full strength. By the statutes of 1638 this consisted of an organist, a master of the choristers, eight lay vicars and six choristers. All of these were under the charge of the precentor, who was one of the minor canons. The organist and the master of the choristers each held the place of a lay vicar, making the number of that rank ten in all. On paper, at any rate, the 1638 statutes had adjusted the number of lay vicars from the twelve at the 1541 foundation to ten, and the number of choristers had been reduced from ten to six, but this seems to have reflected what had been common practice over the earlier years of the century, for there had rarely been more than six choristers since the 1590s. The major change, which was to prove short-lived after 1660, had been to divide the posts of organist and master of the choristers. The Lord Chamberlain from London had appointed Christopher Gibbons, son of Orlando, and had named his salary to the Dean and Chapter,[1] so that they had had to juggle with the finances rather more than usual in order to pay John Silver appropriately as master of the choristers. Of those lay vicars reassembling in the cathedral choir after the Commonwealth six, including Gibbons and Silver, had been in the earlier establishment which had limped on until its last recorded statutory meeting in June 1645.[2] Two of the pre-Commonwealth lay vicars are recorded as having died during the 15-year gap, and two seem not to have returned, while of the four newcomers one was a former chorister. Of the new choristers two may have been sons of lay vicars.

The tasks of reconstruction were limited by the available money. Those of repairs to the cathedral fabric and the housing of the dean and canons took priority, and it was not until early in 1666 that the first moves were made to acquire new music for the choir. The Dean and Chapter had not been accustomed to recording their less important decisions in detail, their prime concern being to ensure that business relating to their estates, from which they derived the majority of their income, was noted in the Chapter Books, but from 1666, perhaps feeling the want of such lesser records, they established a secondary book of Chapter Orders in which were written the majority of minor administrative decisions concerning all aspects of the cathedral during the remainder of the century and, in a more haphazard way, to 1738. From these records it is possible to view at close hand the changes which were made.

On 6 February 1665/6 it was ordered that 'A set of printed singing bookes for the service of the Quire to bee bought in Quires with a quier of ruled paper to every booke

& be sure the Organ part be among them'.[3] The only printed collection at this time was that originally produced by John Barnard, a minor canon of St Paul's in London, in 1641. No organ book has survived, and, indeed, it is probable that none was ever produced. From similar accounts at other cathedrals,[4] it would seem that Barnard's *First Book of Select Cathedral Music* formed the mainstay of the first Restoration repertoire in Winchester. A few months later a further order was made, but subsequently erased, 'that Mr Quarterman of S Pauls, now in Oxfordshire be sent for, & agreed with ye Dean & Prebendarys of this Church for ye pricking out of severall services in bookes necessary for ye use of ye Quier'.[5] Clearly, unrestrained by any copyright legislation, having purchased a set of books, further manuscript copies were normally made for everyday use; but it is at first sight extraordinary that it was immediately assumed that Winchester did not possess anybody with the skills to make such copies. Perhaps this is in part explained by the fact that John Silver, having taken on Christopher Gibbons's duties in addition to his own, had himself fallen victim to the plague which had struck Winchester in 1666, silencing the 'chanting service'[6] and forcing the dean and canons to sojourn at Alresford. Gibbons had remained but a short time in Winchester after 1660, if he returned at all. Finding no organ, possibly no music, and little sign of either being reinstated in the immediate future, he had quickly moved back to London, where he had already established himself and had received royal preferment.

The care of the music books seems largely to have been the responsibility of the organist and master of the choristers, who may well have had them at his home until it was ordered specifically in 1800 that they be kept in the cathedral.[7] Following Silver's death the chapter was anxious to retrieve these precious items, and on 29 November 1666 they required his daughter to deliver to them 'all ye singing bookes together with ye Organ part late in her fathers Custody'.[8] There seems, however, to have been another set of books, for the chapter ordered 'further that ye aforesaid singing bookes together w[t] ye ten old singing bookes' were to be received by the vice-dean and that he was to arrange for them 'to be made up & New Services to be prickt where any fault shal be, at such rates as Mr ViceDeane shall contract for ye same & so farre prepared (if not p[er]fected) as to be usefull for ye Quire on Christmas Eve next. At which time it is Ordered that ye Chanting service shall begin, & all ye Ornaments to be there used as formerly'. Were the ten 'old bookes' survivals from before 1645, or were the new ones the copies made from the recently-acquired Barnard set, as opposed to 'old' books produced between 1660 and 1666? This latter argument seems unlikely. Although treasurers' accounts from the immediate post-Commonwealth period survive only from 1662-63,[9] the insistence that copying be agreed only at vice-decanal level, and subsequent orders displaying great concern that payments and orders for copying had to be sanctioned only after careful consideration, seem to show that this represented a new phenomenon to the chapter at this time, of which, perhaps because of their own inexperience in that field, they were very wary. It would seem most unlikely that during the period 1660 to 1666, when all available money had been spent on essential building and repairs, the Dean and Chapter had agreed to music-copying. The only conclusion can then be that, despite the propaganda pamphlets of Bruno Ryves, *alias* 'Mercurius Rusticus', who wrote of the total destruction of organ and singing-books in 1642,[10] something had been salvaged, possibly in a very incomplete state, which had provided the basis for the choir's repertoire in the years immediately following the Restoration.

If there was no organ, and nothing was done until the year 1666-67, how was the choir accompanied, if at all? During the years 1618 to 1640, for which treasurers' accounts survive spasmodically, it can be seen that viols were used, although there is no indication as to who actually played them. There is no mention of viols in the accounts after 1660, except for one entry in 1675-76, so they may not have been used regularly, even from 1660 to 1668 when the new organ built by Thomas Thamar of Cambridge was probably completed. Another possibility is the survival of what had been termed 'the Rigoll' in 1629,[11] which may have been a smaller portable (if not portative) organ, perhaps used in the Lady Chapel where, it would appear, weekday services were held.[12] This might have been removed before Cromwell's troops arrived, dismantled and hidden, and then pressed back into service as a temporary measure in 1660.

The Dean and Chapter viewed the earnings from music-copying as a privilege which they offered in the first place to the precentor. In December 1669 a committee of any three of the vice-dean and canons was to decide what rates to allow the precentor, or, at his refusal, one of the lay vicars, for copying. They were to decide this with a precision which reveals their distrust for the process: 'the rates agreed upon shall be by sheet or side & ... there shall be a patern giuen of the largeness of the sheet & number of ye lines & other materiall Circumstances'.[13] Unfortunately their final decision was not recorded, but they ordered further 'that scobs be made under ye desks for ye preservation of such books of Services when made & bound'. On 11 January 1668/9 William Webb, one of the lay vicars, had been paid 12s. for '24 sheets pricking by order of Chapter'.[14] This is the only indication of a copying rate in the 17th century, and may bear relation to that agreed by the 'Copying Rates Committee' later that year. If by a 'sheet' is intended a folio which, when bound, would give four pages, then Webb's rate is equivalent to only three ha'pence a page. This is probably too low, since between 3d. and 4d. was a common rate in the 18th century. Possibly the '24 sheets' were folios stabbed into the book by their left-hand edges, and thus being of only two pages each. This sort of binding is very prone to dismantling itself, and may be an additional reason for the lack of survival of any manuscript of this period. It is also a method which would suit the addition of material into books which had already been bound.

From this date there appear sizeable payments for copying music, which must show more than replacements as a result of dilapidations. There are specific entries for copying organ parts to the precentor in 1674-75 and annual amounts to the choristers for what are termed 'dittie books'. These, costing around 6s. 8d. a dozen, were perhaps used for the choristers to write out their own parts themselves for use both in the cathedral and wherever they were then being 'taught'—possibly over the Cheyney Court by the Close gate. It would not have been at all unusual for the choristers' 'education' to have included preparing their own copies of the music. In 1667 the chapter had felt it necessary to stipulate that 'none shalbe received or continued Choristers ... but such as ... come to be duely instructed and educated both in singing & good manners by ye Master of the Choristers',[15] and their daily instruction obviously consisted of little else.

If the precentor was by statute in charge of the choir, then it was not until the late 1670s that the organist came to be acknowledged as the person best able to augment the repertoire. In 1676 Randolph Jewett's widow had to deliver the 'Church's Virginall' to the new organist (possibly an instrument used for the boys' training) and it was further decreed that 'the Copys of Services, now in her hands, but wanting in ye Quire be lent to ye Church to be transcribd'.[16] There was still great control over exactly what would be copied, and, a few days before, the precentor had been allowed £12 'for pricking the Organ parts & such services & anthems as are included in a note reposed with Dr Bradshaw'.[17] Perhaps it was during John Reading's time that the close control was relaxed a little. In December 1678 it was ordered 'that the Organ books written & pricked by Mr Reading bee inscribed & kept as books belonging to this Church & that for his payns in procuring & pricking these Services & Anthems to this day there bee payd unto Him ... ten pounds'.[18]

It is not until well into the 18th century that we have any clearer view of the choral repertoire. With the advent of subscription publishing the cathedral began to purchase the editions which were subsequently employed to generate the manuscripts for daily use in the choir-stalls. Although we can see from the amount of copying done that, from 1666, the organists Jewett, Reading, Roseingrave and Richardson must have introduced new material, accounts entries are limited to the enigmatic: 'scribenti libros musicos £3 4s. 6d.' or 'Hymnos inscribenti £2' tell us nothing of what was copied, and the Latin terminology probably bears little resemblance to the job paid for. The words 'Libris symphoniacis' might occur as readily as 'novis Anthymnis', and both probably mean music for the choir. From 1724, subscriptions appear for Croft's Musica Sacra, followed by payments for copying work. In most cases, the actual printed books survive, and show a system of marginal ticks in the indexes which may indicate either approval to copy, or the completion of such work. There is only one surviving manuscript for this period, which consists of the vocal parts only of verse and full anthems.[19] The first seven items are by Croft, all from Musica Sacra, vol. ii, and the book would thus seem to date from 1726 or after when, on receipt of the second volume, both were bound in one. There are items by Clarke, Lawes, Turner, Weldon and Wise, and locally-produced anthems by Richardson and Bishop. The latest item seems to be by Greene, from his Forty Select Anthems of 1743.

In 1765 a book of anthem texts was produced as a private venture in which the cathedral seems to have had no financial interest. A Collection of Anthems, as the same are now performed in the Cathedral Church, College, and St Maurice Church, Winchester was obviously designed to appeal to a wider market than just those who might attend the cathedral,[20] and while inclusion of an anthem might not imply that it was part of the cathedral choir's repertoire, it is reasonable to assume that, of the three establishments, the cathedral might have performed all the music, since, at this date, the organist, James Kent, was also organist of Winchester College, and the assistant, Peter Fussell, officiated at St Maurice's Church, the fashionable town church which used to stand in the High Street, to the north of the outer Close. An analysis of the 122 anthems in this collection reveals a heavy bias towards Croft and Greene (both of whose works had been subscribed to by the cathedral) and Kent. Of those composers represented by three or more items, in descending order there are: Kent (21); Croft (18); Greene (14); Purcell (7); Aldrich, Bishop and King (6); Clarke and Fussell (5); Boyce, Rogers and Weldon (4); Wise (3). No further collection of anthem words was published until that edited by the lay vicar William Garrett, in 1827, when the cathedral actually purchased one copy for the library.[21] A comparison of the two reveals that of the 122 items in the 1765 collection, 106 remained in the repertoire in 1827 which was 37 per cent of the 289 pieces listed. The disposals include all the works by Fussell (who obviously was not held in high regard by his pupil, George Chard, the organist in 1827) and, more curiously, Handel's Zadok the Priest, which was to reappear in the anthem book published in 1843.[22] Stalwart survivors with local connections included

Haste thee O God by Roseingrave, three of the anthems by John Bishop and both of those by Vaughan Richardson. The main sources for the remaining music dating from the 1720s onwards can be shown by tabulating the cathedral's subscription purchases during that period (Table 1).

Accounting years	Title
1723-24 to 1725-26	William Croft, *Musica Sacra,* vols. i and ii
1726-27	William Croft, *Funeral Sentences*
1741-42 to 1743-44	Maurice Greene, *Forty Select Anthems*
1756-57 and 1759-56	William Boyce (ed.), *Cathedral Music,* 1st edn. (3 sets), vols. i and ii
1768-68	'Boyce's Anthems' 2nd subscription paid to Kent
1770-71	Richard Woodward, *Cathedral Music*
1772-73	James Kent, *Twelve Anthems*
1773-74	William Boyce (ed.), *Cathedral Music,* vol. iii (1778)
1778-79	James Nares, *Twenty Anthems*
1780-81	William Boyce, *Fifteen Anthems*
1787-88	'Jackson's Services and Hymns'
1790-91 and 1795-96	Samuel Arnold (ed.), *Cathedral Music*, 3 vols.
1797-98	James Kent (ed. Corfe), *Anthems*

Table 1. 18th-century subscriptions and purchases[23]

If from the 1827 titles one extracts all those which were decidedly 19th-century in their acquisition—all the compositions of George Chard, arrangements of Mozart pieces by John Pratt, organist of King's College, Cambridge, music by Matthews and probably those by Crotch—then, not counting the anthems already listed in 1765, there remain some 142 which represent the augmentation of repertoire from 1765 to 1800. When these titles are compared with the indexes in the volumes subscribed to by the cathedral, a further 82 can be accounted for directly, and, in many cases, these are marked 'copy' or have a symbol against them to indicate their absorption into the repertoire. It is thus likely that much of the music was prepared for performance as soon as it had been received. Eighteen more anthems were available in the Handel copies, or were 'local', being by Kent, and one came from a set of the English version of Marcello's *First Fifty Psalms* of 1757, given to the cathedral in 1770. There thus remain only 42 titles in the 1827 collection which cannot be traced to any identifiable Winchester source within the 18th century. The pattern shown, then, is of a steady increase in the music performed by the choir from just over 120 anthems in 1765 to almost 250 by 1800.

In many cases the Dean and Chapter subscribed for more than one copy, and, where there were multiples, it would seem from the markings on the copies that the back row of the stalls on each side of the choir was home to one of them for the men to share, while the third was presumably for the organ. It is generally the men's copies which have survived. A further examination of the subscription lists shows that the organist, and sometimes even his assistant, subscribed to these and other contemporary publications, and, in this way, Kent in particular would seem to have amassed a sizeable library. The subscription rates themselves may in some cases have been negotiable. For Boyce's *Cathedral Music* the Winchester payment was £1 11s. 6d. per instalment per set, whereas

Boyce himself issued a receipt to King's College, Cambridge in 1763 for £1 1s. 6d. for the same item![24] It has been said that with this representative cross-section of services and anthems from the cathedral repertoire, *Cathedral Music* did not have any substantial success until the second edition was produced.[25] The number of cathedrals listed among the subscribers to the first edition is far less than in the second edition published in the 1780s, but certainly Winchester was prepared to join this and other ventures at the start, and the cathedral authorities may have thought that using multiple copies in the choir-stalls would reduce the expenditure of some of the copying.

Period	Purchases	Materials	Copying	Total
1665-70	£15 0s. 0d.	£1 7s. 6d.	£2 12s. 0d.	£18 19s. 6d.
1671-80	£0 0s. 0d.	£1 15s. 0d.	£37 0s. 0d.	£38 15s. 0d.
1681-90	£3 0s. 0d.	£2 10s.10d.	£9 0s. 0d.	£14 10s.10d.
1691-1700	£0 0s. 0d.	£3 0s. 6d.	£4 0s. 0d.	£7 0s. 6d.
1701-10	£0 0s. 0d.	£8 9s. 6d.	£6 4s. 6d.	£14 14s. 0d.
1711-20	£0 0s. 0d.	£2 0s. 0d.	£20 10s. 0d.	£22 10s. 0d.
1721-30	£4 2s. 0d.	£34 8s. 0d.	£18 11s.11d.	£57 1s.11d.
1731-40	£1 11s. 0d.	£2 8s. 0d.	£14 4s. 8d.	£18 3s. 8d.
1741-50	£4 4s. 0d.	£3 17s. 6d.	£37 15s. 2d.	£45 16s. 8d.
1751-60	£4 14s. 6d.	£0 8s. 0d.	£26 17s. 9½d.	£32 0s. 3½d.
1761-70	£9 13s. 9d.	£3 1s. 2d.	£5 1s. 7d.	£17 16s. 6d.
1771-80	£16 7s. 0d.	£2 7s. 6d.	£4 19s. 6d.	£23 14s. 0d.
1781-90	£4 14s. 6d.	£0 0s. 0d.	£23 15s. 0d.	£28 9s. 6d.
1791-1800	£24 17s. 4½d.	£8 17s. 0d.	£30 3s. 9d.	£63 18s. 1½d.
	£88 4s. 1½d.	£74 10s. 6d.	£240 15s.10½d.	£403 10s. 6d.

Table 2. Expenditure on music for the choir 1665-1800, by decades[26]

It will be seen that the copying of music was carried out in waves. The 1670s were a particularly active time, and this can easily be explained by the need felt to broaden the repertoire beyond the diet of pre-Commonwealth music found in Barnard, and possibly also in the 'ten old books'. What perhaps is surprising is the relatively small amount of copying work done during the period 1681-1710. One might have expected that at this time the cathedral would have wished to be gathering works by Purcell and Blow, to name but two composers, and it is strange that Roseingrave and Richardson seem not to have had a more concerted policy towards expanding the repertoire. In fact, if one examines the 1827 Anthem Book, the majority of pieces by these two composers must have been introduced from the retrospective collections of Boyce's *Cathedral Music* and Arnold's similar volumes in the 1780s and 1790s. Even works such as Byrd's *Bow thine ear* and Gibbons's *Lift up your heads,* which had been in Barnard's collection, seem to have dropped out of sight by 1765, only to reappear when they were republished in the 18th-century anthologies. Perhaps this shows that little Jacobean music was considered suitable in the 1660s and 1670s, and Barnard's anthology was used only as a very temporary expedient. This would reinforce the urgency felt in the 1670s to gather as much as possible which was new, and so, among this material, if it was not yet Purcell and Blow, may have come such as Rogers, Locke and Wise.

It has to be remembered that musical taste at almost any time before the second half of the 19th century was limited to a fairly short span, since many would have held that the music of the day was a constant 'improvement' over that of the past. In many ways the three-volume collections of Boyce and Arnold broke new ground, reflecting the awakening interest in the old and curious, as is shown in musical literature with Burney's and Hawkins's histories of music. Both Boyce and Arnold looked back to Tallis and Tye as founding fathers of Anglican church music, although both editors transmitted rather dubious versions of the four pieces representative of these composers. If the 16th-century origins of music for the Church of England had been tersely acknowledged by this time, the real meat was considered to embody those 18th-century works, many of which which we might today view as possessing an insipidness which must have made services musically bland and monotonous. Yet we should not blame past musicians for their conviction that new was best. Those whose beloved style was of neat and dainty short phrases in dotted rhythms supported by tinkling organ accompaniments would have been well-nigh affronted at the austerity of lengthy polyphonic *melismata* such as found in Tallis's *With all our hearts* (the English-words version to the music of *Salvator mundi*) which had been in Barnard.

That there was good music in the latter half of the 18th century is not in question. Of these composers William Boyce probably represents the best, while there is much to be admired in Greene's anthems and in those of Croft. If we would not wish to take

Fig. 20.1   Three Winchester Cathedral lay vicars in 1820. *Dean and Chapter of Winchester*

Tucker, Tudway or Travers to our desert island, that is because we can make our judgements against a far broader span of church music than could those who limited themselves to fashionable music in one particular style, almost regardless of quality. A century ago a cathedral music-list would have been proud to offer *Praise ye the Lord* by Garrett, *Rejoice greatly* by Gadsby or *Unto thee have I cried* by Elvey, yet, however worthy these Victorian settings were, we should be disinclined to make the time to rehearse and perform them today. Winchester cannot be blamed if its long-serving 18th-century organist, James Kent, contributed many sincere but ultimately insignificant works, and it is only natural that his output should have been so solidly represented by his choir. Apart from this local distortion there was some balance in the repertoire which did not merely reflect the good sense of Doctors Boyce and Arnold: John Bishop, even with his local connections as organist 1729-37, had his representation pruned by half by 1827, and it has already been remarked that Fussell's works seem to have disappeared from the daily services soon after his death.

It has been possible to view only the anthems which formed the Winchester repertoire. The service music, which represents in numbers of pages almost half the contents of the Boyce and Arnold collections and approximately three-quarters of Barnard's, must have been assumed more or less in its entirety. It is perhaps reassuring that works such as Gibbons's *Short Service* (called 'Gibbons in F' by the tonally-centred) continued in popularity throughout this period. It is certainly true that if each Mattins and Evensong required canticles and anthem there were far more anthems to choose from than canticles. Barnard's 14 mostly-complete services (morning, communion and evening canticles) could be augmented by ten more settings from Boyce and a further ten from Arnold. Allowing for 'natural wastage' and the possible amassing of around ten more settings from other sources, this probably meant that the repertoire for services might not have been larger than a choice of some three dozen sets of canticles, but this must, at best, be conjectural.

The expenditure on the music had then, as now, to be seen as part of an overall music budget. In any year, to the figures extracted for music need to be added those for stipends, which, for the majority of the period, came to £57 5s. 0d. for the organist and £13 10s. 0d. for each lay vicar; the choristers' parents received £1 6s. 8d. per boy. Thus a total of around £187 *per annum* was required, together with overheads such as washing of surplices, heating of the boys' schoolroom and the meagre pay of their schoolmaster. When this is added to the sum of approximately £400 for the music, about £27,600 was used to keep the choir in existence. The considerable money spent on various building, rebuildings and repair of the organ has not been included or discussed, as this really represents the fabric of the cathedral, and will be the subject of another study.[27] To appreciate the value represented by this expenditure it is necessary to attempt an equivalent for the value of money in Winchester at this time. For much of the period from 1650 to 1760 the ten-year mean of the value of consumables in the country fluctuated between 558 and 675 (taking the years around 1450 as 100).[28] In the main, these fluctuations correspond to cycles in the cost of wheat, and, on a more local scale, these same variations can be seen almost exactly in the prices paid by Winchester College.[29] If the average of this overall index, carried forward to this century, is spliced on to the prices indexes, we might compute that in 1993 values we should multiply by about 75 to obtain an equivalent for the period 1650 to 1760. For the remaining 40 years of the 18th century there was a steady upward movement in the cost of consumables, caused in part by the Napoleonic wars, so that, instead of the average of 614 for the 110 years from 1650 we have 850, and by 1800 the ten-year mean of the index had topped 1,100. The pressure which this caused on Winchester spending-power can be seen in the introduction of a system of 'augmentations' and 'rewards' to members of the choir to supplement their small stipends. Music provision—that is the purchase and copying, and the basic salaries—was little affected, so we can probably take the whole £27,600 at the lower index average, and this gives us £2.07 million equivalent, or about £15,000 *per annum*. This seems insignificant in today's terms, but it must be remembered that the choir was far smaller, with almost half the number of men, and less than a third of the number of choristers, provision for whose education was negligible in comparison with today. A salary of £1,012 for a lay clerk nowadays would hardly be countenanced, and so any values realised by this computation must be tempered with an understanding of the far lower expectations of the time. Nevertheless, it can be demonstrated that for a large part of the late 17th century and for the majority of the 18th, the Dean and Chapter valued and invested in its choir and its music, and in no way should it continue to be thought that this period represents a nadir in the cathedral's life and witness across the centuries.

Notes

1. Day-book of Dean John Young, MS, WCL, 23 and 25 June 1638.
2. CA, 1622-1645, fo. 83v ff.
3. CO, 6 February 1666.
4. See J. Morehen's introduction to the facsimile of Barnard's *First Book of Select Church Music,* dated 1641 (Farnborough, 1972).
5. CO, 26 November 1666.
6. CA, 8 June 1666.
7. CA, 25 November 1800.
8. CO, 29 November 1666.
9. Loose 17th-century treasurers' accounts, MS, WCL, currently boxed as T4/3/7/4.
10. Mercurius Rusticus (pseud.) (Bruno Ryves) XX week, p. 161, dated 24 February 1643/4, 'The Countries Complaint of the Sacriledges ... committed by the Rebells on the Cathedrall Churches ...'.
11. TA 1628-29, p. 17, 2 April 1629: 'for 4 newe pipes & tuning of the Rigoll x^s'.
12. The day-book of Dean Young refers to processions for statutory chapter meetings during Mattins held in the Lady Chapel on a weekday: *vide* 23 June 1638.
13. CO, 9 December 1669.
14. TA 1668-69, *varia*: 11 Jan 1668/9.
15. CO, 11 December 1667.
16. *Ibid.,* 7 December 1676.
17. *Ibid.,* 1 December 1676.
18. *Ibid.,* 20 December 1678.
19. MS, WCL.
20. WCL, Ea.5.
21. TA 1823-1837, p. 150: various 1827, 'Garrett for Anthem Book 3s. 0d.'.
22. *A Collection of Anthems, Psalms, and Hymns, as sung by the Choir of Winchester Cathedral compiled by William Garrett, Lay Vicar of the Cathedral* (Winchester, 1843). Private property of Mrs. Brenda Kipling to whom I am indebted for this information.
23. Of these, only the publications by Greene and Jackson are no longer in the cathedral library. As well as those to which the cathedral subscribed, there appear to have been copies acquired at an early date of Handel's *Chandos Anthems* and *Messiah,* and William Hayes's *Cathedral Music* of 1795.
24. King's College, Cambridge, Library, Modern Archives Centre, Lib. 11/3. Misc. vouchers for library and chapel binding, etc., 1746-96.
25. See H. Watkins Shaw, 'William Boyce', in E. W. Blom (ed.), *Grove's Dictionary of Music and*

Musicians, 5th edn., 9 vols. (London, 1954) and 1961 (supplement), i, pp. 860-64, at p. 862.

26. The figures for purchases comprise the acquisition of already-complete manuscripts (e.g. those offered by a Mr. Standish in 1670 and those of Roseingrave's in 1684); later, they represent the subscriptions for or purchase of printed editions. Materials include blank music books and repairs. Not all the treasurers' accounts survive for the earlier years of this period. Those lacking are for the years ending November 1666, 1668, 1670, 1671, 1673, 1677 and 1680. In some cases it has been possible to fill the gaps to a degree by interpolating sums voted in the Chapter Orders book, and these include all but £10 of payments for copying 1671-1680. It is especially frustrating not to have the accounts for 1665-66, and so not to see what was paid for the set of Barnard purchased that year.

27. Andrew Parker, *A Short History of the Organs in Winchester Cathedral,* Friends of Winchester Cathedral, forthcoming.

28. E. H. Phelps Brown and S. V. Hopkins, 'Seven Centuries of the Price of Consumables Compared with Builders' Wage-Rates', *Economica,* new ser., 23 (1956), p. 296.

29. Sir W. Beveridge and others *Prices and Wages in England from the Twelfth to the Nineteenth Century* (London, 1939), i, p. 81ff, 'Price Tables'.

GEORGIAN AND VICTORIAN RESTORATIONS AND REPAIRS, 1775-1900

Philip Barrett

Frederick Bussby's monumental history of Winchester Cathedral describes the period from 1775 to 1825 as 'fifty years of feverish building, repair and alteration'.[1] Although that is an exaggeration, there was certainly great concern about the building in those years, and the Dean and Chapter made considerable progress in repairing and embellishing it.

By the late 18th century the cathedral was in a very poor state. The masonry over the west porch was in ruins, while a visitor in 1789 noted that on the north side of the nave 'I everywhere saw broken pinnacles, architraves and mullions of windows; innumerable quarries of glass were wanting ... a scene of generall devastation'.[2] Before this, however, the Dean and Chapter had received a report from the architect James Essex drawing attention to the damaged vaulting in the retrochoir, and recommending repairs to the choir buttresses, the nave vaulting and the arch over the west door.[3] Essex gave the chapter some further advice about the nave vaulting in 1782,[4] but little was done until 1794 when, at a special chapter called 'to consider the repairs of the Church', several of the repairs which James Wyatt had recommended to the chapter (chiefly about the nave roof) were authorised.[5]

Meanwhile inside the cathedral the dais and nave steps had been repaired in 1774,[6] and new furnishings for the sanctuary, including Benjamin West's painting, *The Raising of Lazarus,* were provided in 1781.[7] John Wesley was disappointed when he saw this painting, and described the colours as 'far too glaring'.[8] It remained in place behind the high altar until 1899, when it was sold for £1,500.[9] John Milner, Winchester's Roman Catholic priest, published his *History and Survey of the Antiquities of Winchester* in two volumes which first appeared in 1798-99.[10] The first three chapters of the second volume contain a detailed description of the cathedral at the beginning of the 19th century. Although Milner was in favour of paintings in churches, 'for informing and exciting the minds of the people, as well as for the decoration of the churches themselves', he found West's painting insipid:

> The apostles here are mere ordinary men, or at most thoughtful philosophers, or elegant courtiers studious of their attitudes ... Christ himself ... appears more like a physician, prescribing a medicine for the recovery of his patient, than the great Messiah, who is working an astonishing miracle for the conversion of a nation.[11]

Cardinal Beaufort's chantry chapel was 'neglected and consigned to dust and ruin', and a 'horse-load' of pinnacles had fallen or been taken down from the canopy and were stored in a neighbouring chapel.[12]

315

Fig. 21.1   The choir, 1801. Watercolour by James Cave. *Dean and Chapter of Winchester/John Crook*

Within a few years of the publication of Milner's book, there was a renewed interest in the condition of the cathedral fabric. The cathedral archives contain a series of reports on the building by the architect William Garbett. There are nine reports, spanning the years 1809 to 1815.[13] They give a remarkably detailed account of repairs recommended and actually carried out. The work of restoration was particularly encouraged by one of the prebendaries, George Frederick Nott (Fig. 21.3), who was appointed to the chapter in 1810 at the age of forty-three.[14] In 1815 the Dean and Chapter asked another architect, William Porden, for a second opinion on the condition of the south transept,[15] and eventually Garbett's more modest proposals were authorised.[16] At the same time the west aisle of the north transept, which had been used as a 'common workshop', was 'cleaned out and put in a decent state', the windows glazed and the door stopped up. The east end of the cathedral was also renovated at this time.[17] The leading role taken by Nott was recognised at the time, for a paper found in the roof of the presbytery said that he 'had done more for the repair of the church than had been done by his predecessors in the course of two or three centuries'.[18] Although injured by a fall from a ladder in January 1816, he continued to take a close interest in all that was being done in the cathedral. He is generally credited with the removal from the Great Screen in around 1820 of the baldachino and Prebendary Harris's urns, which had filled some of the vacant niches since the early 18th century, and with the resiting of several of the older monuments in the cathedral.[19]

According to Nott's own memorial in the north transept, the injuries he sustained in his fall obliged him 'to spend some years in Italy in pursuit of health'. This meant that he was largely absent from Winchester while two protracted matters were being discussed—the repairs to the nave piers and the position of the organ. In fact, a whole series of repairs and improvements were being carried out at this time. The choir-stalls were rearranged, cleaned and varnished,[20] and Garbett designed the present massive episcopal throne to replace Bishop Trelawney's throne, although it was some years before it was installed. The *Gentleman's Magazine* described it as being 'one of the most splendid and elegant compositions in woodwork of the present age'.[21] Inigo Jones's stone screen at the western entrance to the choir was removed in 1819,[22] and galleries were erected above the stalls on both sides of the choir.[23]

The debate about the choir-screen and the position of the organ began in November 1819, when the Dean and Chapter resolved to remove

Fig. 21.2   Engraving of the Inigo Jones screen by Charles Greenfeild, published in S. Gale, *History and Antiquities of the Cathedral Church of Winchester* (London, 1715)

Fig. 21.3   Portrait of Prebendary G. F. Nott aged 25, painted in Italy in 1794. *Dean and Chapter of Winchester/John Crook*

Inigo Jones's screen, replace it with 'a Gothic Screen' and transfer the organ from the north side of the stalls to 'the centre of the proposed screen'.[24] The new stone screen, designed by Garbett, was based on the west doorway of the nave (Fig. 21.4). The mason was James Gillingham, and the foundation stone was laid on 22 July 1820.[25] Although the organ was removed from the north side of the stalls, Dean Rennell's dis-approval, and the urgent work needed to the nave piers, led to a prolonged discussion of its proper position. By 1823 the pipes were suffering damage through being laid on a damp floor, and the Dean and Chapter decided (by a majority of five votes to three) to rescind their previous decision and replace the organ in its original posi-tion. The cost of this was assisted by a donation of £100 from Dean Rennell, and in 1824 the Dean and Chapter entered into an agreement with the organ builder James Blyth of Isleworth to build a new instrument.[26] Dean Rennell was assisted in this debate by the architect Edward Blore, who sent him a printed report on the proposed moving of the organ. Blore objected to the central position for the organ principally because it would interfere with the view of the whole length of the cathedral from the west end.[27] But others disagreed with him. Prebendary Nott wrote to the Dean and Chapter from Rome on 6 March 1824, protesting against the change of policy about the organ. If the organ were replaced in its original position, the choir would be unable 'to perform the service with that precision and effect, which they would otherwise be able to do'. The new gallery seats on the north side of the stalls would have to be removed and the wooden partitions replaced. Fourthly, the lateral position would be less effective for concerts in the nave. If the organ were put back in its old position, the new choir-screen and galleries 'must now be considered as an almost useless waste of time and money'. The 'security and mutual confidence' which ought to exist between members of the chapter was at risk.[28] Prebendary James Hook sent a formal protest to the Dean and Chapter at midsummer 1824 and said that 'the general opinion of the Public is decidedly hostile to the measure of restoring the organ to its late position in the choir'.[29] The appeal which the prebendaries sent to Bishop Tomline in December 1824

Fig. 21.4   William Garbett's Gothic screen (1820), reproducing the design of Bishop Edington's west porch block. *Winchester City Museums*

stressed that a central position for the organ would bring Winchester into line with 'all the other Cathedral choirs in the Kingdom'.[30] The lateral position 'had produced inconveniences that had often been complained of as well by the organist as by the members of the choir'. They considered Garbett's new screen as 'incongruous, disproportionate, and unsightly'. An anonymous pamphlet referred to the former difficulties experienced by having the organ above the north side of the stalls.[31] Wooden partitions, visible in Cave's watercolour of the choir painted in 1801 (Fig. 21.1), had been erected at the entrances to both transepts in order to contain the sound of the organ, but, according to the author of the pamphlet, succeeded only in bouncing it from side to side, 'so that one part of the choir must necessarily be out of tune with the other'.[32] 'All this maudlin sensitiveness and vapouring about clear unobstructed views,' he continued, 'is founded on the grossest ignorance of the principles of art'.[33] The central position would have ensured 'the equal distribution of sound'.[34] Despite this opposition, the views of Dean Rennell and Edward Blore prevailed,[35] and Blore designed the new organ case, which was erected in 1825[36] (Fig. 21.4).

Around the same time as the debate about the organ, flat ceilings were placed in the north and south transepts,[37] and steps were taken to repair some defective piers in the nave: two on the south side, by the Edington chantry chapel, the fourth pier on the south side and the second on the north. Dean Rennell was especially anxious to have a second opinion about the nave piers. As he failed to secure the agreement of the canons, he appealed to Bishop Pretyman Tomline.[38] Although the canons complained that this was 'an undisguis'd attempt to make the opinion of the Dean prevail over that of an unanimous chapter through the instrumentality of your Lordship',[39] William Garbett, the architect, changed his mind and

Fig. 21.5   John Flaxman's memorial to Joseph Warton,
installed November 1804. *John Crook*

said that he would welcome further advice. Rennell suggested various names to the chapter in October 1821, but they outvoted him and chose instead John Nash.[40] Garbett submitted his report on the nave piers on 29 September 1821, but agreed to meet Nash. They decided together that the core of the piers should be strengthened with iron columns.[41] Other work done by Garbett included the renewal of two flying buttresses on the south side of the presbytery and the vaulting of the retrochoir. The doorways to the former cloister on the south side of the nave were blocked and a new south door opened between them.[42] Some repairs to the nave roof and vaulting were also carried out.[43]

The early part of the 19th century also saw the introduction of several notable monuments in the cathedral. The best known of these (now in the south nave aisle) is John Flaxman's memorial to Joseph Warton, a former headmaster of Winchester College (Fig. 21.5)[44]. Prebendary Philip Williams praised this memorial: 'Flaxman has infinite merit in having transferr'd so strong a likeness of Dr Warton as copied from Sir Joshua's picture into marble'.[45] Flaxman's other memorial in the cathedral was to the wife of Bishop North, while North's own memorial, now in the south choir aisle, and that of Prebendary Iremonger in the north transept were the work of Sir Francis Chantrey.[46] Chantrey also designed the monument to Sir George Prevost in the south nave aisle.[47]

The most substantial addition to the cathedral in the middle years of the century was the installation of a new organ in 1854. This comprised the greater part of an organ which Henry Willis had exhibited at the Great Exhibition of 1851. It has been described as 'the most advanced cathedral organ in England at the time', and 2,000 people attended its opening, when special music by the cathedral organist, Samuel Sebastian Wesley, was sung and played.[48] The west front of the cathedral was repaired in 1860,[49] but little else was done until 1874, when it was proposed to replace Garbett's stone choir-screen with a wooden screen matching the stalls, as a memorial to both Bishop Wilberforce and Dean Garnier.[50] This was designed by Sir George Gilbert Scott. A glass case on the north side of the new screen was incorporated in the design in order to display Wilberforce's crozier.[51] Neither Bishop Sumner nor Bishop Wilberforce was buried in the cathedral, but monuments to them, designed by H. Weekes in 1876 and H. H. Armstead in 1878, were erected

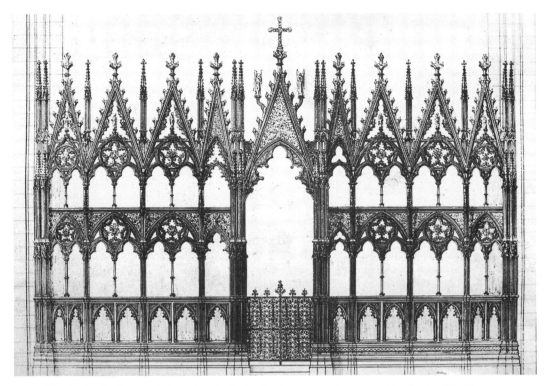

Fig. 21.6 Sir George Gilbert Scott's design for the new choir-screen. *Winchester City Museums*

at this time.[52] The huge Wilberforce cenotaph in the south transept was paid for by a committee established to erect a suitable memorial, but Dean Bramston tried to resist their plans and incurred their displeasure. 'Oh, the Dean', wrote the Member of Parliament for North Hampshire, Melville Portal, to Lord Henry Scott in December 1875, describing him as 'dishonest' and 'shuffling', 'we had the greatest difficulty today with him'.[53] Portal played an important part in the life of the cathedral in the late 19th century, chiefly over the plans to restore the Great Screen.

A certain amount of work had been done to repair the Great Screen in 1835-36.[54] Some parts of it had been restored with plaster of Paris and Roman cement. In 1878 Dean Bramston called for its complete restoration, including new figures in the niches, and circulated a printed paper to suggest what might be done. He proposed that the first step should be the insertion of eight statues in the central niches, while 'the plain stone of the great cross in the screen should be covered with enamel'.[55] The architect G. E. Street told Bramston in 1880 that quite substantial repairs to the screen would be needed before new statues could be inserted, as it was in 'a most mutilated and unfinished condition'.[56] When Archdeacon Philip Jacob died in 1884, a deputation led by the mayor of Winchester called on Dean Kitchin to suggest that a public meeting should be held to consider the best form of a memorial to the late archdeacon. It was decided to embark on the restoration of the Great Screen, and an appeal was launched, which resulted in £2,055 being available to repair the central portion of the screen. The architect J. D. Sedding arranged for the stonework to be repaired, but by 1886 there was insufficient money for any statues to be commissioned.[57]

In fact, a great deal of debate about the whole subject took place during these years. In November 1884 the Dean and Chapter appointed a 'Cathedral Committee' to advise them 'as to all improvements, restorations or ornamentations which may appear to them desirable to be carried out in the cathedral and the Close'.[58] The committee included the bishop, the Dean and Chapter, one honorary canon, Lord Henry Scott, and Melville Portal. There were therefore three bodies interested in the matter—the Jacob Memorial Committee, the Cathedral (Advisory) Committee, and the Dean and Chapter. Although this was a praiseworthy early attempt to involve leading lay people in the administration of the cathedral, in practice it led to much frustration and irritation, since all three bodies claimed to be responsible for the restoration of the screen.

The cathedral archives contain copies of several letters from Melville Portal to Lord Henry Scott (later Lord Montagu). These letters provide an interesting commentary on the more official records in the Chapter Act Book and the minute book of the Cathedral Committee. It is clear that Portal was a formidable personality, who took his membership of the Cathedral Committee very seriously. On 9 February 1885 he told Scott that the subscription to Archdeacon Jacob 'must, I think, be considered a failure, and I always expected that it would be so'.[59] Apparently the proposal to restore the Great Screen in Jacob's memory had been controversial:

> Many ardent admirers of Jacob do not think the screen a worthy symbol of the late Archdeacon. Many others, ardent admirers of the screen, think that it is an affront to the memory of Cardinal Beaufort and Bishop Fox to connect the name of Jacob, in any way whatsoever, with their noble work.[60]

The controversy was not just local. On 23 February 1885 Thackeray Turner, the secretary of the Society for the Protection of Ancient Buildings, wrote to the Dean and Chapter:

> These alterations, whether they be in themselves things of beauty, or, as the Committee think, merely disfigurements, can only be carried out at the cost of irreparable damage to the original work. The modernizing of the screen and its consequent discord with its surroundings is probably not desired, but similar restorations have conclusively proved that such a result is inevitable. Nor will this be atoned for by any intrinsic merit in the new work. Those who engage in the trade of supplying the demand created by the wish to restore old monuments are neither original nor trained artists but merely copiers ... The Committee would therefore urge you to withdraw your consent to the proposed alterations to a work whose antiquity and merit entitle it to exemption from such rough usage.[61]

Portal felt that to have Sedding in charge of the work with John Colson as his 'coadjutor' was 'perfectly appalling'. Two days later he wrote again to Scott:

> We were invited to serve on the Cathedral Committee for a very definite purpose—and we have been made fools of. The most important work that has been attempted in the cathedral for centuries is to be undertaken without consulting the Cathedral Committee.[62]

The reason for this outburst was the publication of an open letter by Dean Kitchin to the members of the Jacob Memorial Committee, thanking them for their work and informing them of the plans of the Dean and Chapter for the restoration of the Great Screen under the direction of Sedding and Colson.[63]

Scott and Portal wrote a joint letter of protest to Dean Kitchin on 11 April 1885, complaining that the Cathedral Committee had not been consulted.[64] Portal sent a covering letter in which he explained that he hoped the dean would find in their joint letter

> nothing hostile or discourteous to yourself, nothing tending in any way to alter that pleasant relationship in which, I trust, we stand towards each other ... it will always be a real pleasure to me to be acting in unison with you for the good of our great Church.[65]

Kitchin's letter to Scott in reply to the joint letter shows the difficulties he had in trying to reconcile the interests of the Jacob Memorial Committee and the Cathedral Committee with the executive responsibility of the Dean and Chapter:

> The matter has been a very difficult one: and (to tell the simple truth) I thought, rightly or wrongly, that the memorialists had, not quite to my liking, stepped in for the moment between us and the Cathedral Committee, and that I could not well invite the Committee to meet till the Chapter could properly turn to them for very valuable advice ... We are bound to show all consideration towards those who had raised this considerable subscription: and I think that though what will be done may not be all we should like, it will not in fact commit the Cathedral Committee or the Chapter to any wrong course of action.[66]

The early stages of the restoration of the Great Screen were also clouded by difficulties over the design of statues for its central section. The Cathedral Committee severely criticised trial statues of St Paul and St Peter modelled by the London sculptor Onslow Ford, and declined even to see an unsolicited statue of St Michael, which had been sent by a Mr. Bates.[67] This fruitless exercise had cost quite a lot of money, and Sedding's connection with the work was terminated.[68]

In November 1886 Lord Montagu protested to Dean Kitchin about a proposal to include a statue of Izaak Walton in the restored screen,[69] and in the following summer he and Portal were again harrying the dean. They felt that they had the strong support of many in the diocese. As Portal told Montagu:

> I saw many men at the Conference who were perfectly boiling over with fury at the work which is going on in the Cathedral and also expressed themselves very strongly in favour of our exposing the real facts of the case.

> The Dean's drawing-room is, I am told, full of statues of angels, saints and martyrs, which are destined for the screen, by all sorts of artists, and in every variety of tone and feeling. He is proposing to represent Canute's Crown over the Cross, and I suppose he will purchase one for 1s. 6d. from the Gaiety Theatre for the purpose.[70]

In November 1887 the Dean and Chapter and the Cathedral Committee agreed that the remaining statues on the Great Screen should all be by one sculptor, and Mr. Nichols was asked to prepare plaster models of six larger and four smaller figures. It was further agreed that the remainder of the central part of the screen should be completed before work began on the lateral portions.[71] Under the supervision of Dean Kitchin's son, Mr. G. H. Kitchin, all the canopies and pedestals in the screen were repaired or replaced, and towards the end of 1888 the Dean and Chapter launched an appeal for all the remaining statues. Nichols eventually completed eight of them, two were executed by Miss M. Grant, ten by Mr. Geflowski, and the remaining 36 (mainly smaller ones) by Mr. R. Boulton of Cheltenham. The work was completed, apart from the central cross, in time for the enthronement of Bishop Thorold on 3 March 1891.[72]

In May 1891 the Dean and Chapter accepted a resolution of the Cathedral Committee that the central cross should be completed, and agreed to ask Bishop Thorold's advice about the character of the figure on the cross.[73] Models of two figures showing 'The

Fig. 21.7   The Great Screen in 1894, showing the short-lived figure of 'The Lord in Glory' and the Benjamin West painting still in position. *Winchester City Museums*

Crucified Christ' and 'The Lord in Glory' were obtained, and Dean Kitchin consulted Bishop Thorold about them.[74] Thorold in turn consulted the eminent lawyer, Sir Lewis Dibdin, who said that while the crucified figure would not be illegal if it were 'an architectural decoration', many people might be offended if either figure were erected on the screen. Although objections might diminish in a year or two, the matter ought to be postponed.[75] Thorold wondered whether any figure was necessary, as he felt that an empty cross would be such an eloquent symbol of the Resurrection: 'His ever present absence may console and strengthen us more than carved stone can do'. In the end, Thorold followed Dibdin's advice and counselled the Dean and Chapter to let the matter rest for a while, though the figure of 'The Lord in Glory' was displayed on the Great Screen over Easter 1894 (Fig. 21.7).[76]

In 1895 the Dean and Chapter consulted the architect G. F. Bodley and the stained glass artist C. E. Kempe about the figure on the cross. Both of them were strongly in favour of a crucified figure and also suggested that Benjamin West's painting should be removed. Another suggestion which they put forward was that the screen should be coloured, but the Dean and Chapter did not accept this idea.[77] As the nave roof needed urgent attention, the matter was again postponed, but in October 1897 Canon Valpy offered to pay for a new central figure on the cross in memory of his wife.[78] The Dean and Chapter gratefully accepted this offer, and the new work was finally dedicated on 24 March 1899.[79] Below the central figure there were placed new statues of the Holy Family and six saints: Margaret, Catherine, Anne, Agnes, Cecilia, and Faith. Benjamin West's painting was at last removed and sold.[80]

The repairs to the nave roof mentioned above were long overdue.[81] Both the external lead covering and the internal timber framing needed substantial repairs. From Easter 1896 to Easter 1898 a tall scaffolding and gantry were erected on the north side of the nave, with a crane at the top and a 'lofty and graceful travelling bridge scaffolding spanning the nave, running on tram rails supported on cantilever brackets projecting from the triforium arches...'[82] At the same time repairs were also made to the nave roof vaulting, the choir roof, the south choir aisle roof, the east and west aisle roofs of the north transept, the belfry floor and various windows.[83] The great west window was also repaired.[84] According to the figures given by J. B. Colson, the cathedral architect, 9,678 cubic feet of new timber weighing over 198 tons was required for the repairs to the roof, with 16,274 cubic feet of pitch pine weighing over 326 tons, 40 tons of iron and 197.5 tons of lead.[85]

In addition to the major work to the Great Screen and the nave roof, the closing decades of the 19th century saw several other notable additions to the cathedral. The fine tomb of Bishop Edward Harold Browne was designed by Messrs. Bodley and Garner in a medieval style, executed by Messrs. Farmer and Brindley, and placed immediately west of Edington's chantry chapel in the nave in 1894.[86] The windows of the Lady Chapel were filled with glass by C. E. Kempe between 1897 and 1900. The south window is a memorial to Bishop Thorold, while that on the north side was paid for by the proceeds of the sale of Benjamin West's picture. The east window commemorated the Diamond Jubilee of Queen Victoria.[87] The processional cross (usually kept in the south transept) was given to the cathedral by Canon A. S. Valpy in 1897.[88]

By 1900 the cathedral was on the eve of a further great restoration which dominated the early years of the present century. Yet much had been achieved since the late

18th century. If we may regret the loss of the Inigo Jones choir-screen, and even its successor, Scott's wooden screen admirably matches the choir-stalls, and the restoration of the Great Screen, protracted as it was, gave back to the cathedral one of its great glories. The building was tidier and more cherished than it had been a hundred years earlier, and some notable memorials and windows had been added. The labours of George Frederick Nott and Dean Rennell in the early years of the century, and Dean Kitchin and Canon Valpy towards its close, can be appreciated both for their care for the cathedral fabric and also for their restraint in preserving its character. In fact, Winchester Cathedral survived the 19th century remarkably well. It avoided such catastrophes as the two fires which badly damaged York Minster, or the collapse of the spire which devastated Chichester. It escaped the radical Victorian restorations which so transformed cathedrals like Ely, Hereford, Lichfield and Worcester. But beneath the apparent calm great danger was lurking, as the next chapter but one makes plain.[89]

Notes

1. F. Bussby, *Winchester Cathedral 1079-1979* (Southampton 1979), p. 194.
2. G. Cobb, *English Cathedrals: The Forgotten Centuries* (London, 1980), p. 126, quoting *Gentleman's Magazine* supplement 1798, p. 1105.
3. 'Surveyors' Reports', MS, WCL, W40/3, pp. 1-3, Report of James Essex, dated 8 August 1775.
4. *Ibid.*, pp. 4-5 (letter dated 12 April 1782).
5. *Ibid.*, pp. 6-10 (undated report by James Wyatt); CA, 21 April and 23 June 1794.
6. CA, 25 November 1774.
7. CA, 23 June and 25 November 1781.
8. Quoted in Bussby, *Winchester Cathedral,* p. 213.
9. *Ibid.*, p. 248; CA, 6 April and 28 November 1899; E. Sabben-Clare, 'The Raising of Lazarus, by Benjamin West', *WCR* 60 (1991), pp. 42-3.
10. Milner, *Winchester.* In a supplement published in 1830 Milner described early 19th-century alterations and repairs.
11. *Ibid.*, ii, pp. 38-9.
12. *Ibid.*, ii, p. 59.
13. 'Cathedral Chronicle, 1800-65', pp. 226-37; see also 'Surveyors' Reports', pp. 47-114.
14. For Nott, see Bussby, *Winchester Cathedral,* p. 200.
15. CA, 2 February 1815; 'Cathedral Chronicle, 1800-65', pp. 1-2.
16. CA, 25 November 1816.
17. *Ibid.*
18. G. H. Blore, 'George Frederick Nott, D.D., 1767-1841', *WCR* 19 (1950), pp. 13-15.
19. S. H. Blake, 'The Great Screen of Winchester Cathedral', *WCR* 29 (1960), p. 14; R. N. Quirk, 'The Monuments of Prior Basing and the "Old Bishop in Marble"', *WCR* 23 (1954), pp. 15-17.
20. CA, 25 November 1818. Nott was absent from 1821 to 1833.
21. S. Jervis, *Woodwork of Winchester Cathedral* (Winchester, 1976), p. 25; CA, 25 November 1819, 23 June 1824, 23 June and 25 November 1826.
22. CA, 25 November 1819; J. M. G. Blakiston, 'The Inigo Jones Screen, Part II', *WCR* 46 (1977), p. 16. John Britton, writing in 1817, described this screen as 'a bad and unsightly object ... It is discordant and highly displeasing and betrays a deplorable lack of feeling': Britton, *Winchester Cathedral,* p. 80.
23. CA, 25 November 1819, 23 June 1822. See also the Appeal by the Prebendaries to Bishop Tomline, 4 December 1824 in 'Cathedral Chronicle, 1800-65', p. 44.
24. CA, 25 November 1819.
25. Blakiston, 'Inigo Jones Screen', p. 17, note 54.
26. CA, 25 November 1819, 23 June, 21 July and 25 November 1823, 10 April 1824. See also B. Matthews, *The Organs and Organists of Winchester Cathedral* (Winchester, undated), p. 8.
27. 'Cathedral Chronicle, 1800-65', p. 42.

28. Nott to Dean and Chapter, 6 March 1824,'Cathedral Chronicle, 1800-65', p. 254.
29. *Ibid.,* p. 42.
30. *Ibid.,* p. 44.
31. *An apology for those who object to the lateral position of an organ in Winchester Cathedral* (London, 1825), Southampton University Library, Cope Collection.
32. *Ibid.,* p. 10, footnote.
33. *Ibid.,* p. 21.
34. *Ibid.,* p. 20.
35. For Edward Blore's views about various contemporary alterations in the cathedral, see his 'Report of the alterations and repairs made and projected in Winchester Cathedral from observations made on the 3rd and 4th of July, 1820', MS, WCL, Goodman Collection, III.3; and G. H. Blore, 'The Cathedral in 1820', *WCR* 7 (1938), pp. 12-14.
36. Jervis, *Woodwork,* p. 22.
37. CA, 25 November 1819; Jervis, *Woodwork,* pp. 8, 15; Cobb, *Forgotten Centuries,* p. 127.
38. CA, 27 March, 23 June, 15 August 1821. Rennell's letter to Pretyman Tomline, dated 30 August 1821, is copied in 'Dean and Chapter Letter-Book, 1814-38', MS, WCL.
39. *Ibid.,* Chapter to Bishop Pretyman Tomline, 29 September 1821.
40. CA, 15 October 1821.
41. For details, see 'Reports and Correspondence Relative to the Failing Piers in Winchester Cathedral, 1822', MSS, WCL, W49/16/3; see also 'Cathedral Chronicle, 1800-65', p. 36; Blore, 'Prebendary Nott', p. 14; and W. J. Carpenter Turner, 'The Nave Pillar', *WCR* 34 (1965), pp. 8-11.
42. Cobb, *Forgotten Centuries,* p. 127; Jervis, *Woodwork,* p. 6.
43. CA, 25 November 1824, 25 November 1825; see also Nash's letter to Dean Rennell, dated 11 February 1825, reproduced in 'Cathedral Chronicle, 1800-65', p. 46.
44. J. M. G. Blakiston, 'Flaxman's Monument to Joseph Warton: its Genesis and Evolution', *WCR* 42 (1973), pp. 22-39.
45. Quoted in P. L. S. Barrett, 'Philip Williams: the Acceptable Face of Pluralism', *WCR* 57 (1988), p. 20.
46. Vaughan, *Winchester Cathedral,* pp. 124, 139, 142; F. Bussby, 'Winchester Cathedral, 1789-1840', *WCR* 44 (1975), pp. 25-6.
47. Vaughan, *Winchester Cathedral,* p. 194.
48. Matthews, *Organs and Organists,* pp. 8-11; S. Webb, 'The Organs of Winchester Cathedral', *Musical Times,* CXXIX, No. 1745 (July 1988), p. 369.
49. CA, 25 November 1858, 25 November 1859, 1 February 1860, 25 March 1861; see also Ewan Christian's report, dated January 1860, in 'Cathedral Chronicle, 1800-65'; and 'Records of Winchester Cathedral and Close', MS compiled 1913, WCL, under year 1860-61.
50. CA, 28 May 1874.
51. *Hampshire Chronicle,* 13 March 1875 and 13 April 1878; Bussby, *Winchester Cathedral,* p. 230.
52. Vaughan, *Winchester Cathedral,* pp. 299-300; CA, 3 August 1875.
53. Portal to Scott, 2 December 1875, in 'Correspondence regarding the Wilberforce Memorial and Screen', MS, WCL, W49/15/3.
54. CA, 25 November 1835, 23 June 1836.
55. 'Cathedral Chronicle, 1873-91', pp. 6-7.
56. Street to Bramston, 13 January 1880, reproduced in *ibid.,* p. 93; see also F. Bussby 'The Great Screen, Part II', *WCR* 48 (1979), p. 12.
57. G. W. Kitchin, *The Great Screen of Winchester Cathedral* (3rd edn., revised and completed by W. R. W. Stephens, Winchester, 1899), pp. 24-6; CA, 25 March 1885.
58. CA, 25 November 1884; 'Winchester Cathedral Committee Minute Book, 1884-91', MS, WCL, W49/3, pp. 1-2.
59. Portal to Scott, 9 February 1885, MS, WCL (Great Screen Boxes).
60. Portal to Scott, 29 March 1885, *ibid.*
61. Thackeray Turner to Dean and Chapter, 23 February 1885, *ibid.,* partially quoted in Bussby, *Winchester Cathedral,* p. 246.
62. Portal to Scott, 31 March 1885, MS, WCL (Great Screen Boxes).
63. Copied in CA, 25 March 1885.

64. Scott and Portal to Kitchin, 11 April 1885, MS, WCL (Great Screen Boxes).
65. Portal to Kitchin, 10 April 1885, *ibid.*
66. Kitchin to Scott, 16 April 1885, *ibid.*
67. 'Cathedral Committee Minute Book', 10 August, 11 September, 17 December 1885, 20 July 1886, 5 October 1887; CA, 2 November 1887.
68. The settlement of Sedding's account was still troubling the Dean and Chapter two years later: CA, 2 April, 16 July, 5 November 1889.
69. Montagu to Kitchin, 12 and 19 November 1886, MSS, WCL (Great Screen Boxes).
70. Portal to Montagu, 12 June 1887. See also 4 June, 15 June, 21 June 1887, MSS, WCL (Great Screen Boxes).
71. CA, 2 November 1887 (recommendation of Cathedral Committee, 5 October 1887); Portal to Montagu 2 October 1887, MS, WCL (Great Screen Boxes).
72. Kitchin, *Great Screen,* pp. 26-8; CA, 25 November 1889, 4 November 1890; 'Cathedral Committee Minute Book', 7 January, 16 July, 21 November 1889, 22 September 1890.
73. CA, 19 May 1891; 'Cathedral Committee Minute Book', 9 April 1891.
74. CA, 29 September 1891; Kitchin's reply, 12 October 1891, MS, WCL (Great Screen Boxes). A slightly different version was copied in CA, 25 November 1891, with Thorold's reply.
75. Dibdin to Thorold, 14 October 1891, MS, WCL (Great Screen Boxes).
76. Bussby, *Winchester Cathedral,* p. 248.
77. Kitchin, *Great Screen,* p. 29; CA, 30 July 1895, 26 May 1896.
78. Kitchin, *Great Screen,* p. 29; CA, 25 October 1897, 31 May 1898.
79. CA, 6 April 1899.
80. Bussby, *Winchester Cathedral,* p. 249.
81. CA, 1 January 1878, 30 July 1895, 25 February, 23-4 March, 26 May, 28 July, 1 September, 28 September, 28 December 1896, 1 June, 27 July, 28 September 1897, 31 May, 25 November 1898, 28 February, 27 September, 31 October 1899, 26 November 1900.
82. J. B. Colson, *Winchester Cathedral: A Descriptive and Illustrated Record of the Reparation of the Nave Roof, 1896-8* (Winchester, 1898), p. 6.
83. *Ibid.,* pp. 5-6; CA, 28 December 1896, 27 July 1897.
84. CA, 25 November 1897, 21 February 1898.
85. Bussby, *Winchester Cathedral,* p. 249.
86. CA, 27 Sept 1892; Vaughan, *Winchester Cathedral,* p. 300; G. H. Blore, *The Monuments of Winchester Cathedral*, 3rd edn. (Farnborough, 1983), p. 21; for date of installation of memorial, *Hampshire Chronicle,* 1 December 1894.
87. Vaughan, *Winchester Cathedral,* p. 305; A. K. Walker, 'Kempe's Jesse Window in the Lady Chapel', *WCR* 59 (1990), pp. 36-44; Bussby, *Winchester Cathedral,* p. 250.
88. A. K. Walker, 'Arthur Sutton Valpy, the Epiphany Chapel and its Stained Glass', *WCR* 58 (1989), p. 16.
89. For further information about the cathedral in the 19th century, see P. L. S. Barrett, 'Winchester Cathedral in the Nineteenth Century', in D. Marcombe and C. S. Knighton (eds.), *Close Encounters: English Cathedrals and Society since 1540* (Nottingham, 1991), pp. 115-136.

CARING FOR THE COLLECTIONS

John Hardacre

'Churches aren't museums, you know, and we aren't curators.' It was with this quotation, attributed to a series of unidentified clergymen, that Claude Blair, then keeper of metalwork at the Victoria and Albert Museum, prefaced a paper on cathedral and diocesan museums in 1979. He found the remark irritating, fatuous even, because, as he explained, it suggested that the care of historical collections and the care of souls are mutually exclusive, that no-one could possibly do both. At Winchester we hope to prove that both can be achieved.

For the past fifteen or sixteen years, museums and similar institutions have shown an increasing interest in material held in churches. Conferences in Norwich (1976), London (1979) and, more recently, Winchester (1990), have all attempted to establish links or strengthen those existing between churches and museums. This is not because museums are acquisitive but because curators feel a responsibility for objects of historical value no matter in whose care they are, especially if those objects are at risk from neglect or theft. Winchester Cathedral is not a museum—the very word museum now encompasses such a

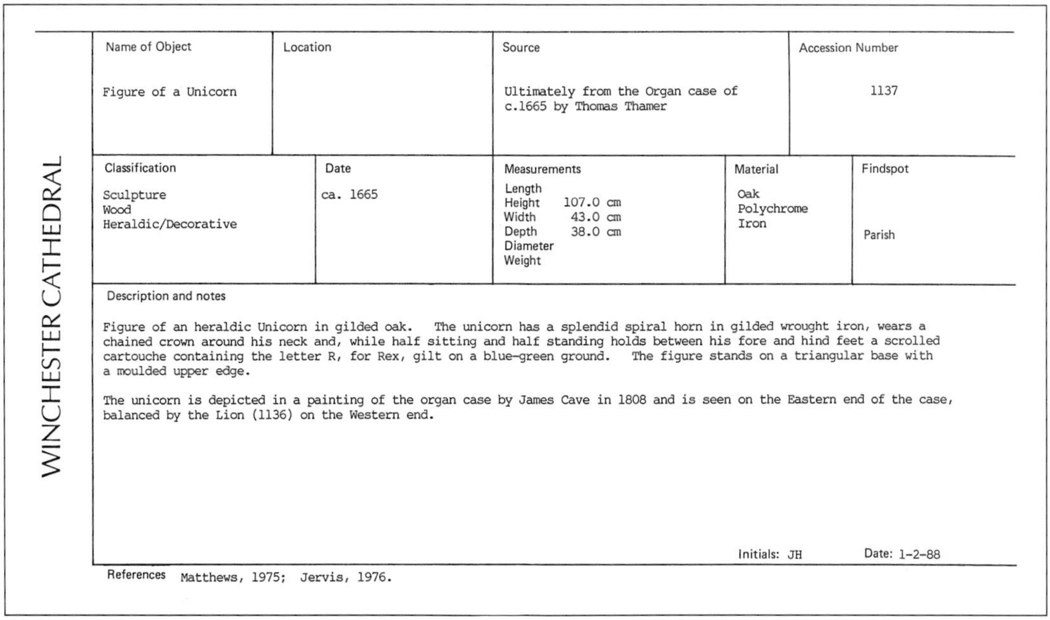

WINCHESTER CATHEDRAL	Name of Object	Location	Source	Accession Number
	Figure of a Unicorn		Ultimately from the Organ case of c.1665 by Thomas Thamer	1137

Classification	Date	Measurements	Material	Findspot
Sculpture Wood Heraldic/Decorative	ca. 1665	Length Height 107.0 cm Width 43.0 cm Depth 38.0 cm Diameter Weight	Oak Polychrome Iron	Parish

Description and notes

Figure of an heraldic Unicorn in gilded oak. The unicorn has a splendid spiral horn in gilded wrought iron, wears a chained crown around his neck and, while half sitting and half standing holds between his fore and hind feet a scrolled cartouche containing the letter R, for Rex, gilt on a blue-green ground. The figure stands on a triangular base with a moulded upper edge.

The unicorn is depicted in a painting of the organ case by James Cave in 1808 and is seen on the Eastern end of the case, balanced by the Lion (1136) on the Western end.

Initials: JH   Date: 1-2-88

References Matthews, 1975; Jervis, 1976.

Fig. 22.1 A specimen catalogue card.

wide variety of institutions and concepts that it may have outlived its usefulness—but it is a building full of objects. This much it holds in common with a museum.

So in 1984 the decision taken by the Dean and Chapter to appoint a full-time, qualified curator was greeted with some delight by the museums community. It was the first such post in the country and was advertised initially for a three-year period, and shortly afterwards extended indefinitely. For the first three years the cost was borne in equal portions by the Dean and Chapter, the Pilgrim Trust and the Area Museum Service for south-east England, and after that by the Dean and Chapter alone. The brief comprised three distinct sections: to catalogue the cathedral's collection of moveable objects, estimated then to number about five thousand; to prepare a design brief for a cathedral 'museum' in the gallery of the south transept; and to offer advice on the care of historic objects in churches in the diocese.

The cataloguing process was supervised in its initial stages by the directors of the Area Museums Service and the Hampshire County Museum Service, and proceeded according to current museum practice. Each object is allocated a unique number and classified according to material: woodwork, sculpture, metalwork or textile, for example. A card bearing the object's number and classification is prepared (Fig. 22.1), together with its description, notes about its provenance, dimensions, date, storage or display location and any references in publications or notes elsewhere. With these cards are stored associated material, such as photographs, conservation notes, correspondence and descriptive labels from previous exhibitions. The cards are stored in number order.

Access to the information in these cards is gained via a series of computer-generated indices according to date, name, material and class, perusal of which will reveal the object's unique number. Knowledge of that number will enable the enquirer to return to the master cards and retrieve the information stored there.

The catalogue was complete at a *pro-forma* stage by 1989, although we are still working towards its final form. The Care of Cathedrals Measure (1990), Section 13 (1), makes the following provision:

Fig. 22.2   Heads and other sculptural fragments displayed in the feretory, *c.*1907. The small, crowned head resting on the torso in the top left of the picture had disappeared by the 1930s. *Dean and Chapter of Winchester*

It shall be the duty of the administrative body of a cathedral church to compile and maintain an inventory of all objects in possession of the chapter which the Fabric Advisory Committee considers to be of architectural, archaeological, artistic or historic interest ... and to complete the compilation of that inventory before the expiration of the period of five years...

If the Dean and Chapter had not been sufficiently far-sighted to begin this process five years in advance of its becoming mandatory, the completion of an inventory of collections as extensive as those at Winchester would have proved very difficult.

The information available on each object of course varies enormously. Some of the collection has been subjected to close scholarly examination and the results published in depth—other objects have merely been measured and described by the curator to the best of his ability, and in some cases this amounts to no more than 'Bronze Object. L: 3.2 cm. W: 0.1 cm.'. In such instances the catalogue entry will remain brief until a future scholar turns his or her attention to the object; and it is perhaps here that a curator can contribute most to the pursuit of scholarship.

His role is one of an enabler, a catalyst that allows a reaction to take place between the scholar and the object. A curator with an intimate knowledge of the collection should be able to do more than just make the object available for study; he should be able to draw the ends together from parts of the collection that at first sight have no connection with the object in question. He will recognise the handwriting of previous scholars, know of the existence of photographs or drawings, be aware of the circumstances of the finding of an object, refer the scholar to others who may have worked on other elements of the collection and with whom it may be helpful to talk.

The role of enabler is matched with the role of housekeeper, with the oversight of the objects in daily use in the cathedral—plate, textiles, woodwork—to advise on their handling and storage, and occasionally to organise their repair. In this way the Dean and Chapter have, in recent years, made it clear that they have made more effective arrangements for the safekeeping, daily treatment and display of the historic objects in their possession, and have gone a long way towards proving that Christian witness and curatorial responsibility are not incompatible.

Nowhere is this attitude better expressed than in the Triforium Gallery, a small 'museum' in the south transept, containing sculpture, woodwork and metalwork from the 9th to the 19th century. The Dean and Chapter had recognised for many years that the collections in their care were of high quality (Fig. 22.2), and equally they had realised that the high gallery in the south transept, with its three sides open to the cathedral, would make a wonderful setting for the finest objects in the collections. In the catalogue of the exhibition, *Winchester Saxon and Norman Art,* held in the Cathedral Treasury in 1972, Dean Michael Stancliffe adumbrated the Triforium Gallery when he wrote, '... It is greatly to be hoped that in due course ways and means will be found of creating a new museum to enable [the collections of "finds"] to be enjoyed by the public.'

The first demonstration of the commitment of the Dean and Chapter to this project was the building of a staircase from the library lobby to the gallery so that public access could ultimately be allowed; the second was the commissioning of an initial brief from the newly-appointed curator. This took the form of a feasibility study, to assure or convince the chapter that the material was of sufficiently high quality and general interest to make the construction of the gallery worthwhile. It dealt with previous attempts at displaying the collections (Fig. 22.3), the nature of the site and of the material; it listed eight objectives which it hoped

Fig. 22.3   Part of T. D. Atkinson's lapidarium in the south transept gallery, *c.*1932. The heads on the bench rest on their cast-cement bases; some of those illustrated are now missing. *Dean and Chapter of Winchester*

the gallery would achieve; it looked at possible themes for the gallery, at the intended audience, and the objects likely to be included, and the physical constraints within which the work would be carried out. The brief was accepted by the chapter in February 1986, and work began on a detailed design brief, which would be submitted to a short-list of six designers with wide experience of building exhibitions in sensitive surroundings.

As soon as the Dean and Chapter approved the brief, in consultation with the sculpture conservation department of the Victoria and Albert Museum, a report was commissioned from Harrison Hill, sculpture conservators, on those items from the collection which were candidates for inclusion. The report looked at the physical condition of these sculptures, their chemical stability, and the rate of their deterioration, and set out a programme of work for their consolidation and cleaning. At the same time a presentation was made to the Winchester Cathedral Trust Development Committee for access to a Hampshire County Council grant channelled through the Trust for this purpose. It was this grant of £20,000, allowing the initial conservation work to go ahead (Fig. 22.4), that proved crucial to the success of the whole project: not only did it make clear to other potential sources of grant aid that the County Council was taking the gallery project seriously, it also enabled the cathedral's own fund-raisers to present grant-giving bodies with the results of work already undertaken. As the best of the sculpture was conserved first, they were invariably impressed.

It was decided at an early stage that the gallery should not be overtly didactic, and to this end labelling and explanatory text should be kept to a minimum; further discussion and interpretation would be found in an illustrated catalogue. The intention was that the gallery should be a visual delight in itself, and that the objects should be offered as works of art in their own right rather than as illustrations of aspects of the cathedral's history. It was also envisaged that visitors should positively feel that they were in part of the building, rather than in a separate museum annexe, as is the case in some of the great continental cathedral museums. The need for visitors to see the architectural space in as uninterrupted a way as possible, to admire the views into the nave and transept, and be aware that hourly prayers and the daily services of the cathedral were taking place, was also stressed in the design brief.

The designer chosen was Paul Williams, partnered by Alan Stanton, and their solutions of the problems posed in the brief were inspired. The Triforium Gallery is there for all to see, has been much admired and has received much critical acclaim; the cases are elegant and understated, the metalwork is restrained and the labelling discreet and informative. The objects, the *raison d'être* of the gallery, are wonderfully displayed and lit, and positioned with extraordinary sensitivity. It was principally due to the genius of the Stanton-Williams partnership that the gallery was given the award for 'the best fine and applied art museum' in the National Heritage Museum of the Year awards in 1990 and was a finalist in the National Art Collections awards in the same year.

What, of course, is not visible is the preparatory work, the cleaning of the gallery stonework, the removal of unsightly cement stains from the brick floor, the strengthening of the floor to take the weight of the cases, the largest of which—without its contents—is estimated to weigh fourteen tons (Fig. 22.5). The balustrades around the perimeter wall-tops were required to conform to conditions applied to barriers in places of public assembly, and needed to be massively counterweighted (Fig. 22.6), and all specifications were minutely examined by structural engineers and the cathedral architect.

A donors' board in the gallery lists those individuals and organisations which provided financial

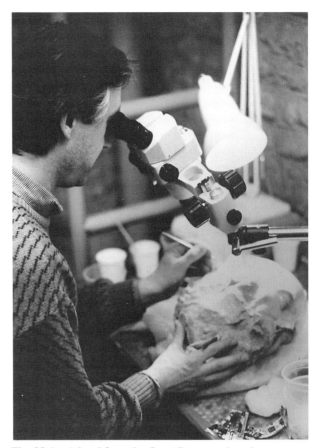

Fig. 22.4   A head from the Great Screen undergoing conservation by Harrison Hill Ltd. at Little Oakley in 1986. *John Hardacre*

Fig. 22.5   The skeleton of the central and northernmost cases in the west range of the Gallery. *John Hardacre*

Fig. 22.6   Preparations for the reinforced concrete counterweight to the balustrade along the south perimeter of the Triforium Gallery. *John Hardacre*

Fig. 22.7   The Triforium Gallery, west range. *John Crook*

assistance for its building, and anyone who has been connected with fund-raising at any level will know how much effort that entails on the part of those involved.

Fortunately the scholarly detective work which enabled the sculpture to be identified and grouped together, and which formed the basis of the labels and the catalogue text, is written up elsewhere in this book. This research was the foundation upon which everything else was built, and the fact that the project had a sound basis in scholarship permeated all our presentations and applications for grand aid, giving them a definite authority.

The Triforium Gallery (Fig. 22.7) opened to the public on 29 April 1989, and received some very good reviews. It is managed in conjunction with the cathedral library under the canon librarian and is warded, as is the library, by trained and dedicated volunteers. Since it opened, between 20,000 and 25,000 people have visited it each year, which has brought a significant income to the Dean and Chapter.

This short paper opened with a quotation attributed to an unidentified clergyman. It will close with another from the Very Reverend Alan Webster, dean of St Paul's, during the 1979 Conference on Cathedral Treasures and Museums: a seminal conference if ever there was one. He said,

> Our treasures are ... intended to move us, to give this world gleam. The gleam in the treasure is not justified by its value in cash or its rarity. It is justified if it saves us from disenchantment with God and with each other.

Acknowledgements

The author is grateful to the Dean and Chapter and to many friends and colleagues for their help, support and advice, but special thanks are due to Canon Paul Britton, father of the project.

THE 20TH CENTURY AND THE FUTURE

Keith Walker

At the beginning of the century Randall Davidson, lord bishop of the Winchester diocese, held a visitation of the cathedral and made his charge on 19 October 1900. His perspicacious words will surprise some by their urgency and accuracy. The cathedral is the diocese's 'centre and its heart'. The cathedral body is answerable to God and man for the part the cathedral takes 'in the whole corporate life, first of the diocese, and then of the English Church and realm'. Since its new foundation at the Reformation the cathedral has had opportunity to develop sacred and secular learning, works of charity, and material progress. It must be in the diocese a 'white-hot focus' of Christian force for good. Its worship must be of the highest, its gospel message the most practical, its concern for the young unremitting, and its commitment to help solve the social questions of the day plain. The future archbishop of Canterbury's words remain a yardstick against which the cathedral's achievements this century must be measured.

At the outset of our period the cathedral was served by a dean, five residentiary canons, an organist and master of the music, seven lay vicars, 16 choristers, two sub-sacrists, four virgers, 12 bell-ringers and 12 bedesmen. Dean Stephens died in 1902 and was succeeded the year following by Canon William Mordaunt Furneaux, an affable High Churchman of the old school, who had been headmaster of Repton until 1900, and was living at the Friary at Winchester as examining chaplain to the bishop of Winchester when he was made dean in 1903. The cathedral was variously active, as the programmes for Lent and Holy Week, 1900, amply demonstrate (Fig. 23.1).[1]

During the first decade of the century routine repair work continued in cathedral and Close. The trees in the outer Close were pruned, a bell was recast, fire-fighting equipment was installed, a practice organ was purchased, four stops were added to the main organ, hassocks were bought, repairs began on the south aisle roof, the weight of the organ was lifted from the roof of the Holy Sepulchre Chapel, the glass in the west window was repaired by Messrs Powell, and the chapter room was refitted and improved as a memorial to Canon Arthur Valpy. The 'stupendous' (the diocesan bishop's word) achievement in what Dean Furneaux insisted on calling 'reparation' fell between the years 1905 and 1912.[2] The cathedral was discovered to be falling apart, and, but for the ardent, intelligent effort of Dean Furneaux, the architectural surveyor, J. B. Colson, the consultant architect, Thomas Jackson, the consultant engineer, Francis Fox, and the diver, William Walker—and a team of up to 150 builders in various trades—parts might actually have collapsed. What may be described as the artistic licence in mistakenly supplying the present statue commemorating Walker with Francis Fox's face at least serves the purpose of emphasising the excellent team-work that prevailed during the anxious, labouring period.

Widening cracks had been discovered throughout the building, masonry actually falling from the vaulting near Bishop Waynflete's chantry chapel. The retrochoir had

335

Fig. 23.1   Holy Week Services in Winchester
Cathedral, 1900. *Dean and Chapter of Winchester*

moved five inches to the east and was sinking unevenly. The south wall of the presbytery was eight or nine inches out of plumb, daylight could be seen through the wall of the north transept, the gable of the south transept overhung its base by 4 ft. 6 ins., and the nave walls were shifting outwards. In addition it was discovered that the extensive repairs to the west front some fifty years earlier would have to be repeated as the Caen stone used had betrayed poor weathering qualities.

The 13th-century retrochoir had been built on a raft of beech logs, lying on a layer of peat, above a solid gravel bed. The peat had compressed under the weight of the walls, which had shifted. The response was to underpin the outer walls of the cathedral by placing layers of sacks of cement concrete above the gravel, concrete blocks above that, then brickwork. After initial difficulties caused by the high water-table, two divers were brought in; one of them stayed on for over five years and became a living legend (Fig. 23.2). William Walker worked two three-hour shifts a day under water, mainly in the dark, clearing away sections of logs and peat and placing the bags of cement in place. The Greathead grouting machine or hand labour injected 1,600 tons of liquid cement into cracks (25 tons going into one corner of the north transept alone), metal tie-rods were introduced into the tower, retrochoir and transepts, flying buttresses were built against the south nave wall, spent or dislodged stone was replaced, and major repair was repeated to the west front.

The Dean and Chapter had no special repair fund. A major appeal was launched, first local, then national and international. The national newspapers took up the cause, and the required £113,000 was eventually raised, despite difficulties until the last moment. The *Hampshire Observer* wondered if this was the largest sum ever raised for the preservation of a cathedral.[3] On St Swithun's Day 1912 a Thanksgiving Service was held for the completion of the work, attended by King George V and Queen Mary.

Embellishments to the cathedral continued even while the massive appeal and repair work were in progress. In 1900 an altar cross was provided by Canon Valpy, 400 chairs were added to the choir and nave, and C. E. Kempe glazed the window in the 11th bay of the north aisle of the nave as a memorial for the Rifle Brigade. He was also responsible for the north window of the Lady Chapel (the last window in the chapel to be re-glazed), and a window in the eighth bay of the north aisle of the nave commemorating Jane Austen.

The pavement and woodwork in the Lady Chapel were renewed and repaired. In 1904 Powell's War Memorial window in the south aisle of the nave was added, commemorating those who fell in the South African war. In 1905 a reredos, designed by Kempe, was placed behind the Lady Chapel altar. Two years later Canon Valpy provided the money and inspiration for creating the Epiphany Chapel out of the western aisle of the north transept, and in 1910 the Morris and Burne-Jones windows were completed (Fig. 23.3).[4] That year one of the last windows that Kempe designed was added in the south presbytery aisle, dedicated to the soldiers of the King's Royal Rifle Corps who had fallen in the South African war.

If normal congregations were modest, great occasions produced crowds. In 1901 4,000-5,000 were reckoned to attend the millenary commemoration of King Alfred. Very large congregations attended the services celebrating the coronation of King Edward VII and Queen Alexandra in 1902, and about five thousand were present for the king's memorial service in 1910.

Fig. 23.2   William Walker, the diver. *Dean and Chapter of Winchester*

Since the time of Samuel Sebastian Wesley the function of music in the ministry of the Church had won new regard. In 1902 William Prendergast succeeded Dr. Arnold as organist and master of the music. Arnold had been a pupil of Wesley, and Prendergast had been Arnold's pupil and later his assistant organist at Winchester. Reports suggest that Dr. Arnold was a remarkable musician. The rendering of the choir was described by the *Hampshire Chronicle* on one occasion as 'near perfect'. Regulations for lay clerks, published in 1909 over Dean Furneaux' name, inform us that the salary was £72 19s. 2d.—much above the requirement. It was their duty to sing Mattins at 10.00 a.m. and Evensong at 4.00 p.m. daily; on Sundays they were to sing Mattins at 11.00 a.m. (with choral celebrations on Greater Festivals) and Evensong at 3.15 p.m. Full practices were held twice weekly after service. The choir was excused singing one day a week, and enjoyed five weeks' holiday a year, but only one Sunday absence. Lay clerks were recommended to take other employment.

The onset of hostilities in 1914 was met by a pastoral letter from Bishop Talbot that appreciated the pain to come, the need for Christians to love their enemies, and the waywardness of England as being partly responsible for the horror. The Dean and Chapter and others associated with the cathedral would doubtless have echoed these sentiments, but the depth of moral thinking about the war to be found in the writings of Albert Schweitzer and Bertrand Russell was beyond their scope. These were King and Country men, reared in the public school and Empire tradition.

Within the limits of their beliefs they did what they could. Intercession services were held, there was participation in National Days of Prayer, services for soldiers were instituted at 8.00 p.m. on Sundays. In December 1914 a Mission for soldiers billeted nearby was held. Allied troops from Bohemia and the USA were welcomed. The presence of the latter caused bugles to be sounded in the cathedral, perhaps for the first time since the Civil War; American and British flags were on display, and 700 black American troops formed a cross in the nave and sang hymns.

There was also immediate suffering. One of the most moving services conducted this century took place in the ringing chamber of the tower, in 1918. The dean presided and Canon Braithwaite preached. The service remembered ringers who had died in the conflict, and especially Sergeant C. H. Russell, who had died of pneumonia. Mr. J. W. Elkins, virger and ringer, accompanied the singing on the violin, muffled bells began the service, and the knell of the tenor bell tolled 31 times at the end, marking Russell's age. Canon Braithwaite's voice broke throughout his sermon. His son had recently been killed in action. Quite different was the service celebrating the end of the war, attended by five to six thousand people, some standing outside, which was marked, according to the *Hampshire Chronicle,* by 'heartiness and brightness throughout'.

Fig. 23.3   Annunciation Window in the Epiphany Chapel, by the William Morris workshops after designs by Edward Burne-Jones. *John Crook*

Furneaux resigned in 1919, and in December that year William Holden Hutton was instituted and installed. Hutton was a rapid and fluent writer, an historian with 34 publications to his credit. He was a conservative in politics, a disciple of the Caroline Divines, and believed it inappropriate for a priest to marry. Hutton's particular and needed contribution to the life of the cathedral lay in the renewal of the liturgy. A chapter minute for 30 November 1920 informs us that a majority of members were in favour of the use of eucharistic vestments and that they accepted a gift of money for their purchase. A certain E. G. Selwyn was in fact the benefactor.[5] On Easter Day 1921, chasuble, dalmatic and tunicle were worn for the first time since the Reformation. Early in July that year Hutton wrote to the greater chapter saying that the Dean and Chapter wished to celebrate St Swithun's tide with more emphasis. The bishop would use the occasion of the greater chapter meeting to speak about the relation of cathedral to diocese and Hutton ventured his own views: worship must be offered 'as reverently and beautifully as it can be', music being a special assistance. Historic monuments from the past should be preserved and others added. Diocesan groups were welcome in the cathedral and education must be stimulated. Lastly, hospitality was a statutory requirement. The meeting of the greater chapter with the bishop confirmed Hutton's priorities. From this meeting came the practice of the cathedral's praying for parishes, deaneries and the greater chapter, development of musical festivals, and the communication of cathedral and parishes with each other when significant developments were planned.

There were many other innovations during Hutton's decanate. Twelve sculpted saints were replaced in the niches of Fox's chantry chapel. A pair of standard candlesticks was provided for the choir sanctuary in 1921 and two treble bells were added. Two years later Cardinal Beaufort's chantry chapel was refurnished for liturgical use, with an altar table, hangings and ornaments; the wooden statue of St Joan of Arc was set in place, designed by Sir Ninian Comper, and it was decided that silver-gilt eucharistic plate and wafer bread should be used at all but 'late plain' services. A carpet was provided for the sanctuary, and the chapter ordained that choristers should wear ruffs. The following year a stone altar was placed in Bishop Waynflete's chantry chapel and a set of copes was purchased. An altar was provided for the nave dais in 1925 and the ironwork screen was moved to the head of the steps leading from the south transept. The metal railing and gates commemorating Dean Furneaux were approved and installed at the junction of the south aisle of the nave and the south transept. It was resolved to terminate payment for visiting the cathedral and to rely on voluntary offerings. In 1927 there were experiments with loudspeakers, and in that year, too, problems in the music department came to an explosive head. They were resolved by the intervention of Bishop Woods, and it was agreed that communications should be improved and that the organist and lay clerks should be paid more money.

Dean Hutton had his gravestone inserted in the floor of the south presbytery aisle near Bishop Fox's chantry chapel well before his death in 1930. His obituary in *The Times* said that he combined interest in current affairs with 'something of that benign detachment from them which characterised dignitaries of the English Church in its peaceful and opulent past'.

Canon Edward Gordon Selwyn (Fig. 23.4) succeeded Hutton as dean in 1930. Only 45 years of age, with remarkable and varied talent, but for an imperiousness of manner he might have adorned any post in the Church of England. A liberal catholic, he had edited *Theology* since 1920, *Essays Catholic and Critical* in 1926, and his commentary on *I Peter* (1946) is a classic work.

Selwyn was immediately busy. The Friends of Winchester Cathedral was launched in 1931. The policy was to undertake or assist in schemes of repair deemed necessary by the Dean and Chapter, for which funds were insufficient; to collaborate on works of restoration and enrichment deemed desirable; to support the Dean and Chapter in cases of financial emergency; to build up a reserve fund.[6] In 1934 there were already 1,000 members, today almost 4,000. Since 1931 the Friends have contributed nearly £1 million towards the maintenance and beautification of the cathedral.[7] The value of the Friends to cathedral life continues to be incalculable, not least in the fellowship and communication the organisation enables.

In 1931 also an Advisory Committee was formed 'to advise the Dean and Chapter respecting architectural and decorative alterations or additions made in the cathedral or Close

Fig. 23.4   Portrait of Dean Edward Gordon Selwyn.
The Pilgrims' School/John Crook

buildings to which the Dean and Chapter may desire advice'. This committee of seven persons had representatives of the arts, architecture and the diocese.

That same year The Pilgrims' School was founded, constituting a thorough reorganisation of the previous Choir School. The house adjacent to the Pilgrims' Hall was utilised, and a preparatory school of Anglican foundation, with some boys to supply the cathedral choristers, was formed. Selwyn took a marked interest in its progress, and it was fortunate in its first headmaster, Humphrey Salwey. The school has expanded in numbers, achievement and buildings ever since.[8]

Selwyn was busy that year cogitating the idea presented to him that a number of cathedral textiles needed renewing and that local effort should be engaged. Soon the Winchester Cathedral Broderers were formed and included 200 members. Louisa Pesel and Sybil Blunt guided the work and trained broderers. In April 1934 Queen Mary paid a private visit to examine and admire the work. Miss Pesel saw the possibilities for the diocese and country as a whole. In five years they had refurbished the choir, making 360 kneelers, 96 alms bags, 34 long bench cushions, 62 stall cushions, and 55 other pieces. The enthusiasm and skill were as remarkable as the designs were conventional.[9]

Tolerance over what in this period was High Church practice could have its limits. In 1927 a visiting group of pilgrims had been refused the use of thurifers in the cathedral. For seven or eight years prior to Selwyn's arrival the Sacrament had been reserved in the Langton Chapel for the sick. Selwyn and the chapter introduced permanent reservation and a sanctuary lamp. The bishop of Southampton believed that this was the point where the line between reserving for the sick and reserving for devotion was crossed. Bishop Garbett expressed his uneasiness and eventually, after a petition was received by the bishop in 1933 signed by 400 people objecting to the practice on the grounds of illegality and divisiveness, the Dean and Chapter slowly bowed to the inevitable and by 1935 permanent reservation ceased.[10]

In 1932 the first public appeal for money was launched since 1912. Its purpose was to provide an adequate heating system, improve the electric lighting, reconstruct the organ, and endow the choir. Special music and drama festivals were held in the coming years and the choir visited the Channel Islands in 1935, when £4,000 was still outstanding. By 1938 the required sum of £12,202 was realised. Other important restorative and improvement work included the recasting and rehanging of the bells (1936-37), the nativity figures for the niche behind the high altar by Sybil Blunt (1937), the completion by Professor Tristram of restoration work on the mortuary chests and the Lady Chapel frescos, the addition in 1938 and 1939 of two windows in the south and north aisles of the nave, commemorating respectively King George V and the coronation of George VI and Queen Elizabeth.

The Second World War necessitated a vast reduction of work on the cathedral. The crypt became a shelter for members of the Close, the Winchester Bible went to Hereford Cathedral for safekeeping and then to the British Museum shelter near Bradford-on-Avon, the bells were reserved to give warning of parachute attack, a night watch was kept, intercession services and National Days of Prayer were observed, allied troops from home and abroad were welcomed and entertained, and musical festivity was not quelled.

In 1945 public appeal and a legacy permitted the purchase of a large oak Annunciation group by Alan Durst, which was first placed north-west of the nave altar. If we compare this artefact with Henry Moore's *Madonna and Child* in St Matthew's Church, Northampton, created at the same time, we cannot but see the radically different perception of the nature of sacred art obtaining at Winchester and in the mind of Walter Hussey.

In the years immediately after the war extensive repairs to the west front and to the clerestory windows on the south side of the nave were undertaken. The vault of the choir and tower were repainted and the bosses were cleaned and recoloured. The most significant work of restoration of this period related to the cathedral library, which Walter Oakeshott believed to be 'probably the earliest library in the country still in use for its original purpose'. Oakeshott was the honorary librarian, and to him we owe the initiative and main lines of the work, in which he was ably assisted by the cathedral architect, Wilfrid Carpenter Turner. In 1951 Bishop Morley's library was restored to its 17th-century condition, a plaster vault of the outer room was constructed replicating the medieval tunnel vault of the inner room, and the exhibition cases were installed for the Winchester Bible and other treasures. It was hoped that students would use the Morley Library.[11] In 1959 Professor and Mrs. Robert Baker from the Royal College of Art were working in the Guardian Angels Chapel, restoring the painted vault. They worked innovatively, for the plaster was crumbling and they had to transfer the painting on to silk, repair the plaster, then re-attach the paintings. In 1963 they worked in the Holy Sepulchre Chapel, proving the existence of suspected 12th-century paintings under the 13th-century Deposition painting on the east wall. The latter was removed and transferred to the west wall. Dr. Oakeshott regarded the find as 'one of the most important ever made of a Romanesque wall painting in England'.[12]

During the 1950s reference is more frequently found to orchestral concerts being performed in the cathedral. The Hallé Orchestra came several times with Sir John Barbirolli as conductor and the Birmingham Symphony Orchestra gained entrance. The Dean and Chapter were less convinced about drama. An application by Winchester College to perform a play by Christopher Fry was rejected 'on the grounds that it was not suitable'.[13] In September 1955 full Choral Mattins was abandoned as the secular employment of lay clerks increasingly meant that they were unable to attend.

Dean Selwyn retired in 1958. At his departure he stated that without the financial contribution of the Friends the cathedral would be unable to maintain itself. In 1953 a deficit in the General Account of £1,100 was recorded, which by 1961 had risen to £4,237.

Selwyn was succeeded in the same year by Professor Norman Sykes, Dixie Professor of Ecclesiastical History in the University of Cambridge, one of the most distinguished ecclesiastical historians of his day (Fig. 23.5). He believed that worship was the heart of the cathedral's life and that it should be a home for the arts, and he reiterated the importance of the Friends. He died within three years. Sykes was succeeded by Archdeacon Oswin Gibbs-Smith (1961-69) (Fig. 23.6), who brought to his work a keen understanding of practical matters, successfully managed an appeal for over £405,000, opened the nave to regular Sunday worship, increased the size of the choir, and encouraged the organist and master of the music to extend the Southern Cathedrals Festival to three days. He was followed by Canon Michael Stancliffe (1969-86) (Fig. 23.7), who emphasised prayer and the arts, and had a deserved reputation as a preacher. These were qualities he shared with Bishop John Taylor, and together they created programmes combining the arts in sacred presentation. During his tenure of office successful appeals for money were launched, fresh ecumenical links were forged, not least with the French Benedictine community at Fleury (1978), and the striking Creation banners of Thetis Blacker were unveiled in the nave (1979).

Canon Trevor Beeson became dean in 1987 (Fig. 23.8). During his decanate we have witnessed a heroic endeavour to overcome the nagging problem of shortage of money, with an appeal for £7 million, almost realised within two economically difficult years. Visitors have been newly welcomed, and planning approval has been gained for a visitors' centre, with restaurant, bookshop and education centre. Sacred visual art of high quality has been encouraged and the work of Peter Eugene Ball (Fig. 23.9) and Antony Gormley is justly praised. Education work has increased, with seminars, Lent lectures and theology days. The choir has maintained its enviable reputation under the successive direction of Martin Neary and David Hill. Attention has been given to the administrative structure of the cathedral staff. In all these matters the support of Bishop Colin James has been as discreet as enabling. So much remains to be done, but the paid staff, augmented by over six hundred voluntary helpers, take courage from past achievements while seeing in their labour a means to glorify God.

Epilogue—The Future

That Winchester Cathedral has a future is as certain as any contingent fact. Assurance about its future arises from its architectural magnificence, its expression of history, and its religious character. Despite the temporary weakness of religion in British culture today, the history of humanity and such research as has been done into contemporary recognition of the transcendent suggest the perennial importance of signs of the transcendent in our midst. The cathedral is one such sign. What is unknown is how the character of

Fig. 23.5 Dean Norman Sykes with Bishop Alwyn Williams (1953-62), outside the Deanery.
Dean and Chapter of Winchester

Fig. 23.6 Dean Oswin Gibbs-Smith with Viscount Montgomery, Cathedral Gift Day, 30 April 1966.
Dean and Chapter of Winchester

that sign may change. A dictum of Paul Tillich was that religion is the substance of culture, and culture the form of religion. We must expect continuity and change.

The values celebrated permanently by the cathedral are essentially obvious but difficult sometimes to exercise: worship, education and hospitality. These values reflect Benedictine wisdom on human nature and culture, and express the office of the bishop whose *cathedra* is in the cathedral. Just as the bishop has both a local ministry to the diocese and a wider ministry to the nation and Church, so the cathedral has a local and general reference.

The cathedral is essentially a eucharistic house. It is constructed round the altar and the tone of its structure and ornaments reflects this dignity. It is a symbol of the Kingdom of God, and crossing the physical threshold of the entrance we are intended to cross a metaphysical threshold. The soaring arches, the stained glass, the aisles and the progress to the altar are a journey of communion that ends in exaltation. George Herbert's poem *Love bade me welcome* describes the experience.

We must hope for the continuation of the present emphasis on dignity and order in corporate worship and maintenance of our excellent choral foundation and organ. But I expect to see the Eucharist become the corporate focus of Sunday worship, and I expect renewed attention to be given to the quality of the rite. Rite A (the Alternative Service Book) and all that goes naturally with it, including now the Revised English Bible and

Fig. 23.7   Dean Michael Stancliffe. *John Crook*   Fig. 23.8   Dean Trevor Beeson. *John Crook*

inclusive language, are pioneer attempts to forge a liturgy worthy of our time. The future lies here, and defence of Cranmer's prose cannot mask the inadequacy of his theology nor the changes in the English language itself. The thinking of Cranmer in the 16th century would make him a radical liturgist today.

We must hope that the renewed regard for music in the cathedral since the mid-19th century as a support for and expression of worship will be increasingly reflected in the quality of textiles, silverware, statuary and paintings. Beauty must be understood again as one of the eternal values and attributes of God. The visual sense must be understood again as co-equal with the auditory sense as a channel of grace and devotional aspiration, as should the sense of smell in regard to the use of incense. Puritanism denies sensuous experience. Grace purifies and uses it. Splendid efforts have been made in this direction under the leadership of the present Dean, but how daunting is the task may be gauged by contemplating the financial commitment or considering the windows of the nave, where the theological sequence and artistic excellence doubtless observed by medieval people have been broken for ever.

Occasional gatherings for music, drama, lectures and similar functions are important elements of worship in the broader sense. So long as they are consonant with the Eucharist they are to be encouraged as expressing the ministry of the cathedral to those who may not be prepared to participate in the Eucharist—or to all of us, in that, while the Eucharist expresses the heart of religion, it does not express all of it.

Worship and education may be distinguished but they cannot be separated. An educative element is acknowledged in a form of worship that makes good intellectual sense and in attendant visual images that lift the hearts and illuminate the minds of those who live in today's world, where feminism, world (including religious) unity, and the supremacy of love as defining God must find their place. P. T. Forsyth equated the sermon with the Bible and the Eucharist in its sacramental potential in communicating the Word of God, and constant care of quality in preaching must be made. But education becomes significant in the lecture, the seminar and similar gatherings. In a world where every belief is controverted, and new knowledge must be assimilated continually, the Church has an urgent task in mediating the Gospel to the world and the world to the Gospel. There is a tragic gap between the work of theologians and

Fig. 23.9   Pietà in the Lady Chapel, by Peter Eugene Ball. *John Crook*

church-goers. The position of the cathedral in the diocese makes it centrally important in this ministry, both because of its ecclesiastical eminence and its professional staffing. Good work has been started in this field, but much more needs to be done, including liaison with sympathetic educational establishments and the facilitating of research in applied theology (for example discernment in and significance of sacred visual art, testimony to spiritual audiences in Hampshire, local unemployment and its human effects). The cathedral stands at many cultural border-points and is well placed for such activity.

The provision of visitors' chaplains, guides, and welcoming stewards are token of the endeavour to introduce visitors to the cathedral. Tourists can become visitors and visitors can become pilgrims, for such is the latent potential of the cathedral. The new visitors' centre will extend welcome and hospitality to a notable degree. Involved in such provisions is the understanding of the cathedral not only as a centre of contemplation but of mission. These ideals are sometimes opposed, but I believe that they are complementary. It is a focus of in-gathered strength and a point from which concentric circles of spiritual energy radiate. The sources of its power are vertical and horizontal, drawn from God and culture.

A recurrent and debilitating problem for the cathedral and one which could prove crippling is finance. The present heroic appeal for £7 million will not solve the problem when it has succeeded. All the professional skill that can be mustered to match decent income and necessary expense needs to be deployed, and we have some distance to go in this endeavour. Although rejected for spiritual reasons at the moment, we may find that the compromise of

Fig. 23.10   Dean Trevor Beeson dedicates the completion of work on the tower. *John Crook*

admission charges such as are exacted at Ely and St Paul's is inevitable. Compromise is inescapable, and this is one likely to be understood by the people. Half a million pounds and more annually is at stake.

Another problem being confronted is that of staffing. The dean is appointed by the Crown after wide consultation, local and national. The bishop appoints the canons. Power is concentrated in the Dean and Chapter. Such is the extent of lay involvement in the running of the cathedral and the multiple forms of our life and decision-making that reform is urgently required. I believe that the dean should be appointed according to a structure similar to that of a diocesan bishop. I believe that canons should be appointed by the mutual agreement of bishop and Dean and Chapter. I believe that canons should be appointed for specific work on the basis of requisite skills. I believe that the recent practice, following the management consultancy exercise (1991), of devolving responsibility and defining roles within the overall authority of the Dean and Chapter, should be strengthened. I believe that a woman or women should find place in the Dean and Chapter. I believe that the present annual congregational meeting should be strengthened as a consultative, but not as a legislative, body. I believe that all the clergy members of the Dean and Chapter should be employed on leasehold terms and should submit to periodic assessment by a committee including the bishop and a lay person. This assessment should determine eventually the length of employment at the cathedral.

Winchester Cathedral is a busy, struggling, and achieving place. The present strong emphasis on method and money is the price to be paid for the larger vision to be possible. The larger vision could be obscured, but if the right men and women lead us, and if all who participate in its life are persons of prayer, that will not happen. God is faithful, and sounding amid our toil will be that which has echoed down the centuries, the Kingdom of God itself.[14]

Notes

1. During Lent 1900 Evensong on Fridays was followed by a special sermon: preachers included the Headmaster of Berkhamsted School and the dean of Peterborough. On Tuesday 6 and 27 March the Revd Canon Bigg, Tutor of Christ Church, Oxford, gave lectures on 'The Mediæval Scholar' and 'The Mediæval Pastor'.
2. For the history of these works, see I. T. Henderson and J. Crook, *The Winchester Diver* (Winchester, 1984).
3. *Hampshire Observer,* 11 March 1911.
4. A.K. Walker, 'Arthur Sutton Valpy, the Epiphany Chapel, and its Stained Glass', *WCR* 58 (1989), pp. 15-23.
5. CA, 31 May 1921.
6. *WCR* 1 (1932), p. 2.
7. *WCR* 61 (1992), p. 58.
8. J. Crook, *A History of The Pilgrims' School*, rev. edn. (Chichester 1991).
9. *WCR* 6 (1936), pp. 8, 9.
10. The whole question is dealt with admirably in T. W. Daykin, 'The Selwyn Papers', unpubl. Ph.D. thesis, University of London, 1992.
11. *WCR* 21 (1952), pp. 4-8.
12. *Hampshire Observer,* 28 May 1966.
13. CA, 29 March 1955.
14. The interested reader is referred to the present Dean's sermon, 'Mission and Management in the Cathedral', 5 May 1992; the Revd. Philip Barrett's lecture, '1541 and All That', 25 May 1991; and the survey of contemporary life in cathedrals published by *The Guardian* between 29 July-26 August 1991, all of which are preserved in the cathedral archives.

LIST OF SHORT TITLES AND ABBREVIATIONS

This list is not intended as a complete bibliography, but lists the short titles employed for second and subsequent occurrences of references in the end-notes to each article. Certain classic works (e.g. Milner's *History*) are cited only in short title form in the endnotes.

Age of Chivalry	Jonathan Alexander and Paul Binski (eds.), *Age of Chivalry: Art in Plantagenet England 1200-1400*, Catalogue, Royal Academy Exhibition (London, 1987)
Anglia Sacra	Henry Wharton (ed.), *Anglia Sacra sive Collectio Historiarum,* 2 vols. (London, 1691)
Anglo, 'Hampton Court Painting'	Sydney Anglo, 'The Hampton Court Painting of the Field of Cloth of Gold Considered as an Historical Document', *Antiq. J.* 46 (1966), pp. 287-307
Anglo-Norman Studies	R. Allen Brown (ed.), *Anglo-Norman Studies: Proceedings of the Battle Conference* (Woodbridge, from 1979)
Antiq. J.	*Antiquaries Journal*
Appleby, 'Richard of Devizes'	J. T. Appleby, 'Richard of Devizes and the Annals of Winchester', *Bulletin of the Institute of Historical Research* 36 (1963), pp. 70-7
Arch. J.	*Archaeological Journal*
Atkinson, 'Figure Sculpture'	T. D. Atkinson, 'Medieval Figure Sculpture in Winchester Cathedral', *Archaeologia,* 85 (1936), pp. 159-67
Atkinson and Goodman, 'Chests'	T. D. Atkinson and A. W. Goodman, 'The Mortuary Chests', *WCR* 2 (1933), pp. 11-14
BAA Winchester	*Medieval Art and Architecture at Winchester Cathedral,* British Archaeological Association Conference Transactions for 1980 (London, 1983)
Baggs, 'Terracotta Tombs'	A. P. Baggs, 'Sixteenth-century Terracotta Tombs in East Anglia', *Arch. J.* 125 (1968), pp. 295-301
Ball, *Historical Account*	Charles Ball, *An Historical Account of Winchester, with Descriptive Walks* (Winchester, 1818)
Barlow, *English Church I*	Frank Barlow, *The English Church 1000-1066*, 2nd edn. (London, 1979)
Baylé, *La Trinité de Caen*	Maylis Baylé, *La Trinité de Caen; sa Place dans l'Histoire de l'Architecture et du Décor Romans* (Geneva, 1979)
Biddle, 'Nicholas Bellin'	Martin Biddle, 'Nicholas Bellin of Modena: an Italian Artificer at the Courts of Francis I and Henry VIII', *JBAA*, 3rd ser., 29 (1966), pp. 106-21
Biddle, *Round Table*	Martin Biddle, *King Arthur's Round Table* (London, 1993)
Biddle, 'Stuccoes of Nonsuch'	Martin Biddle, 'The Stuccoes of Nonsuch', *Burlington Magazine* 126 (July 1984), pp. 411-16
Biddle, *Wolvesey*	Martin Biddle, *Wolvesey: The Old Bishop's Palace, Winchester, Hampshire,* English Heritage Handbook (London, 1986)

349

Binns, *Dedications* Alison Binns, *Dedications of Monastic Houses in England and Wales, 1066-1216* (Woodbridge, 1989)

Bishop, 'Henry of Blois' Edmund Bishop, 'Gifts of Bishop Henry of Blois, Abbot of Glastonbury, to Winchester Cathedral', *Downside Review* 3 (1884), pp. 33-44

Blakiston, 'Inigo Jones Screen' J. M. G. Blakiston, 'The Inigo Jones Screen, Part II', *WCR* 46 (1977), pp. 13-17

Blore, *Monuments* G. H. Blore, *The Monuments of Winchester Cathedral,* 2nd edn. (Winchester, 1983)

Blore, 'Prebendary Nott' G. H. Blore, 'George Frederick Nott, D.D., 1767-1841', *WCR* 19 (1950), pp. 13-15

Blunt, *Art and Architecture* Anthony Blunt, *Art and Architecture in France 1500-1700,* 4th (rev.) edn. (Harmondsworth, 1982)

Blunt, 'Influence française' Anthony Blunt, 'L'influence française sur l'architecture et la sculpture decorative en Angleterre pendant la première moitié du XVIᵉ siècle', *Revue de l'Art* 4 (1969), pp. 17-29

Bogan, 'Figg' Peter Bogan, 'Dom Thomas Figg and the Foot of St Philip', *WCR* 61 (1992), pp. 22-6

Brett, *English Church* M. Brett, *The English Church under Henry I* (Oxford, 1975)

Britton, *Winchester Cathedral* John Britton, *The History and Antiquities of the See and Cathedral Church of Winchester* (London, 1817)

Brooke, 'Cathedral Builders' Christopher Brooke, 'The Normans as Cathedral Builders', in Willis, *Winchester* (1980 edn.), pp. 83-98

Brooke, *Marriage* Christopher Brooke, *The Medieval Idea of Marriage* (Oxford, 1989)

Brooke, *Medieval Church* Christopher Brooke, *Medieval Church and Society* (London, 1971)

Brooke and Brooke, *Popular Religion* Rosemary and Christopher Brooke, *Popular Religion in the Middle Ages* (London, 1984)

Brooke and Keir, *London* Christopher Brooke and Gillian Keir, *London 800-1216: the Shaping of a City* (London, 1975)

Bussby, *Winchester Cathedral* Frederick Bussby, *Winchester Cathedral 1079-1979* (Southampton, 1979)

CA Chapter Act books of the Dean and Chapter of Winchester

Carpenter Turner, 'Lady Chapel' Wilfrid Carpenter Turner, 'Discoveries in the Lady Chapel', *WCR* 39 (1970), pp. 32-8

'Cathedral Chronicle' 'Winchester Cathedral Chronicle'. 12 vols. and 2 supplementary vols., 1800 to present day, MS, WCL

Cave, 'Quire Bosses' C. J. P. Cave, 'The Bosses on the Vault of the Quire at Winchester Cathedral', *Archaeologia* 76 (1927), pp. 161-78

Cave, *Roof Bosses* C. J. P. Cave, *The Roof Bosses of Winchester Cathedral* (Winchester, 1955)

Chibnall, *Historia Pontificalis* Marjorie Chibnall (ed.), *The Historia Pontificalis of John of Salisbury,* rev. edn. (Oxford, 1986)

CO Chapter Order Book, MS, WCL (covering years 1665/6-1738)

Cobb, *Forgotten Centuries* Gerald Cobb, *English Cathedrals: The Forgotten Centuries* (London, 1980)

Colish, 'Twelfth-Century Problem' M. L. Colish, 'A Twelfth-Century Problem', *Apollo,* July 1968, pp. 36-41

Colvin, *Henry III* H. M. Colvin (ed.), *Building Accounts of King Henry III* (Oxford, 1971)

Conant, *Architecture* K. J. Conant, *Carolingian and Romanesque Architecture,* rev. edn. (Harmondsworth, 1978)

Councils and Synods I	Dorothy Whitelock, M. Brett and C. N. L. Brooke (eds.), *Councils and Synods with Other Documents relating to the English Church, 1* (Oxford, 1981)
Country Life, 'Cupboard'	'Cupboard in the Cathedral', *Country Life,* 9 December 1965
Crook, 'East Arm'	John Crook, 'The Romanesque East Arm and Crypt of Winchester Cathedral', *JBAA* 142 (1989), pp. 1-36
Crook, 'Holy Hole'	John Crook, 'Excavating the Holy Hole', *WCR* 58 (1989), pp. 34-42
Crook 'King Edgar's Reliquary'	John Crook, 'King Edgar's Reliquary of St Swithun', *Anglo-Saxon England* 21 (1992), pp. 177-202
Crook, *Monastic Chroniclers*	John Crook (ed.), *Monastic Chroniclers of St Swithun's Priory,* forthcoming
Crook, 'Typology of Shrines'	John Crook, 'The Typology of Early Medieval Shrines—a Previously Misidentified "Tomb-Shrine" Panel from Winchester Cathedral', *Antiq. J.* 70 (1990), pp. 49-64
Crook and Kusaba, 'Transepts'	John Crook and Yoshio Kusaba, 'The Transepts of Winchester Cathedral: Archaeological Evidence, Problems of Design, and Sequence of Construction', *Journal of the Society of Architectural Historians* 50 (1991), pp. 293-310
Draper, 'Retrochoir' 1978	Peter Draper, 'The Retrochoir of Winchester Cathedral', *Architectural History* 21 (1978), pp. 1-17
Draper, 'Retrochoir' 1986	Peter Draper, 'The Retrochoir of Winchester Cathedral: Evidence and Interpretation', *JBAA* 139 (1986), pp. 68-74
Durliat, *Art Roman*	Marcel Durliat, *L'Art Roman* (Paris, 1982)
Eadmer, *Historia Novorum*	Martin Rule (ed.), *Eadmer, Historia Novorum in Anglia,* RS 81 (1884)
Eames, 'Furniture'	Penelope Eames, 'Furniture in England, France and the Netherlands from the Twelfth to the Fifteenth Century', *Furniture History* 13 (1977)
Edington's Register	Dom S. F. Hockey (ed.), *The Register of William Edington, Bishop of Winchester 1346-1366,* 2 vols., Hampshire Record Series, 7-8 (Winchester, 1986-7)
EHR	*English Historical Review*
Emden, *Oxford*	A. B. Emden, *Biographical Register of the University of Oxford to A.D. 1500,* 3 vols. (Oxford, 1957-59)
English Romanesque Art	George Zarnecki, Janet Holt and Tristram Holland (eds.), *English Romanesque Art 1066-1200,* Exhibition Catalogue, Hayward Gallery (London, 1984)
Fowler, *History of Corpus*	Thomas Fowler, *The History of Corpus Christi College,* Oxford Historical Society 25 (Oxford, 1893)
Gem, 'Winchester Cathedral'	Richard Gem, 'The Romanesque Cathedral of Winchester: Patron and Design in the Eleventh Century', *BAA Winchester,* pp. 1-12
Gesta Abbatum Sancti Albani	H. T. Riley (ed.), *Gesta Abbatum Monasterii Sancti Albani,* 2 vols., RS 28 (1867)
Gesta Pontificum	N. E. S. A. Hamilton (ed.), *Willelmi Malmesburiensis De Gestis Pontificum Anglorum,* RS 52 (1870)
Goodman, *Chartulary*	A. W. Goodman (ed.), *Chartulary of Winchester Cathedral* (Winchester, 1927)
Greatrex, *Common Seal*	Joan Greatrex (ed.), *The Register of the Common Seal of the Priory of St Swithun, Winchester, 1345-1497,* Hampshire Record Series, 2 (Winchester, 1978)

Greenhill, *Incised Effigial Slabs*

F. A. Greenhill, *Incised Effigial Slabs; A Study of Engraved Stone Memorials in Latin Christendom, c. 1100 to c. 1700,* 2 vols. (London, 1976)

Hardacre, *Catalogue*

John Hardacre, *Winchester Cathedral: Triforium Gallery,* Catalogue (Winchester, 1989)

Harvey, *Mediæval Architects*

John H. Harvey, *English Mediæval Architects: a Biographical Dictionary down to 1550,* rev. edn. (Gloucester, 1984)

Harvey, 'Winchester College'

John H. Harvey, 'Winchester College', *JBAA* 27 (1965), pp. 107-28

Heads I

Dom. David Knowles, C. N. L. Brooke and V. C. M. London (eds.), *Heads of Religious Houses, England and Wales, I, 940-1216* (Cambridge, 1972)

HFC Proc.

Proceedings of the Hampshire Field Club and Archaeological Society

Hope and Atchley, *Colours*

William St. John Hope and E. G. Cuthbert Atchley, *English Liturgical Colours* (London, 1918)

HRO

Hampshire Record Office, Winchester

HRSoc

Hampshire Record Society (Winchester and London, from 1889)

JBAA

Journal of the British Archaeological Association, 3rd ser.

Jervis, *Woodwork*

Simon Jervis, *Woodwork of Winchester Cathedral* (Winchester, 1976)

Johnson *et al., Hugh the Chanter*

C. Johnson, M. Brett, C. N. L. Brooke and M. Winterbottom (eds.), *Hugh the Chanter, The History of the Church of York, 1066-1127* (Oxford, 1990)

Joy, *Woodwork*

Edward T. Joy, *Woodwork in Winchester Cathedral* (Winchester, 1964)

Kauffmann, *Romanesque Manuscripts*

C. M. Kauffmann, *Romanesque Manuscripts 1066-1190,* Survey of Manuscripts Illuminated in the British Isles, III (London, 1975)

Ker, *Medieval Libraries*

N. R. Ker, *Medieval Libraries of Great Britain: a List of Surviving Books* (London, 1964)

Kitchin, *Compotus Rolls*

G. W. Kitchin (ed.), *Compotus Rolls of the Obedientiaries of St. Swithun's Priory,* HRSoc (1892)

Kitchin, *Great Screen*

G. W. Kitchin, *The Great Screen of Winchester Cathedral,* 3rd edn., revised and completed by W. R. W. Stephens (Winchester, 1899)

Kitchin and Madge, *Documents*

G. W. Kitchin and F. T. Madge (eds.), *Documents Relating to the Foundation of the Chapter of Winchester A.D. 1541-1547,* HRSoc (1889)

Klauser, *Liturgy*

Theodor Klauser, *A Short History of the Western Liturgy* (London, 1969)

Knowles, *Monastic Order*

Dom David Knowles, *The Monastic Order in England, 940-1216,* 2nd edn. (Cambridge, 1963)

Knowles, *Monastic Constitutions*

Dom David Knowles (ed. and trans.), *The Monastic Constitutions of Lanfranc* (London, 1951)

Knowles, *Religious Orders*

Dom David Knowles, *The Religious Orders in England,* 3 vols. (Cambridge, 1948-59)

Kreisel, *Kunst des Möbels, I*

Heinrich Kreisel, *Die Kunst des Deutschen Möbels, I, Von den Anfängen bis zum Hochbarock,* 2nd edn. (Munich, 1974)

Kusaba, 'Treasury of Henry of Blois'

Yoshio Kusaba, 'The Function, Date and Stylistic Sources of the Treasury of Henry of Blois in the South Transept of Winchester Cathedral', *WCR* 57 (1988), pp. 38-49

L & P Henry VIII	*Calendar of Letters and Papers, Foreign and Domestic, Henry VIII*, 21 vols. and addenda (London 1864-1932)
Lapidge and Winterbottom, *Wulfstan*	Michael Lapidge and Michael Winterbottom (eds.), *Wulfstan of Winchester: the Life of St Æthelwold* (Oxford, 1991)
LB	Ledger Books or 'Books of the Common Seal', MSS, WCL
Lees-Milne, *Tudor Renaissance*	James Lees-Milne, *Tudor Renaissance* (London, 1951)
Lindley, 'Figure Sculpture'	P. G. Lindley, 'Figure Sculpture at Winchester in the Fifteenth Century: A New Chronology', in D. Williams (ed.), *England in the Fifteenth Century* (Woodbridge, 1987), pp. 153-66
Lindley, 'Great Screen, I'	P. G. Lindley, 'The Great Screen of Winchester Cathedral, I', *Burlington Magazine* 131 (1989), pp. 604-15
Lindley, 'Great Screen, II'	P. G. Lindley, 'The Great Screen of Winchester Cathedral, II', *Burlington Magazine* (forthcoming)
Lindley, 'Sculptural Discoveries'	P. G. Lindley, 'Sculptural Discoveries at Winchester Cathedral', *HFC Proc.* 46 (1990), pp. 101-11
Lindley, 'Sculptural Programme'	P. G. Lindley, 'The Sculptural Programme of Bishop Fox's Chantry Chapel', *WCR* 57 (1988), pp. 33-7
Lowth, *Life of Wykeham*	Robert Lowth, *The Life of William of Wykeham, Bishop of Winchester*, 3rd edn. (Oxford, 1777)
McCann, *Rule*	J. McCann (ed.), *The Rule of Saint Benedict* (London, 1960)
Matthews, *Organs and Organists*	Betty Matthews, *The Organs and Organists of Winchester Cathedral* (Winchester, undated)
Milner, *Winchester*	John Milner, *The History, Civil and Ecclesiastical, and Survey of the Antiquities of Winchester,* 2 vols. (Winchester, 1798-99)
Morris, 'Thomas of Witney'	Richard Morris, 'Thomas of Witney at Exeter, Winchester and Wells', *Medieval Art and Architecture at Exeter Cathedral,* British Archaeological Association Conference Transactions for 1985 (London, 1991), pp. 57-84
Muller, *Letters of Gardiner*	J. A. Muller, *The Letters of Stephen Gardiner* (Cambridge, 1933)
Munby and Fletcher, 'Carpentry'	Julian Munby and John Fletcher, 'Carpentry in the Cathedral and Close at Winchester', *BAA Winchester,* pp. 101-11
Norton, 'Medieval Pavements'	E. C. Norton, 'The Medieval Tile Pavements of Winchester Cathedral', *BAA Winchester,* pp. 78-93
Oakeshott, *Artists*	Walter Oakeshott, *The Artists of the Winchester Bible* (London, 1945)
Pantin, *Black Monks*	W. A. Pantin, *Documents Illustrating the Activities of the General and Provincial Chapters of the English Black Monks, 1215-1540,* 3 vols., Camden Society, 3rd ser., 45 (i), 47 (ii), 54 (iii) (1931-37)
Park, 'Holy Sepulchre Chapel'	David Park, 'The Wall Paintings of the Holy Sepulchre Chapel', *BAA Winchester,* pp. 38-62
Pevsner and Lloyd, *Hampshire*	Nikolaus Pevsner and David Lloyd, *Hampshire and the Isle of Wight* (Harmondsworth, 1967)
Pontoise's Register	Cecil Deedes (ed.), *Registrum Johannis de Pontissara, Episcopi Wintoniensis, A.D. 1282-1304,* Canterbury and York Society (1915-24)
PRO	Public Record Office, London
Quirk, 'Cardinal Beaufort'	R. N. Quirk, 'The Tomb of Cardinal Beaufort', *WCR* 23 (1954), pp. 6-10
Quirk, 'Prior Basing'	R. N. Quirk, 'The Monuments of Prior Basing and the "Old Bishop in Marble"', *WCR* 23 (1954), pp. 12-21

Quirk, 'Winchester Cathedral'	R. N. Quirk, 'Winchester Cathedral in the Tenth Century', *Arch. J.* 114 (1957), pp. 28-68
Rannie, 'Decorated Architecture'	Alan Rannie, 'Decorated Architecture in the Cathedral', *WCR* 35 (1966), pp. 14-23
Rolland, 'L'expansion tournaisienne'	Pierre Rolland, 'L'expansion tournaisienne aux XIe et XIIe siècles: art et commerce de la pierre', *Annales de l'Académie Royale d'Archéologie de Belgique* 71 (1924), pp. 175-219
Russell, 'Decorated Tracery'	Georgina Russell, 'Decorated Tracery in Winchester Cathedral', *BAA Winchester,* pp. 94-100
Salzman, *Building in England*	L. F. Salzman, *Building in England down to 1540* (Oxford, 1952)
Smith, 'Chantry Chapel'	Angela Smith, 'The Chantry Chapel of Bishop Fox', *WCR* 57 (1988), pp. 27-32
Spear, 'Chanoines'	David Spear, 'Les chanoines de la cathédrale de Rouen pendant la période ducale', *Annales de Normandie* 41 (1991), pp. 135-75
Stone, *Sculpture*	Lawrence Stone, *Sculpture in Britain: The Middle Ages* (Harmondsworth, 1972)
TA	Treasurers' accounts (post-Reformation), MSS, WCL
Tracy, *Choir-Stalls, 1200-1400*	Charles Tracy, *English Gothic Choir-Stalls, 1200-1400* (Woodbridge, 1987)
Tracy, *Choir-Stalls, 1400-1540*	Charles Tracy, *English Gothic Choir-Stalls, 1400-1540* (Woodbridge, 1990)
Tristram, *Thirteenth Century*	E. W. Tristram, *English Medieval Wall Painting: The Thirteenth Century,* 2 vols. (Oxford, 1950)
Tudor-Craig and Keen, 'Screen'	Pamela Tudor-Craig and Laurence Keen, 'A Recently Discovered Purbeck Marble Sculptured Screen of the Thirteenth Century and the Shrine of St Swithun', *BAA Winchester,* pp. 63-72
Vaughan, *Winchester Cathedral*	John Vaughan, *Winchester Cathedral: its Monuments and Memorials* (London, 1919)
VCH Hants	H. A. Doubleday, then W. Page (eds.), *The Victoria History of the County of Hampshire and the Isle of Wight,* 5 vols. (London, 1900-12)
Warton, *Description of Winchester*	[Thomas Warton], *A Description of the City, College, and Cathedral of Winchester* (London, [1760])
WCL	Library and Archives of the Dean and Chapter of Winchester
WCR	*Winchester Cathedral Record,* published annually since 1932 by the Friends of Winchester Cathedral
Whinney, *Sculpture in Britain*	Margaret Whinney, rev. by John Physick, *Sculpture in Britain 1530-1830,* 2nd edn. (Harmondsworth, 1988)
Whittingham, *Portrait Gallery*	Selby Whittingham, *A Thirteenth Century Portrait Gallery at Salisbury Cathedral* (Salisbury, 1979)
Wickham Legg, 'Survey'	L. G. Wickham Legg, 'A Relation of a Short Survey of the Western Counties, Made by a Lieutenant of the Military Company in Norwich in 1635', *Camden Miscellany* 16, Camden Society, 3rd. ser. 52 (1936), pp. 44-9
Willis, *Winchester Cathedral*	Robert Willis, *The Architectural History of Winchester Cathedral,* Proceedings of the Annual Meeting of the Archaeological Institute at Winchester, September 1845 (London, 1846), reprinted by Friends of Winchester Cathedral (Winchester, 1980)
Winchester Annals	H. R. Luard (ed.), *Annales Monastici, II: Winchester and Waverley,* RS 36 (1865)
Winchester Studies 1	Martin Biddle (ed.), *Winchester in the Early Middle Ages,* Winchester Studies, 1 (Oxford, 1976)

Winchester Studies 2	Derek Keene, with a contribution by A. R. Rumble, *Survey of Medieval Winchester,* Winchester Studies, 2, 2 vols. (Oxford, 1985)
Winchester Studies 4.ii	Martin Biddle and Birthe Kjølbye-Biddle, *The Anglo-Saxon Minsters of Winchester, II: The Cult of St Swithun,* Winchester Studies 4.ii (forthcoming)
Windisch-Graetz, *Möbel*	Franz Windisch-Graetz, *Möbel Europas von der Romanik bis zu Spätgotik* (Munich, 1982)
Woodman, 'New Interpretation'	Francis Woodman, 'The Retrochoir of Winchester Cathedral: a New Interpretation', *JBAA* 136 (1983), pp. 87-97
Wulfstan, *Narratio Metrica*	Alistair Campbell (ed.), *Frithegodi Monachi Breviloquium Vitæ Beati Wilfredi et Wulfstani Cantoris Narratio Metrica de Sancto Swithuno* (Zurich, 1950)
Wykeham's Register	T. F. Kirby (ed.), *Wykeham's Register,* 2 vols, HRSoc (1896-9)
Zarnecki, 'Henry of Blois'	George Zarnecki, 'Henry of Blois as a Patron of Sculpture', in S. Macready and F. H. Thompson (eds.), *Art and Patronage in the English Romanesque* (London, 1986), pp. 159-72